D1043861

O-Parts
HunteR™

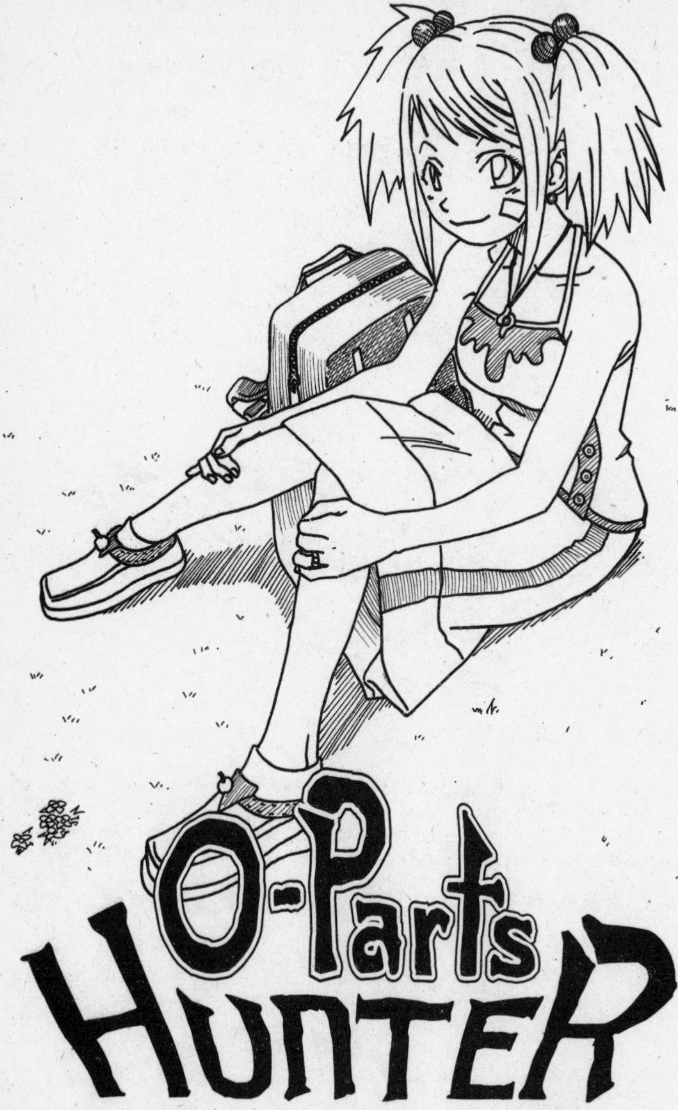

O-Parts HUNTER™

SEISHI KISHIMOTO

2

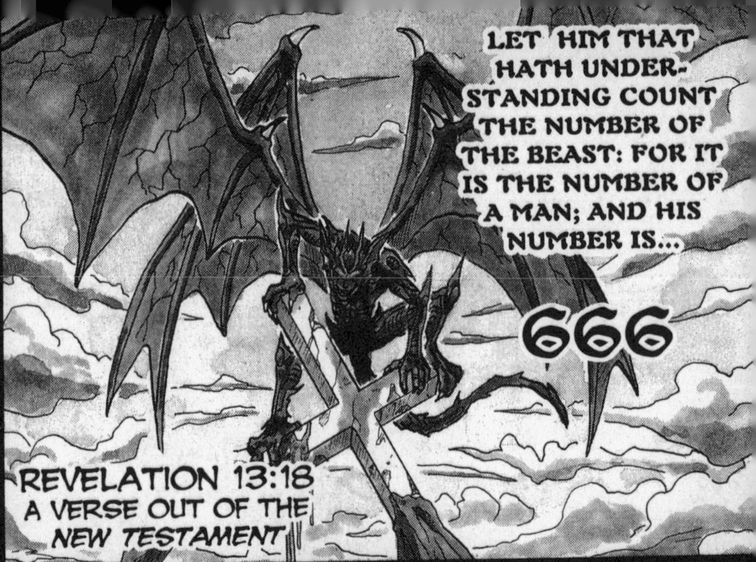
LET HIM THAT HATH UNDER-STANDING COUNT THE NUMBER OF THE BEAST: FOR IT IS THE NUMBER OF A MAN; AND HIS NUMBER IS...
666
REVELATION 13:18
A VERSE OUT OF THE *NEW TESTAMENT*

O-Parts Hunter

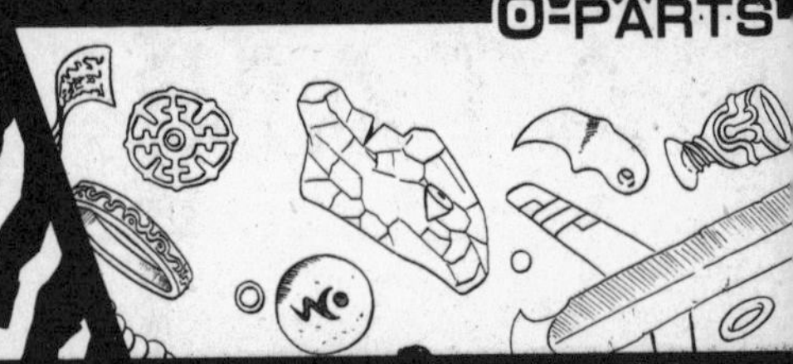
O-PARTS

O-Parts: Amazing artifacts with mystical powers left from an ancient civilization. They have been excavated from various ruins around the world. Depending on its Effect, an O-Part is given a ran from E to SS within a seven-ranking system.

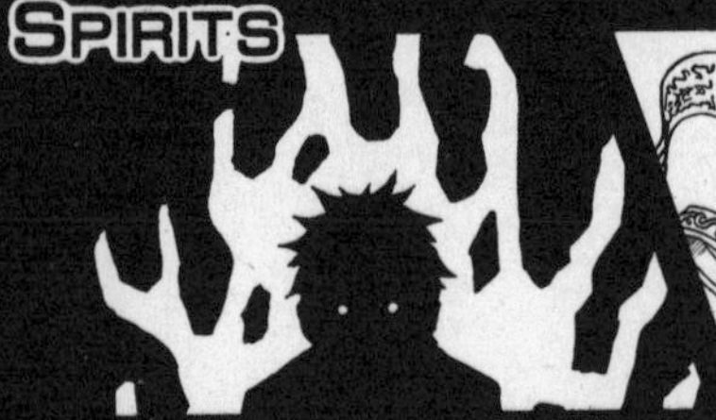
SPIRITS

Spirit: A special energy force which only the O.P.T.s have. The amount of Spirit an O.P.T. has within himself determines how strong of an O.P.T. he is.

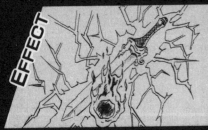

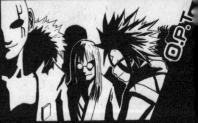

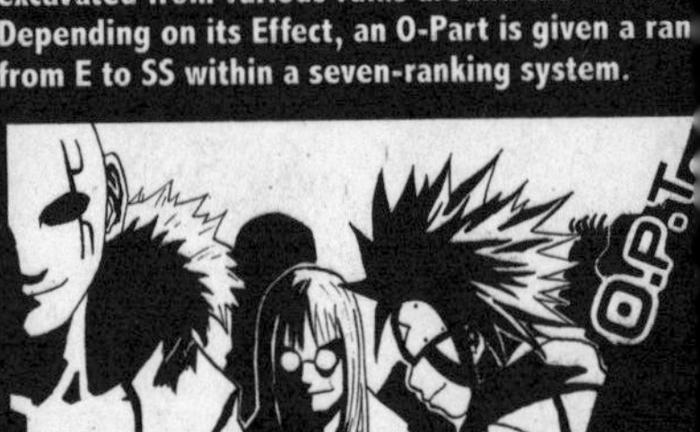
O.P.T.

O.P.T.: Those who have the ability to release and use the powers of the O-Parts. The name O.P.T. is an abbreviated form of O-Part Tactician.

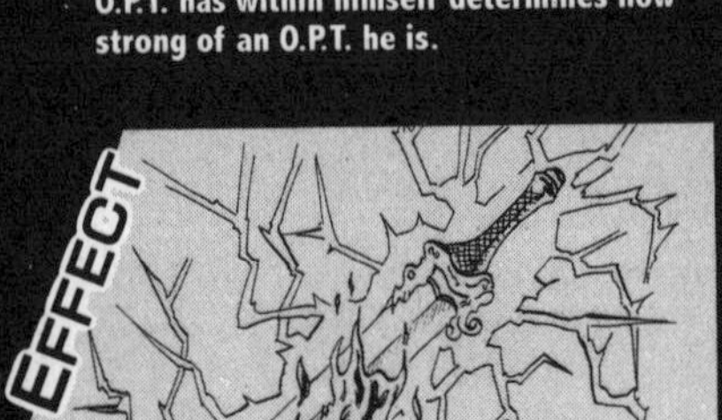
EFFECT

Effect: The special energy (power) the O-Parts hold. It can only be used when an O.P.T. sends his Spirit into an O-Part.

CHARACTERS

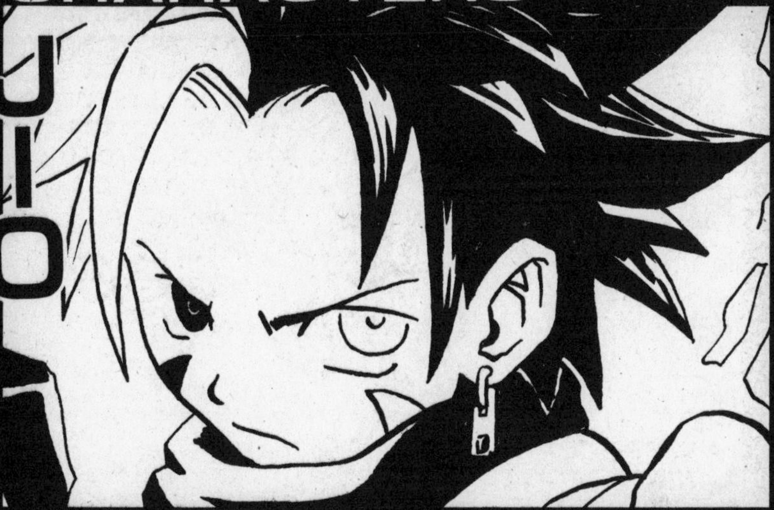
JIO

Jio Freed
An O.P.T. boy whose dream is world domination. He is a wild and powerful youth, but many secrets surround him.
O-Part: Zero-shiki (Rank C) Effect: Double (Increasing Power)

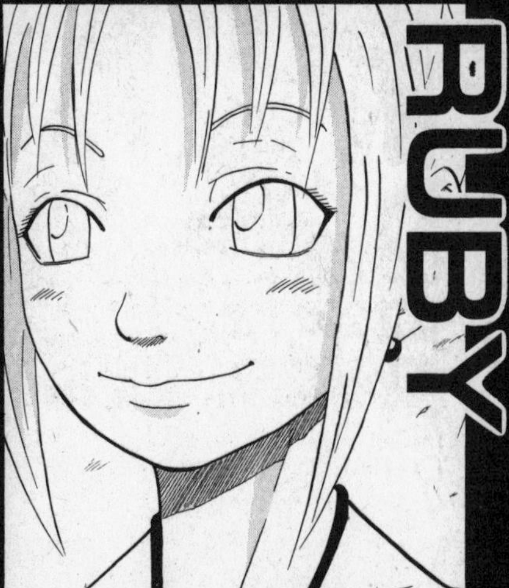
RUBY

Ruby Crescent
A treasure hunter who can decipher ancient texts. She meets Jio during her search for a legendary O-Part.

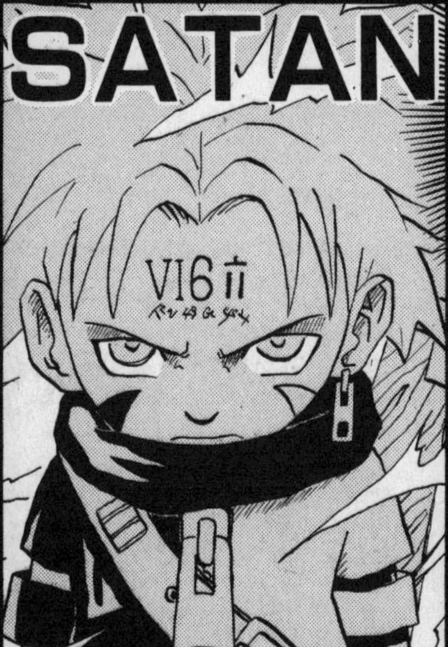
SATAN

????

O-Parts Hunter ™

Table of Contents

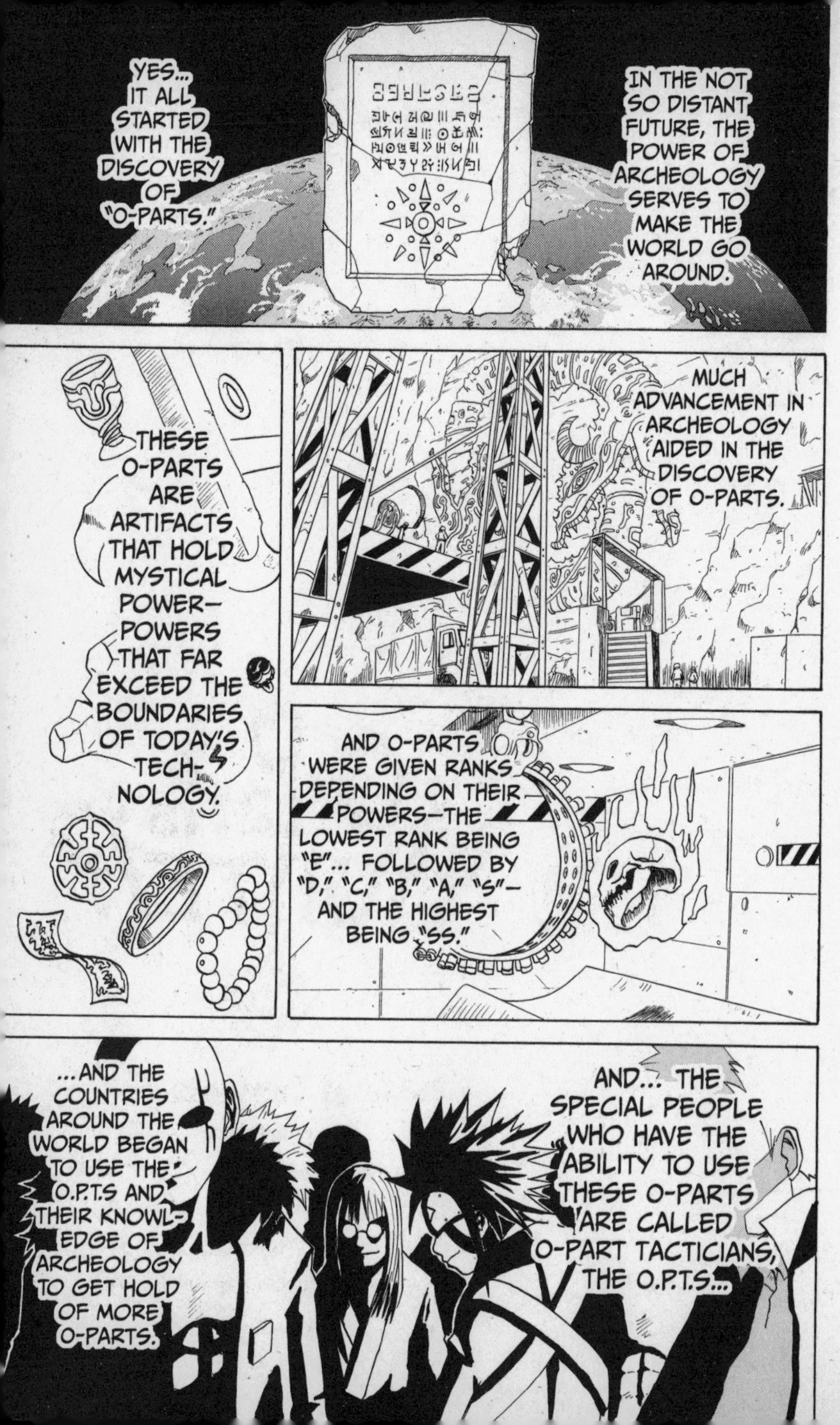
IN THE NOT SO DISTANT FUTURE, THE POWER OF ARCHEOLOGY SERVES TO MAKE THE WORLD GO AROUND.
YES... IT ALL STARTED WITH THE DISCOVERY OF "O-PARTS."
MUCH ADVANCEMENT IN ARCHEOLOGY AIDED IN THE DISCOVERY OF O-PARTS.
AND O-PARTS WERE GIVEN RANKS DEPENDING ON THEIR POWERS—THE LOWEST RANK BEING "E"... FOLLOWED BY "D," "C," "B," "A," "S"—AND THE HIGHEST BEING "SS."
THESE O-PARTS ARE ARTIFACTS THAT HOLD MYSTICAL POWER—POWERS THAT FAR EXCEED THE BOUNDARIES OF TODAY'S TECH-NOLOGY.
AND... THE SPECIAL PEOPLE WHO HAVE THE ABILITY TO USE THESE O-PARTS ARE CALLED O-PART TACTICIANS, THE O.P.T.S...
...AND THE COUNTRIES AROUND THE WORLD BEGAN TO USE THE O.P.T.S AND THEIR KNOWL-EDGE OF ARCHEOLOGY TO GET HOLD OF MORE O-PARTS.

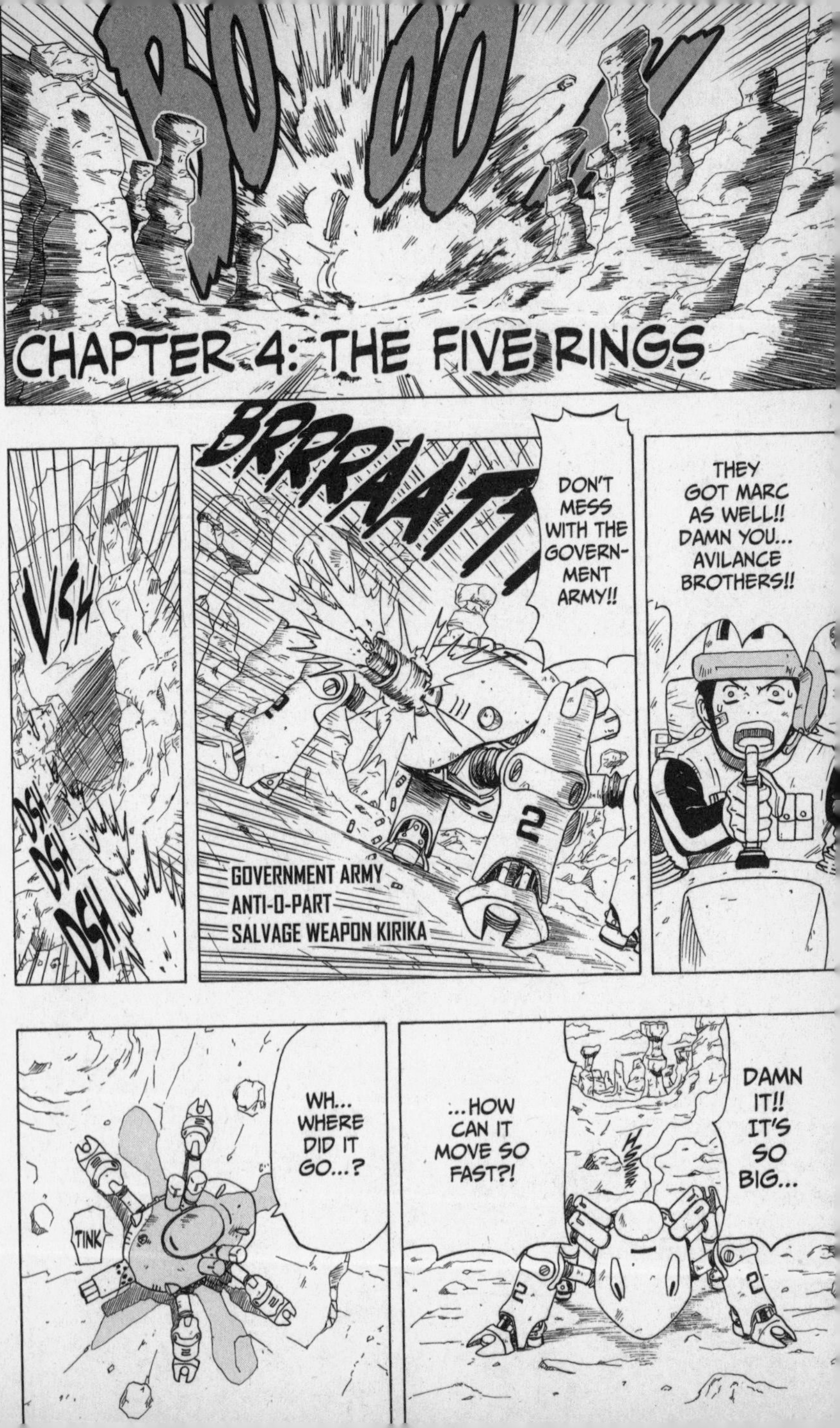
CHAPTER 4: THE FIVE RINGS
THEY GOT MARC AS WELL!! DAMN YOU... AVILANCE BROTHERS!!
BRRRAAT!
DON'T MESS WITH THE GOVERNMENT ARMY!!
GOVERNMENT ARMY ANTI-O-PART SALVAGE WEAPON KIRIKA
VSH
DSH DSH DSH
DAMN IT!! IT'S SO BIG...
...HOW CAN IT MOVE SO FAST?!
WH... WHERE DID IT GO...?
TINK

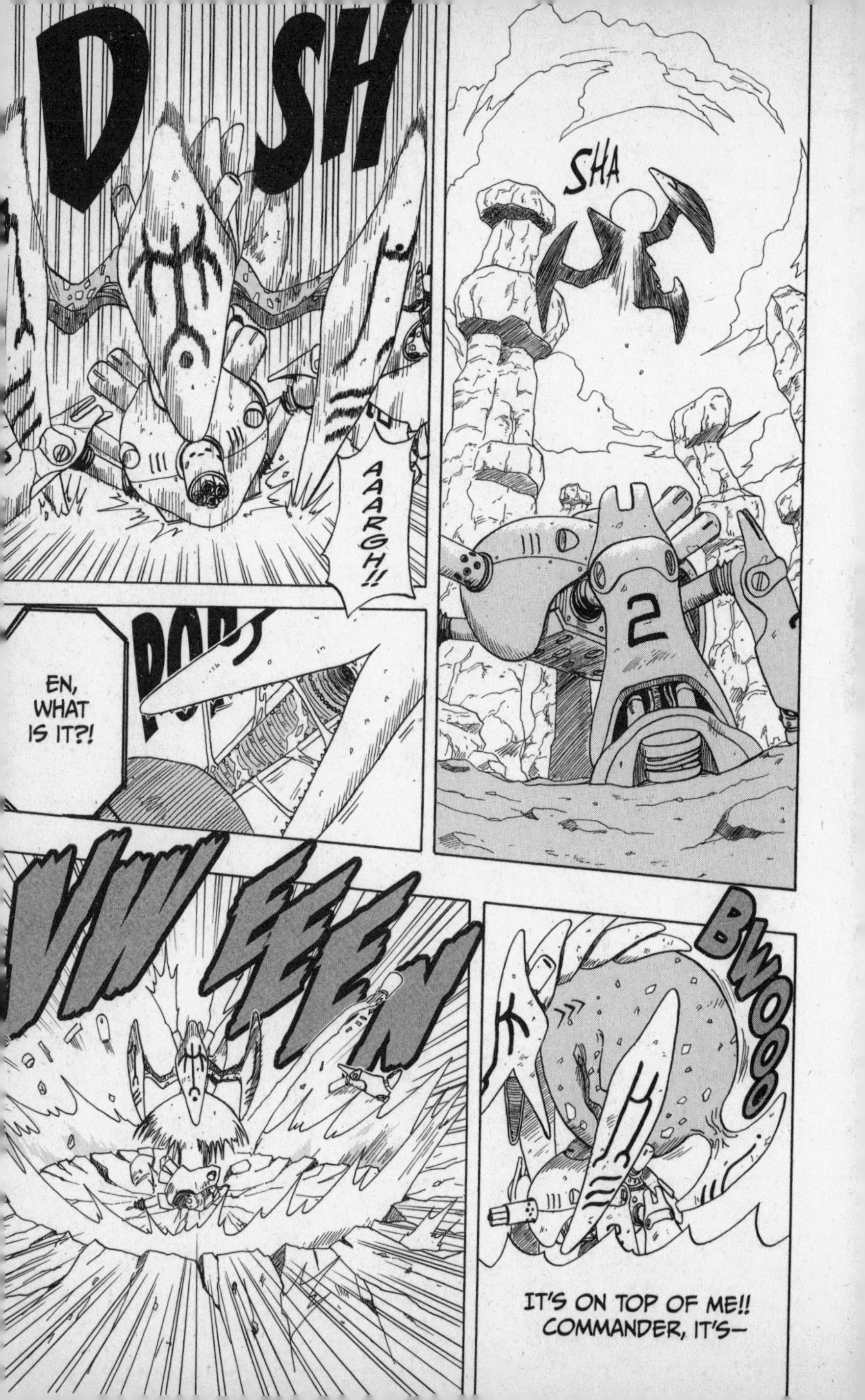
SHA
AAARGH!!
EN, WHAT IS IT?!
BWOOO
IT'S ON TOP OF ME!! COMMANDER, IT'S—

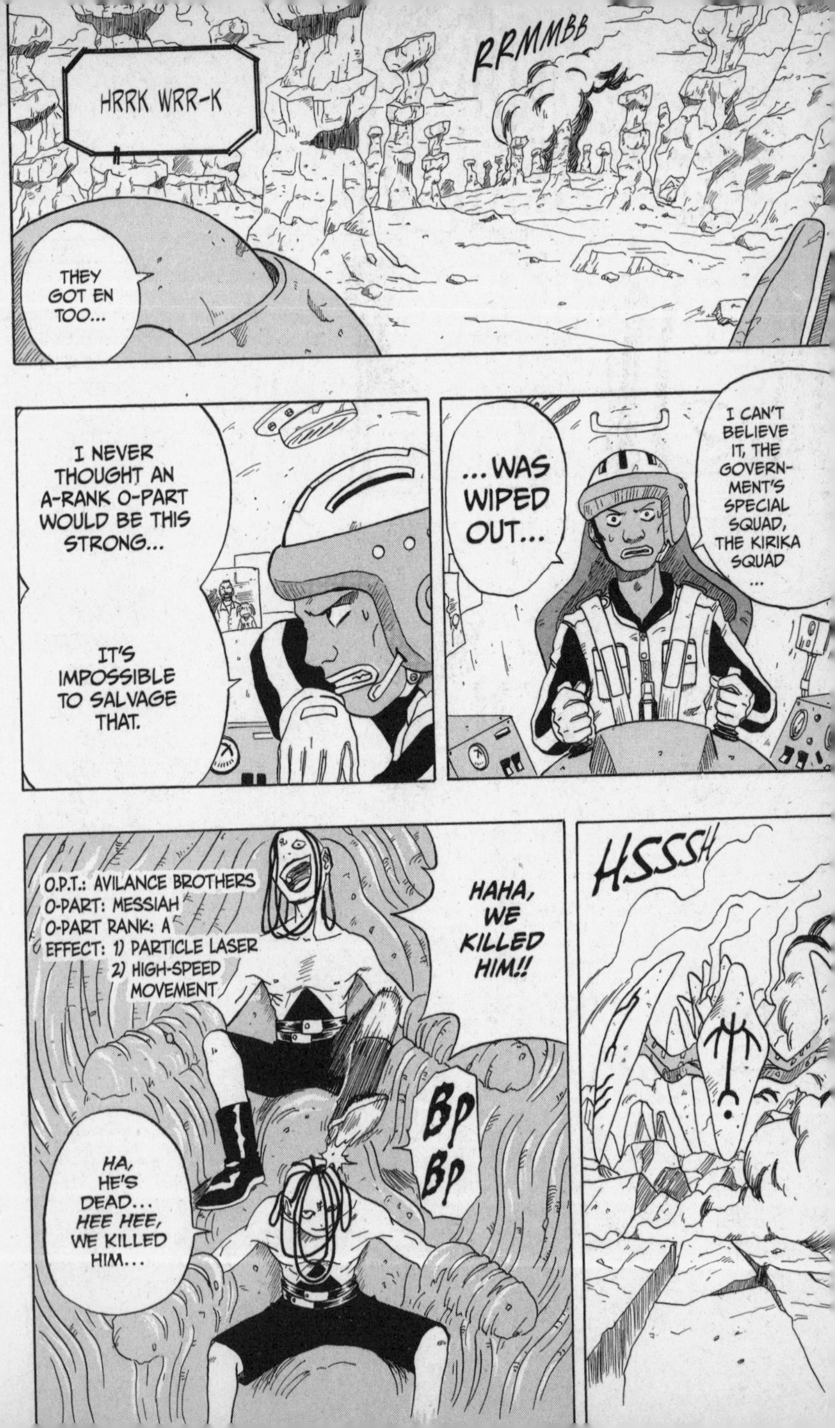
RRMMBB
HRRK WRR-K
THEY GOT EN TOO...
I CAN'T BELIEVE IT, THE GOVERNMENT'S SPECIAL SQUAD, THE KIRIKA SQUAD ...
...WAS WIPED OUT...
I NEVER THOUGHT AN A-RANK O-PART WOULD BE THIS STRONG...
IT'S IMPOSSIBLE TO SALVAGE THAT.
HSSSH
O.P.T.: AVILANCE BROTHERS
O-PART: MESSIAH
O-PART RANK: A
EFFECT: 1) PARTICLE LASER
2) HIGH-SPEED MOVEMENT
HAHA, WE KILLED HIM!!
BP BP
HA, HE'S DEAD... HEE HEE, WE KILLED HIM...

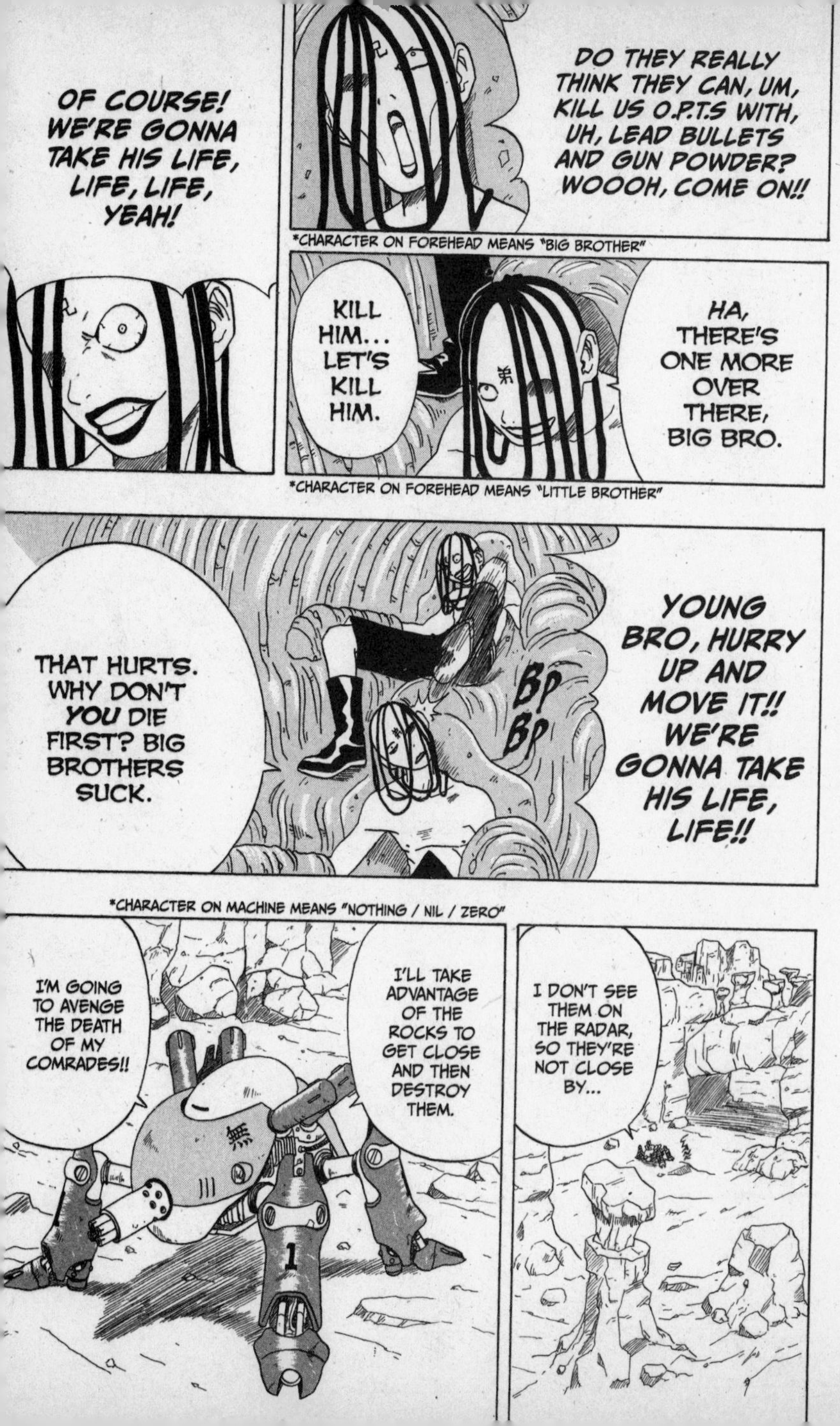
DO THEY REALLY THINK THEY CAN, UM, KILL US O.P.T.S WITH, UH, LEAD BULLETS AND GUN POWDER? WOOOH, COME ON!!
*CHARACTER ON FOREHEAD MEANS "BIG BROTHER"
HA, THERE'S ONE MORE OVER THERE, BIG BRO.
KILL HIM... LET'S KILL HIM.
*CHARACTER ON FOREHEAD MEANS "LITTLE BROTHER"
OF COURSE! WE'RE GONNA TAKE HIS LIFE, LIFE, LIFE, YEAH!
YOUNG BRO, HURRY UP AND MOVE IT!! WE'RE GONNA TAKE HIS LIFE, LIFE!!
BP BP
THAT HURTS. WHY DON'T *YOU* DIE FIRST? BIG BROTHERS SUCK.
*CHARACTER ON MACHINE MEANS "NOTHING / NIL / ZERO"
I DON'T SEE THEM ON THE RADAR, SO THEY'RE NOT CLOSE BY...
I'LL TAKE ADVANTAGE OF THE ROCKS TO GET CLOSE AND THEN DESTROY THEM.
I'M GOING TO AVENGE THE DEATH OF MY COMRADES!!
無
1

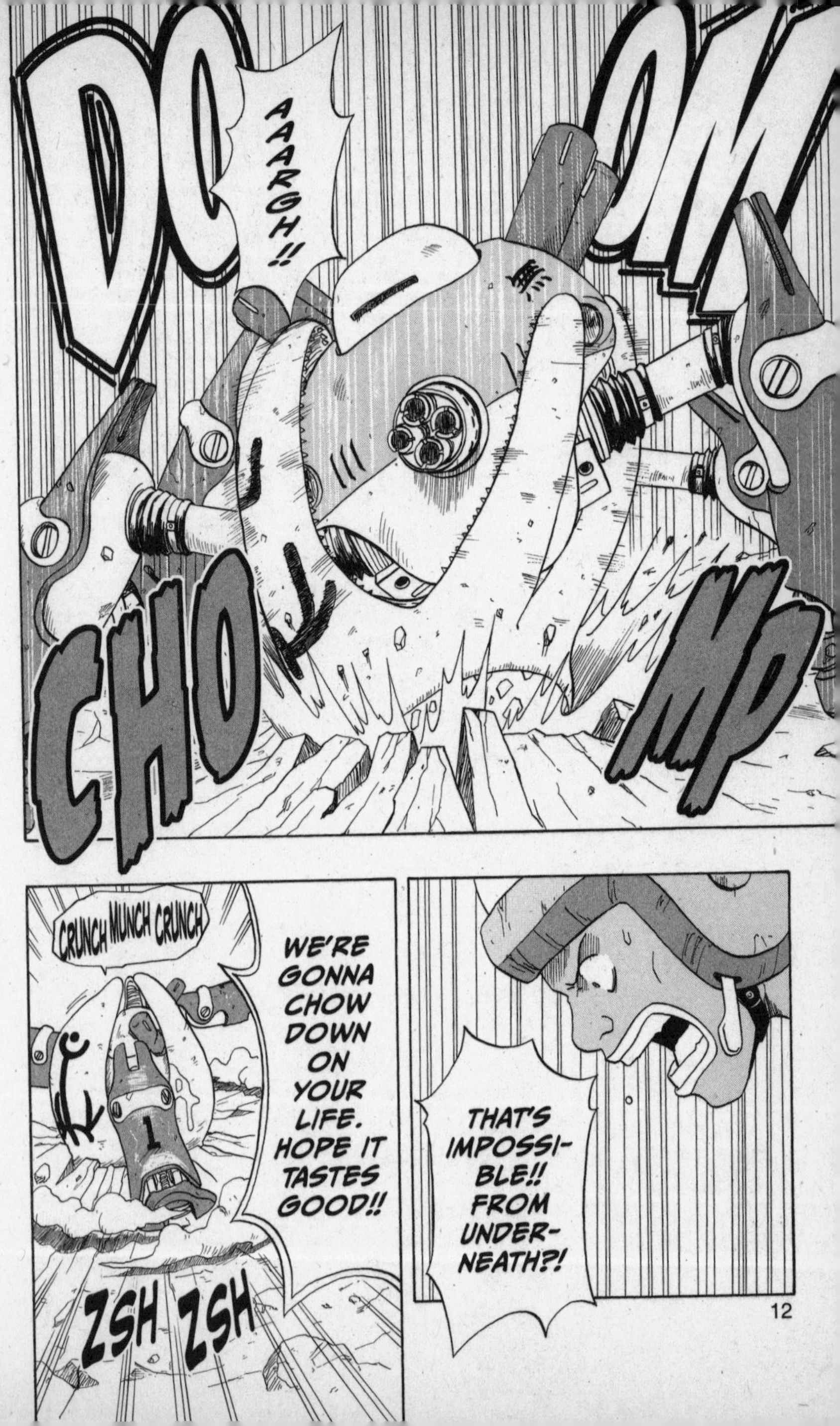
DOOM
AAAARGH!!
CHOMP
THAT'S IMPOSSI-BLE!! FROM UNDER-NEATH?!
CRUNCH MUNCH CRUNCH
WE'RE GONNA CHOW DOWN ON YOUR LIFE. HOPE IT TASTES GOOD!!
ZSH ZSH

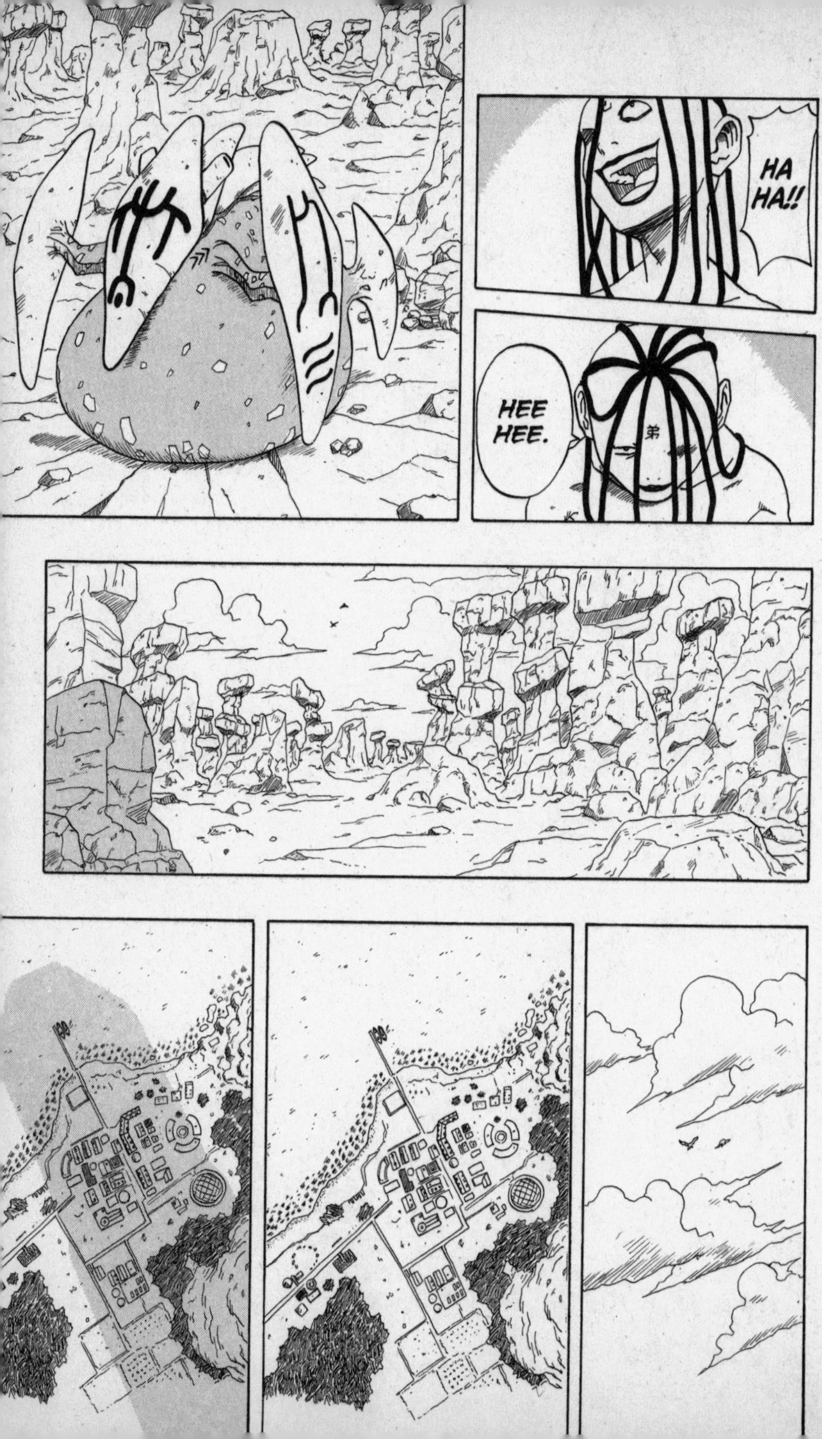
HA HA!!
HEE HEE.

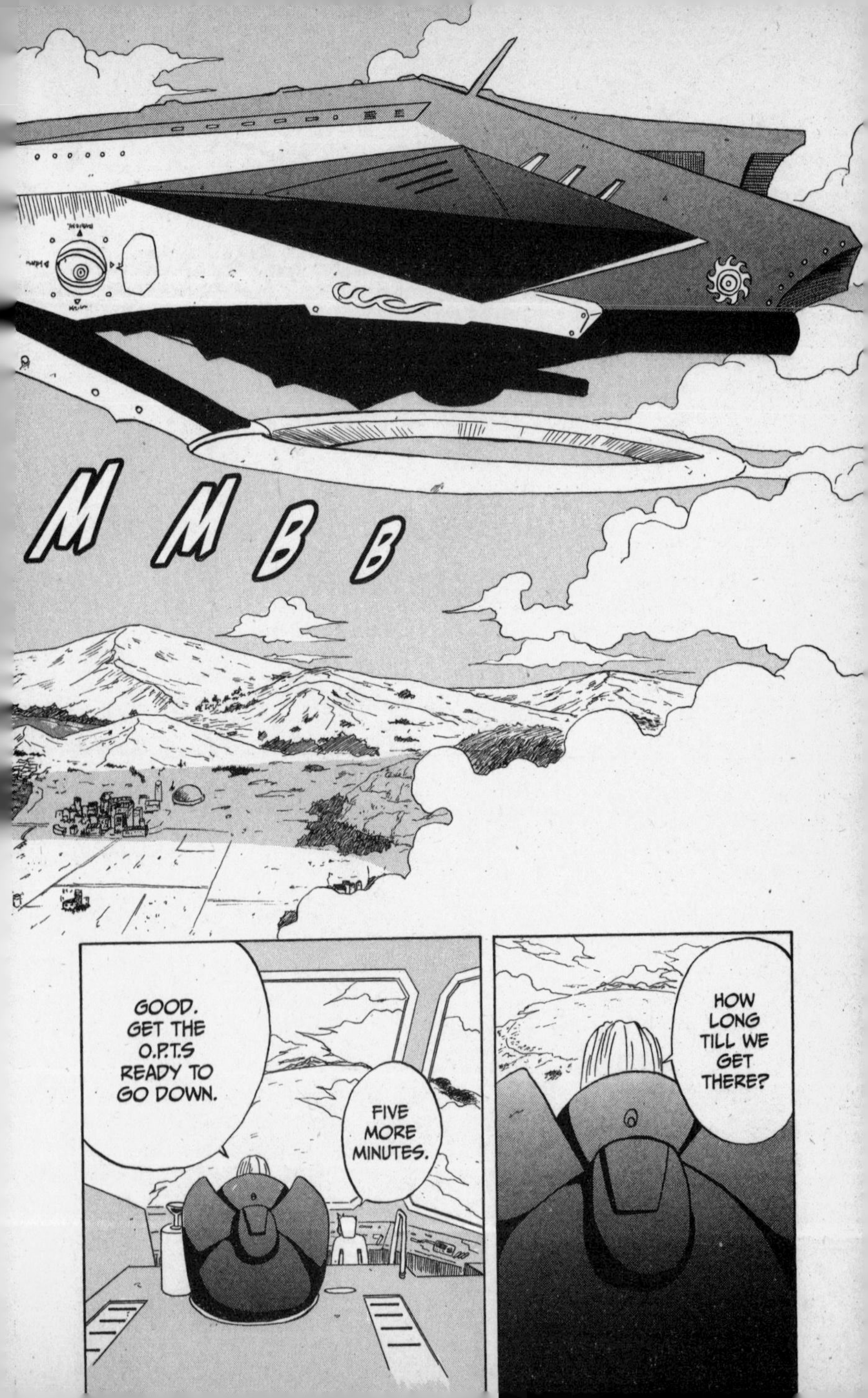
M M B B
HOW LONG TILL WE GET THERE?
FIVE MORE MINUTES.
GOOD. GET THE O.P.T.S READY TO GO DOWN.

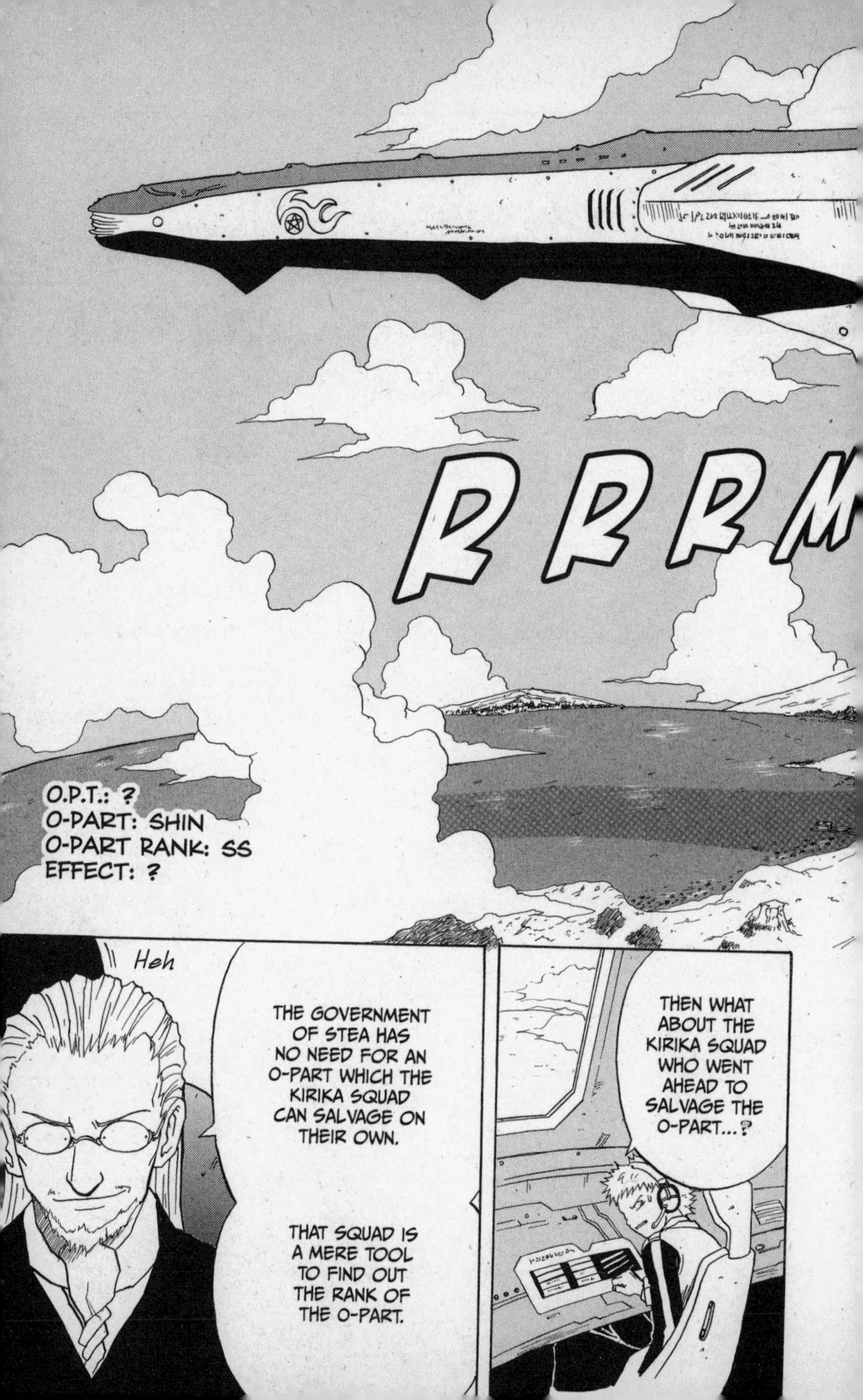
RRRM
O.P.T.: ?
O-PART: SHIN
O-PART RANK: SS
EFFECT: ?
THEN WHAT ABOUT THE KIRIKA SQUAD WHO WENT AHEAD TO SALVAGE THE O-PART...?
Heh
THE GOVERNMENT OF STEA HAS NO NEED FOR AN O-PART WHICH THE KIRIKA SQUAD CAN SALVAGE ON THEIR OWN.
THAT SQUAD IS A MERE TOOL TO FIND OUT THE RANK OF THE O-PART.

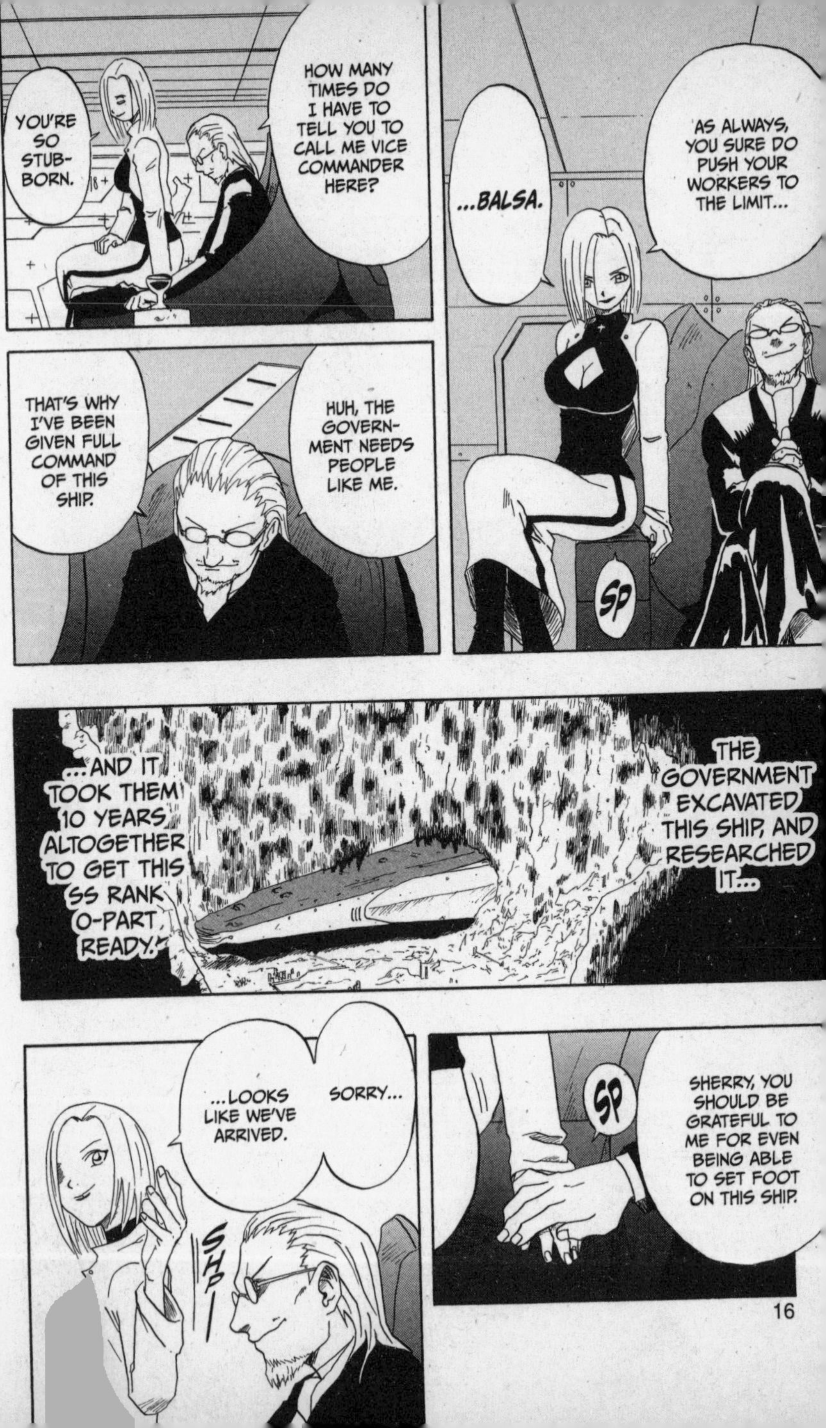
AS ALWAYS, YOU SURE DO PUSH YOUR WORKERS TO THE LIMIT...
...BALSA.
SP
HOW MANY TIMES DO I HAVE TO TELL YOU TO CALL ME VICE COMMANDER HERE?
YOU'RE SO STUB-BORN.
HUH, THE GOVERN-MENT NEEDS PEOPLE LIKE ME.
THAT'S WHY I'VE BEEN GIVEN FULL COMMAND OF THIS SHIP.
THE GOVERNMENT EXCAVATED THIS SHIP, AND RESEARCHED IT...
...AND IT TOOK THEM 10 YEARS ALTOGETHER TO GET THIS SS RANK O-PART READY.
SP
SHERRY, YOU SHOULD BE GRATEFUL TO ME FOR EVEN BEING ABLE TO SET FOOT ON THIS SHIP.
SORRY...
...LOOKS LIKE WE'VE ARRIVED.
SHP!

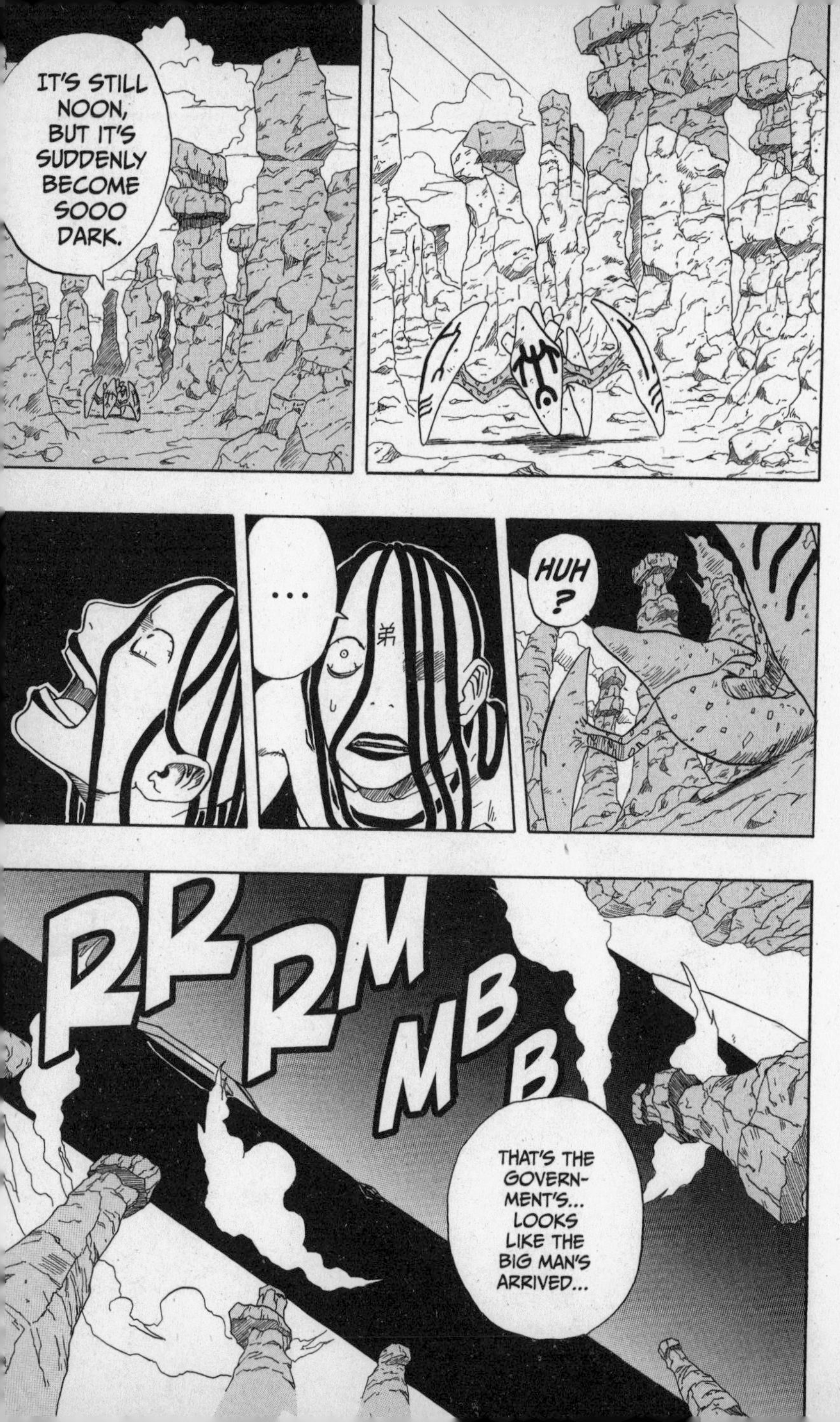
IT'S STILL NOON, BUT IT'S SUDDENLY BECOME SOOO DARK.
HUH?
...
RRRMMBB
THAT'S THE GOVERNMENT'S... LOOKS LIKE THE BIG MAN'S ARRIVED...

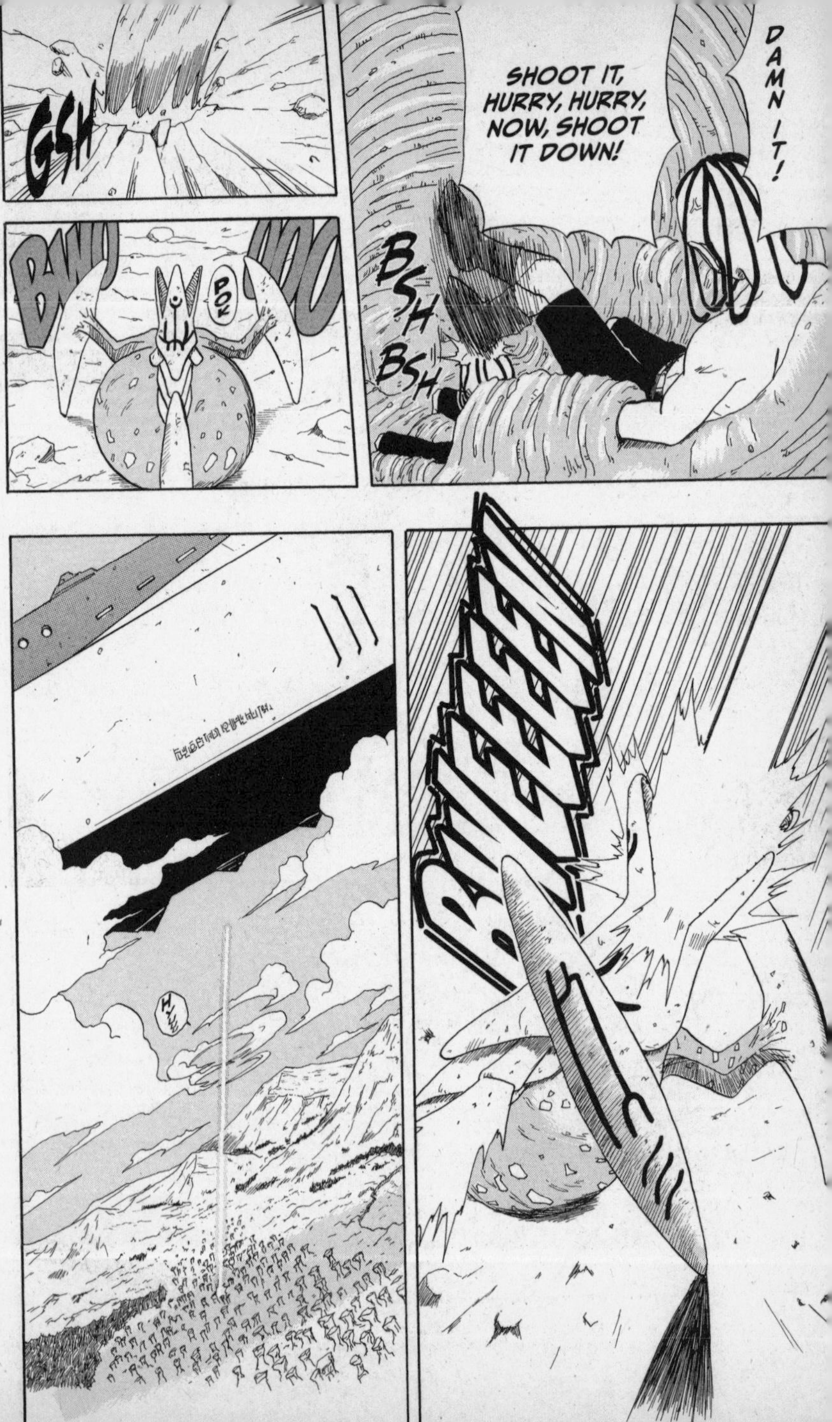
SHOOT IT, HURRY, HURRY, NOW, SHOOT IT DOWN!
DAMN IT!
BSH BSH
GSH
BAWOOO
POK

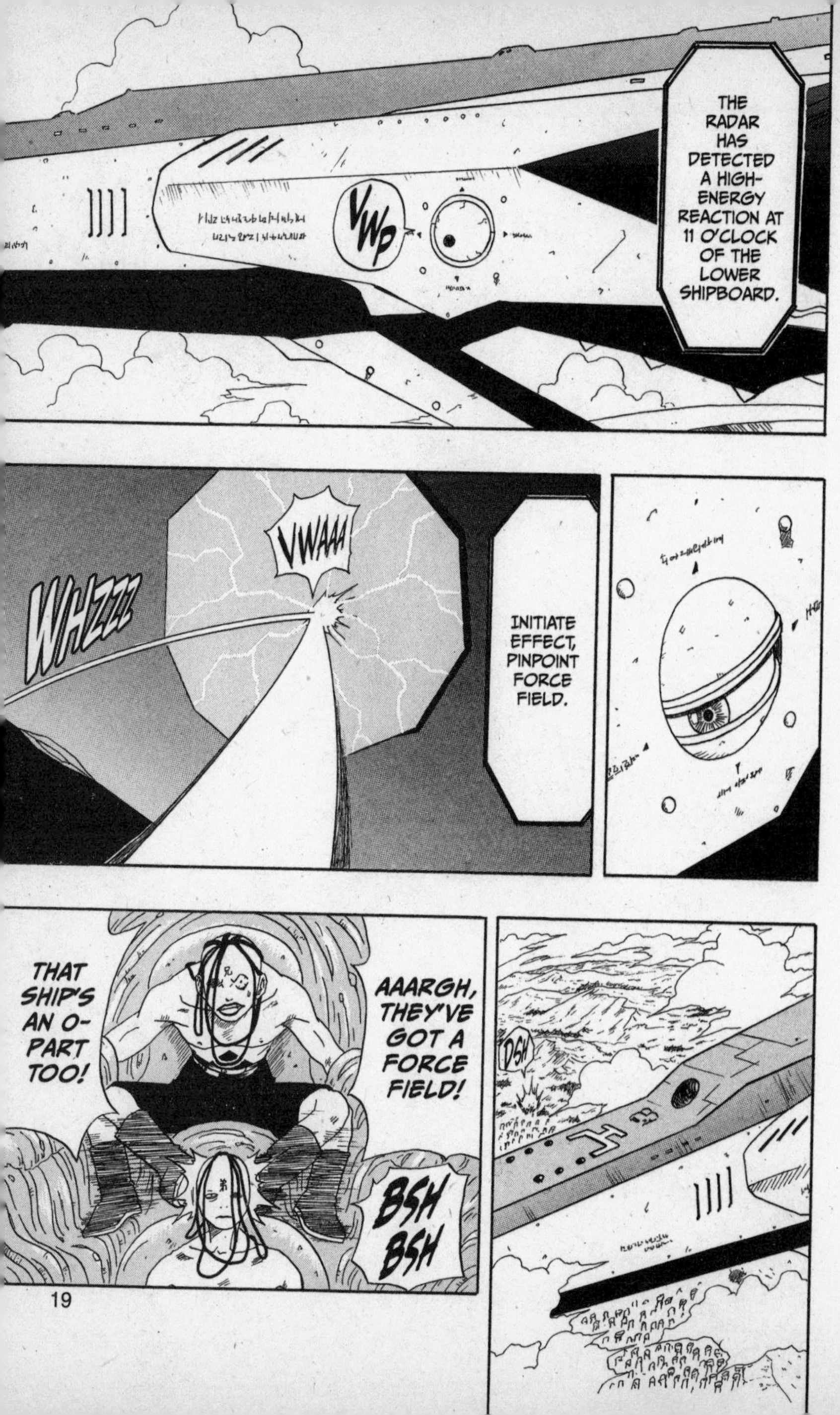
THE RADAR HAS DETECTED A HIGH-ENERGY REACTION AT 11 O'CLOCK OF THE LOWER SHIPBOARD.
VWP
INITIATE EFFECT, PINPOINT FORCE FIELD.
VWAAA
WHZZZ
DSH
AAARGH, THEY'VE GOT A FORCE FIELD!
THAT SHIP'S AN O-PART TOO!
BSH BSH

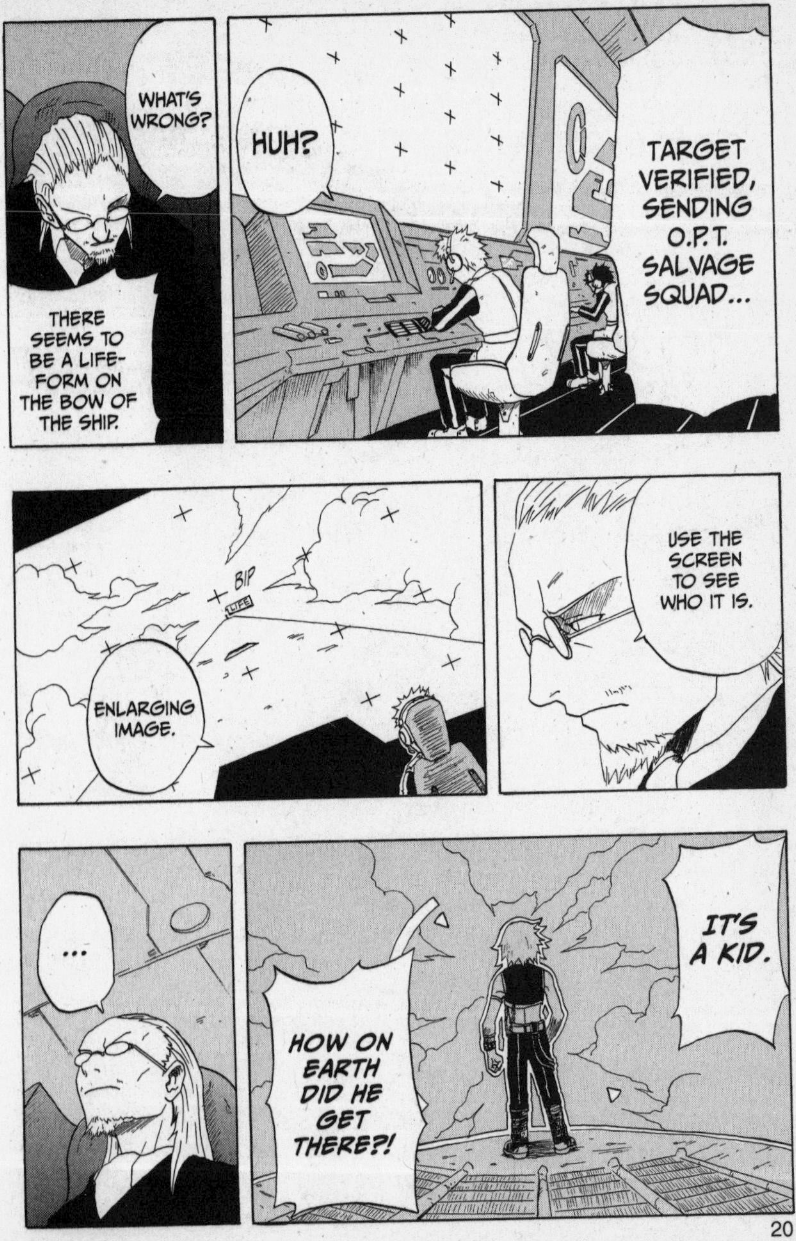
TARGET VERIFIED, SENDING O.P.T. SALVAGE SQUAD...
HUH?
WHAT'S WRONG?
THERE SEEMS TO BE A LIFE-FORM ON THE BOW OF THE SHIP.
USE THE SCREEN TO SEE WHO IT IS.
BIP
LIFE
ENLARGING IMAGE.
IT'S A KID.
HOW ON EARTH DID HE GET THERE?!
...

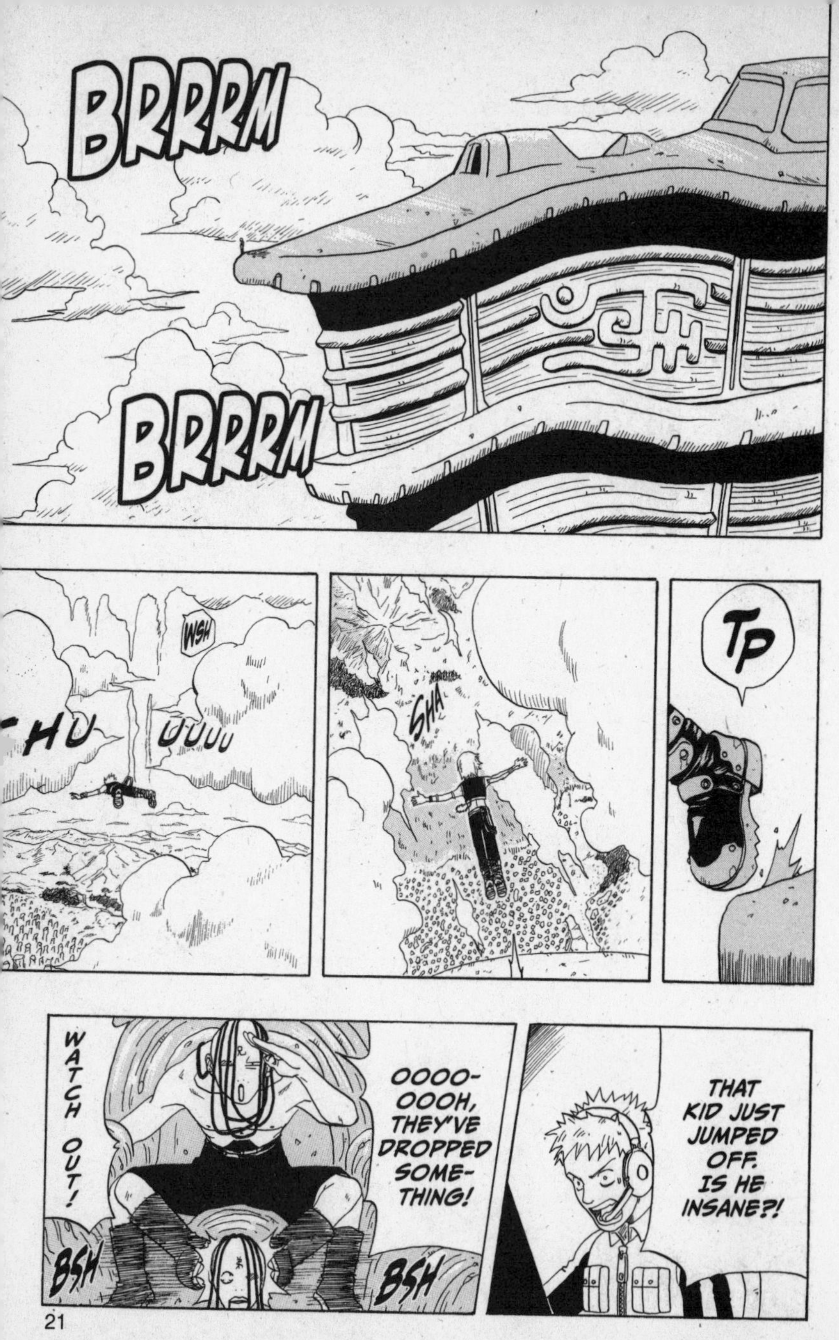
BRRRM
BRRRM
TP
SHA
WSH
HU UUUU
THAT KID JUST JUMPED OFF. IS HE INSANE?!
OOOO-OOOH, THEY'VE DROPPED SOME-THING!
WATCH OUT!
BSH
BSH

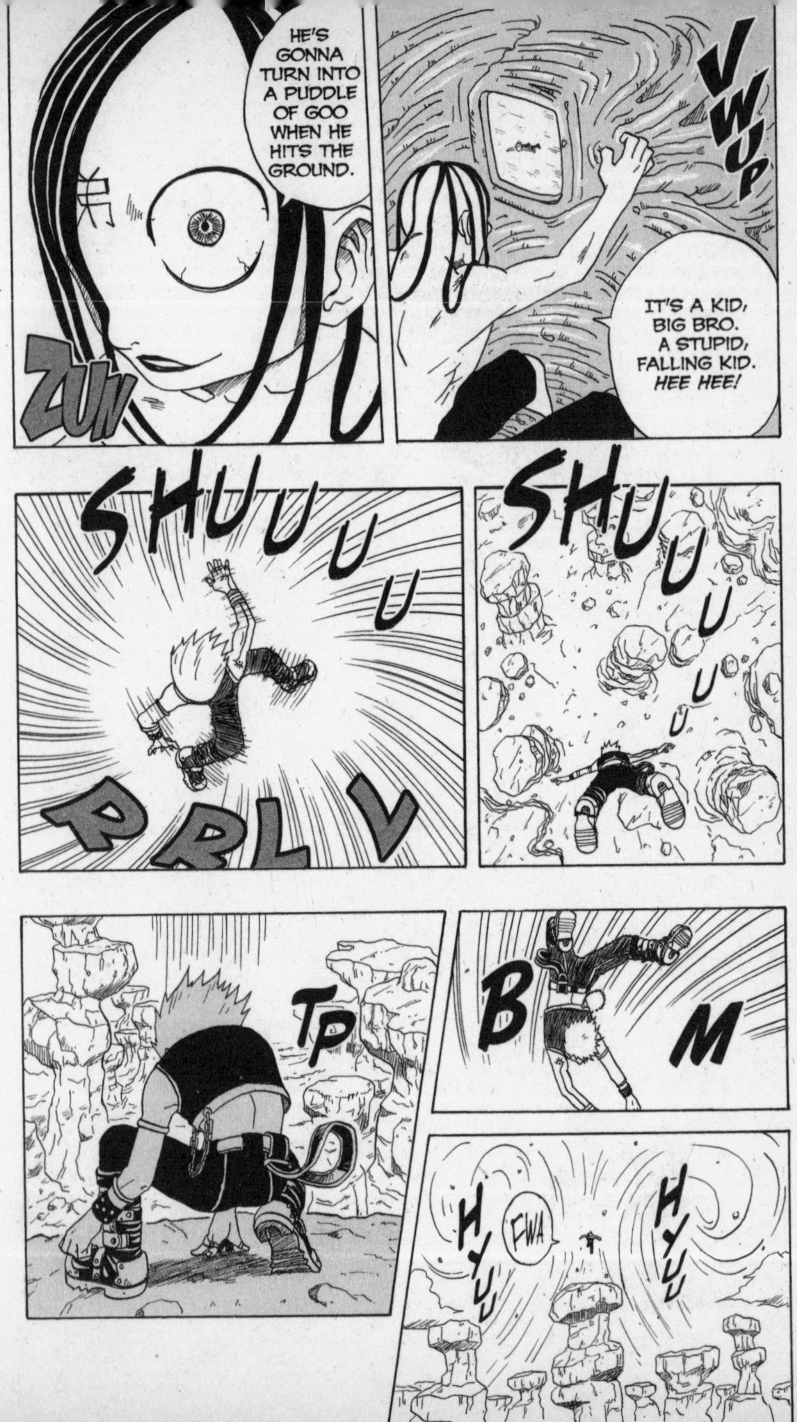

VWUP
IT'S A KID, BIG BRO. A STUPID, FALLING KID. *HEE HEE!*
HE'S GONNA TURN INTO A PUDDLE OF GOO WHEN HE HITS THE GROUND.
ZUN
SHUUUUUU
SHUUUUU
RRLV
BM
HYUU
FWA
HYUU
TP

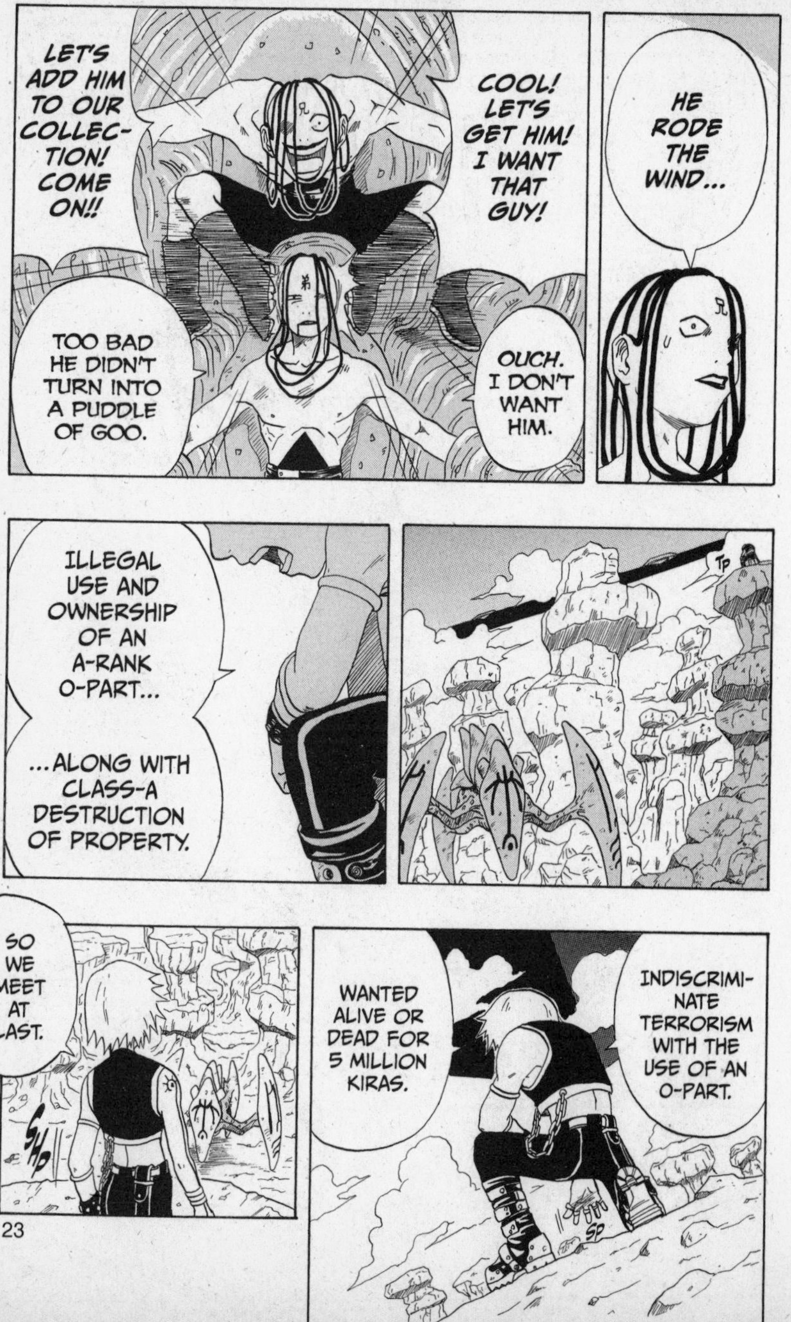
HE RODE THE WIND...
COOL! LET'S GET HIM! I WANT THAT GUY!
LET'S ADD HIM TO OUR COLLECTION! COME ON!!
OUCH. I DON'T WANT HIM.
TOO BAD HE DIDN'T TURN INTO A PUDDLE OF GOO.
TP
ILLEGAL USE AND OWNERSHIP OF AN A-RANK O-PART...
...ALONG WITH CLASS-A DESTRUCTION OF PROPERTY.
INDISCRIMINATE TERRORISM WITH THE USE OF AN O-PART.
WANTED ALIVE OR DEAD FOR 5 MILLION KIRAS.
SP
SO WE MEET AT LAST.
SHP

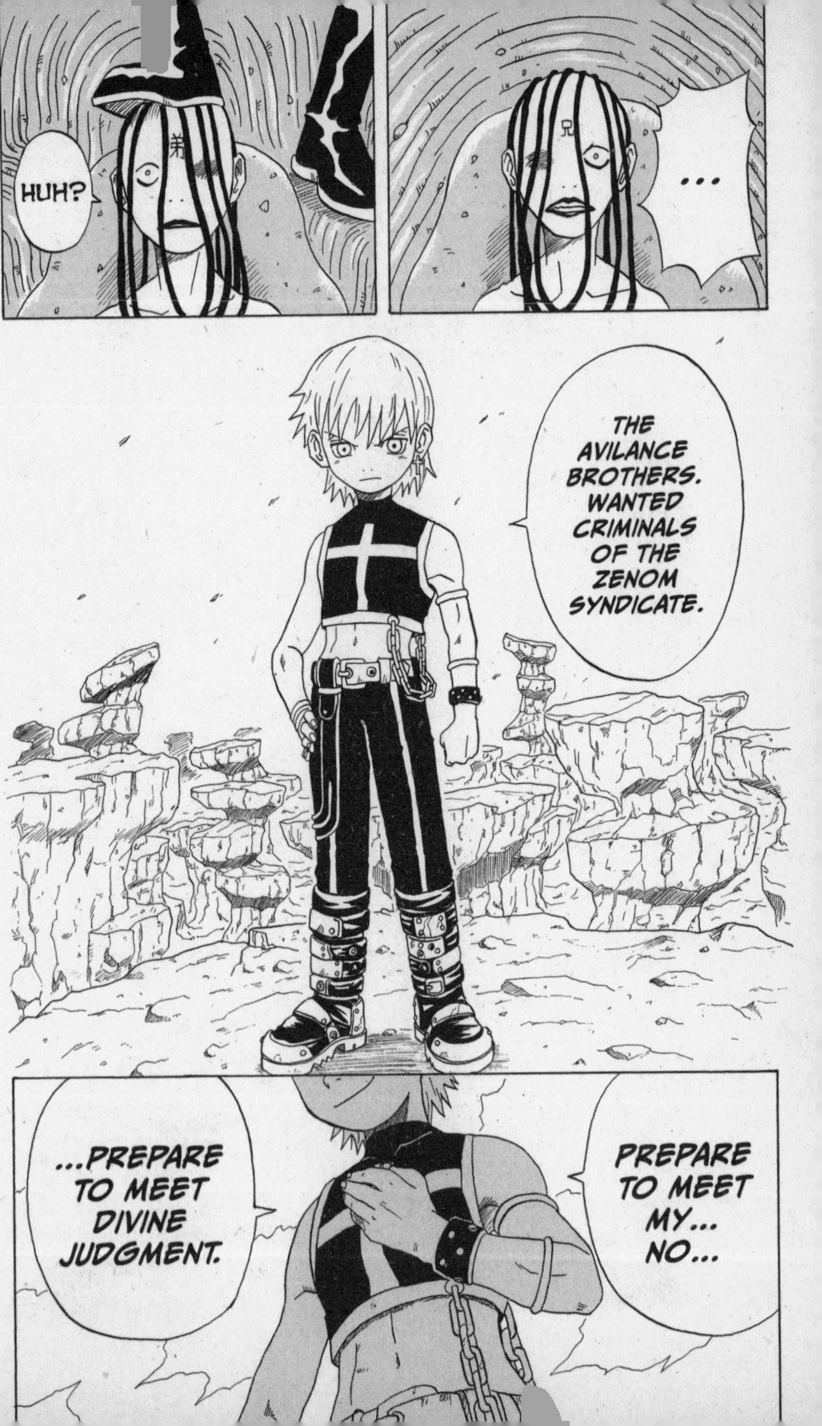
...
HUH?
THE AVILANCE BROTHERS. WANTED CRIMINALS OF THE ZENOM SYNDICATE.
PREPARE TO MEET MY... NO...
...PREPARE TO MEET DIVINE JUDGMENT.

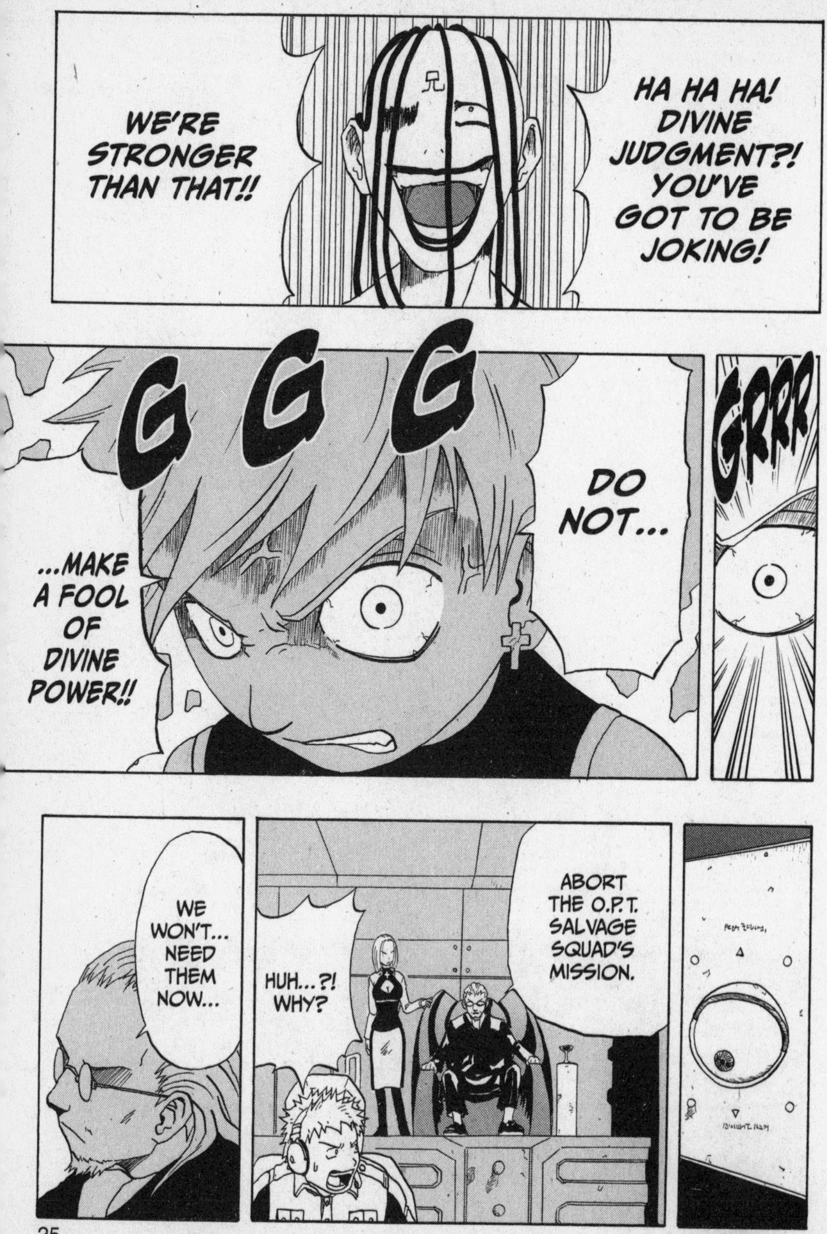
HA HA HA! DIVINE JUDGMENT?! YOU'VE GOT TO BE JOKING!
WE'RE STRONGER THAN THAT!!
GRRR
DO NOT...
G G G
...MAKE A FOOL OF DIVINE POWER!!
ABORT THE O.P.T. SALVAGE SQUAD'S MISSION.
HUH...?! WHY?
WE WON'T... NEED THEM NOW...

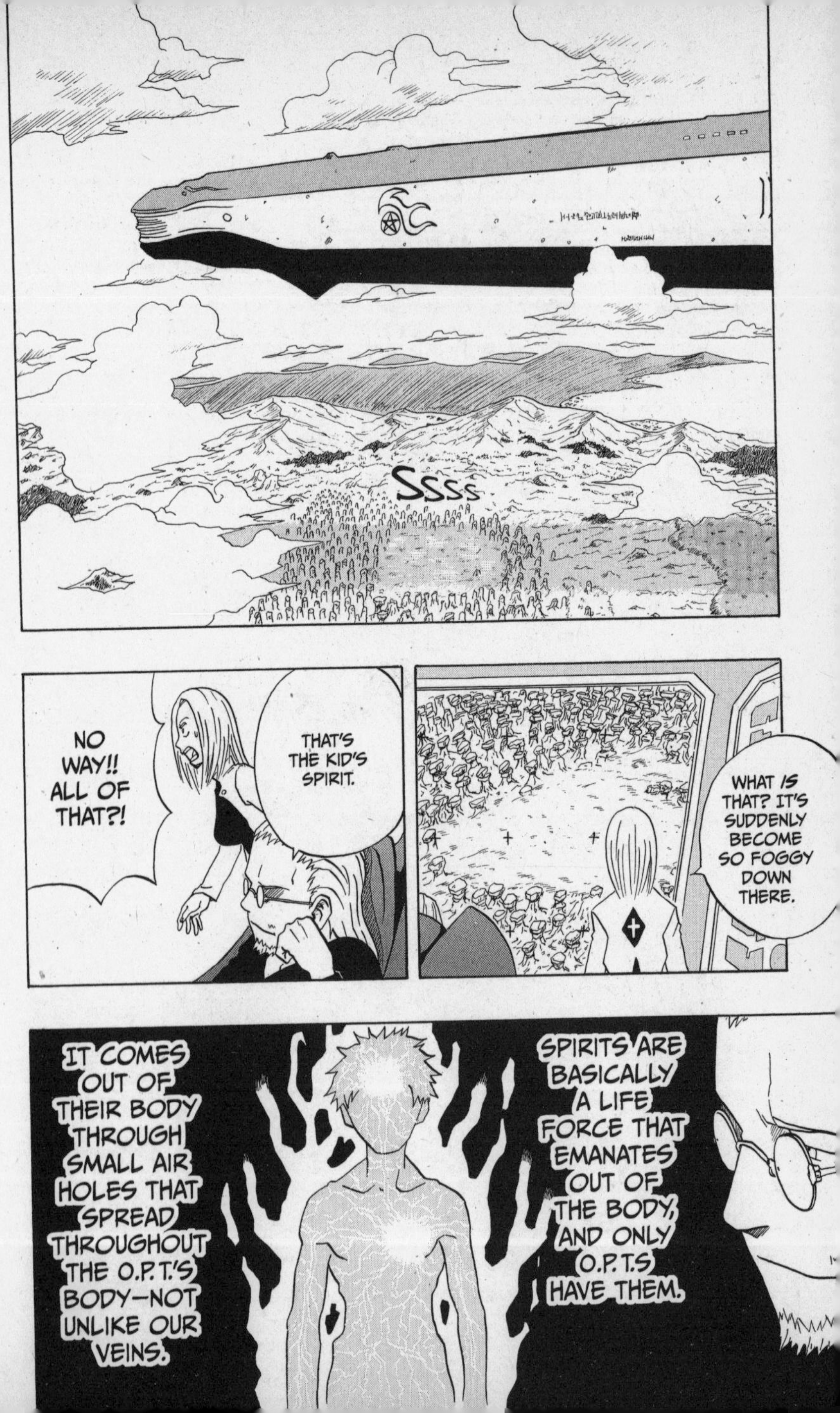
Ssss
WHAT *IS* THAT? IT'S SUDDENLY BECOME SO FOGGY DOWN THERE.
THAT'S THE KID'S SPIRIT.
NO WAY!! ALL OF THAT?!
SPIRITS ARE BASICALLY A LIFE FORCE THAT EMANATES OUT OF THE BODY, AND ONLY O.P.T.S HAVE THEM.
IT COMES OUT OF THEIR BODY THROUGH SMALL AIR HOLES THAT SPREAD THROUGHOUT THE O.P.T.'S BODY—NOT UNLIKE OUR VEINS.

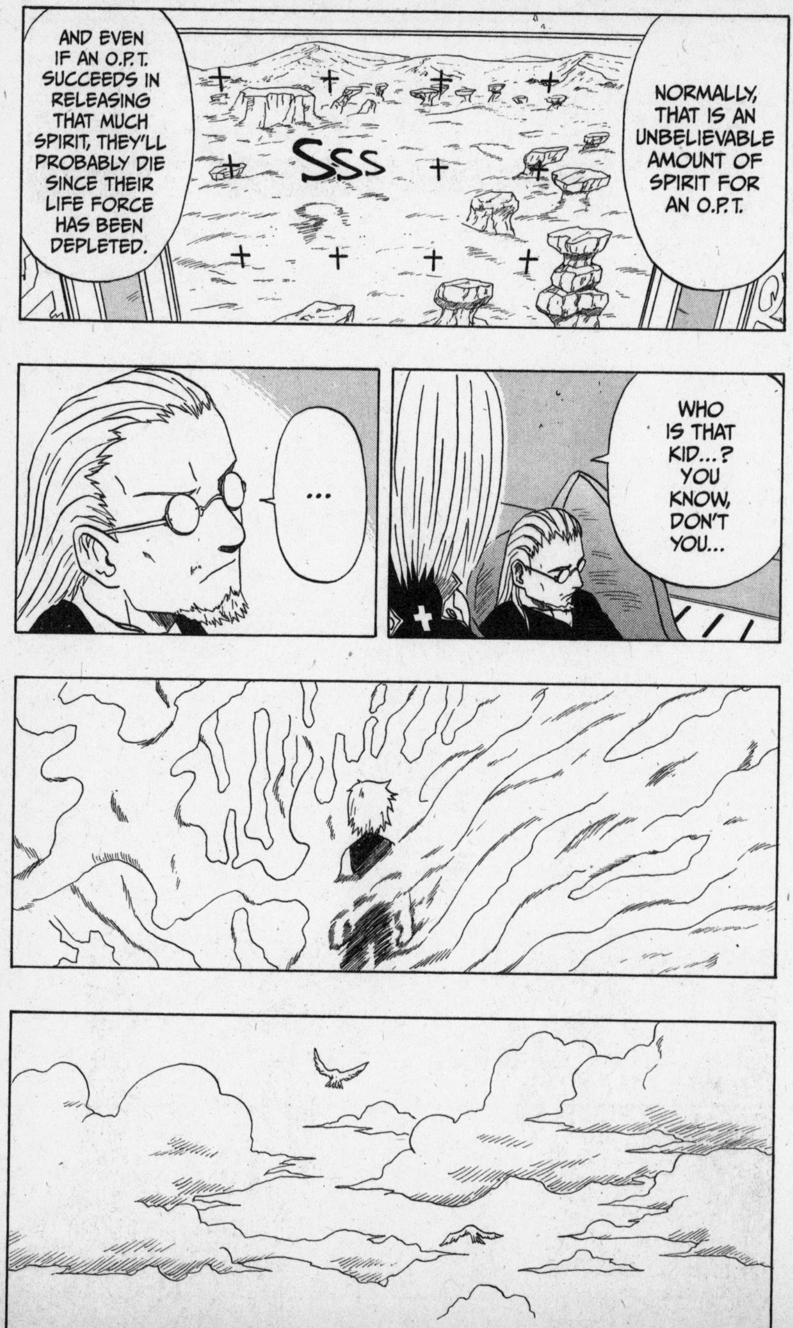
NORMALLY, THAT IS AN UNBELIEVABLE AMOUNT OF SPIRIT FOR AN O.P.T.
SSS
AND EVEN IF AN O.P.T. SUCCEEDS IN RELEASING THAT MUCH SPIRIT, THEY'LL PROBABLY DIE SINCE THEIR LIFE FORCE HAS BEEN DEPLETED.
WHO IS THAT KID...? YOU KNOW, DON'T YOU...
...

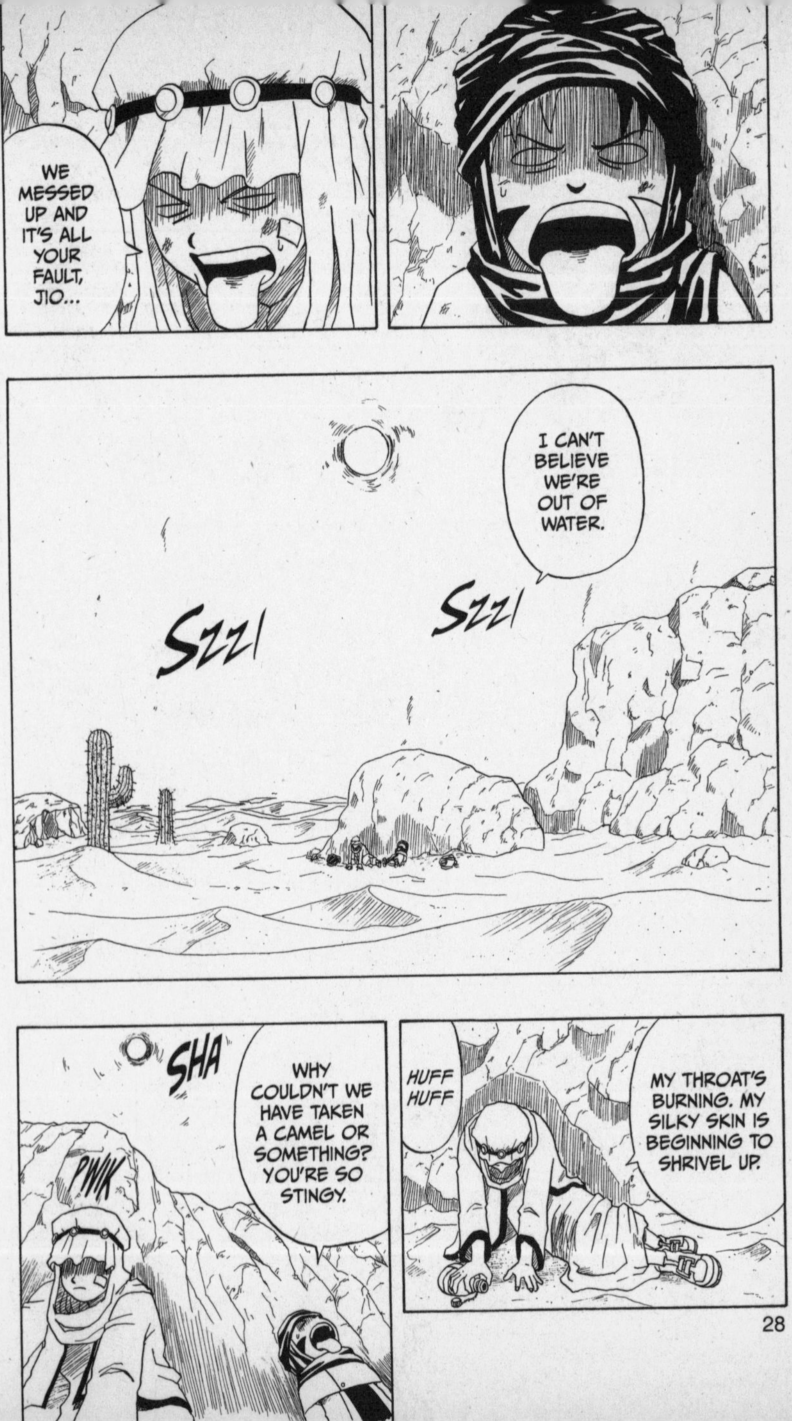
WE MESSED UP AND IT'S ALL YOUR FAULT, JIO...
I CAN'T BELIEVE WE'RE OUT OF WATER.
SZZL
SZZL
MY THROAT'S BURNING. MY SILKY SKIN IS BEGINNING TO SHRIVEL UP.
HUFF HUFF
SHA
WHY COULDN'T WE HAVE TAKEN A CAMEL OR SOMETHING? YOU'RE SO STINGY.
PWIK

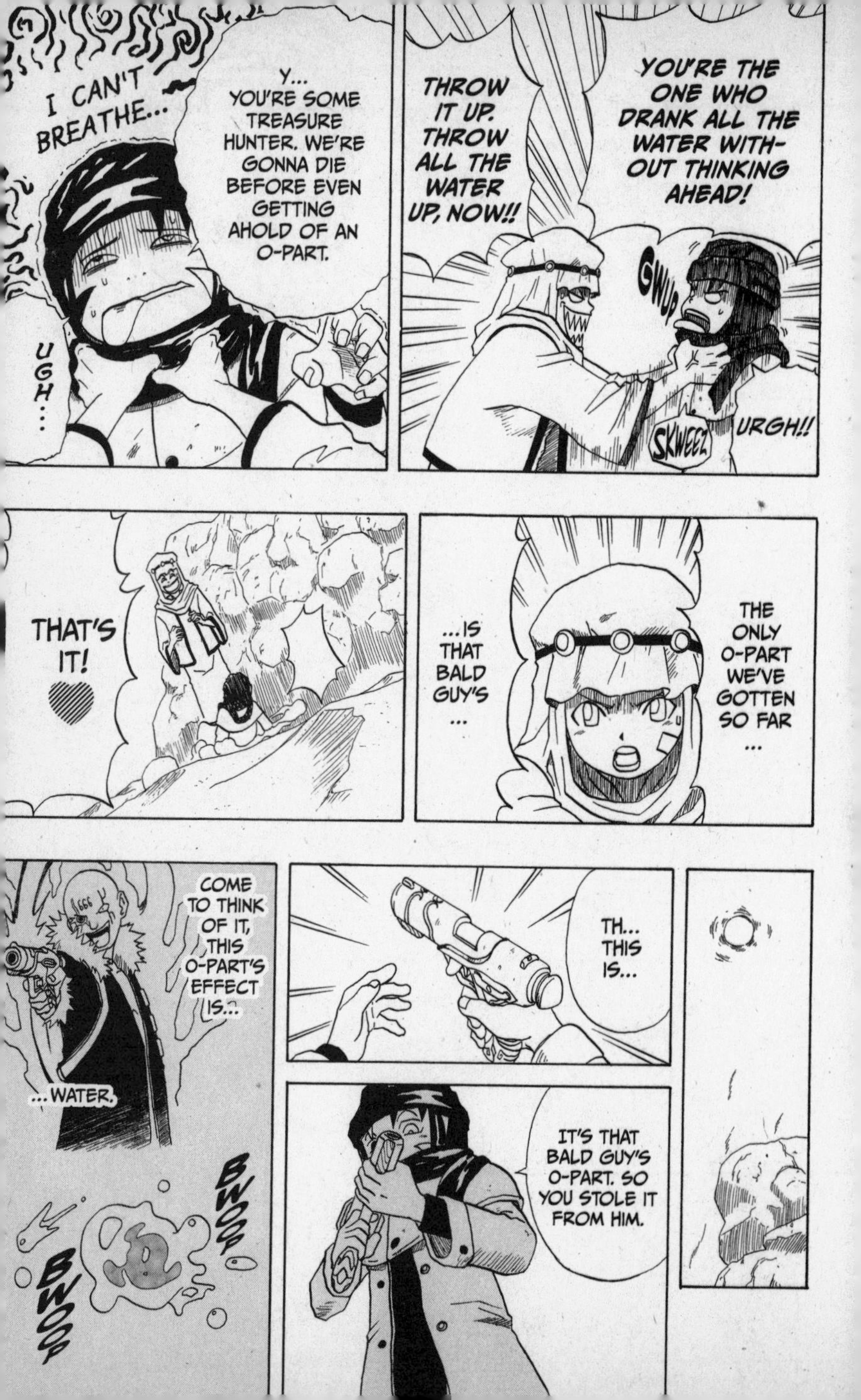
YOU'RE THE ONE WHO DRANK ALL THE WATER WITH-OUT THINKING AHEAD!
THROW IT UP. THROW ALL THE WATER UP, NOW!!
GWUP
SKWEEZ
URGH!!
Y... YOU'RE SOME TREASURE HUNTER. WE'RE GONNA DIE BEFORE EVEN GETTING AHOLD OF AN O-PART.
I CAN'T BREATHE...
UGH...
THE ONLY O-PART WE'VE GOTTEN SO FAR...
...IS THAT BALD GUY'S...
THAT'S IT!
TH... THIS IS...
IT'S THAT BALD GUY'S O-PART. SO YOU STOLE IT FROM HIM.
COME TO THINK OF IT, THIS O-PART'S EFFECT IS...
...WATER.
BWOOP
BWOOP

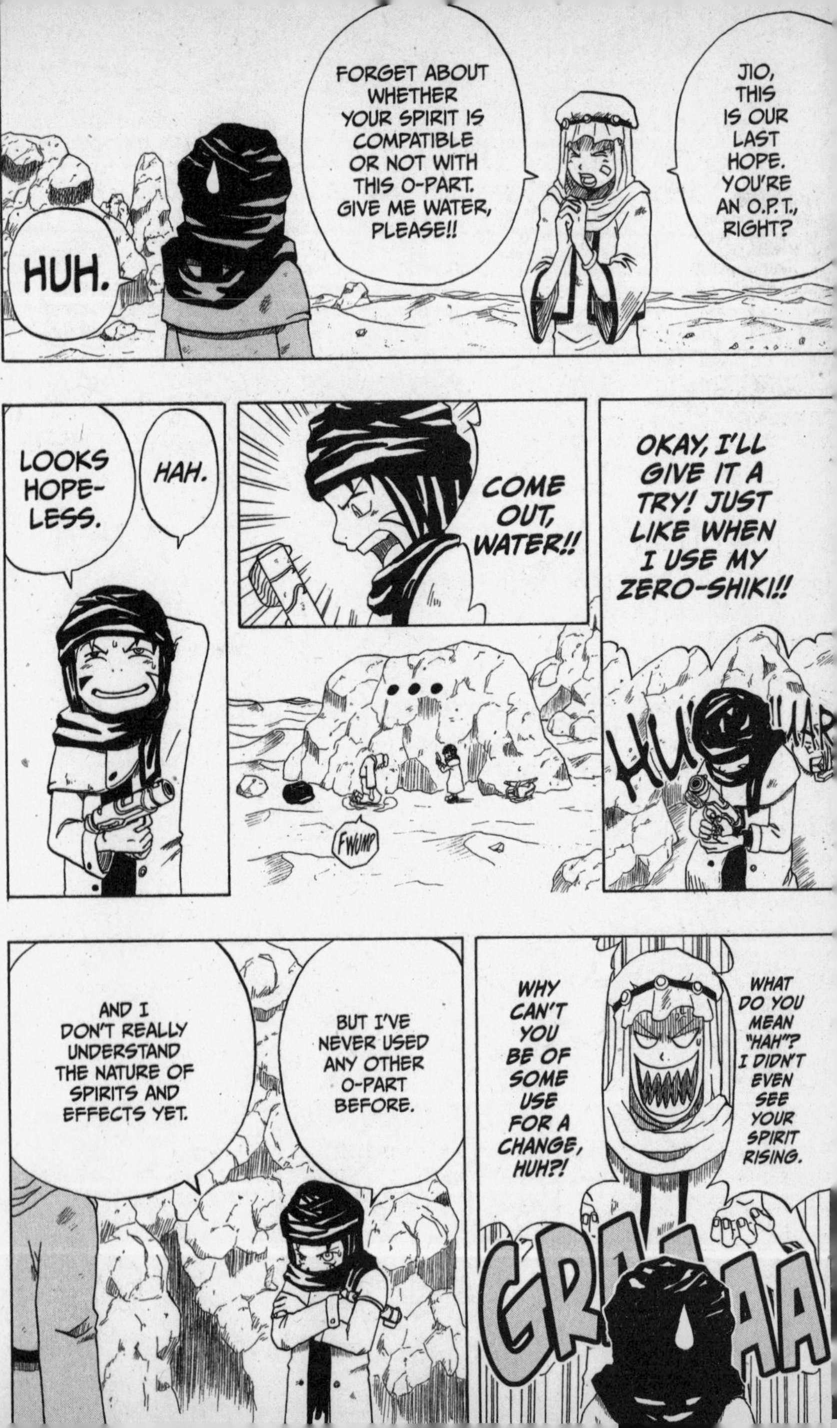
JIO, THIS IS OUR LAST HOPE. YOU'RE AN O.P.T., RIGHT?
FORGET ABOUT WHETHER YOUR SPIRIT IS COMPATIBLE OR NOT WITH THIS O-PART. GIVE ME WATER, PLEASE!!
HUH.
OKAY, I'LL GIVE IT A TRY! JUST LIKE WHEN I USE MY ZERO-SHIKI!!
COME OUT, WATER!!
...
FWUMP
HAH.
LOOKS HOPE-LESS.
WHAT DO YOU MEAN "HAH"? I DIDN'T EVEN SEE YOUR SPIRIT RISING.
WHY CAN'T YOU BE OF SOME USE FOR A CHANGE, HUH?!
BUT I'VE NEVER USED ANY OTHER O-PART BEFORE.
AND I DON'T REALLY UNDERSTAND THE NATURE OF SPIRITS AND EFFECTS YET.

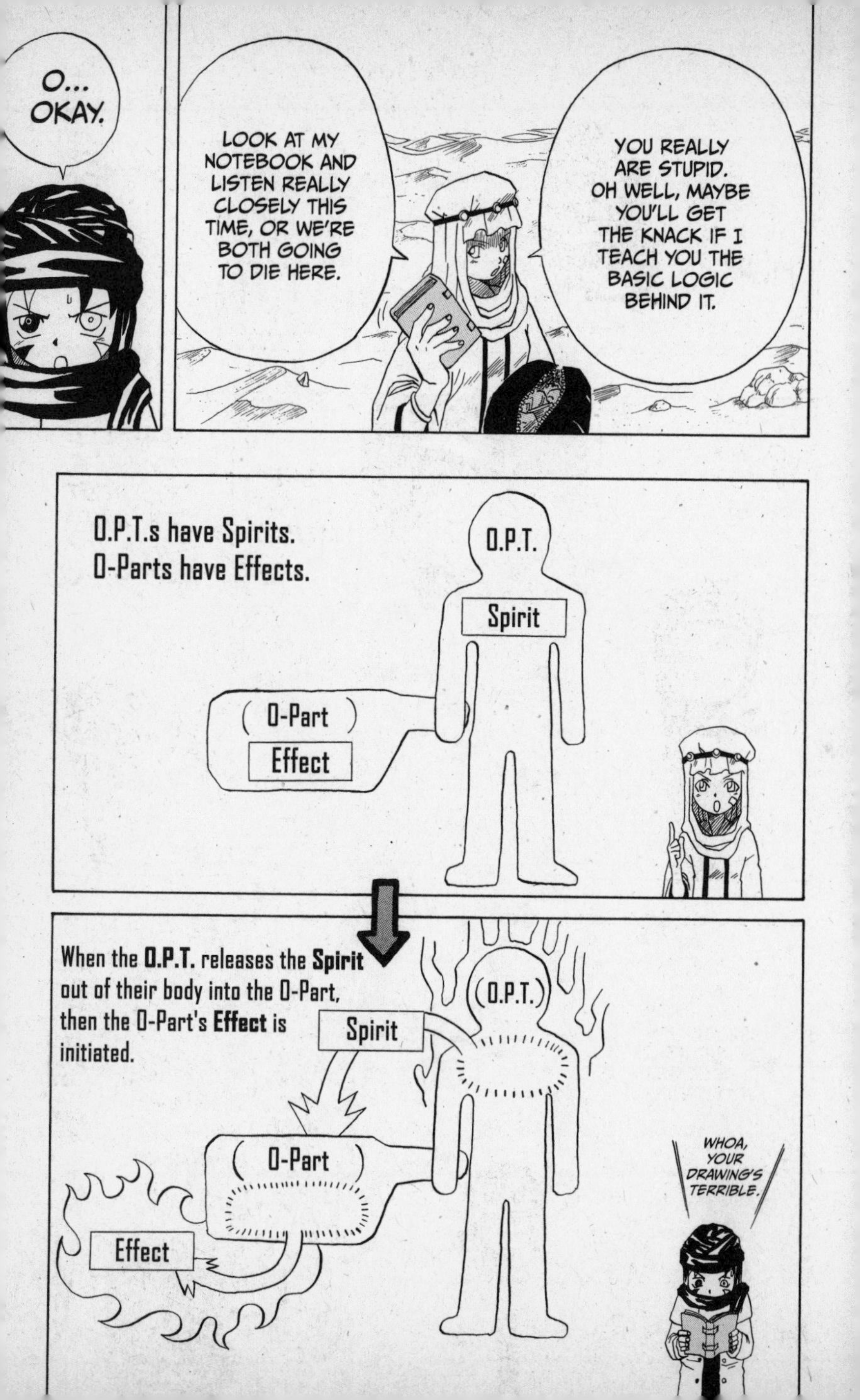
YOU REALLY ARE STUPID. OH WELL, MAYBE YOU'LL GET THE KNACK IF I TEACH YOU THE BASIC LOGIC BEHIND IT.
LOOK AT MY NOTEBOOK AND LISTEN REALLY CLOSELY THIS TIME, OR WE'RE BOTH GOING TO DIE HERE.
O... OKAY.
O.P.T.s have Spirits.
O-Parts have Effects.
O.P.T.
Spirit
(O-Part)
Effect
When the **O.P.T.** releases the **Spirit** out of their body into the O-Part, then the O-Part's **Effect** is initiated.
(O.P.T.)
Spirit
(O-Part)
Effect
WHOA, YOUR DRAWING'S TERRIBLE.

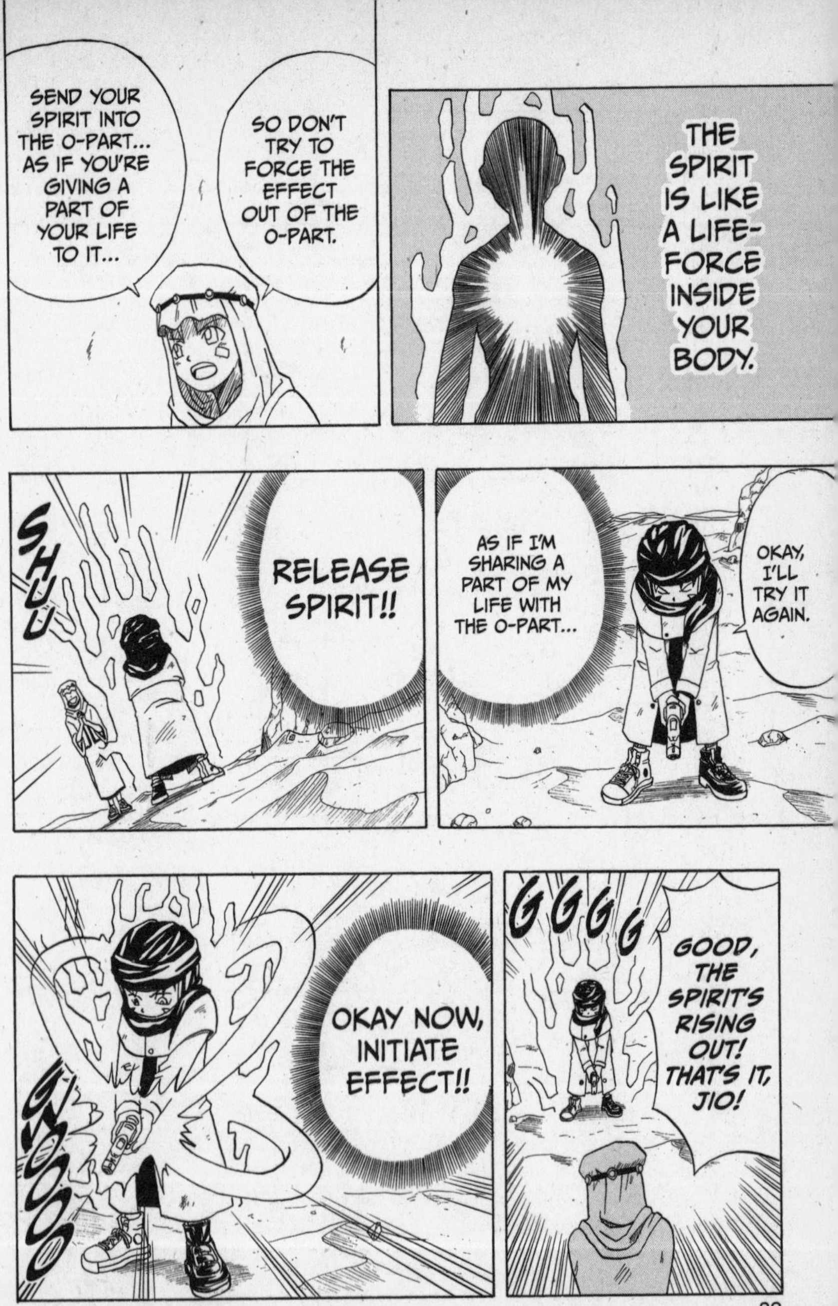
THE SPIRIT IS LIKE A LIFE-FORCE INSIDE YOUR BODY.
SEND YOUR SPIRIT INTO THE O-PART... AS IF YOU'RE GIVING A PART OF YOUR LIFE TO IT...
SO DON'T TRY TO FORCE THE EFFECT OUT OF THE O-PART.
OKAY, I'LL TRY IT AGAIN.
AS IF I'M SHARING A PART OF MY LIFE WITH THE O-PART...
RELEASE SPIRIT!!
SHUU
GGGGG
GOOD, THE SPIRIT'S RISING OUT! THAT'S IT, JIO!
OKAY NOW, INITIATE EFFECT!!
GWOOOO

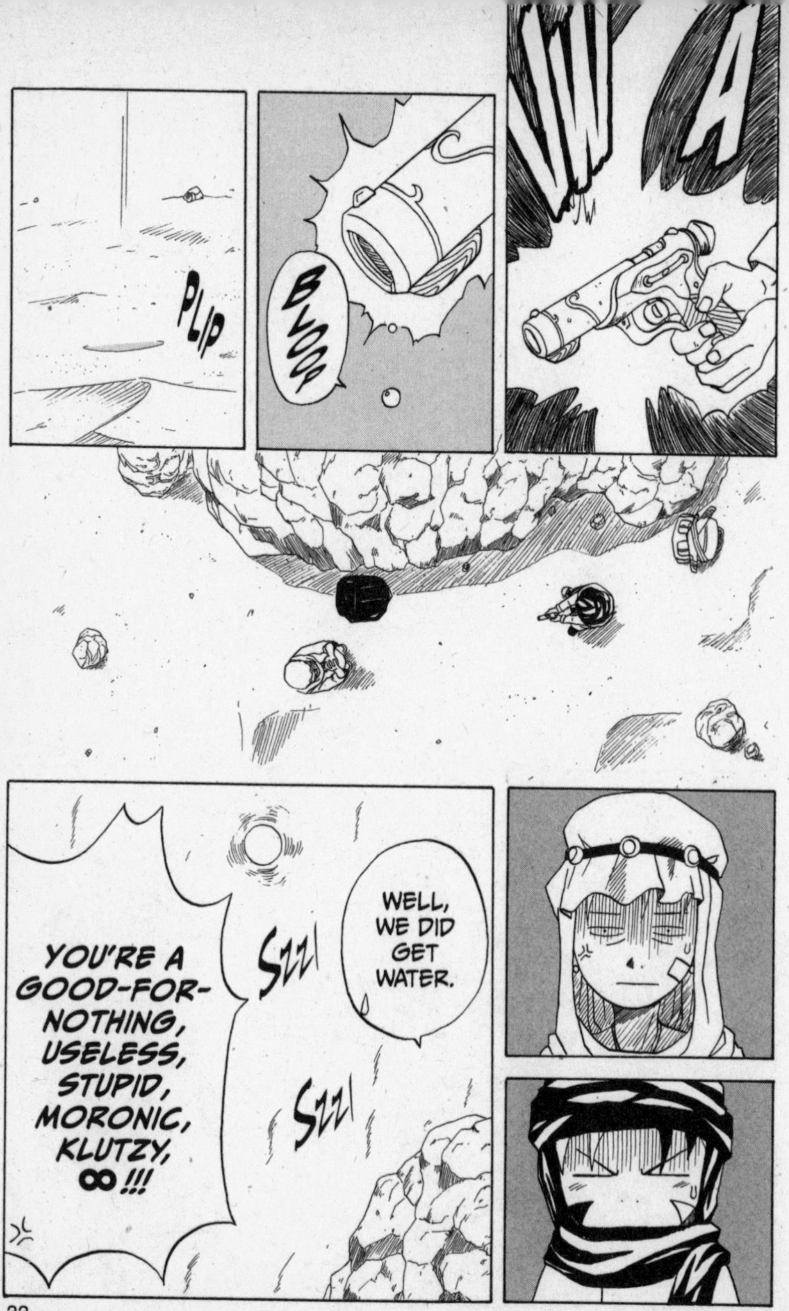
BLOOP
PLIP
WELL, WE DID GET WATER.
SZZI
SZZI
YOU'RE A GOOD-FOR-NOTHING, USELESS, STUPID, MORONIC, KLUTZY, ∞!!!

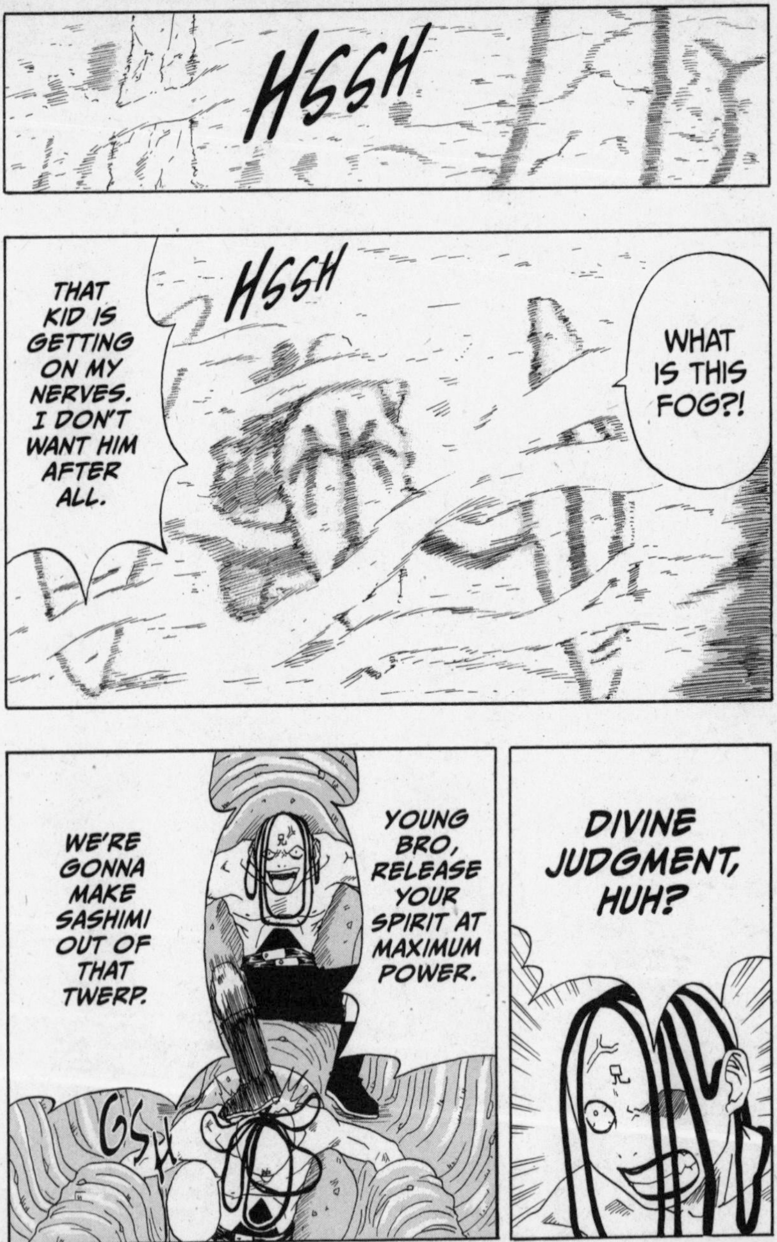
HSSH
WHAT IS THIS FOG?!
HSSH
THAT KID IS GETTING ON MY NERVES. I DON'T WANT HIM AFTER ALL.
DIVINE JUDGMENT, HUH?
YOUNG BRO, RELEASE YOUR SPIRIT AT MAXIMUM POWER.
WE'RE GONNA MAKE SASHIMI OUT OF THAT TWERP.
GSH

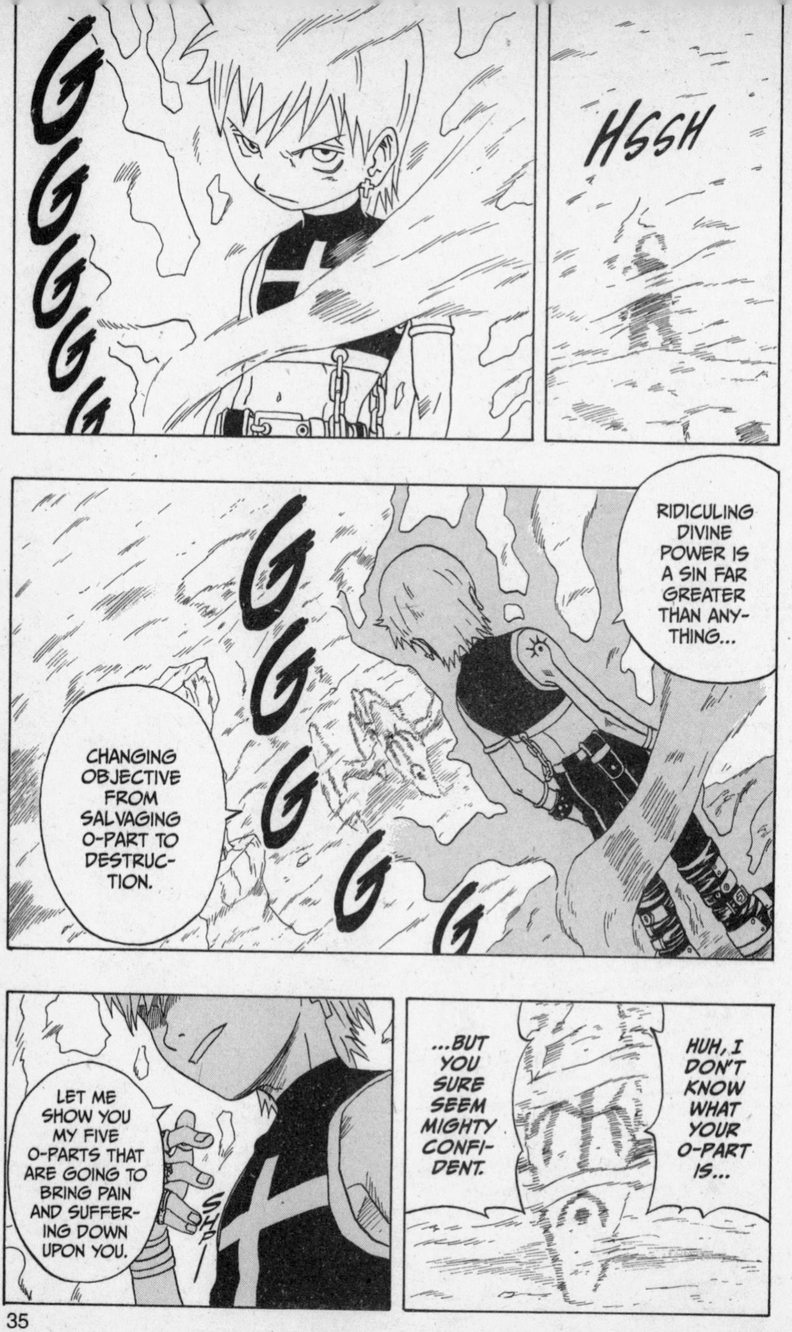
HSSH
GGGGGGG
RIDICULING DIVINE POWER IS A SIN FAR GREATER THAN ANY-THING...
GGGGGGG
CHANGING OBJECTIVE FROM SALVAGING O-PART TO DESTRUC-TION.
HUH, I DON'T KNOW WHAT YOUR O-PART IS...
...BUT YOU SURE SEEM MIGHTY CONFI-DENT.
LET ME SHOW YOU MY FIVE O-PARTS THAT ARE GOING TO BRING PAIN AND SUFFER-ING DOWN UPON YOU.
SHP

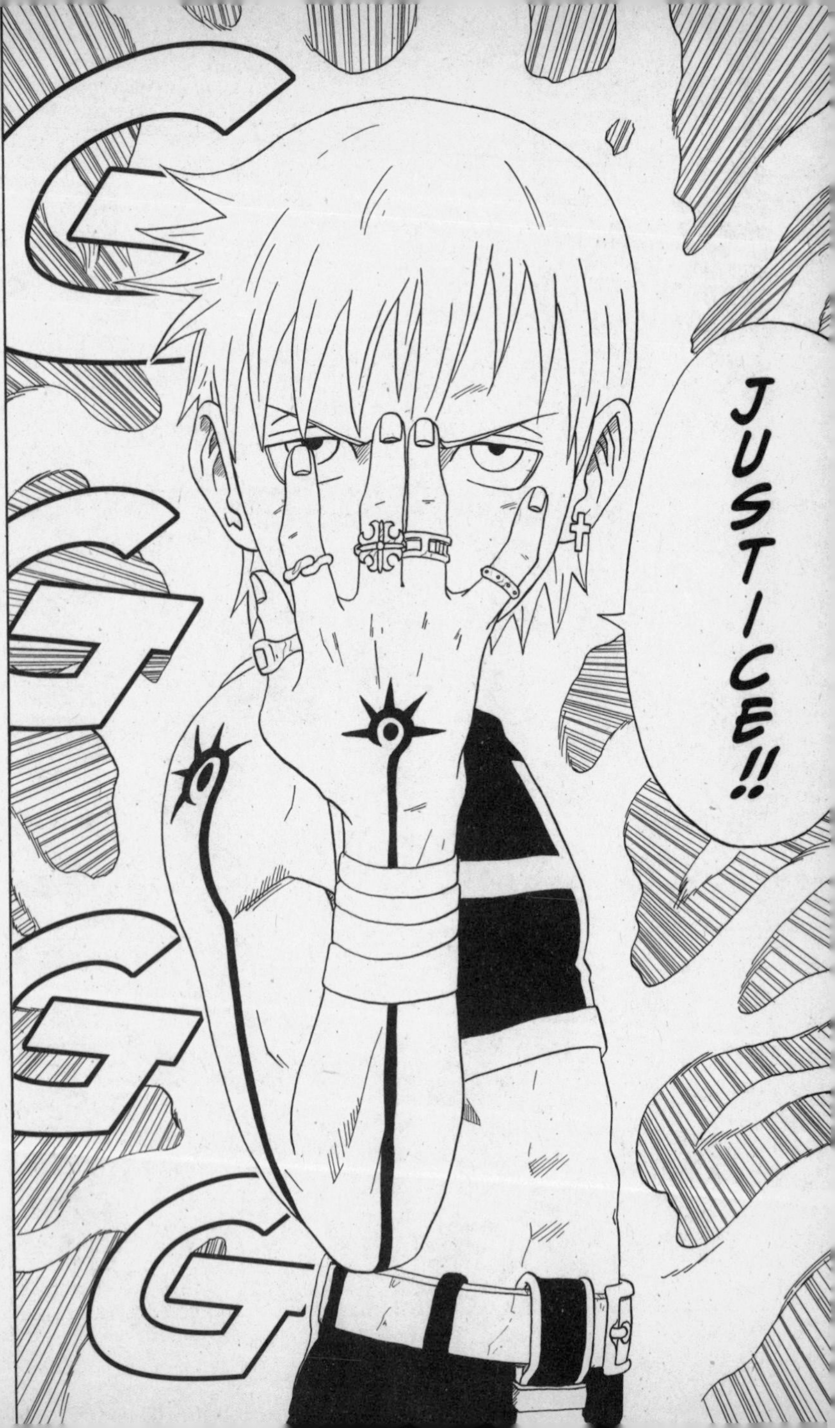
JUSTICE!!

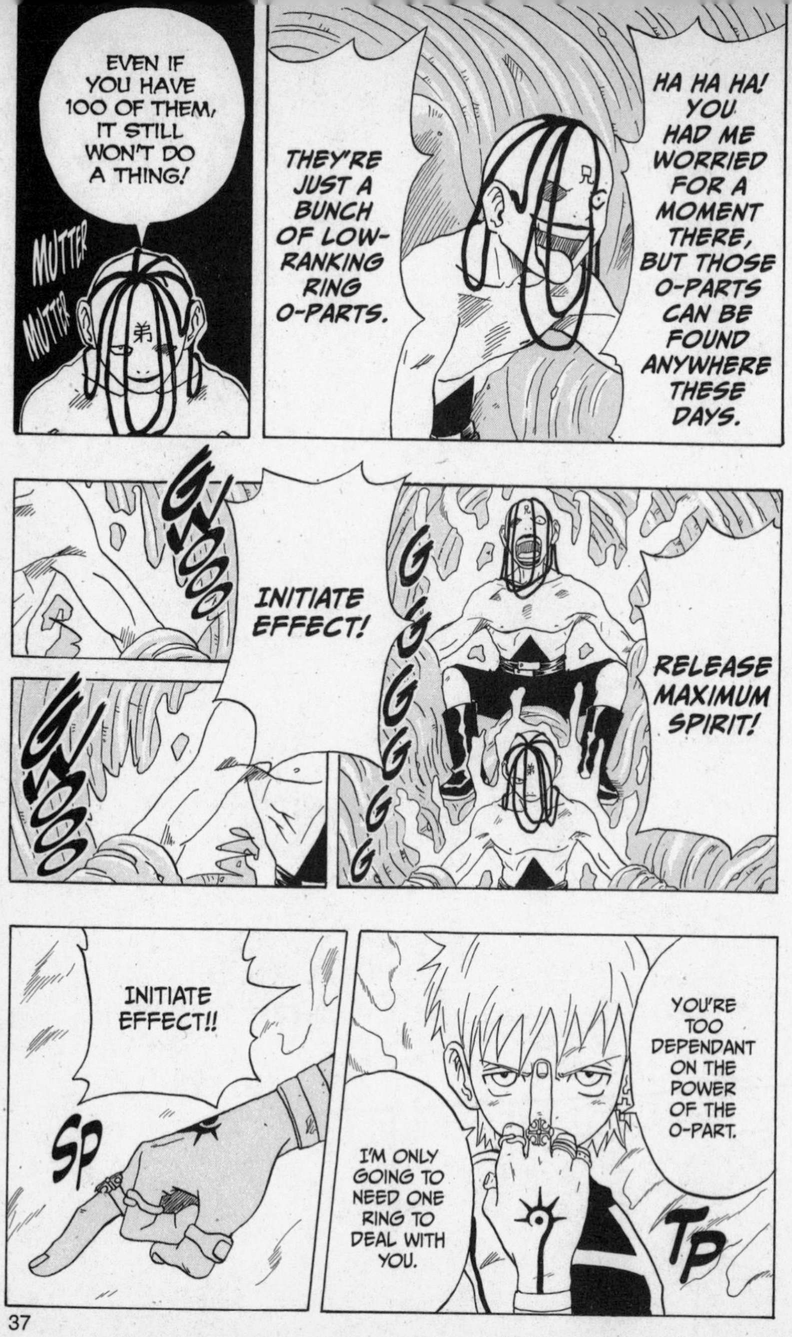
HA HA HA! YOU HAD ME WORRIED FOR A MOMENT THERE, BUT THOSE O-PARTS CAN BE FOUND ANYWHERE THESE DAYS.
THEY'RE JUST A BUNCH OF LOW-RANKING RING O-PARTS.
EVEN IF YOU HAVE 100 OF THEM, IT STILL WON'T DO A THING!
MUTTER
MUTTER
RELEASE MAXIMUM SPIRIT!
INITIATE EFFECT!
GGGGGGGG
WHOOOO
WHOOOO
YOU'RE TOO DEPENDANT ON THE POWER OF THE O-PART.
I'M ONLY GOING TO NEED ONE RING TO DEAL WITH YOU.
TP
INITIATE EFFECT!!
SP

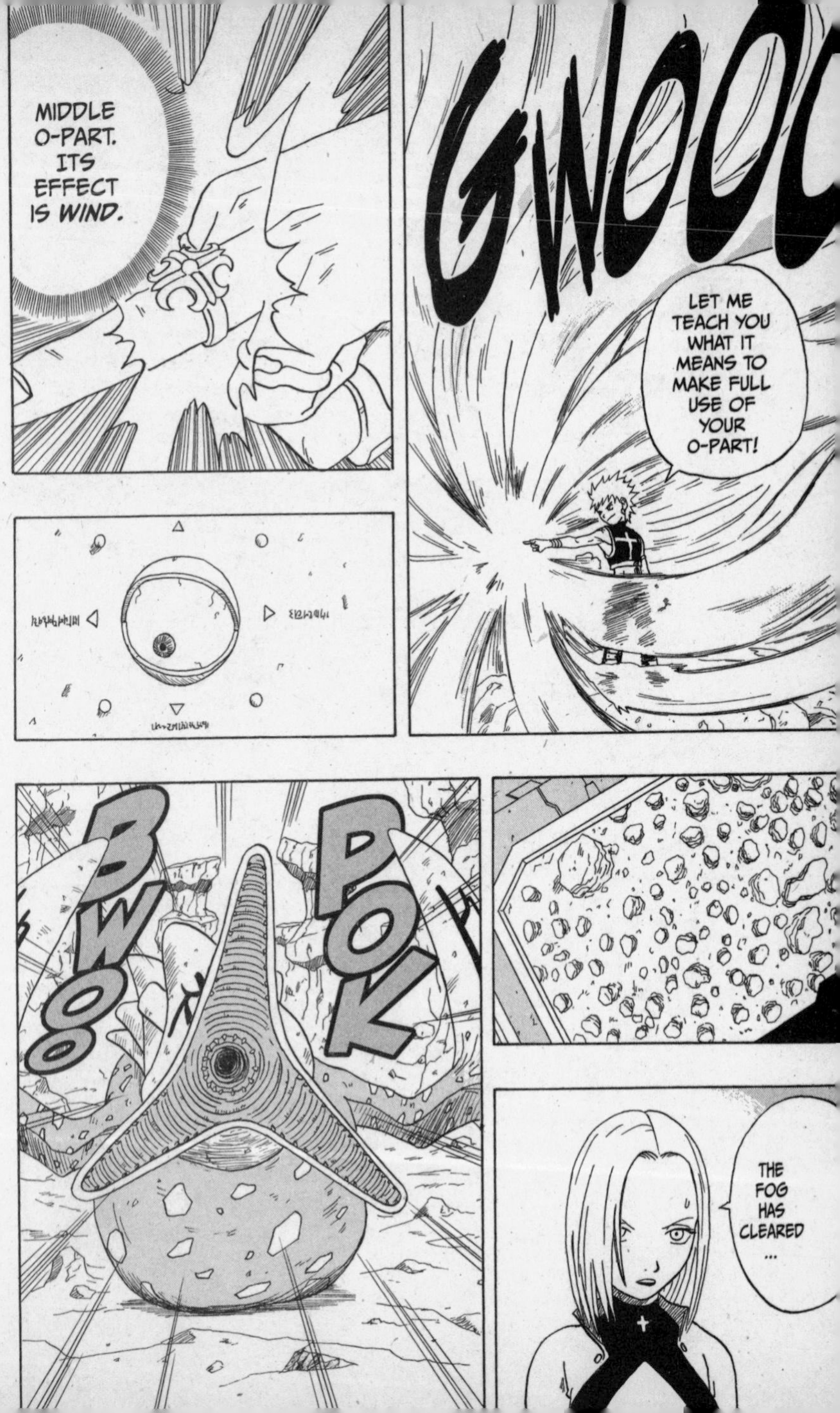
GWOOO
LET ME TEACH YOU WHAT IT MEANS TO MAKE FULL USE OF YOUR O-PART!
MIDDLE O-PART. ITS EFFECT IS WIND.
THE FOG HAS CLEARED ...
BWOOO
POK

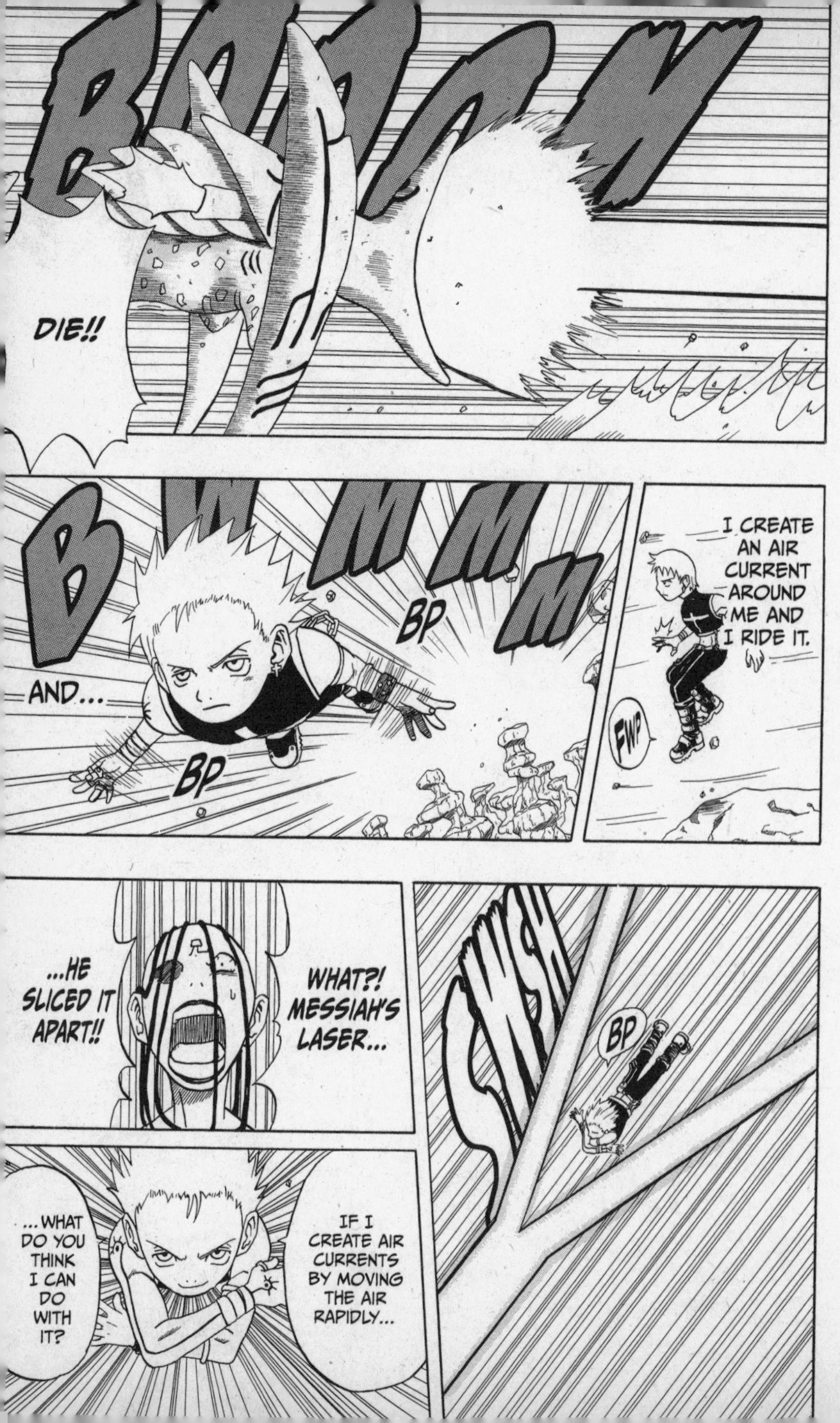
DIE!!
I CREATE AN AIR CURRENT AROUND ME AND I RIDE IT.
FWP
BP
AND...
BP
SWISH
BP
WHAT?! MESSIAH'S LASER...
...HE SLICED IT APART!!
IF I CREATE AIR CURRENTS BY MOVING THE AIR RAPIDLY...
...WHAT DO YOU THINK I CAN DO WITH IT?

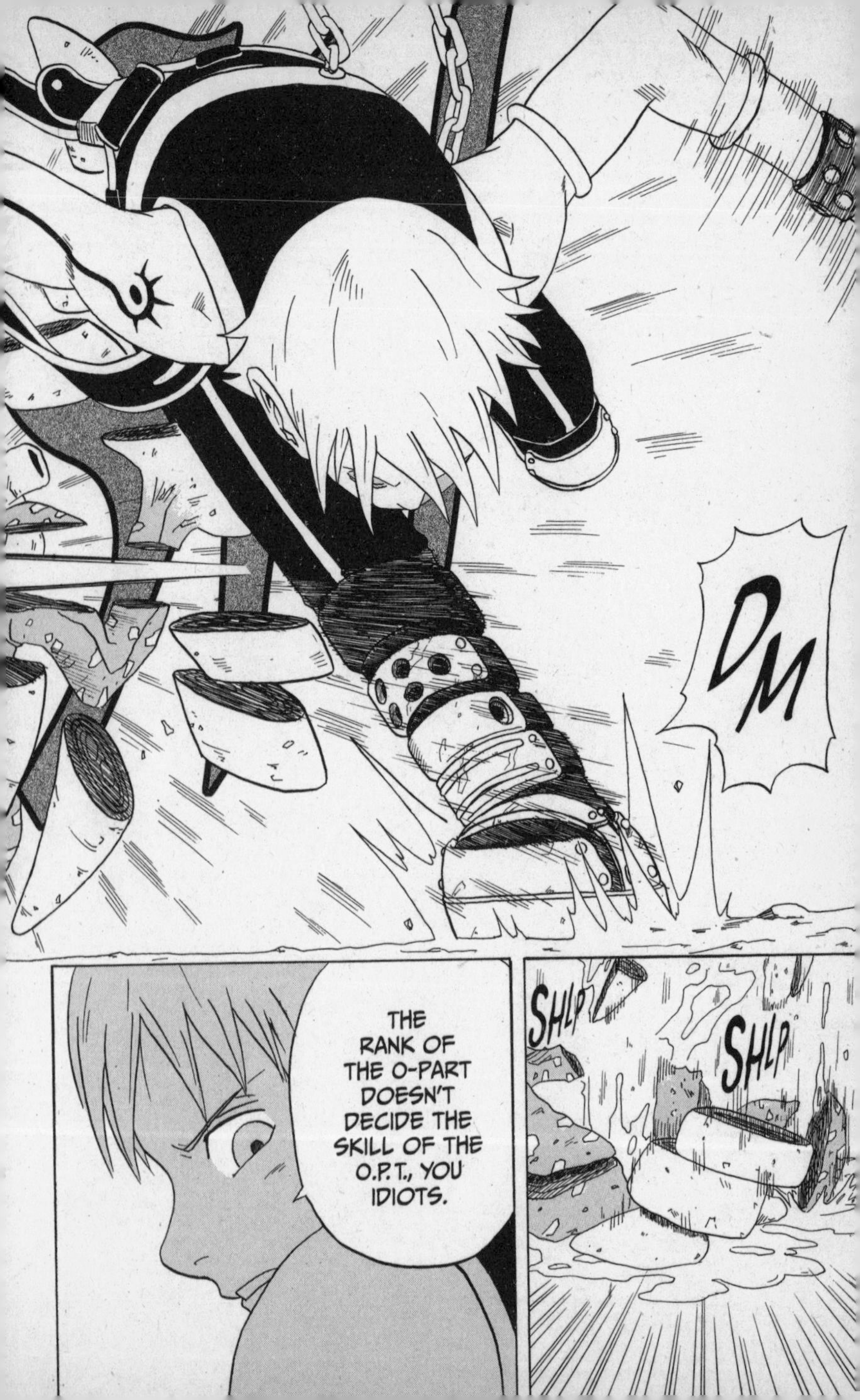
DM
SHLP
SHLP
THE RANK OF THE O-PART DOESN'T DECIDE THE SKILL OF THE O.P.T., YOU IDIOTS.

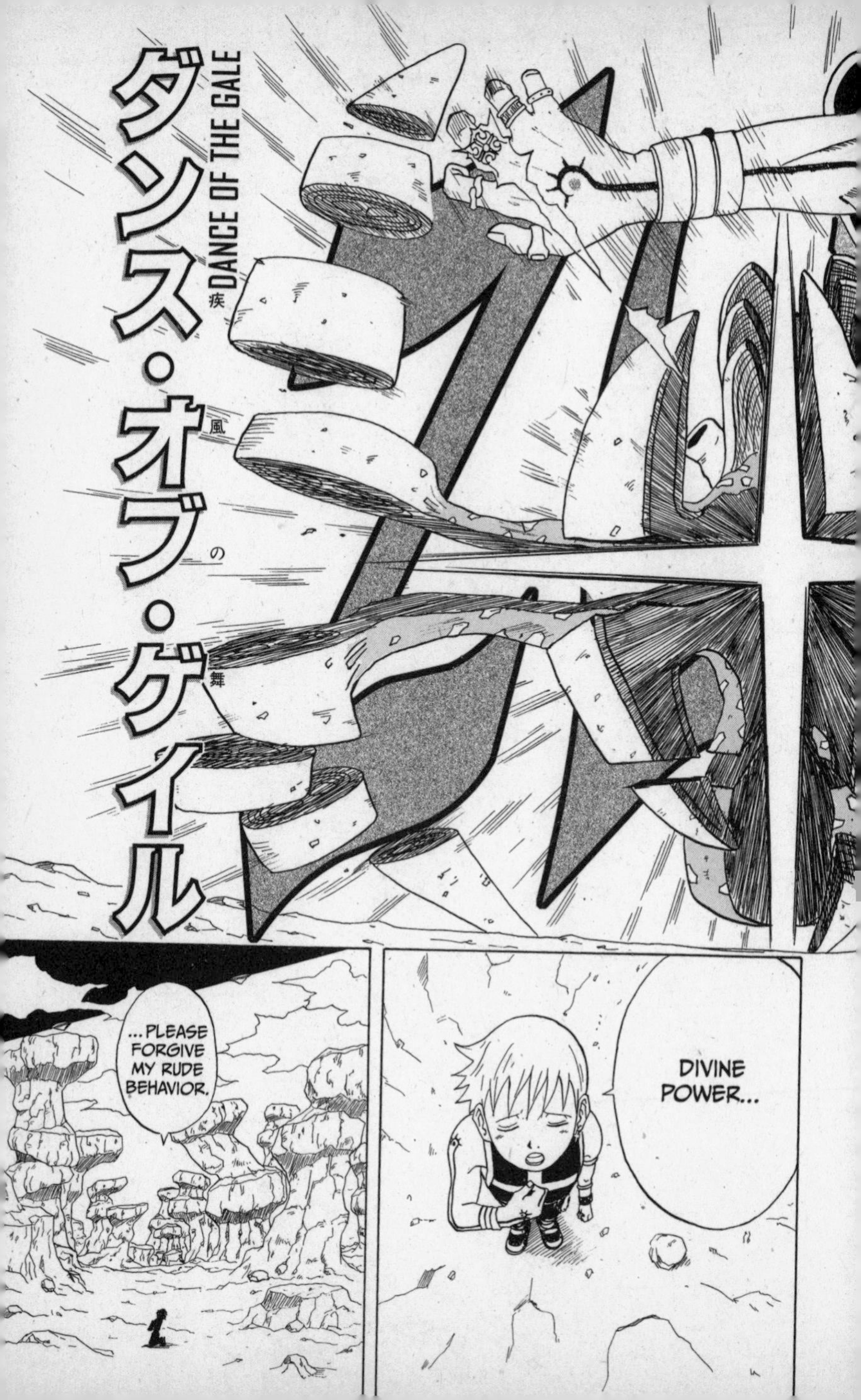
ダンス・オブ・ゲイル
疾風の舞
DANCE OF THE GALE
DIVINE POWER...
...PLEASE FORGIVE MY RUDE BEHAVIOR.

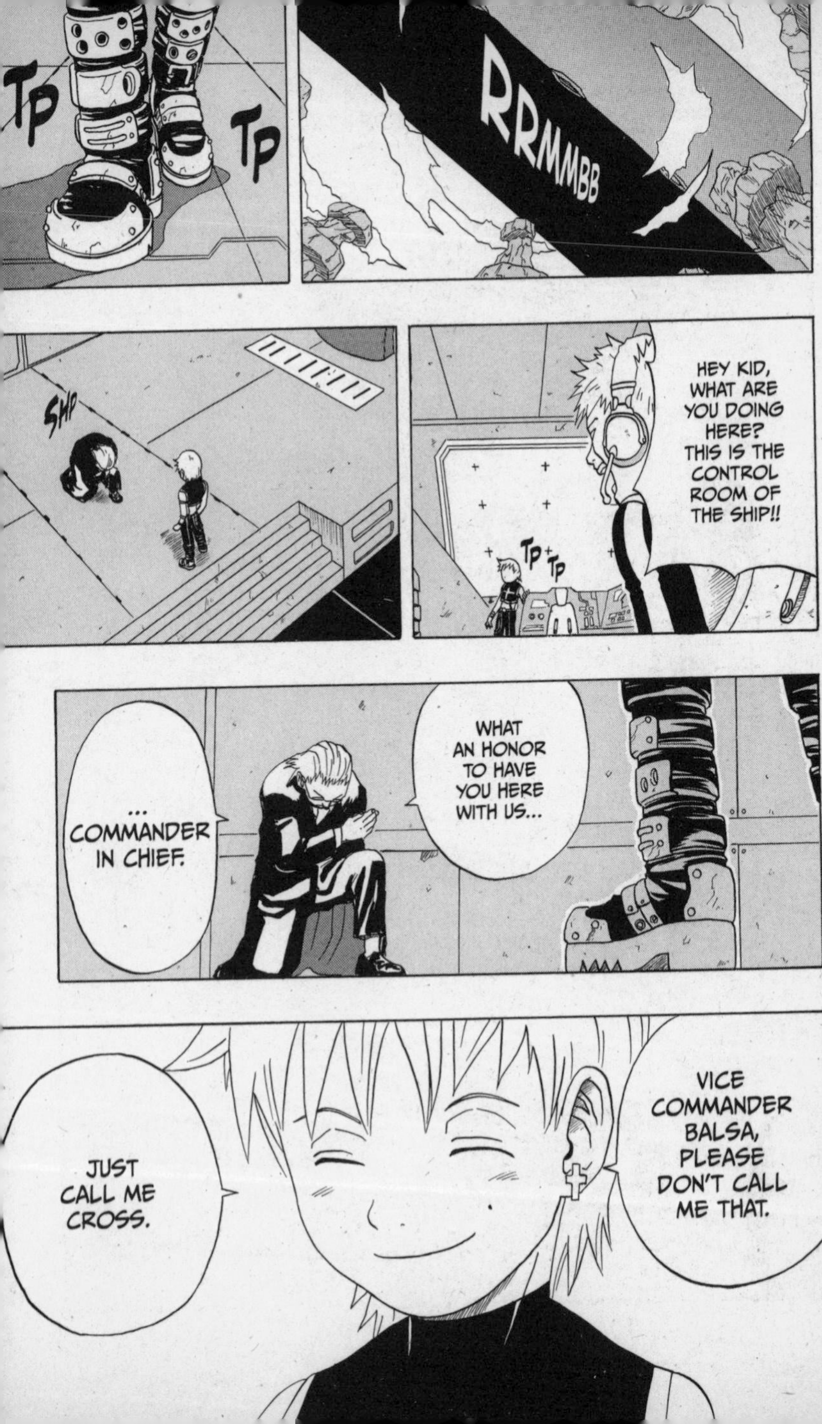
RRMMBB
TP
TP
HEY KID, WHAT ARE YOU DOING HERE? THIS IS THE CONTROL ROOM OF THE SHIP!!
TP TP
SHP
WHAT AN HONOR TO HAVE YOU HERE WITH US...
... COMMANDER IN CHIEF.
VICE COMMANDER BALSA, PLEASE DON'T CALL ME THAT.
JUST CALL ME CROSS.

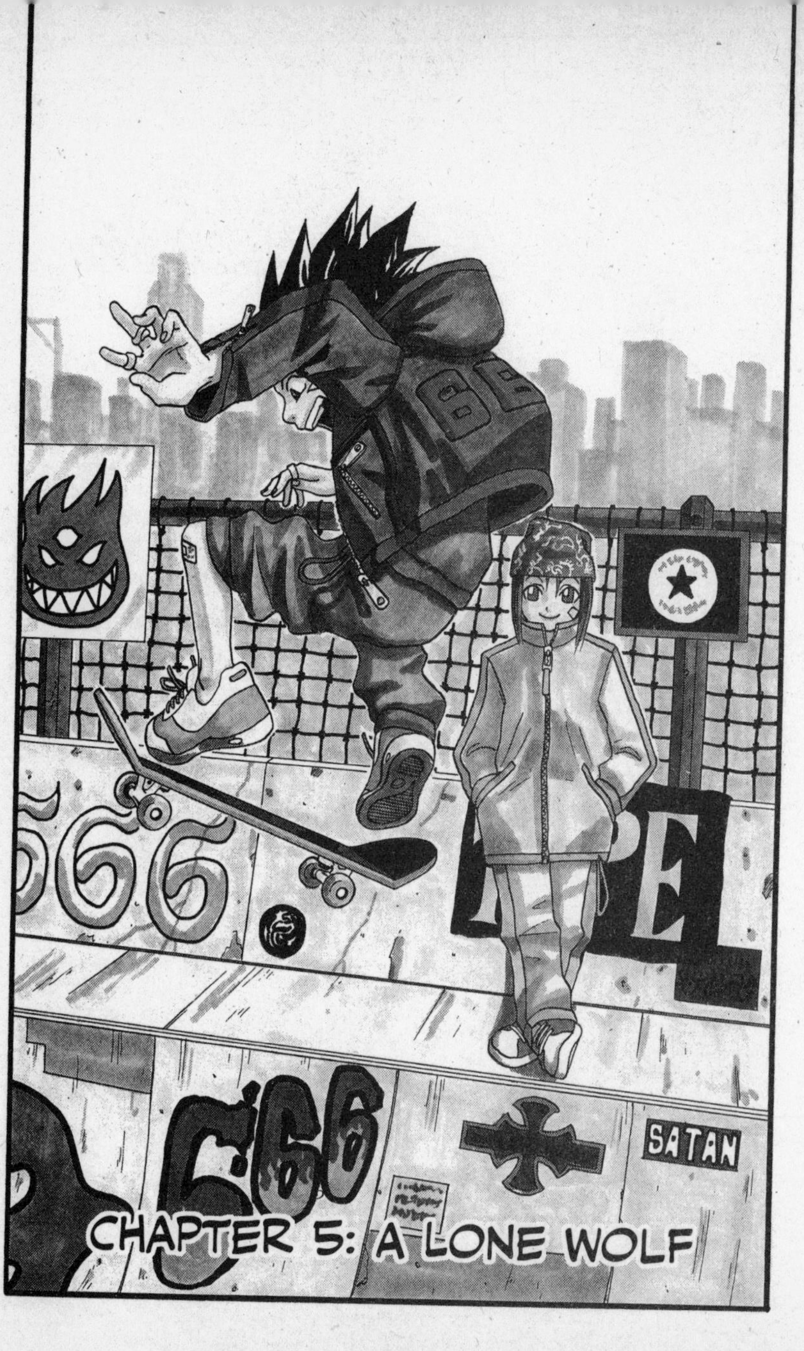
CHAPTER 5: A LONE WOLF
SATAN

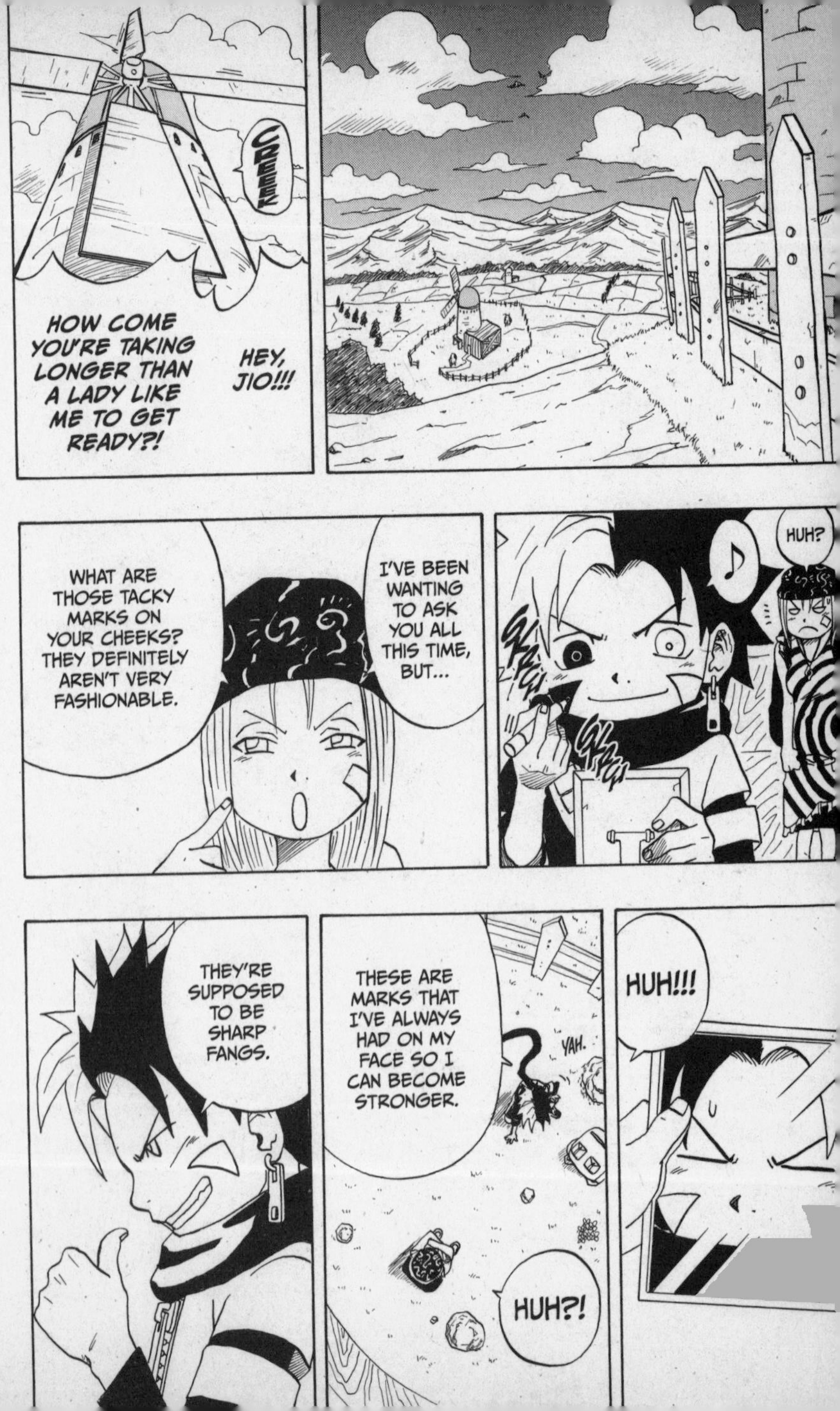
CREEEK
HEY, JIO!!!
HOW COME YOU'RE TAKING LONGER THAN A LADY LIKE ME TO GET READY?!
HUH?
♪
I'VE BEEN WANTING TO ASK YOU ALL THIS TIME, BUT...
WHAT ARE THOSE TACKY MARKS ON YOUR CHEEKS? THEY DEFINITELY AREN'T VERY FASHIONABLE.
HUH!!!
THESE ARE MARKS THAT I'VE ALWAYS HAD ON MY FACE SO I CAN BECOME STRONGER.
YAH.
HUH?!
THEY'RE SUPPOSED TO BE SHARP FANGS.

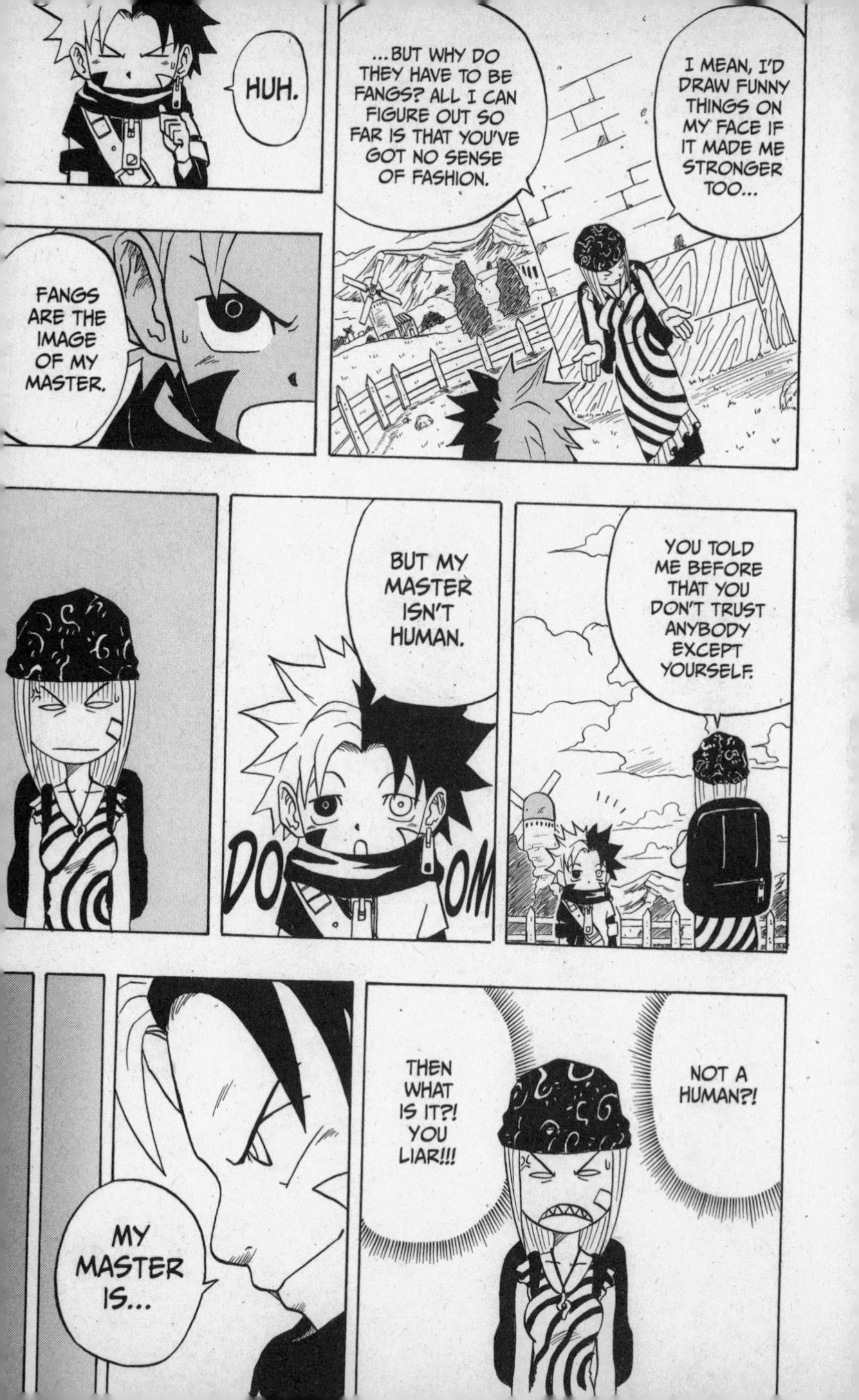
I MEAN, I'D DRAW FUNNY THINGS ON MY FACE IF IT MADE ME STRONGER TOO...
...BUT WHY DO THEY HAVE TO BE FANGS? ALL I CAN FIGURE OUT SO FAR IS THAT YOU'VE GOT NO SENSE OF FASHION.
HUH.
FANGS ARE THE IMAGE OF MY MASTER.
YOU TOLD ME BEFORE THAT YOU DON'T TRUST ANYBODY EXCEPT YOURSELF.
BUT MY MASTER ISN'T HUMAN.
DOOM
NOT A HUMAN?!
THEN WHAT IS IT?! YOU LIAR!!!
MY MASTER IS...

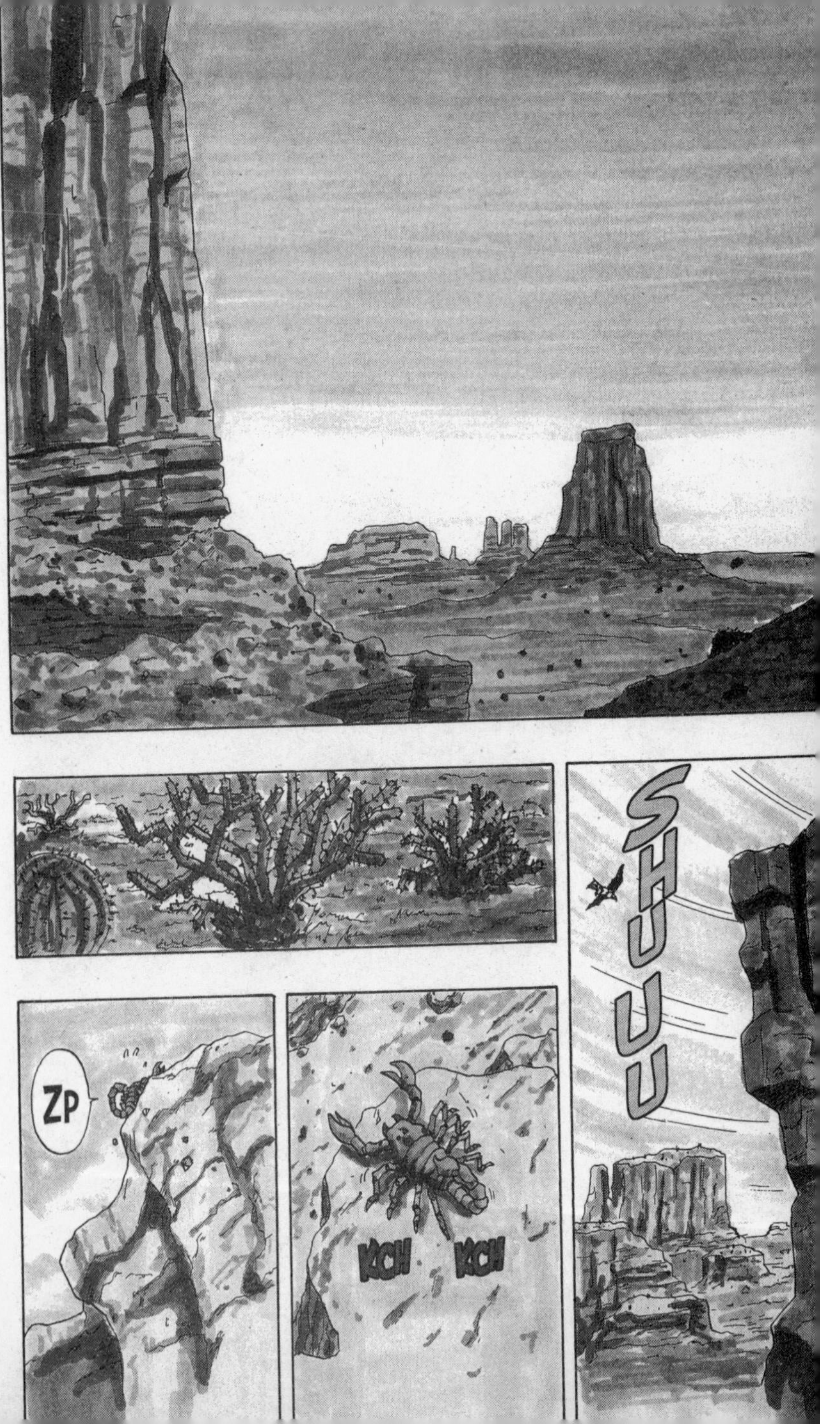
SHUUUU
KCH KCH
ZP

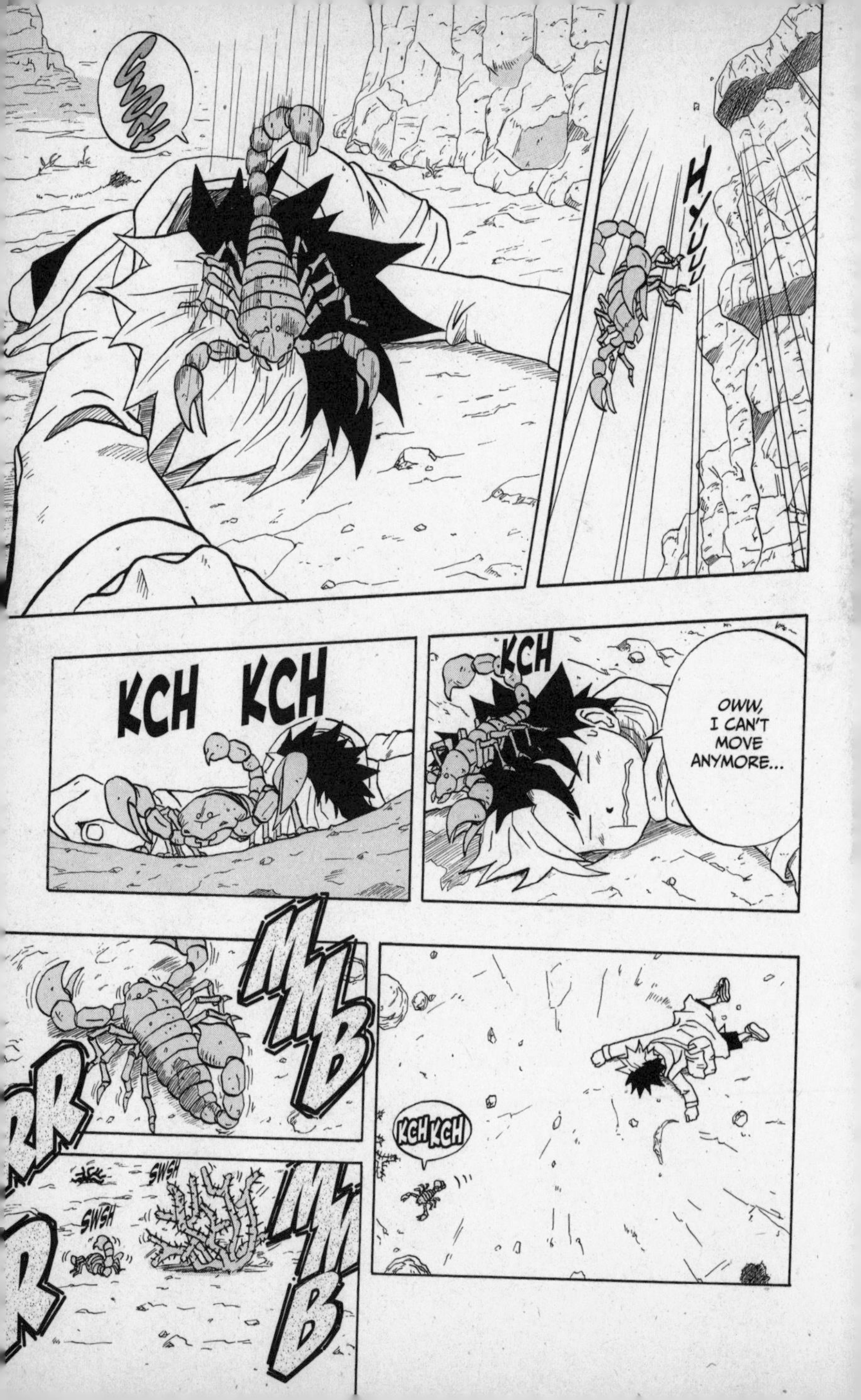
HYUUU
KCH
OWW, I CAN'T MOVE ANYMORE...
KCH KCH
KCH KCH
MMB
SWSH
SWSH
MMB

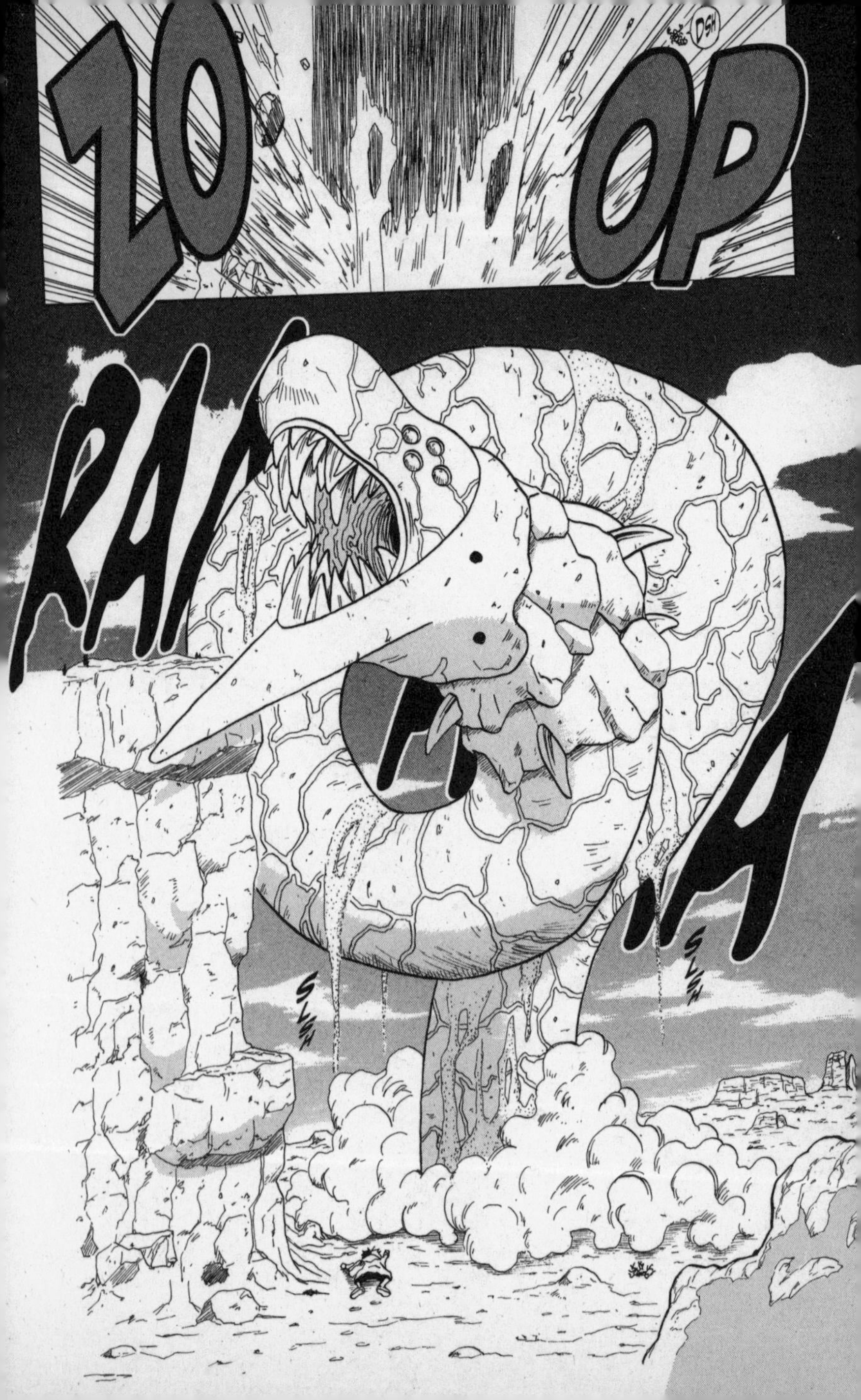
ZO
OP
DSH
RA
SLISH
SLISH

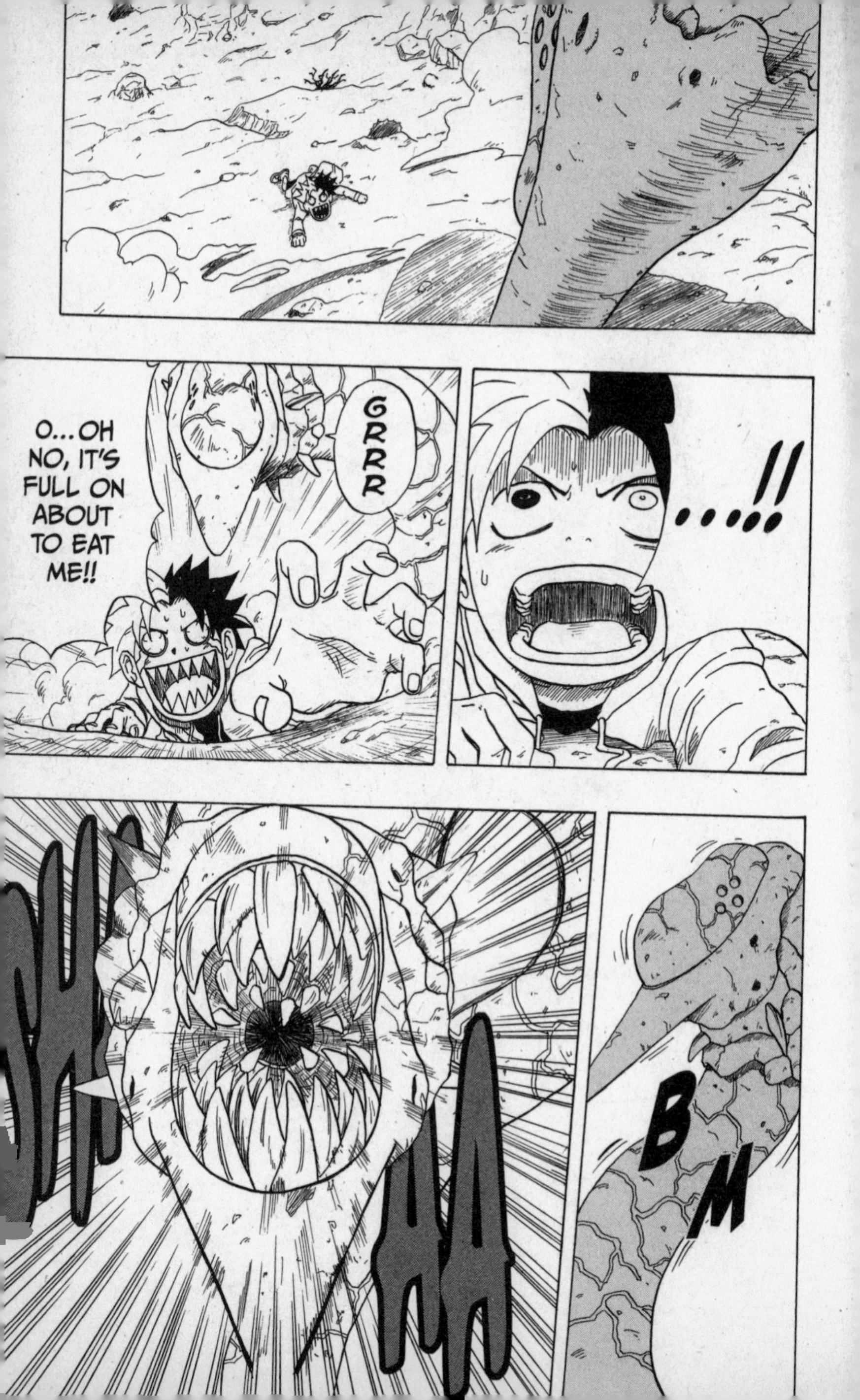
...!!
GRRR
O...OH NO, IT'S FULL ON ABOUT TO EAT ME!!

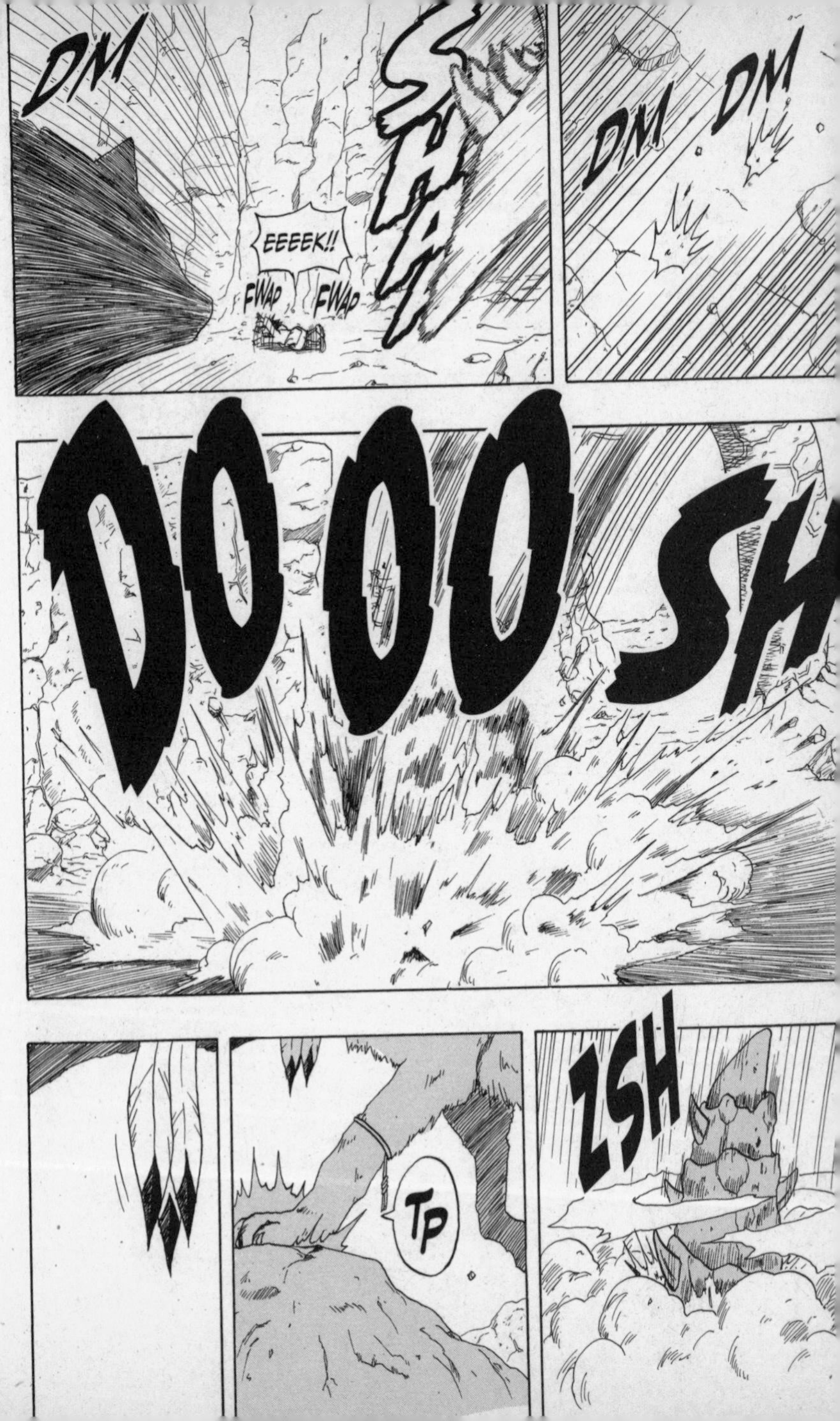
DM DM
EEEEK!!
FWAP FWAP
DM
DOOOSH
ZSH
TP

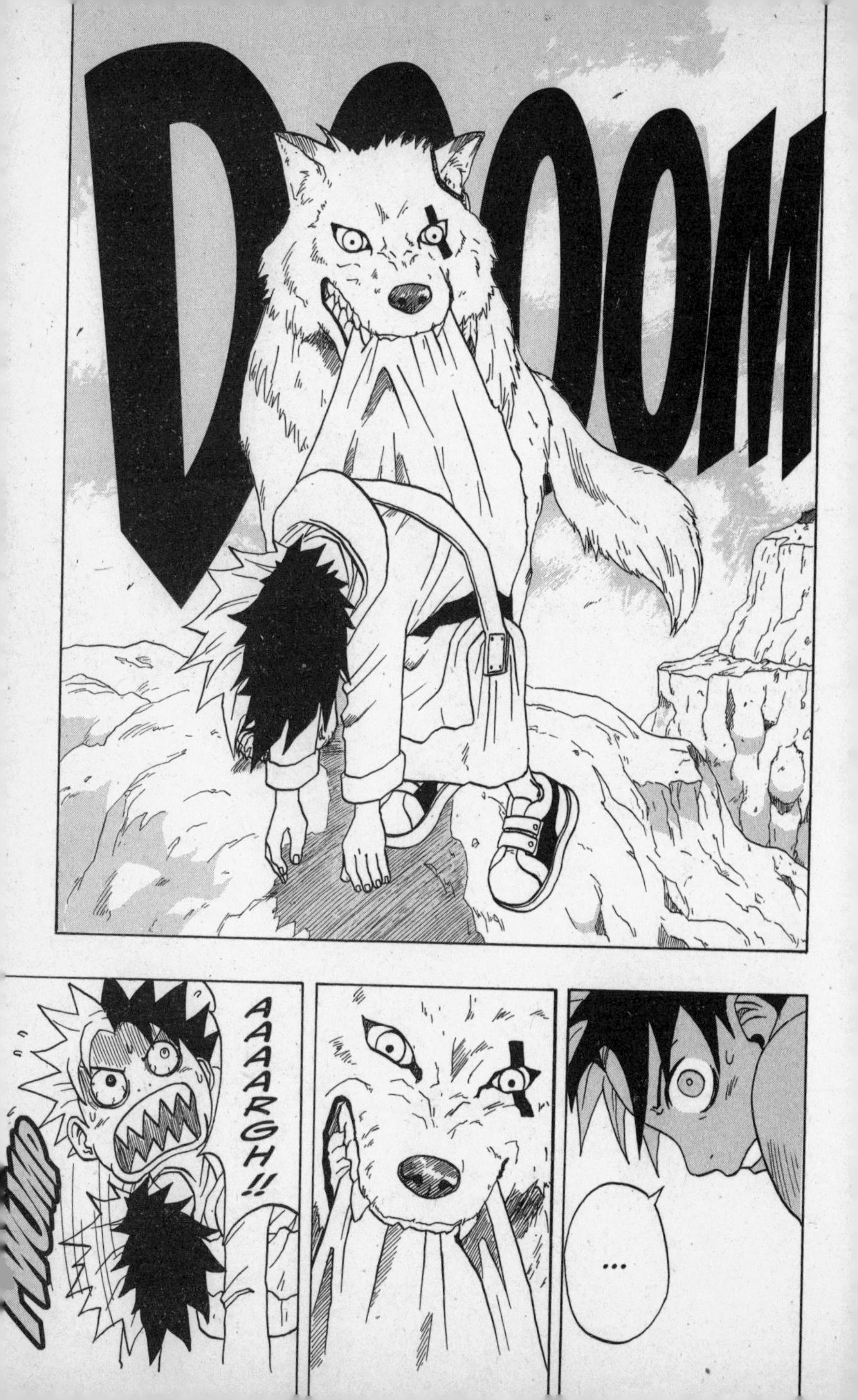
DOOOM
...
AAAARGH!!
HWUMP

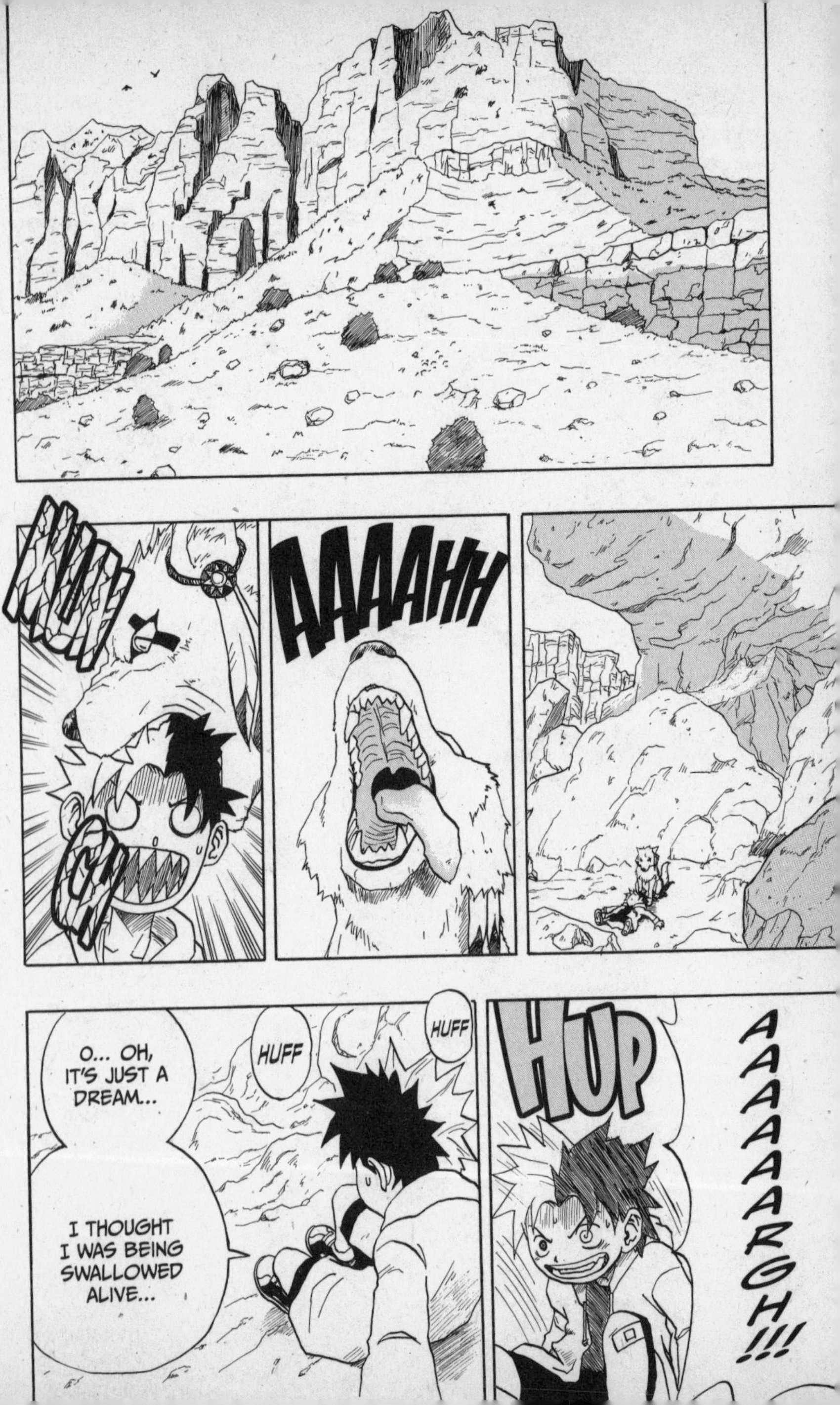
AAAAHH
MUNCH
HUP
AAAAAARGH!!!
HUFF
HUFF
O... OH, IT'S JUST A DREAM...
I THOUGHT I WAS BEING SWALLOWED ALIVE...

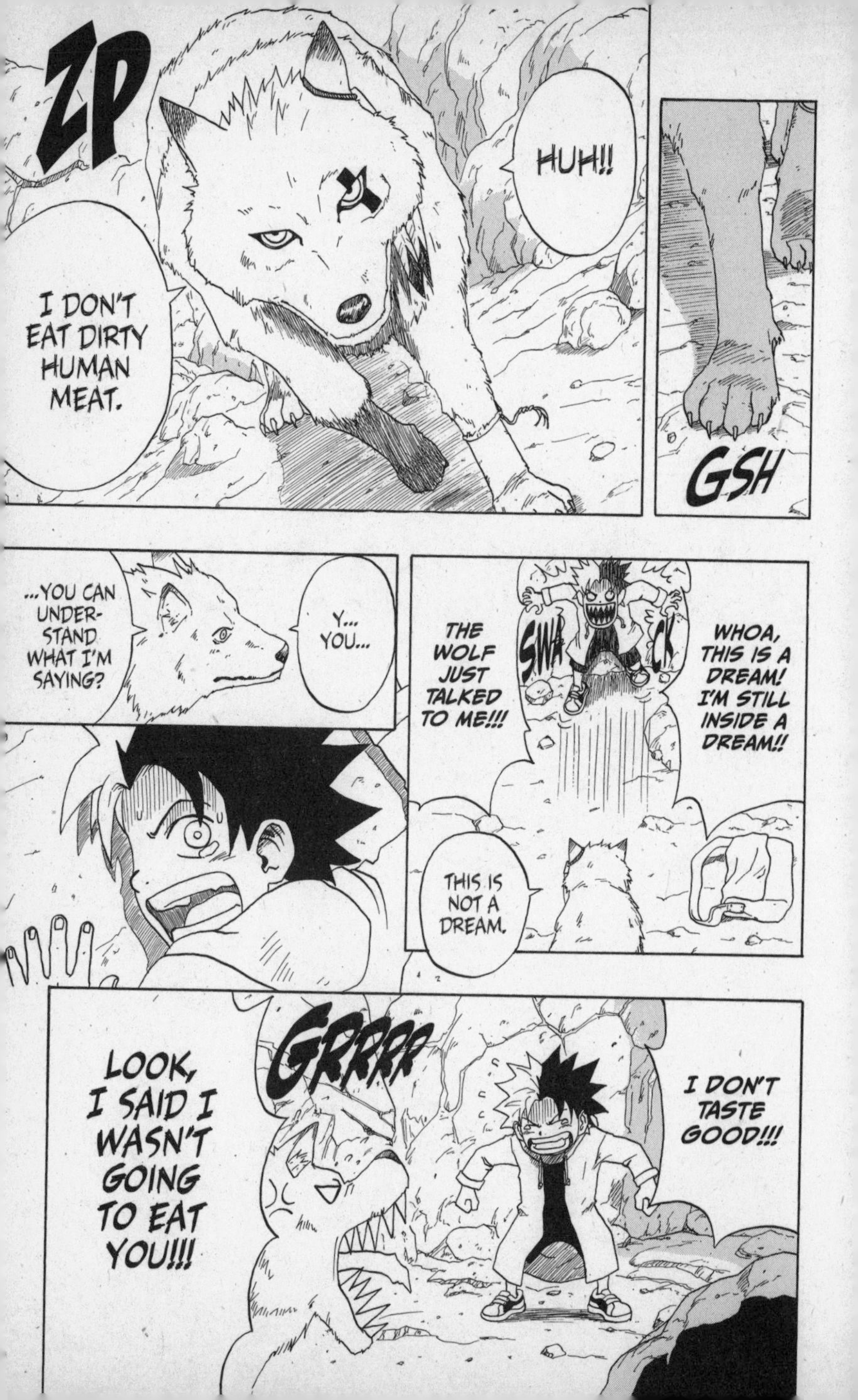
GSH
HUH!!
ZP
I DON'T EAT DIRTY HUMAN MEAT.
WHOA, THIS IS A DREAM! I'M STILL INSIDE A DREAM!!
THE WOLF JUST TALKED TO ME!!!
SWACK
THIS IS NOT A DREAM.
Y... YOU...
...YOU CAN UNDER-STAND WHAT I'M SAYING?
I DON'T TASTE GOOD!!!
GRRRR
LOOK, I SAID I WASN'T GOING TO EAT YOU!!!

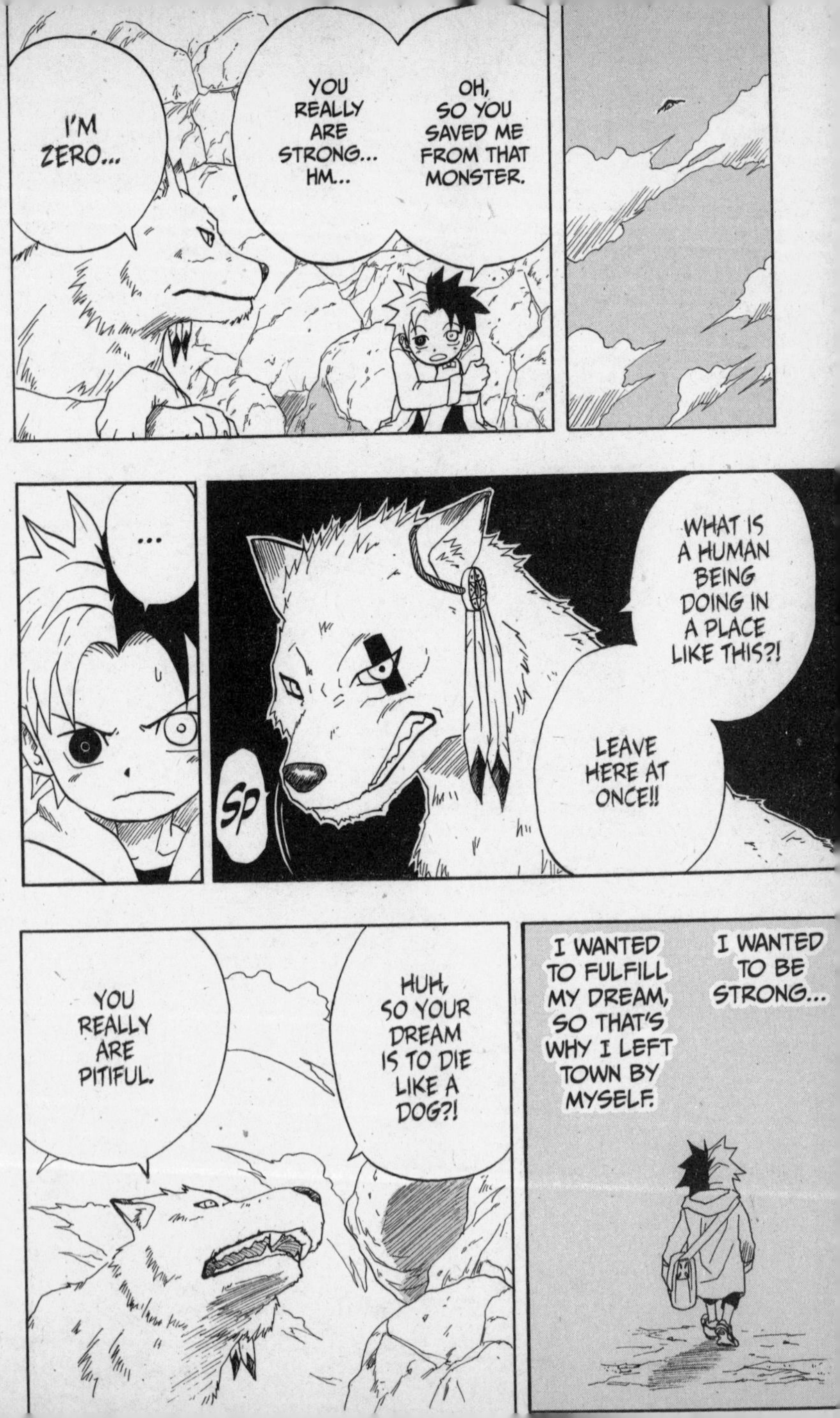
OH, SO YOU SAVED ME FROM THAT MONSTER.
YOU REALLY ARE STRONG... HM...
I'M ZERO...
WHAT IS A HUMAN BEING DOING IN A PLACE LIKE THIS?!
LEAVE HERE AT ONCE!!
SP
...
I WANTED TO BE STRONG...
I WANTED TO FULFILL MY DREAM, SO THAT'S WHY I LEFT TOWN BY MYSELF.
HUH, SO YOUR DREAM IS TO DIE LIKE A DOG?!
YOU REALLY ARE PITIFUL.

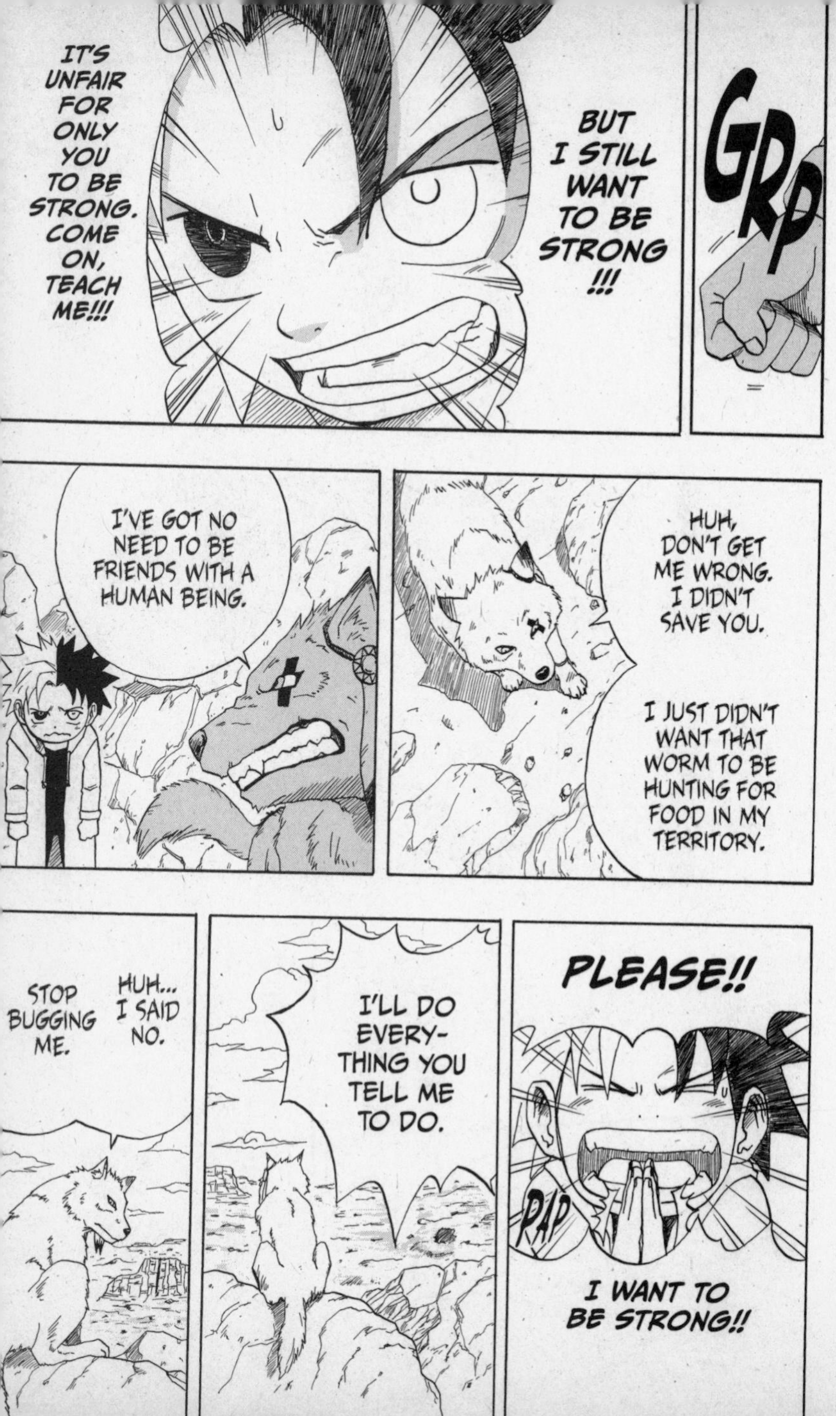
GRP
BUT I STILL WANT TO BE STRONG!!!
IT'S UNFAIR FOR ONLY YOU TO BE STRONG. COME ON, TEACH ME!!!
HUH, DON'T GET ME WRONG. I DIDN'T SAVE YOU.
I JUST DIDN'T WANT THAT WORM TO BE HUNTING FOR FOOD IN MY TERRITORY.
I'VE GOT NO NEED TO BE FRIENDS WITH A HUMAN BEING.
PLEASE!!
PAP
I WANT TO BE STRONG!!
I'LL DO EVERY-THING YOU TELL ME TO DO.
HUH... I SAID NO.
STOP BUGGING ME.

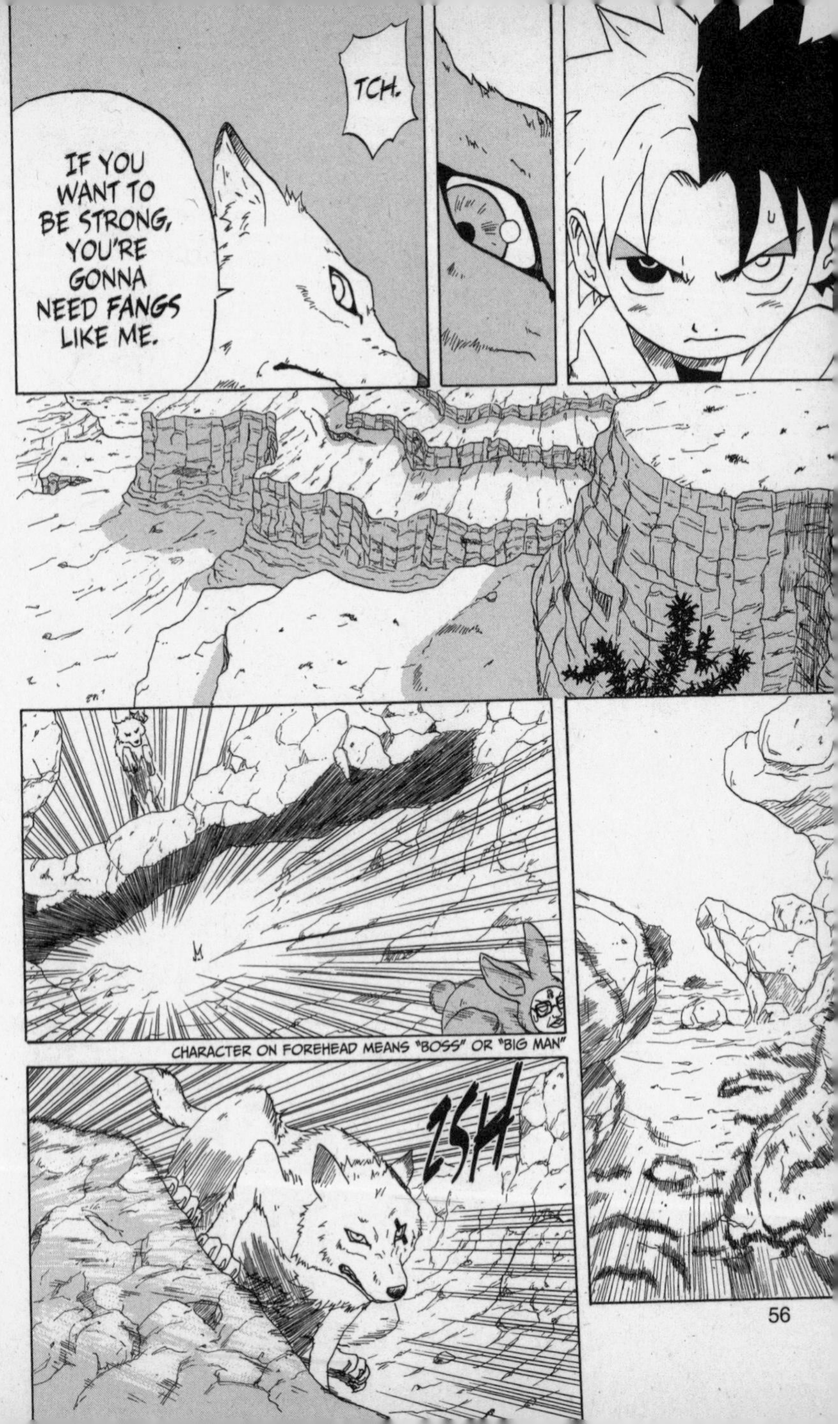
TCH.
IF YOU WANT TO BE STRONG, YOU'RE GONNA NEED FANGS LIKE ME.
CHARACTER ON FOREHEAD MEANS "BOSS" OR "BIG MAN"
ZSH

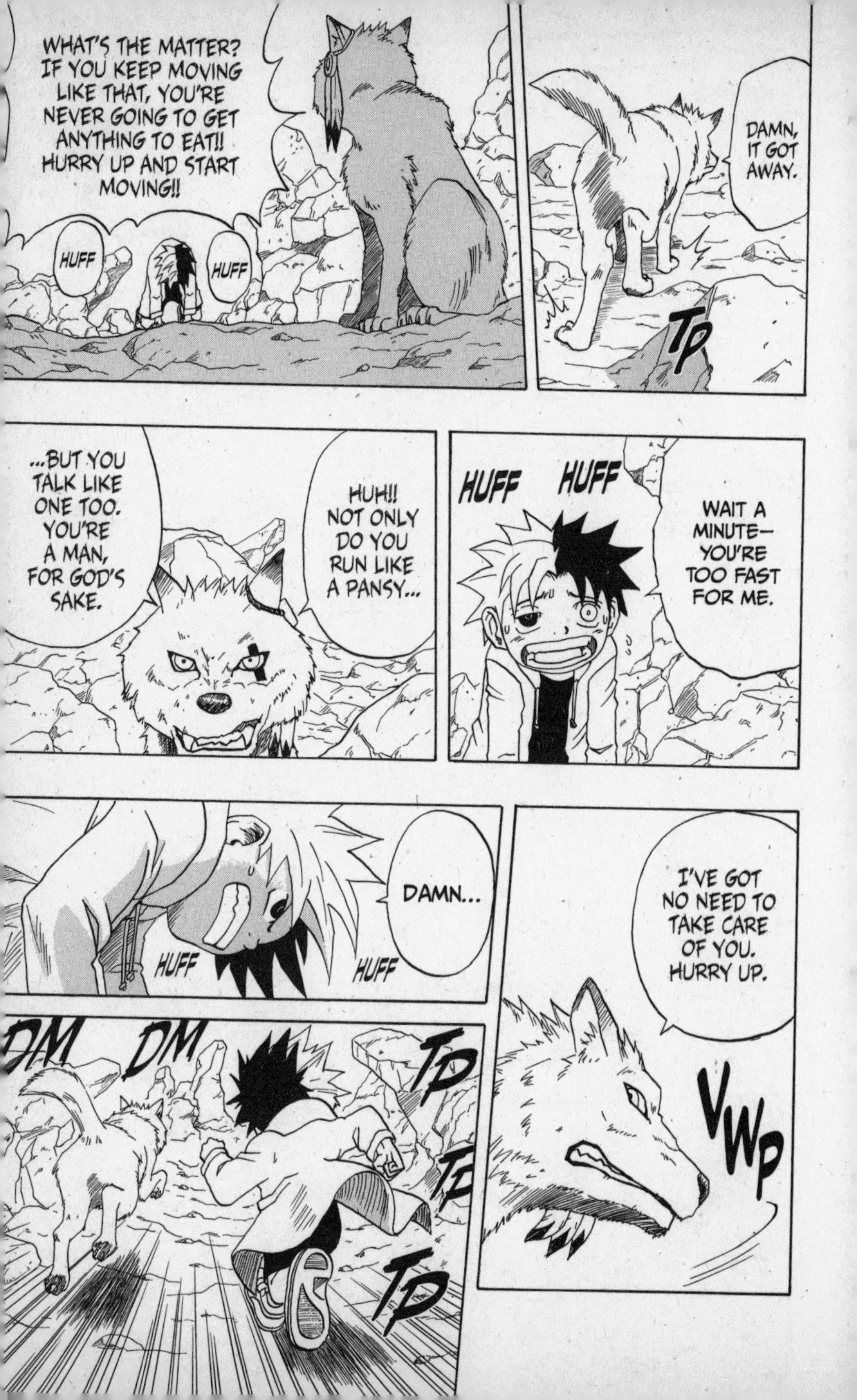
DAMN, IT GOT AWAY.
TP
WHAT'S THE MATTER? IF YOU KEEP MOVING LIKE THAT, YOU'RE NEVER GOING TO GET ANYTHING TO EAT!! HURRY UP AND START MOVING!!
HUFF
HUFF
HUFF HUFF
WAIT A MINUTE— YOU'RE TOO FAST FOR ME.
HUH!! NOT ONLY DO YOU RUN LIKE A PANSY...
...BUT YOU TALK LIKE ONE TOO. YOU'RE A MAN, FOR GOD'S SAKE.
I'VE GOT NO NEED TO TAKE CARE OF YOU. HURRY UP.
VWP
DAMN...
HUFF
HUFF
TP
TP
TP
DM DM

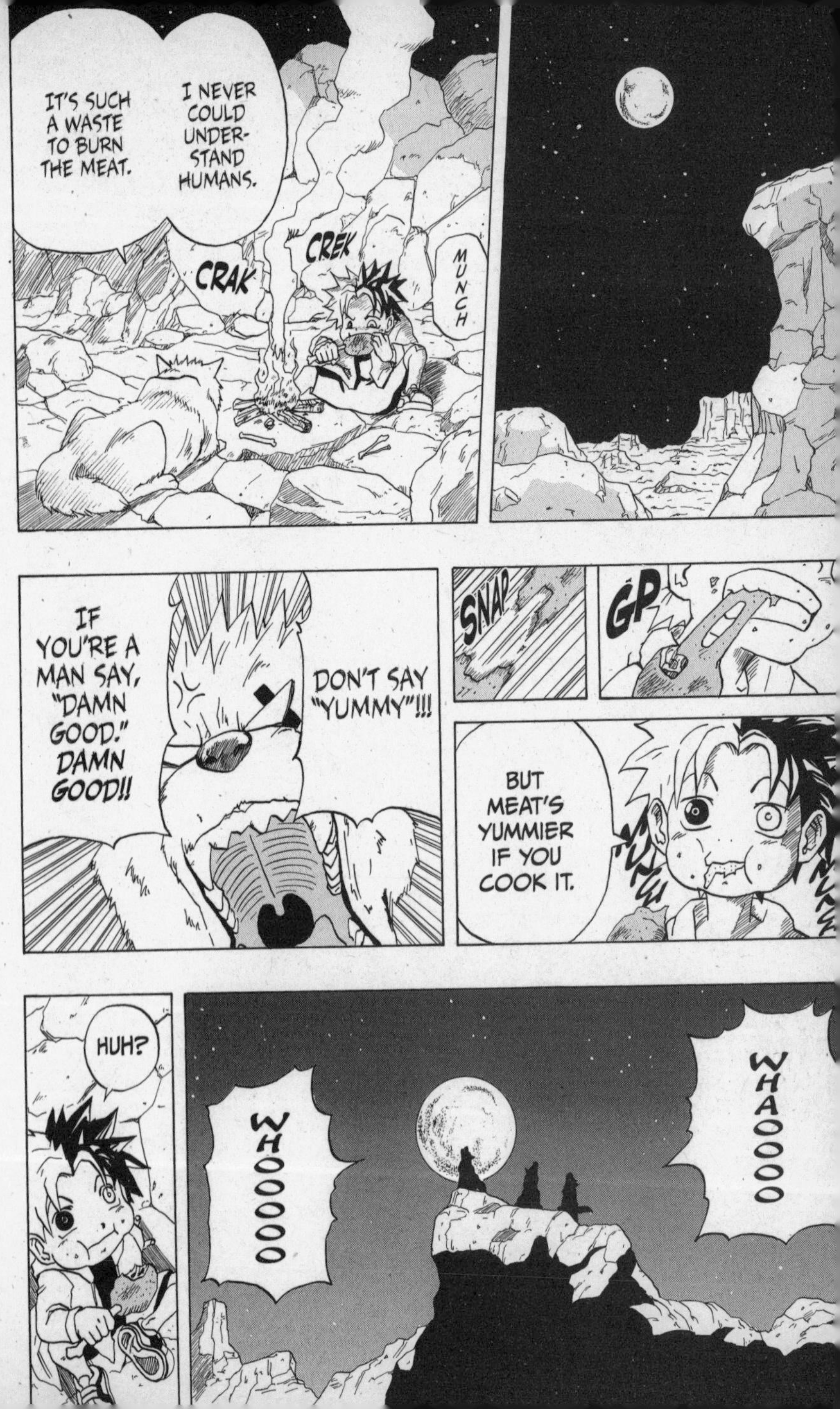
MUNCH
CREK
CRAK
I NEVER COULD UNDER-STAND HUMANS.
IT'S SUCH A WASTE TO BURN THE MEAT.
GP
SNAP
BUT MEAT'S YUMMIER IF YOU COOK IT.
DON'T SAY "YUMMY"!!!
IF YOU'RE A MAN SAY, "DAMN GOOD." DAMN GOOD!!
WHAOOOO
WHOOOOO
HUH?

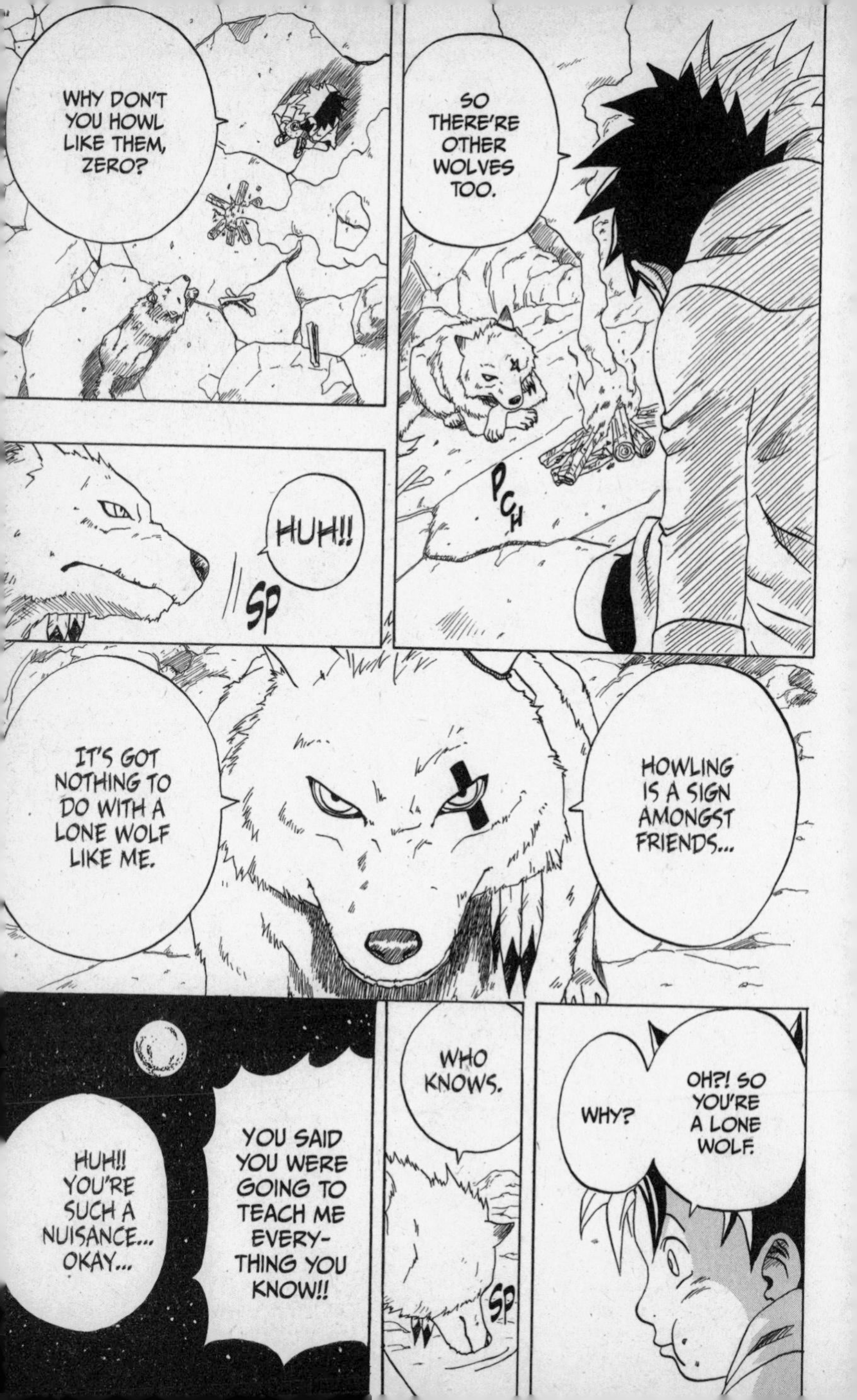
SO THERE'RE OTHER WOLVES TOO.
PCH
WHY DON'T YOU HOWL LIKE THEM, ZERO?
HUH!!
SP
HOWLING IS A SIGN AMONGST FRIENDS...
IT'S GOT NOTHING TO DO WITH A LONE WOLF LIKE ME.
OH?! SO YOU'RE A LONE WOLF.
WHY?
WHO KNOWS.
SP
YOU SAID YOU WERE GOING TO TEACH ME EVERY-THING YOU KNOW!!
HUH!! YOU'RE SUCH A NUISANCE... OKAY...

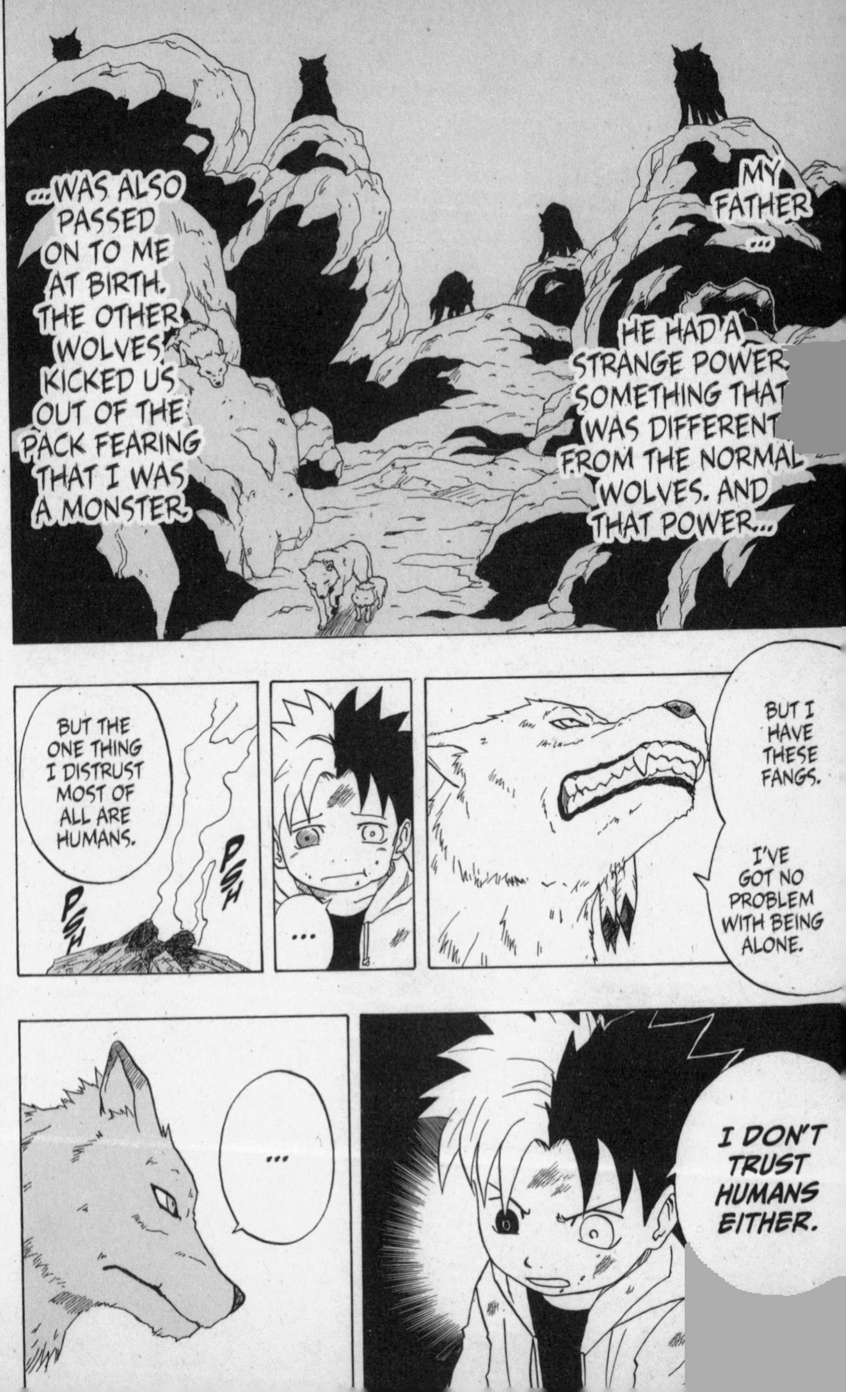
MY FATHER...
HE HAD A STRANGE POWER. SOMETHING THAT WAS DIFFERENT FROM THE NORMAL WOLVES. AND THAT POWER...
...WAS ALSO PASSED ON TO ME AT BIRTH. THE OTHER WOLVES KICKED US OUT OF THE PACK FEARING THAT I WAS A MONSTER.
BUT I HAVE THESE FANGS.
I'VE GOT NO PROBLEM WITH BEING ALONE.
...
BUT THE ONE THING I DISTRUST MOST OF ALL ARE HUMANS.
PSH
PSH
I DON'T TRUST HUMANS EITHER.
...

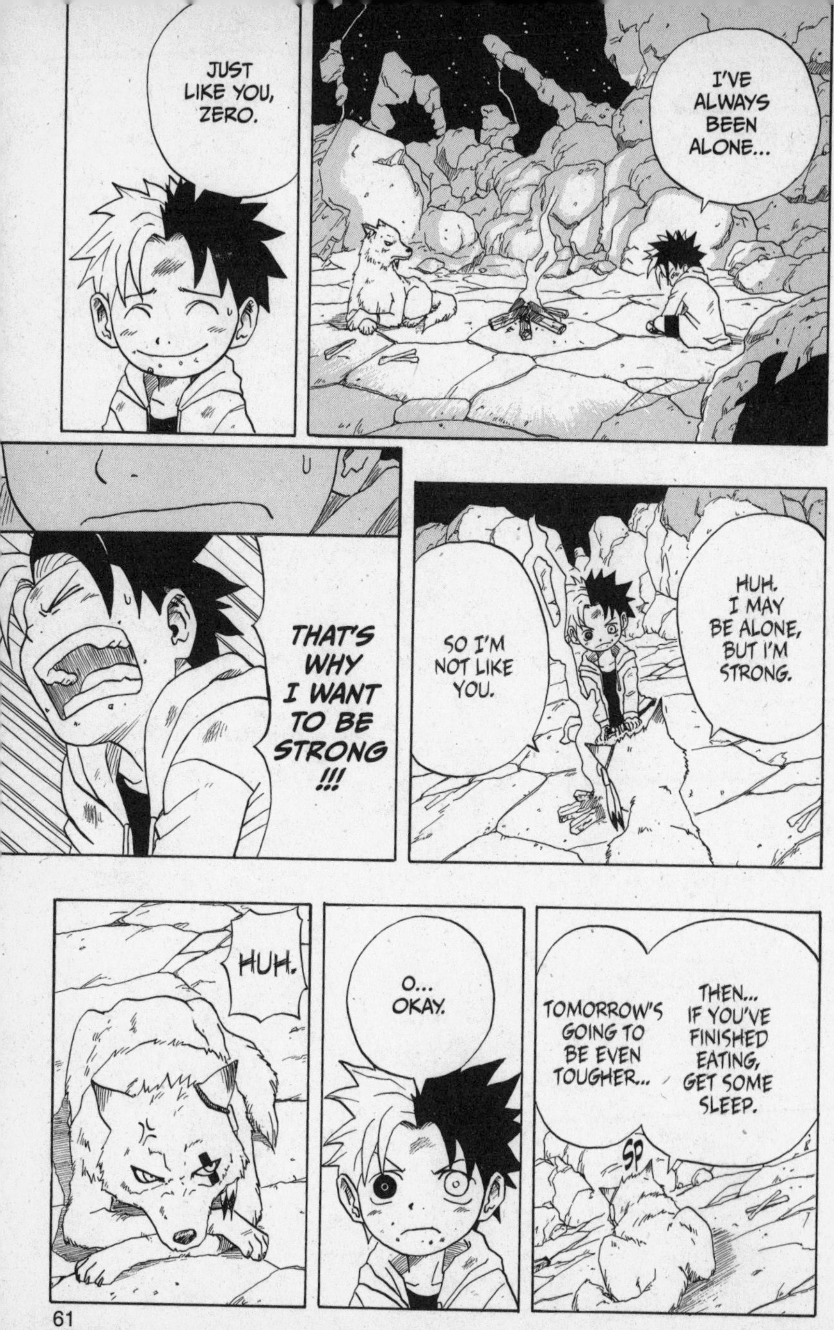
I'VE ALWAYS BEEN ALONE...
JUST LIKE YOU, ZERO.
HUH. I MAY BE ALONE, BUT I'M STRONG.
SO I'M NOT LIKE YOU.
THAT'S WHY I WANT TO BE STRONG !!!
THEN... IF YOU'VE FINISHED EATING, GET SOME SLEEP.
TOMORROW'S GOING TO BE EVEN TOUGHER...
SP
O... OKAY.
HUH.

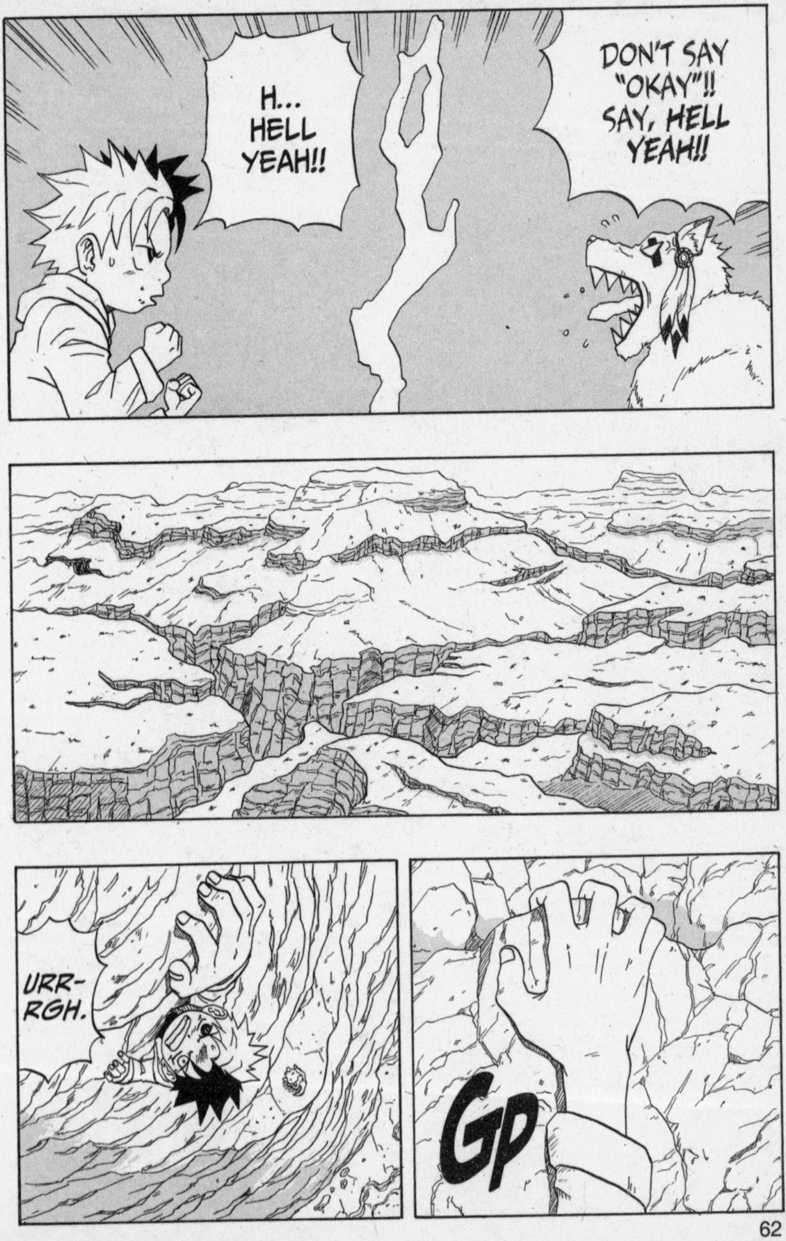
DON'T SAY "OKAY"!! SAY, HELL YEAH!!
H... HELL YEAH!!
GP
URR-RGH.

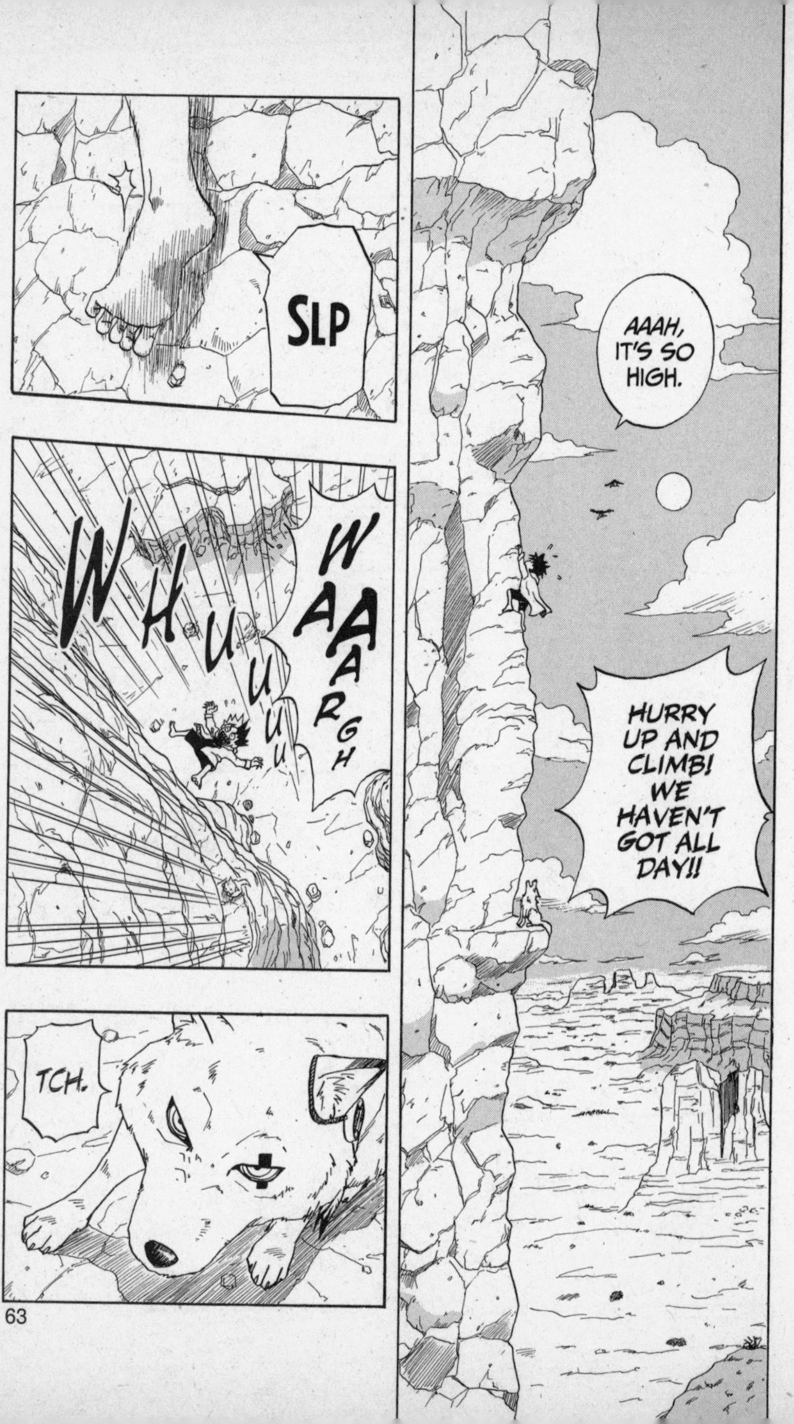
AAAH, IT'S SO HIGH.
HURRY UP AND CLIMB! WE HAVEN'T GOT ALL DAY!!
SLP
WAAAARGH
WHUUUUU
TCH.

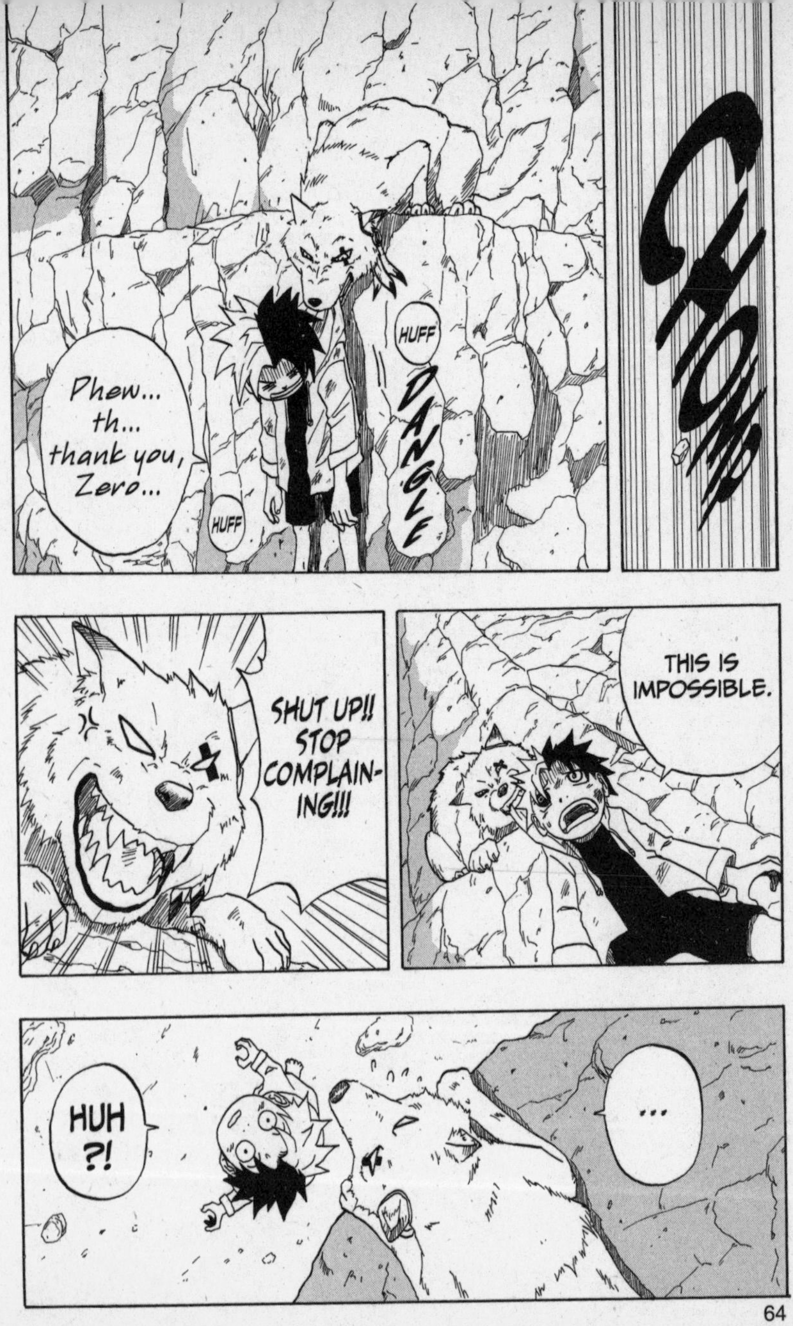
CHOMP
HUFF
DANGLE
Phew... th... thank you, Zero...
HUFF
THIS IS IMPOSSIBLE.
SHUT UP!! STOP COMPLAIN-ING!!!
...
HUH ?!

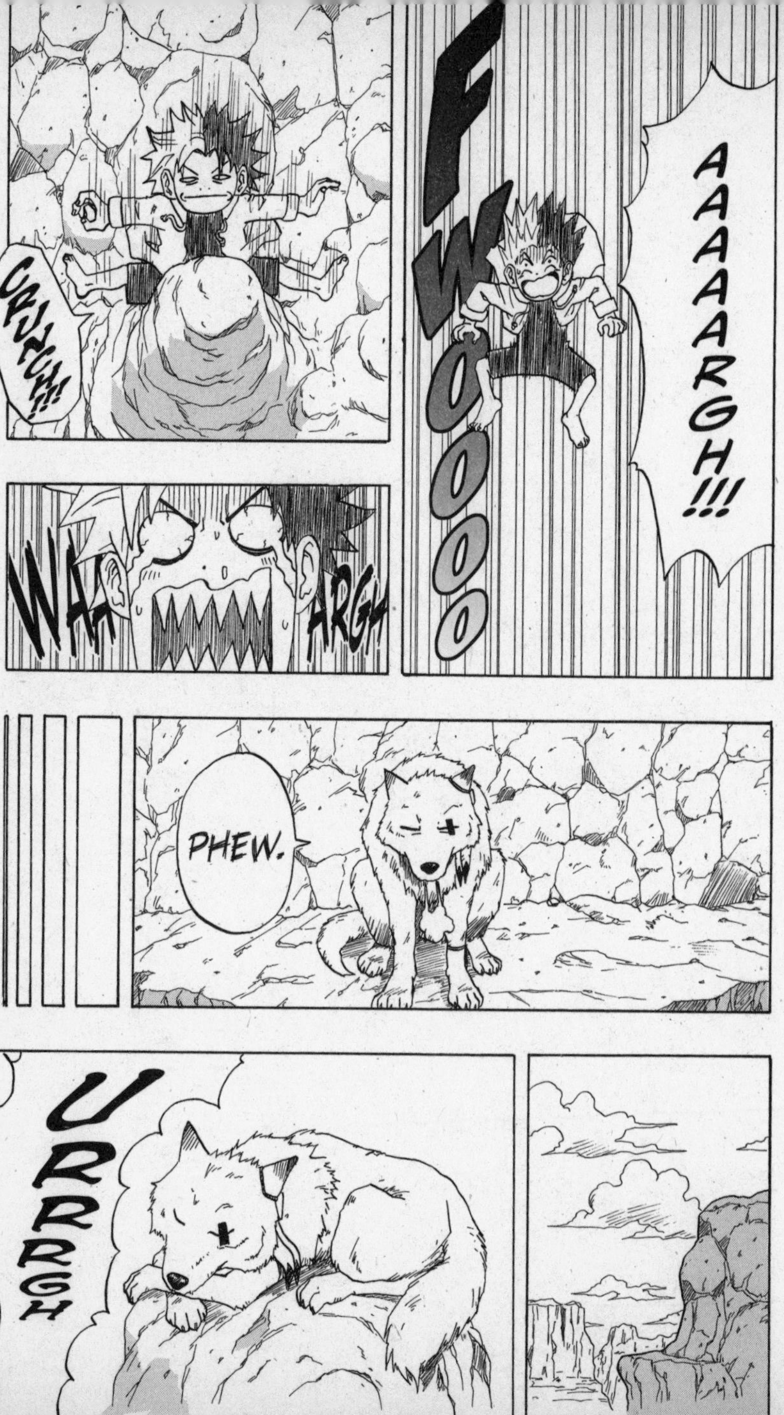
AAAAARGH!!!
FWOOOOO
CRUNCH!!
WAAARGH
PHEW.
URRRGH

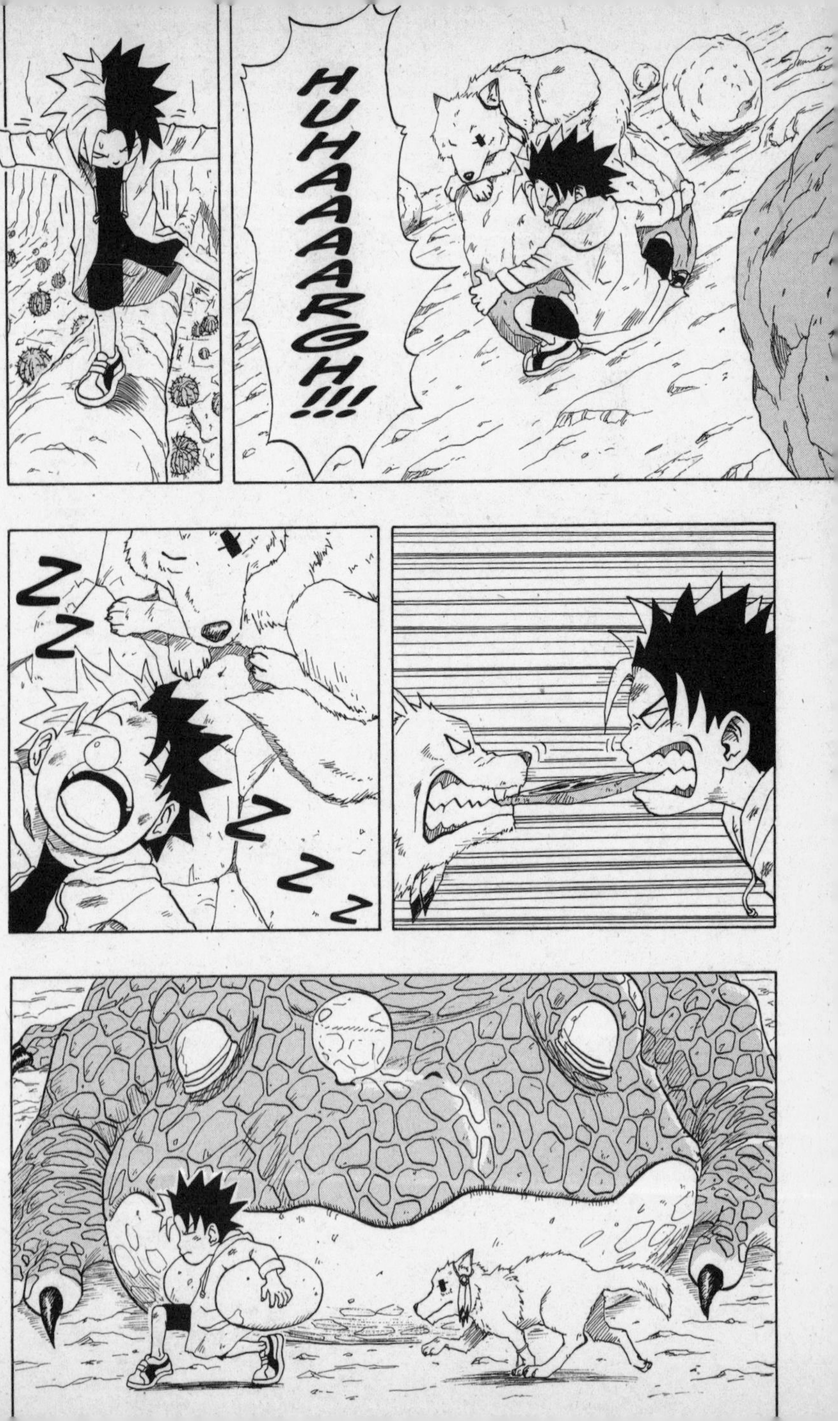
HUHAAAARGH!!!
Z Z
Z Z Z

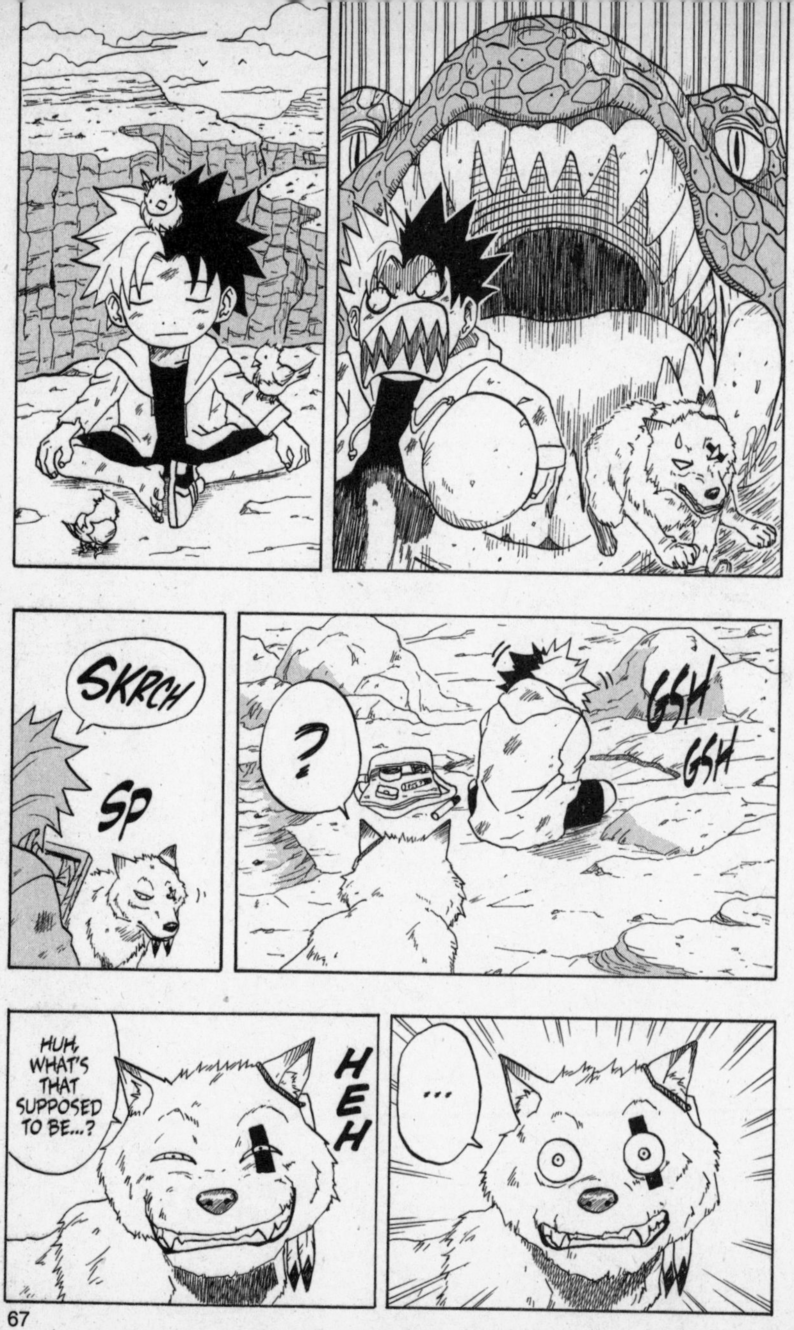
GSH
GSH
?
SKRCH
SP
...
HEH
HUH, WHAT'S THAT SUPPOSED TO BE...?

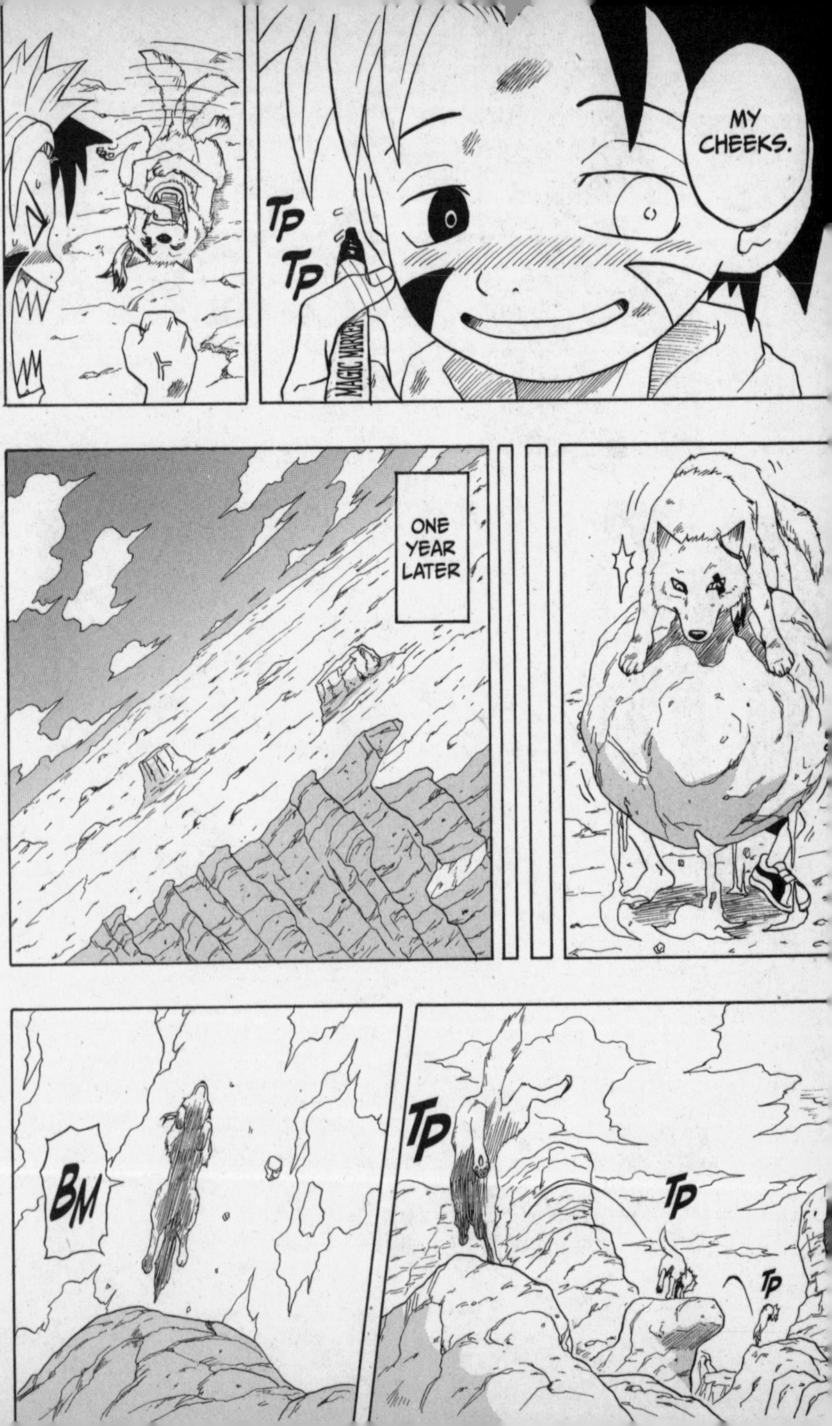
MY CHEEKS.
TP
TP
MAGIC MARKER
ONE YEAR LATER
TP
TP
TP
BM

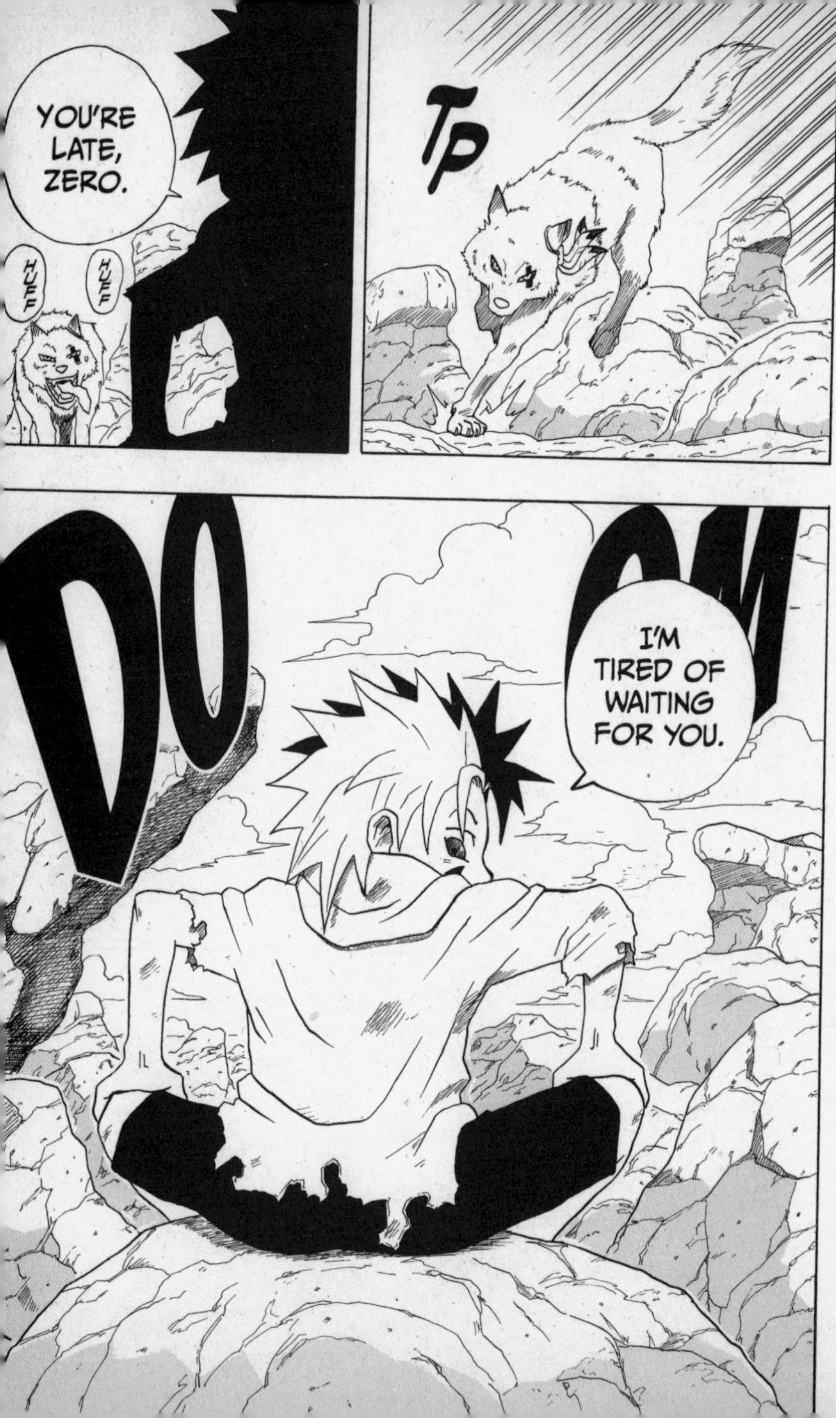
TP
YOU'RE LATE, ZERO.
HUFF
HUFF
DOOM
I'M TIRED OF WAITING FOR YOU.

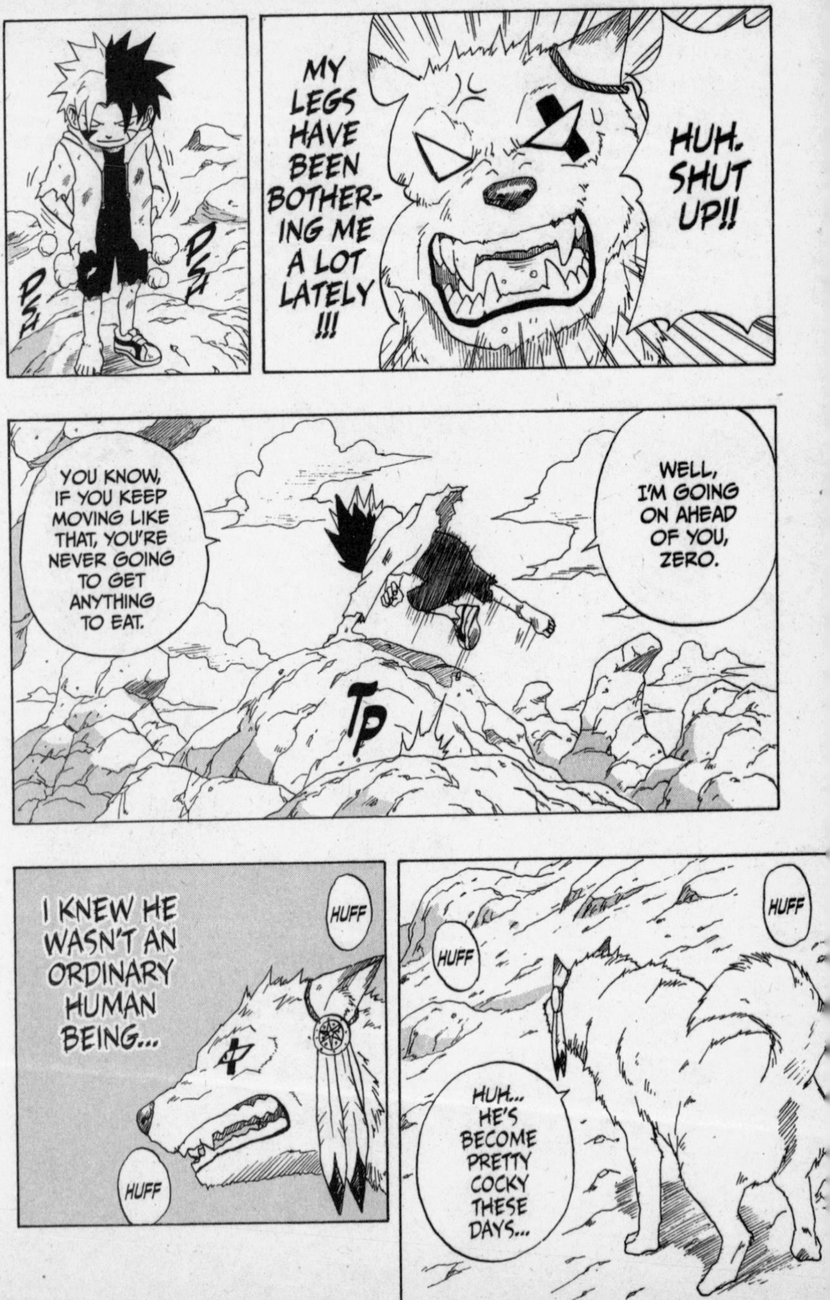
HUH. SHUT UP!!
MY LEGS HAVE BEEN BOTHERING ME A LOT LATELY!!!
DSH
DSH
WELL, I'M GOING ON AHEAD OF YOU, ZERO.
YOU KNOW, IF YOU KEEP MOVING LIKE THAT, YOU'RE NEVER GOING TO GET ANYTHING TO EAT.
TP
HUFF
HUFF
HUH... HE'S BECOME PRETTY COCKY THESE DAYS...
HUFF
I KNEW HE WASN'T AN ORDINARY HUMAN BEING...
HUFF

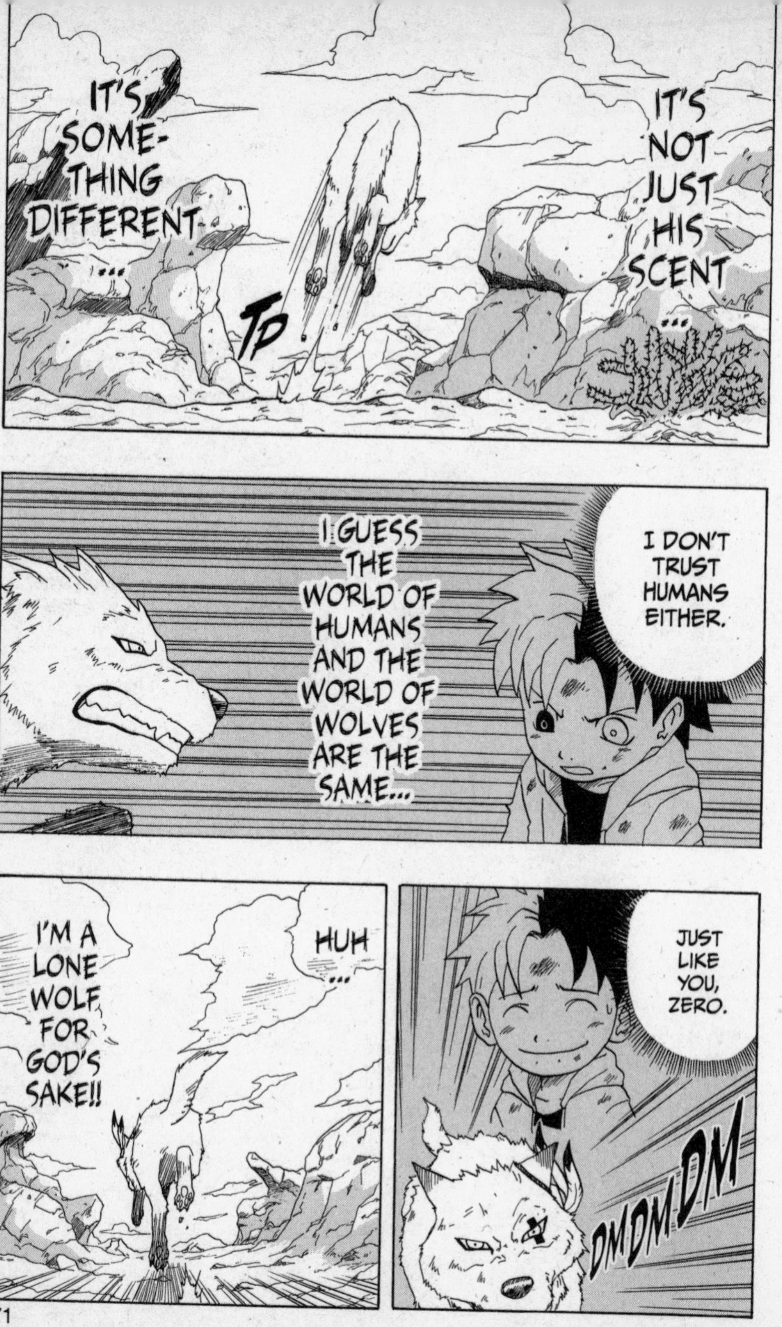
IT'S NOT JUST HIS SCENT...
IT'S SOME-THING DIFFERENT...
TP
I DON'T TRUST HUMANS EITHER.
I GUESS THE WORLD OF HUMANS AND THE WORLD OF WOLVES ARE THE SAME...
JUST LIKE YOU, ZERO.
DM DM DM
HUH...
I'M A LONE WOLF FOR GOD'S SAKE!!

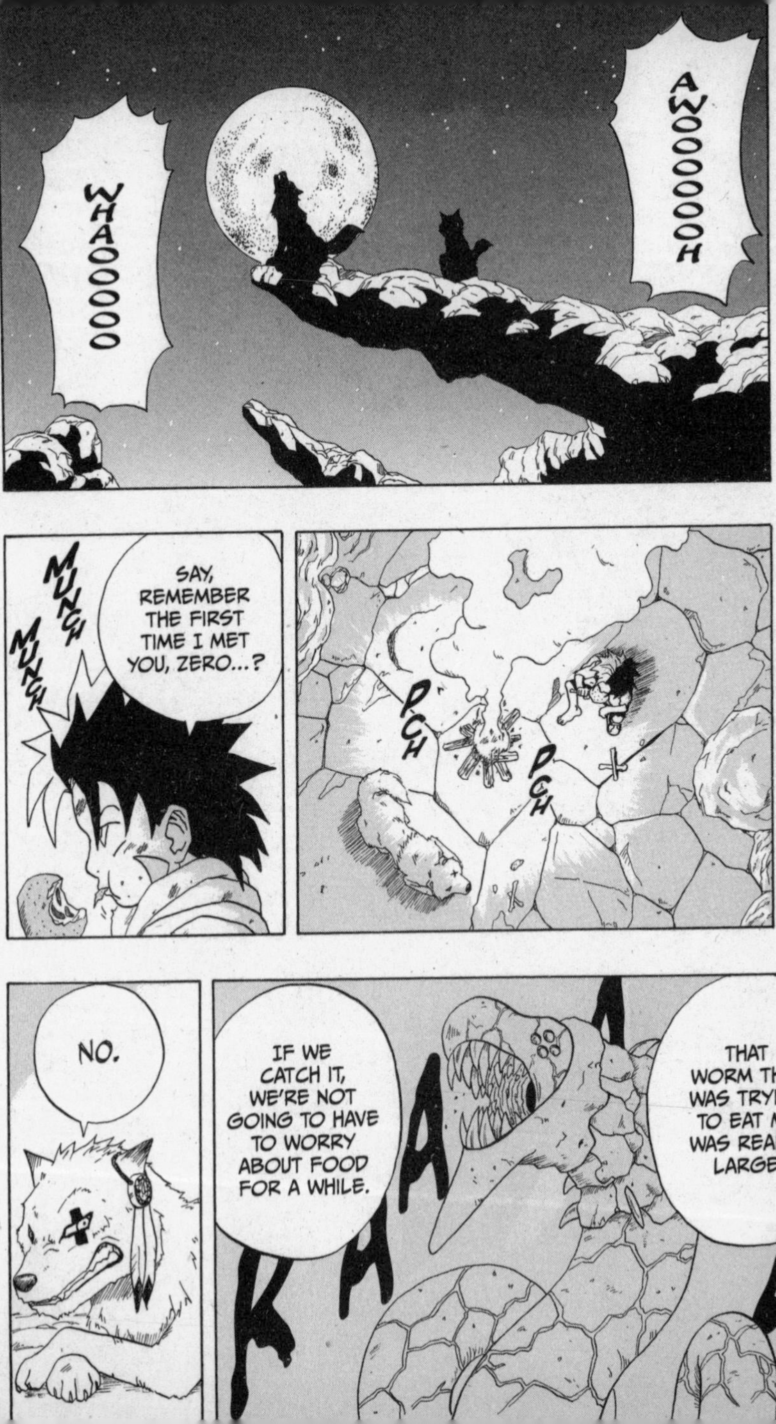
AWOOOOOOOH
WHAOOOOO
PCH
PCH
SAY, REMEMBER THE FIRST TIME I MET YOU, ZERO...?
MUNCH
MUNCH
THAT WORM THAT WAS TRYING TO EAT ME WAS REALLY LARGE.
IF WE CATCH IT, WE'RE NOT GOING TO HAVE TO WORRY ABOUT FOOD FOR A WHILE.
KAAAA
NO.

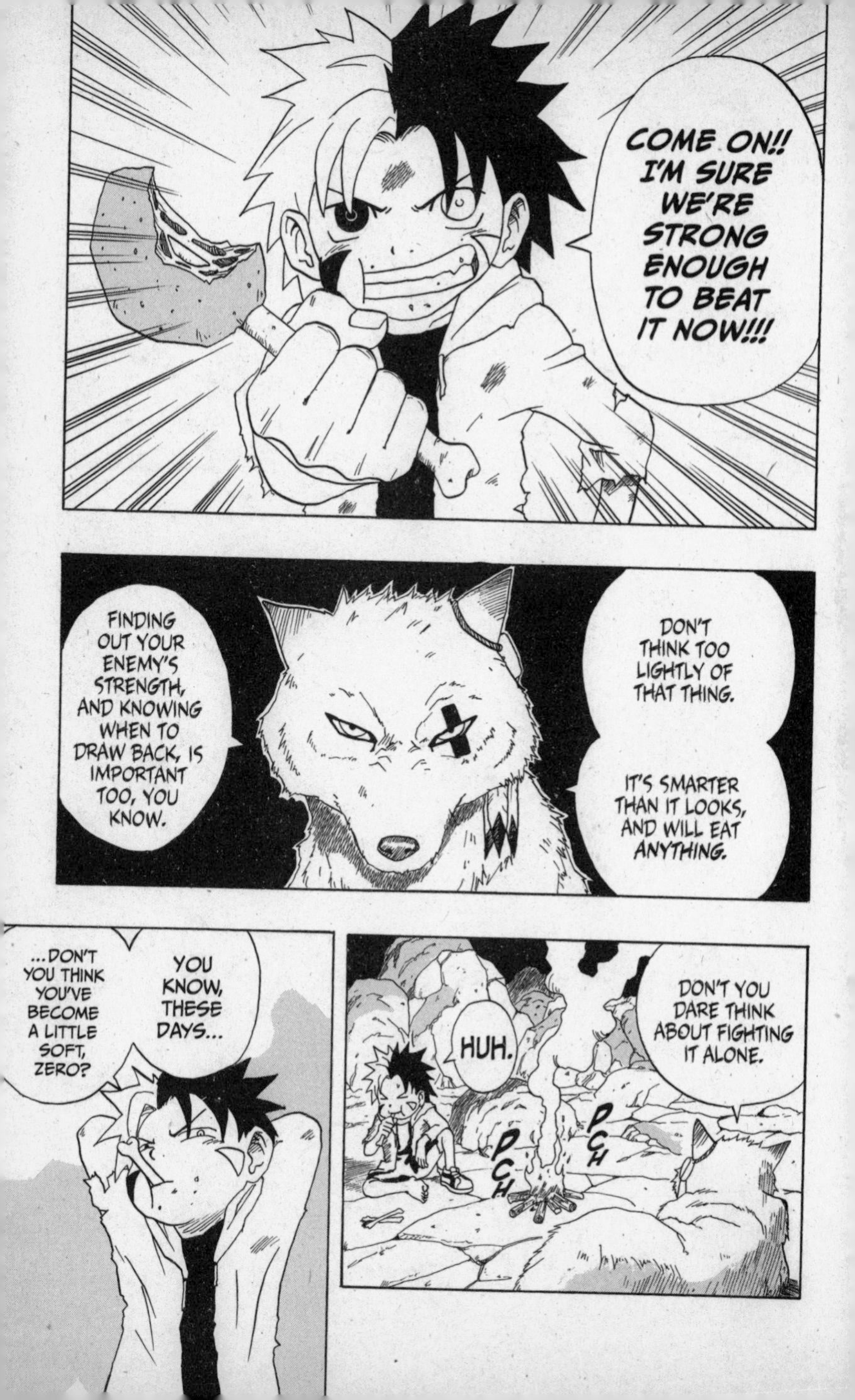
COME ON!! I'M SURE WE'RE STRONG ENOUGH TO BEAT IT NOW!!!
DON'T THINK TOO LIGHTLY OF THAT THING.
IT'S SMARTER THAN IT LOOKS, AND WILL EAT ANYTHING.
FINDING OUT YOUR ENEMY'S STRENGTH, AND KNOWING WHEN TO DRAW BACK, IS IMPORTANT TOO, YOU KNOW.
DON'T YOU DARE THINK ABOUT FIGHTING IT ALONE.
HUH.
PCH
PCH
YOU KNOW, THESE DAYS...
...DON'T YOU THINK YOU'VE BECOME A LITTLE SOFT, ZERO?

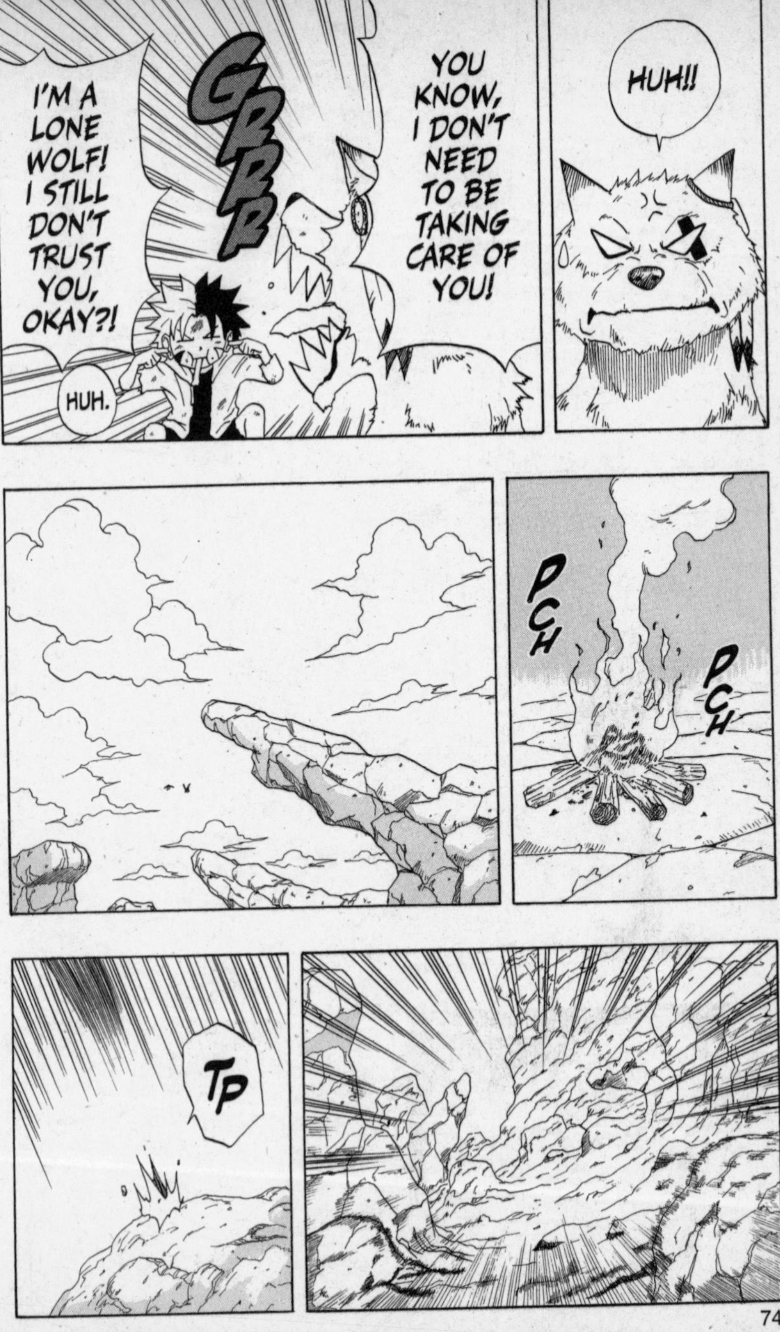
HUH!!
YOU KNOW, I DON'T NEED TO BE TAKING CARE OF YOU!
GRRP
I'M A LONE WOLF! I STILL DON'T TRUST YOU, OKAY?!
HUH.
PCH
PCH
TP

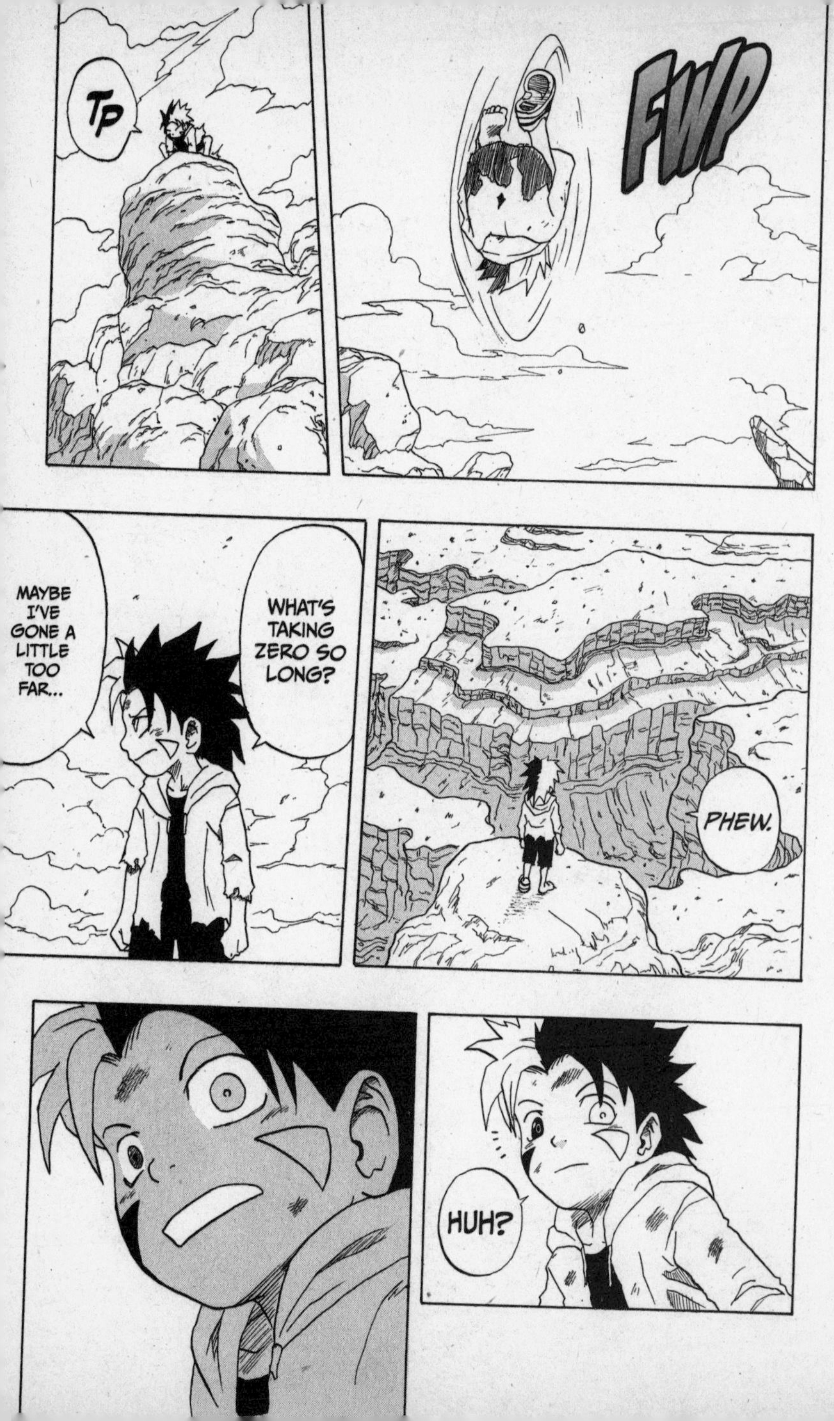
FWP
TP
PHEW.
WHAT'S TAKING ZERO SO LONG?
MAYBE I'VE GONE A LITTLE TOO FAR...
HUH?

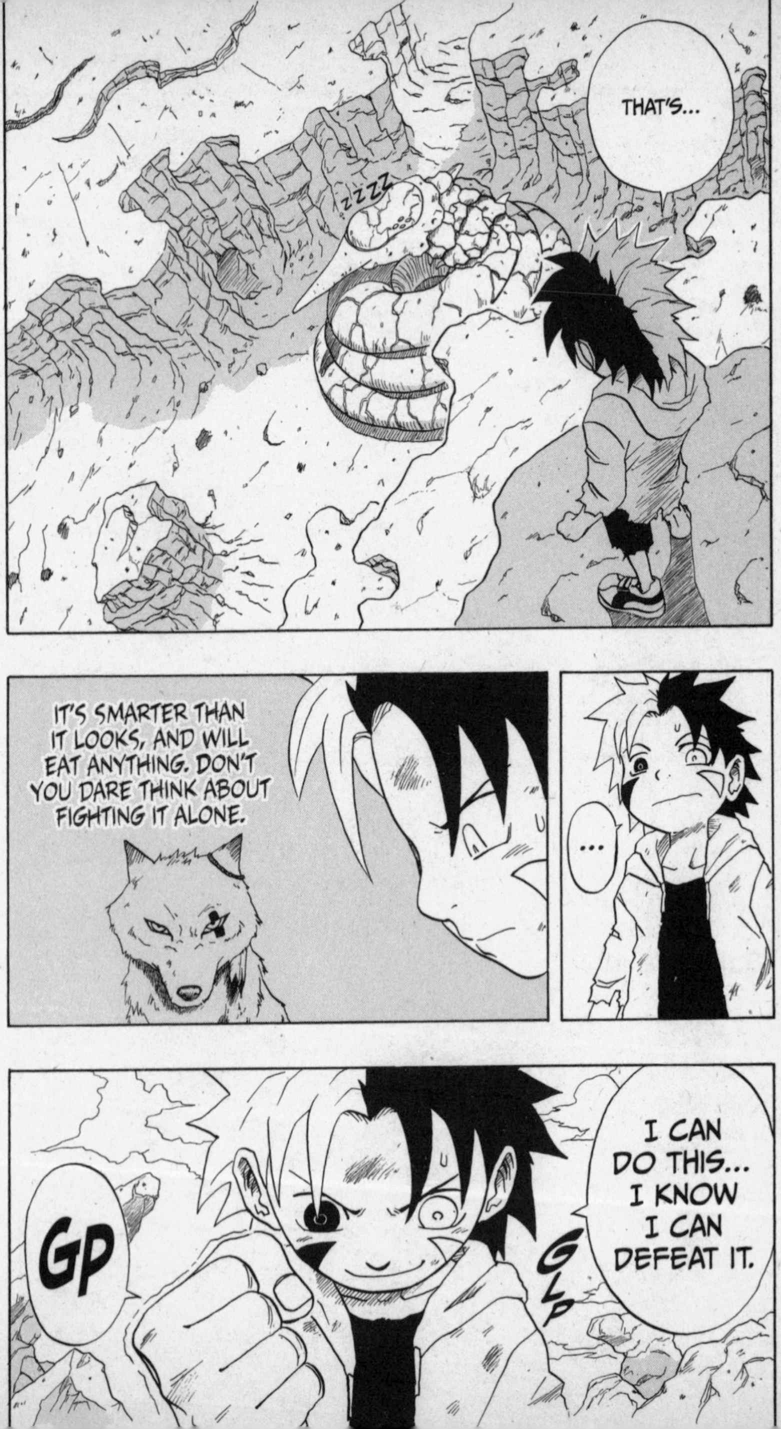
ZZZZ
THAT'S...
...
IT'S SMARTER THAN IT LOOKS, AND WILL EAT ANYTHING. DON'T YOU DARE THINK ABOUT FIGHTING IT ALONE.
I CAN DO THIS... I KNOW I CAN DEFEAT IT.
GLP
GP

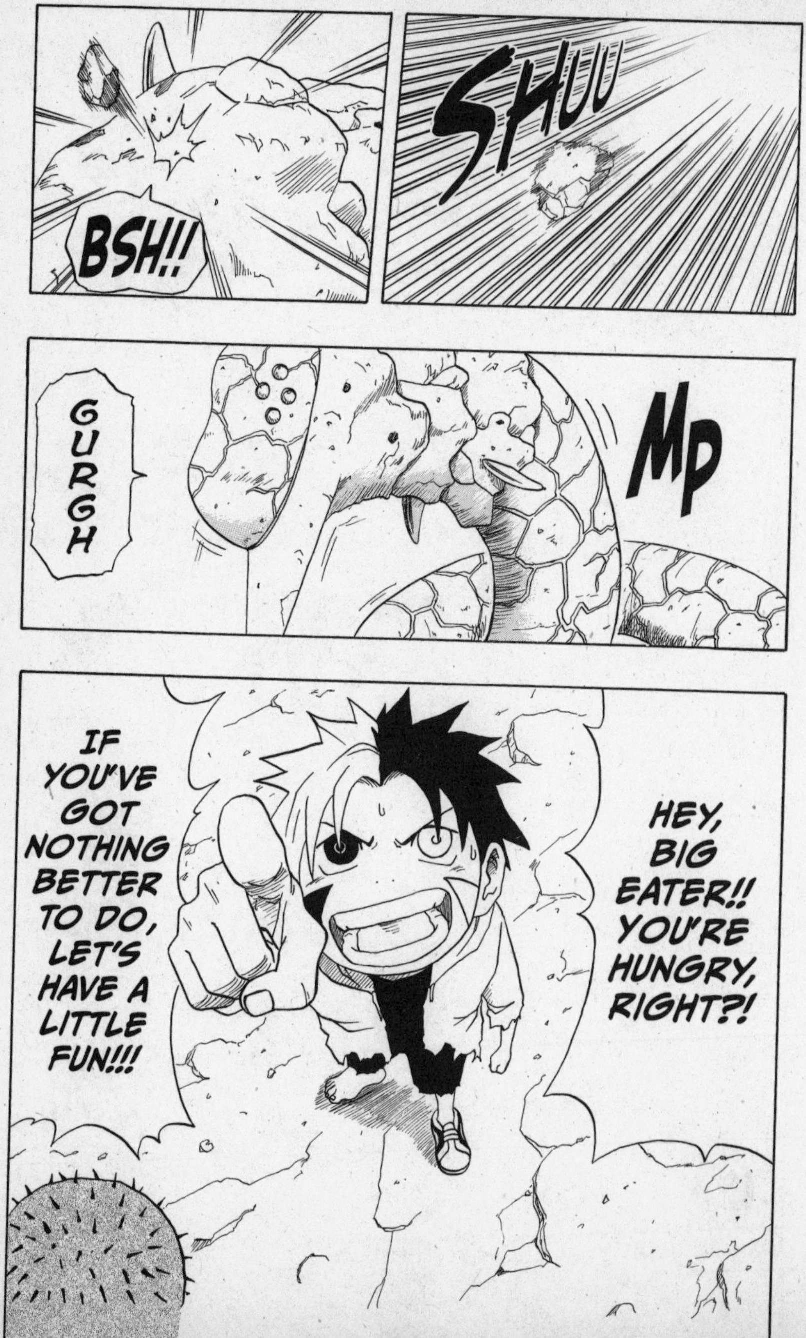
SHUU
BSH!!
Mp
GURGH
HEY, BIG EATER!! YOU'RE HUNGRY, RIGHT?!
IF YOU'VE GOT NOTHING BETTER TO DO, LET'S HAVE A LITTLE FUN!!!

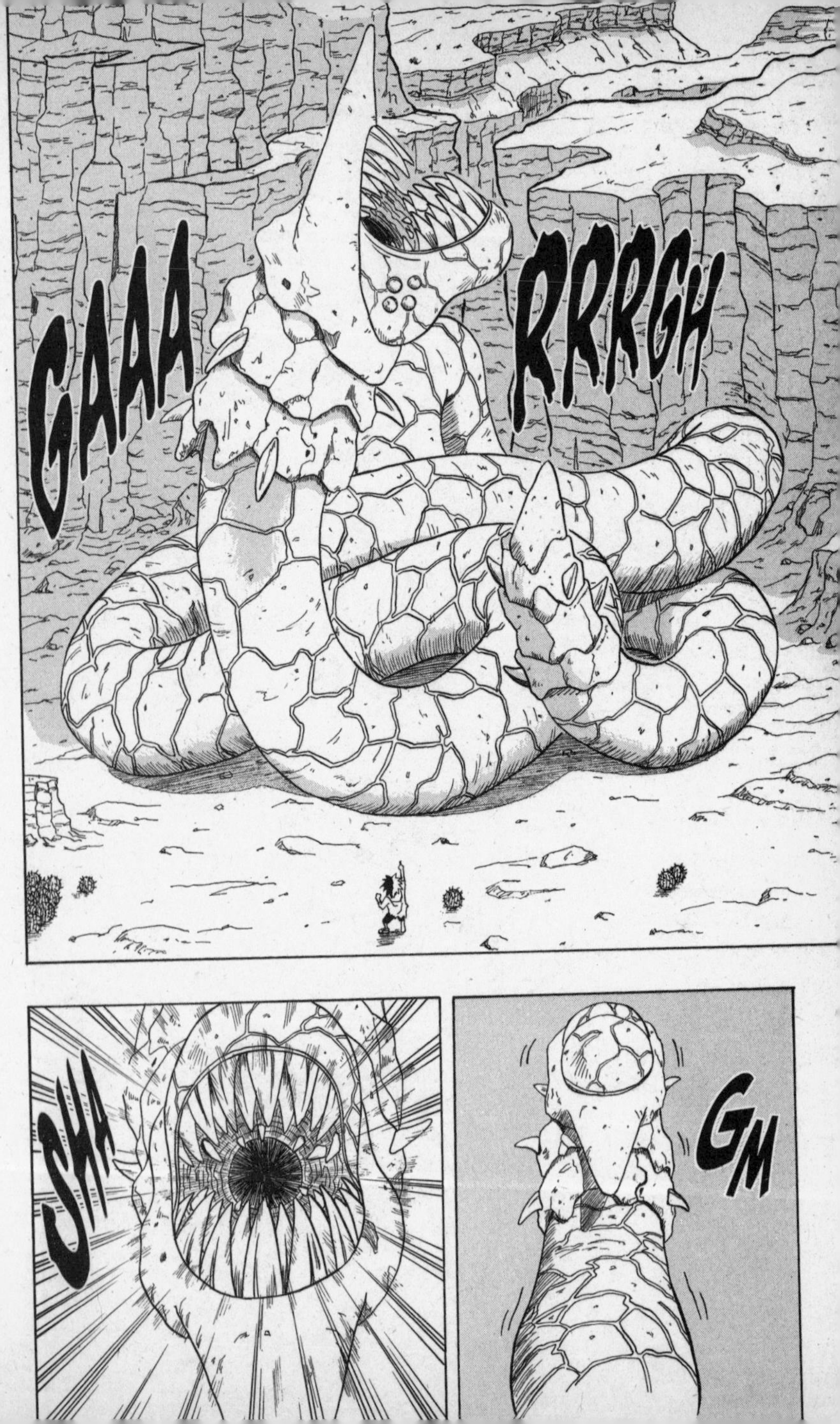
GAAA RRRGH
GM
SHA

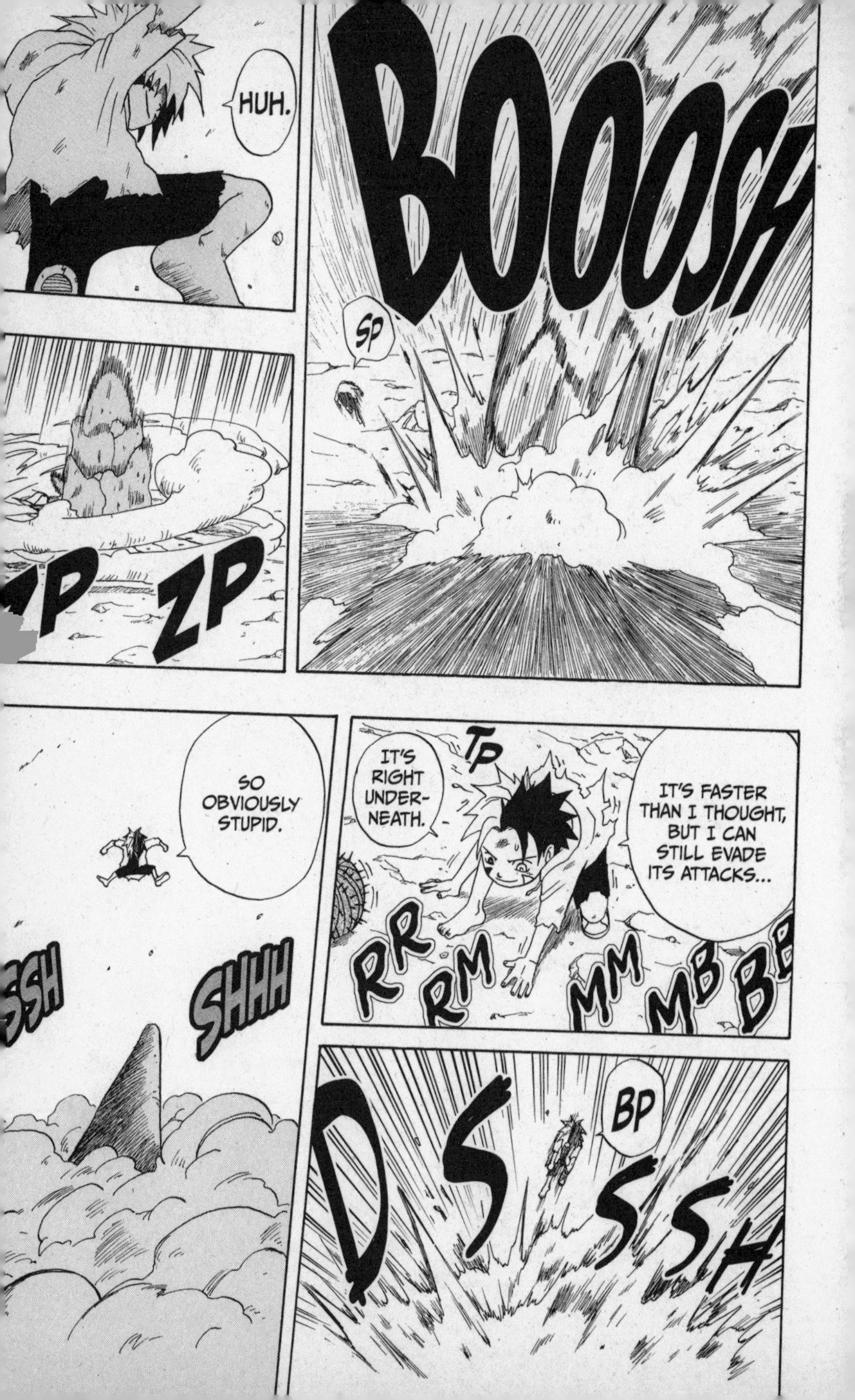
BOOOSH
SP
HUH.
ZP
IT'S FASTER THAN I THOUGHT, BUT I CAN STILL EVADE ITS ATTACKS...
TP
IT'S RIGHT UNDER-NEATH.
RRRM
MMMBB
SO OBVIOUSLY STUPID.
SHHH
SSH
BP
DSSSH

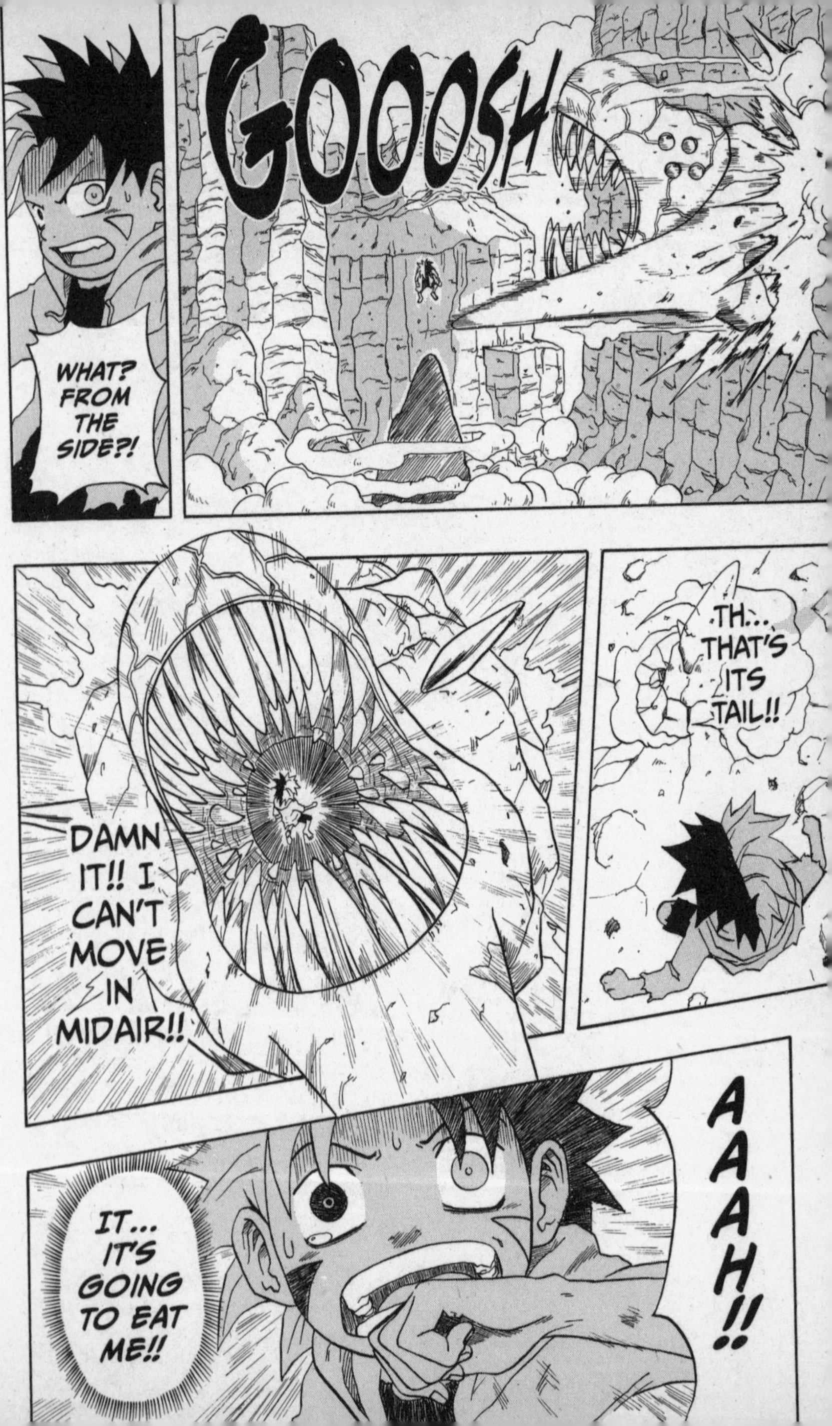
GOOOSH
WHAT? FROM THE SIDE?!
TH... THAT'S ITS TAIL!!
DAMN IT!! I CAN'T MOVE IN MIDAIR!!
AAAH!!
IT... IT'S GOING TO EAT ME!!

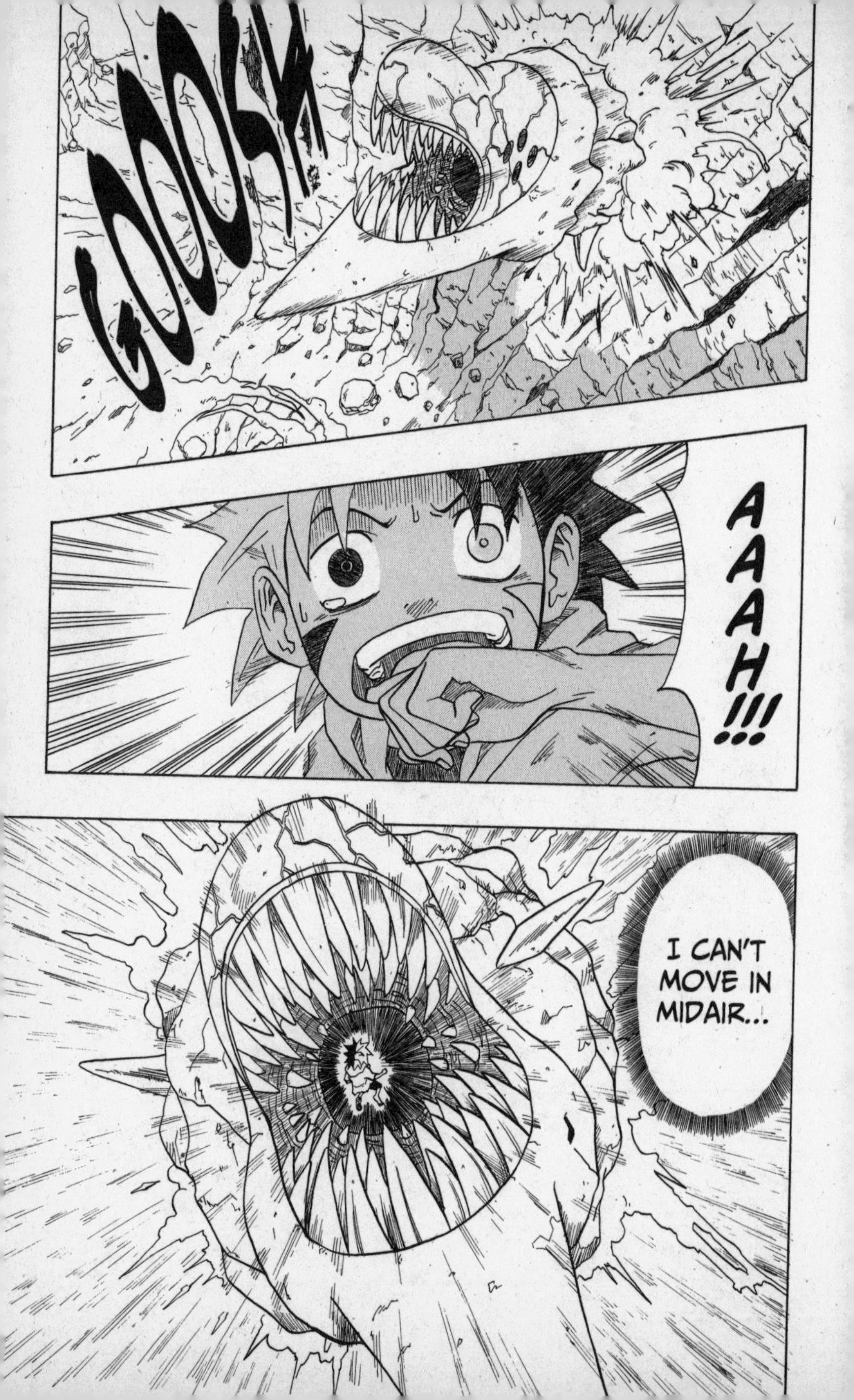
GOOOSH
AAAAH!!!
I CAN'T MOVE IN MIDAIR...

CHAPTER 6: FANGS

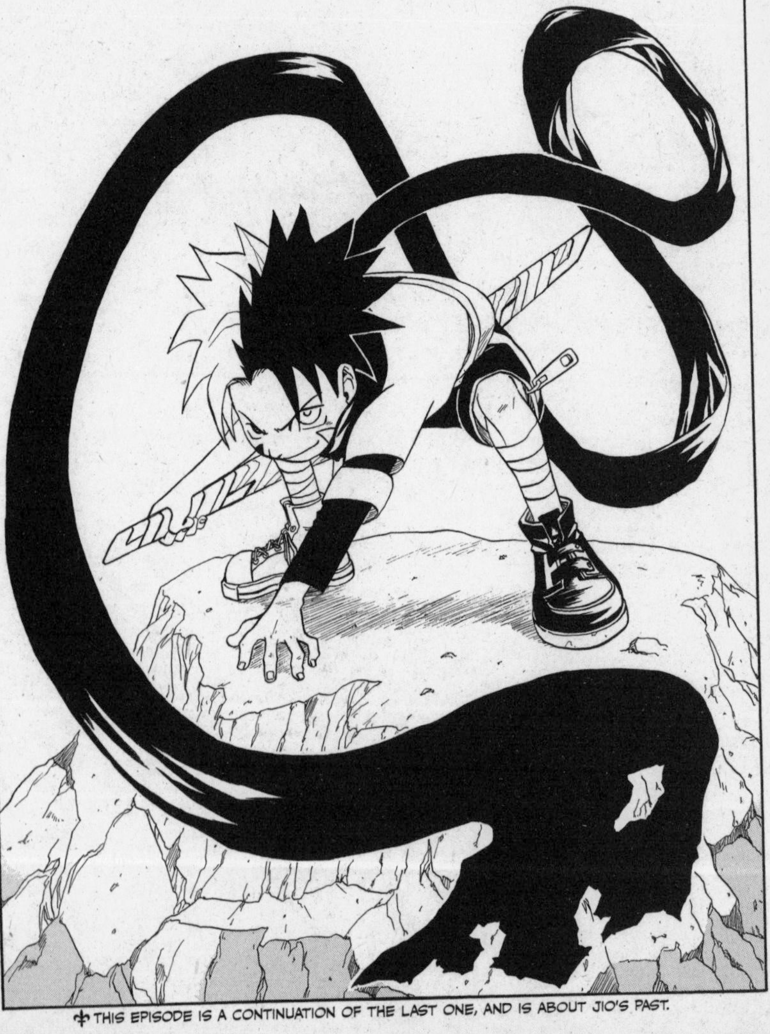

✣ THIS EPISODE IS A CONTINUATION OF THE LAST ONE, AND IS ABOUT JIO'S PAST.

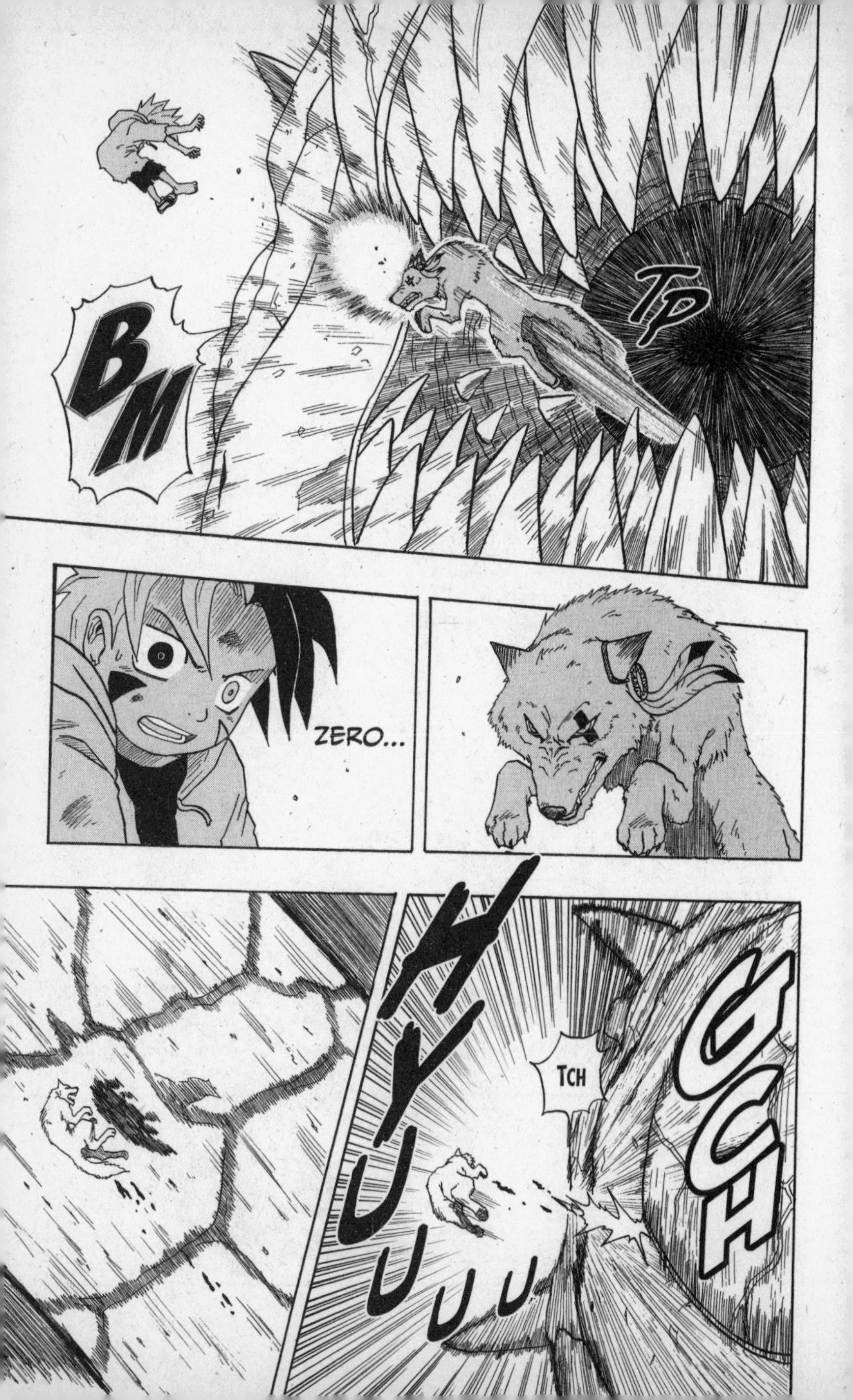
TP
BM
ZERO...
UGH
TCH
HYUUUUU

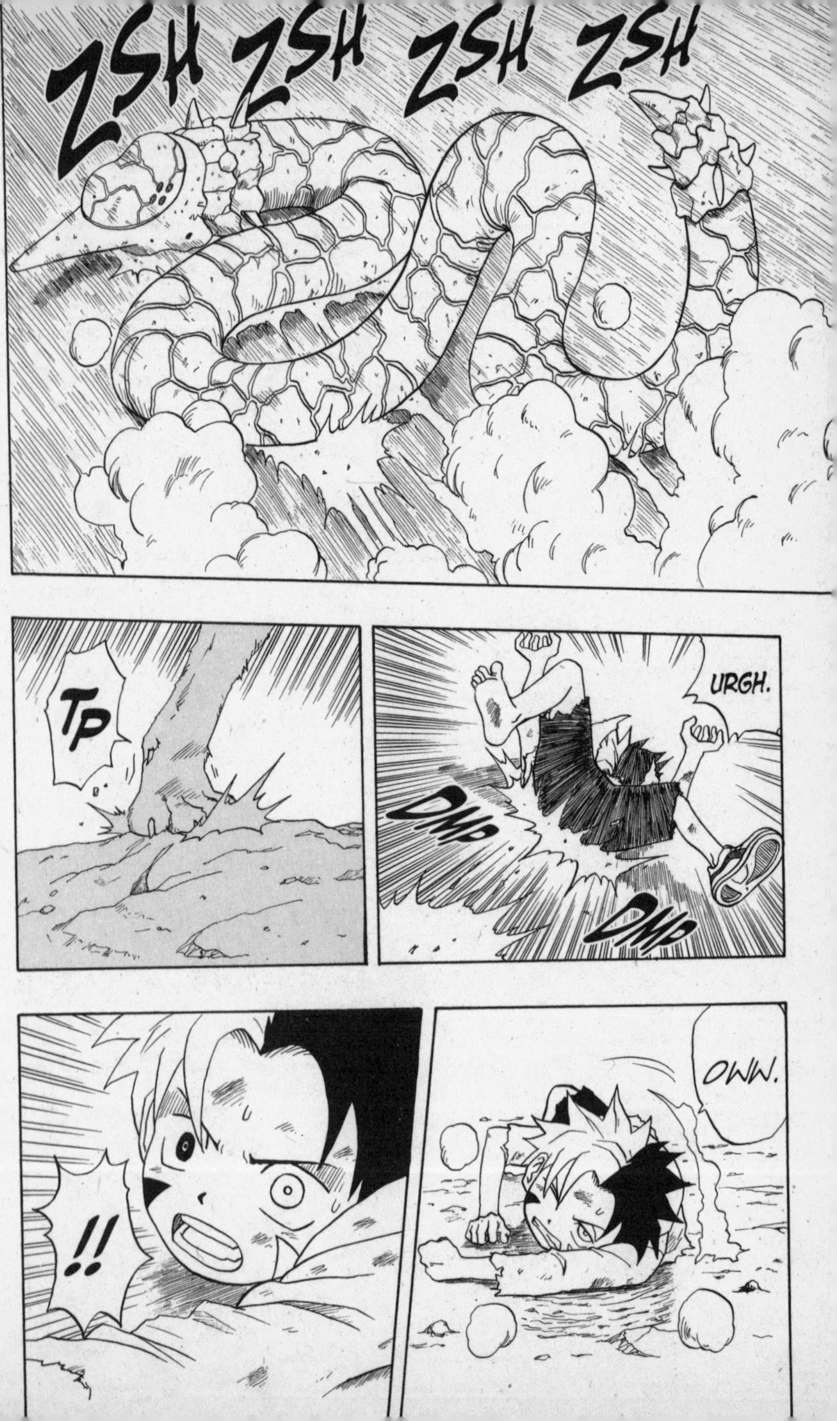
ZSH ZSH ZSH ZSH
URGH.
DMP
DMP
TP
OWW.
!!

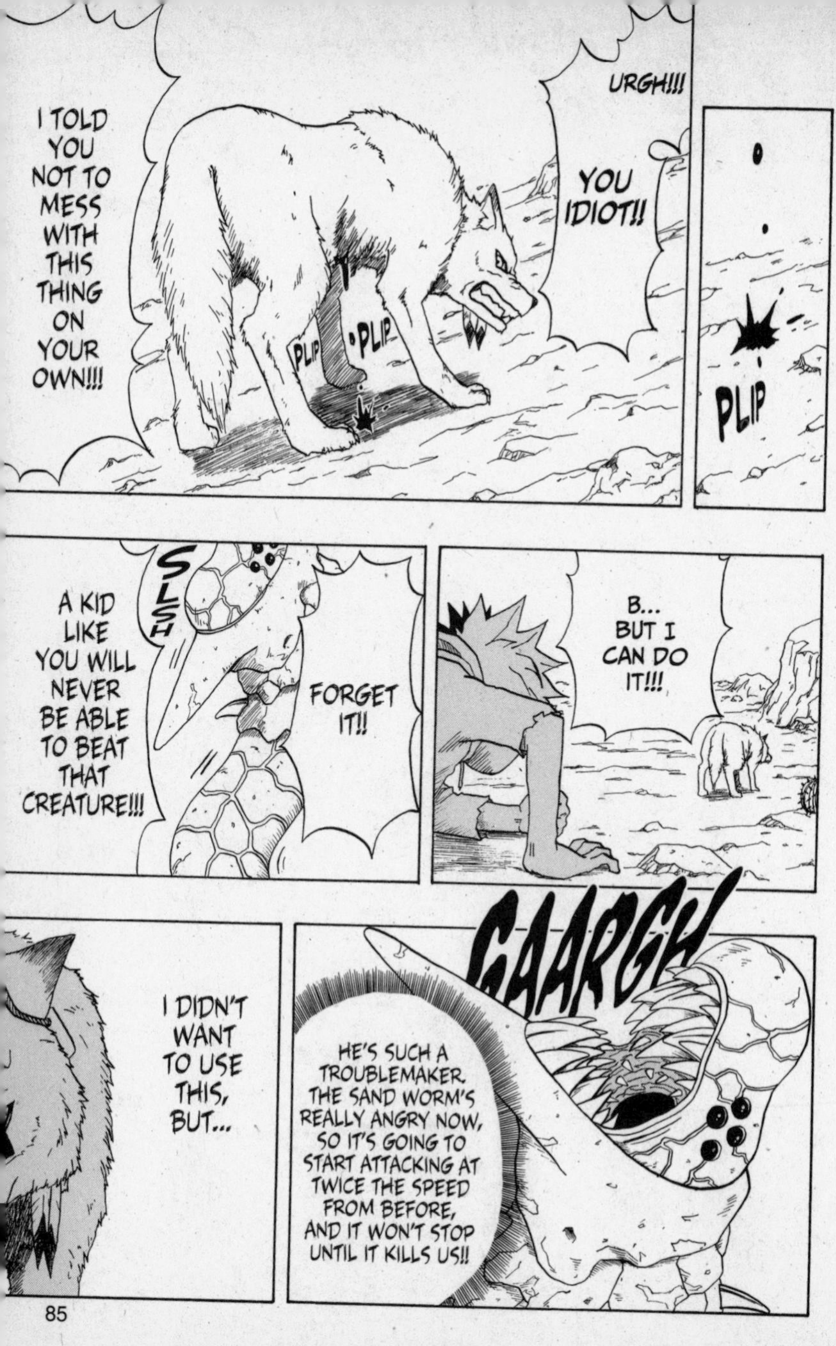
PLIP
URGH!!!
YOU IDIOT!!
PLIP
PLIP
I TOLD YOU NOT TO MESS WITH THIS THING ON YOUR OWN!!!
B... BUT I CAN DO IT!!!
FORGET IT!!
SLSH
A KID LIKE YOU WILL NEVER BE ABLE TO BEAT THAT CREATURE!!!
GAARGH
HE'S SUCH A TROUBLEMAKER. THE SAND WORM'S REALLY ANGRY NOW, SO IT'S GOING TO START ATTACKING AT TWICE THE SPEED FROM BEFORE, AND IT WON'T STOP UNTIL IT KILLS US!!
I DIDN'T WANT TO USE THIS, BUT...

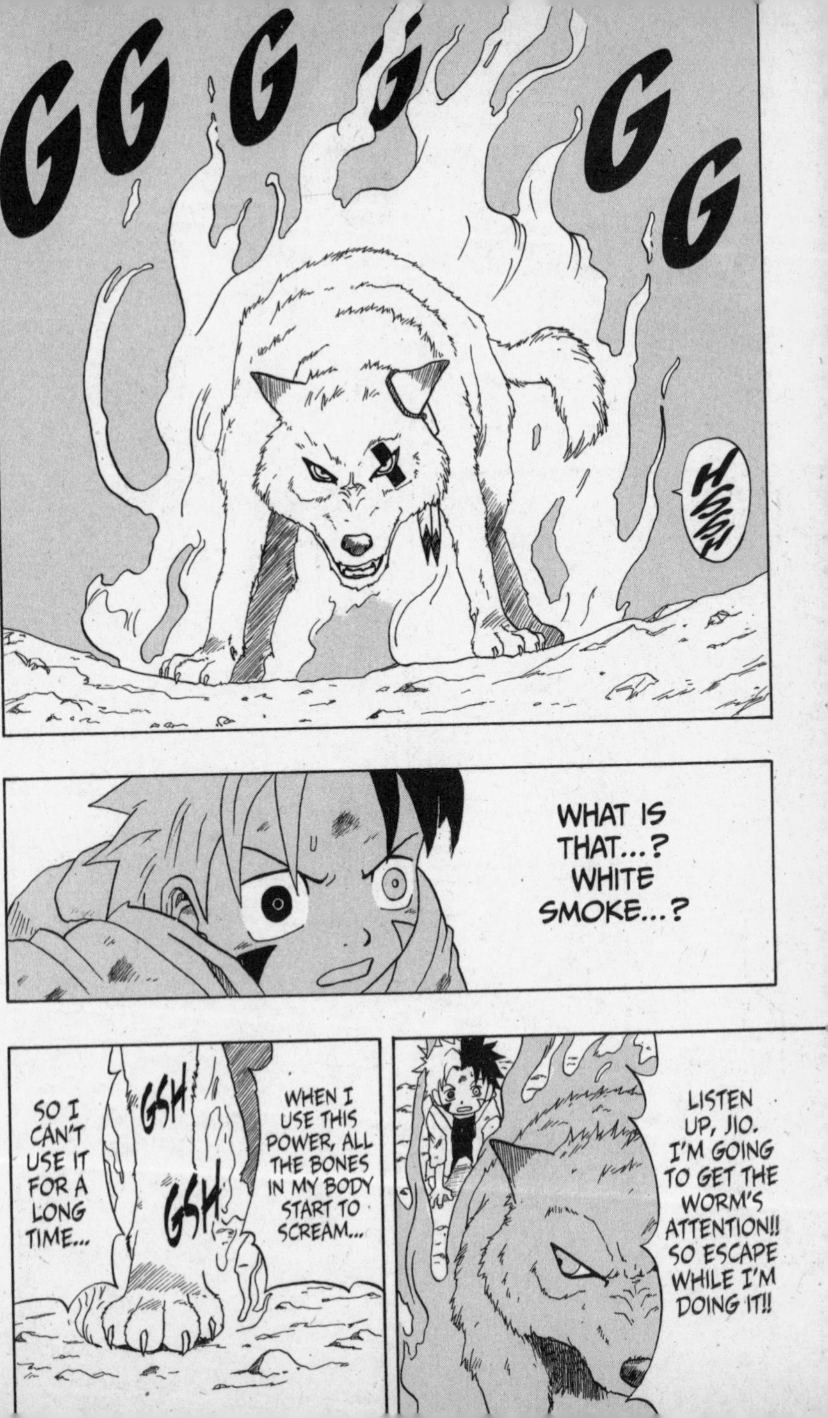
GGGGGG
HSSH
WHAT IS THAT...? WHITE SMOKE...?
LISTEN UP, JIO. I'M GOING TO GET THE WORM'S ATTENTION!! SO ESCAPE WHILE I'M DOING IT!!
WHEN I USE THIS POWER, ALL THE BONES IN MY BODY START TO SCREAM...
GSH
GSH
SO I CAN'T USE IT FOR A LONG TIME...

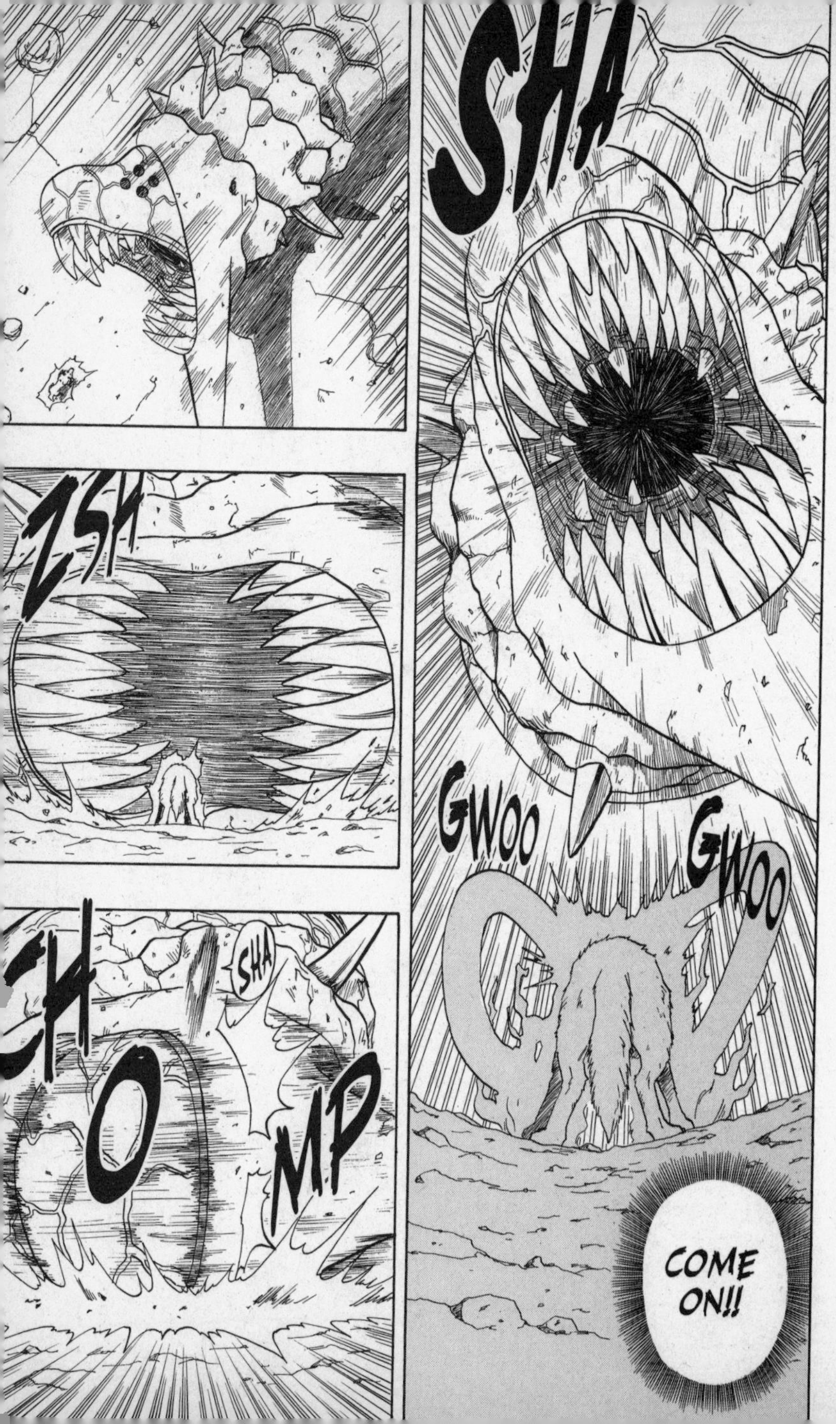
SHA
GWOO
GWOO
COME ON!!
ZSH
SHA
CHOMP

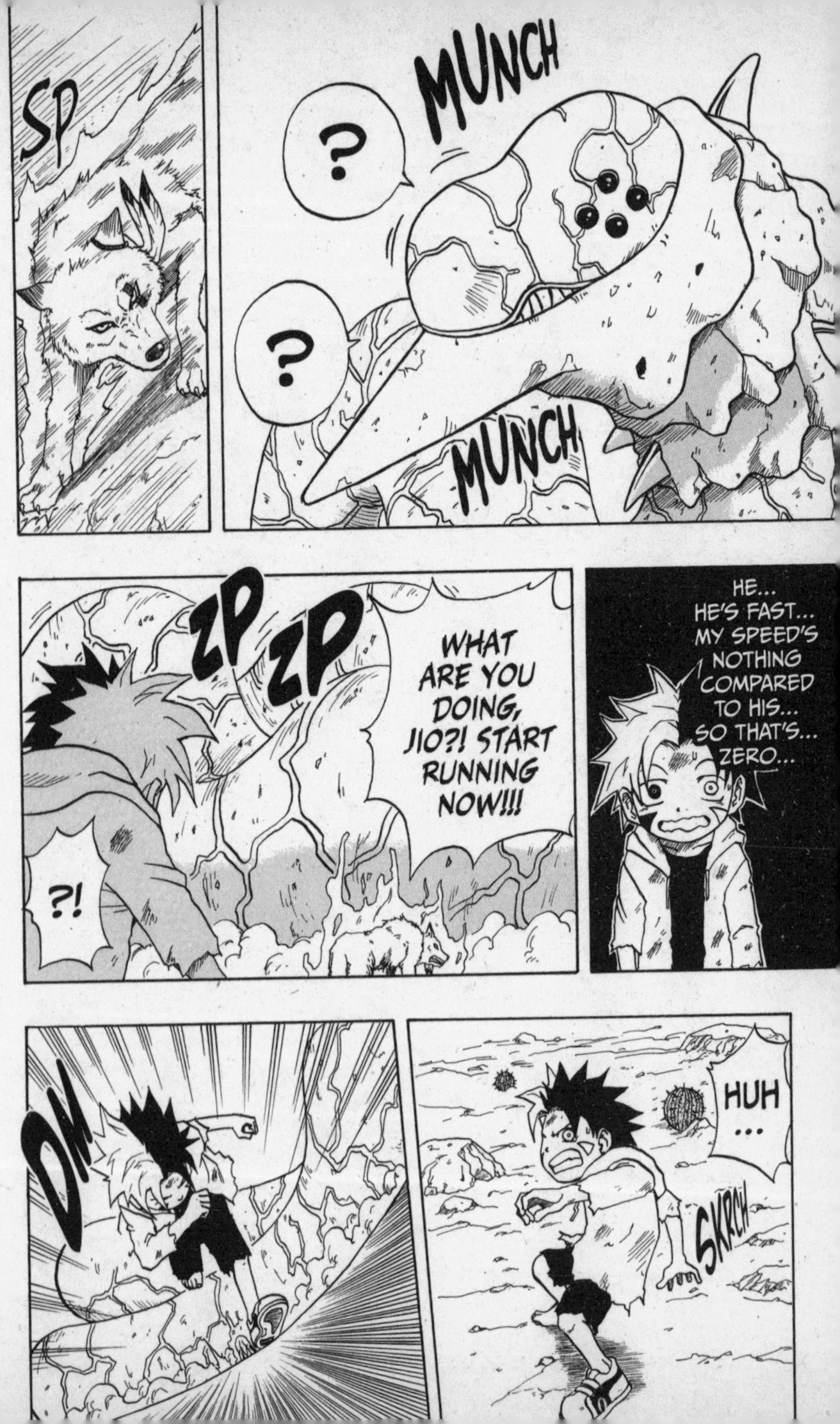
MUNCH
?
?
MUNCH
SP
HE... HE'S FAST... MY SPEED'S NOTHING COMPARED TO HIS... SO THAT'S... ZERO...
ZP
ZP
WHAT ARE YOU DOING, JIO?! START RUNNING NOW!!!
?!
HUH ...
SKRCH
DM

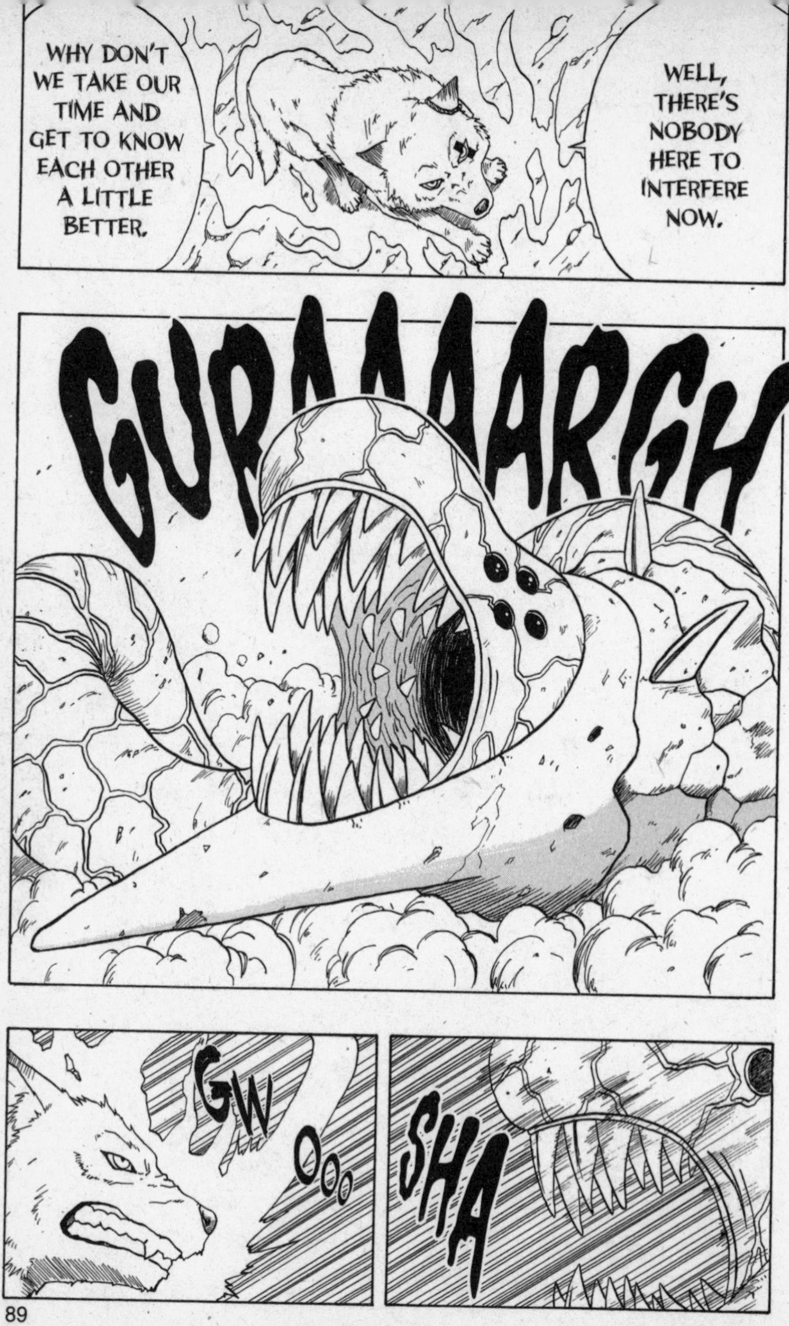
WELL, THERE'S NOBODY HERE TO INTERFERE NOW.
WHY DON'T WE TAKE OUR TIME AND GET TO KNOW EACH OTHER A LITTLE BETTER.
GURAAARGH
SHA
GWOOO

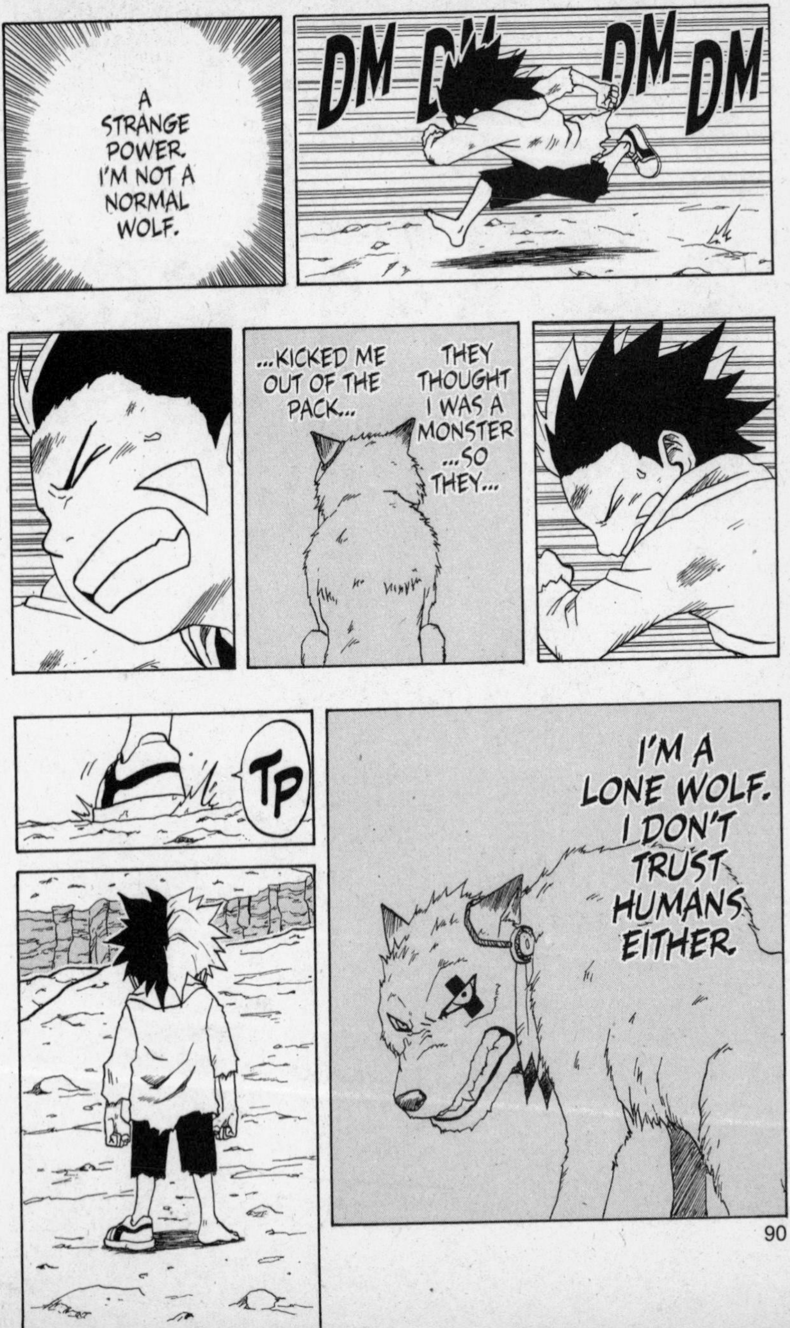
DM DM DM DM
A STRANGE POWER. I'M NOT A NORMAL WOLF.
THEY THOUGHT I WAS A MONSTER ...SO THEY...
...KICKED ME OUT OF THE PACK...
I'M A LONE WOLF. I DON'T TRUST HUMANS EITHER.
TP

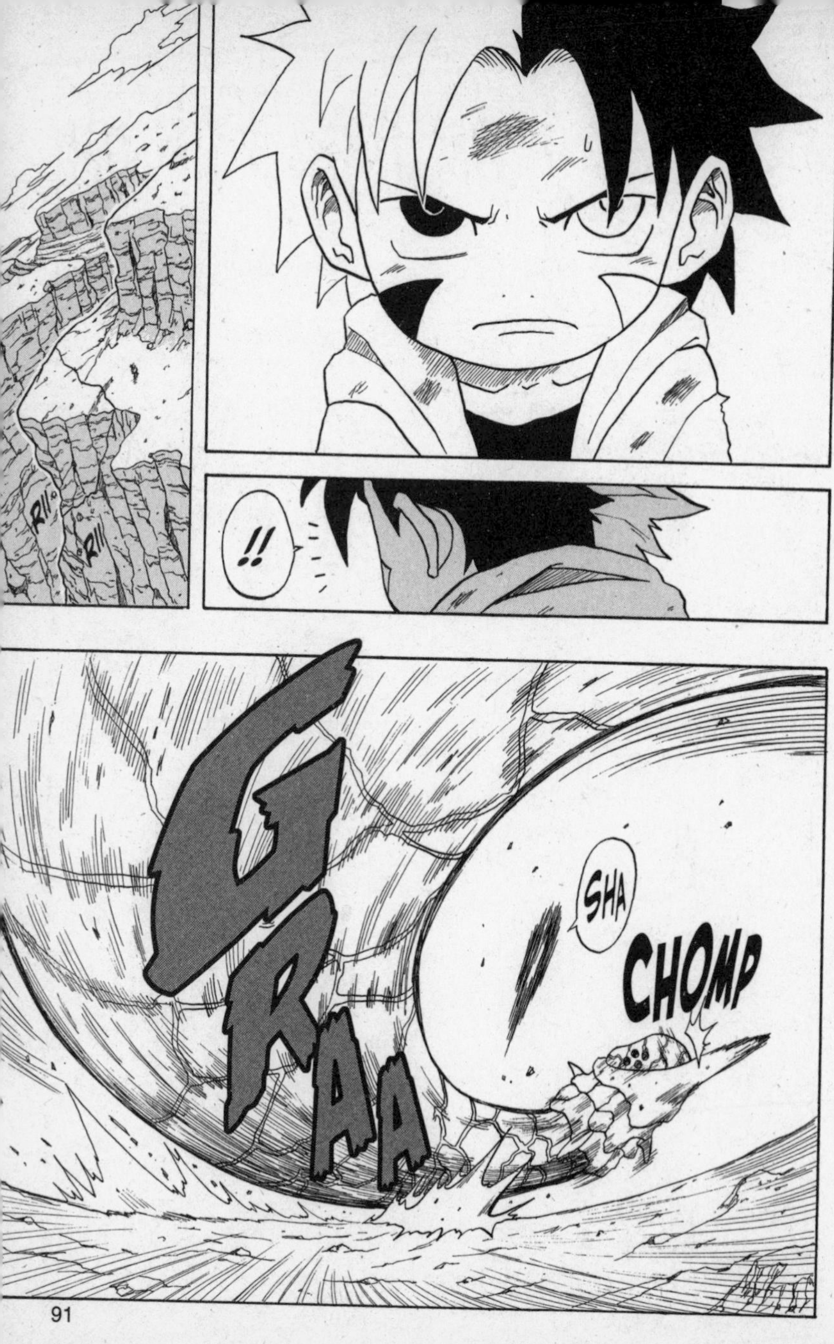
!!
RII
RII
SHA
CHOMP
GRAA

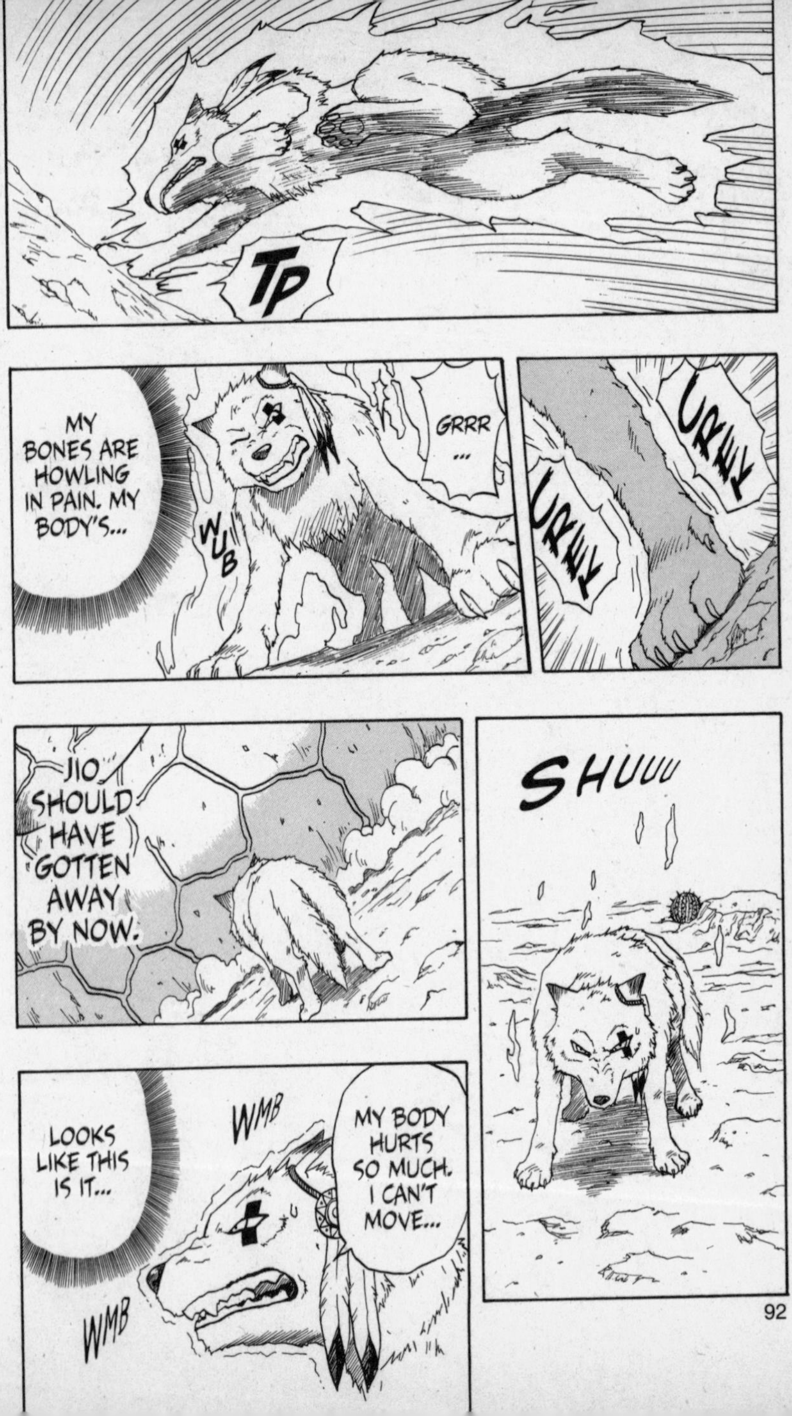
TP
URKY
URKY
GRRR ...
MY BONES ARE HOWLING IN PAIN. MY BODY'S...
WUB
SHUUU
JIO SHOULD HAVE GOTTEN AWAY BY NOW.
WMB
MY BODY HURTS SO MUCH. I CAN'T MOVE...
LOOKS LIKE THIS IS IT...
WMB

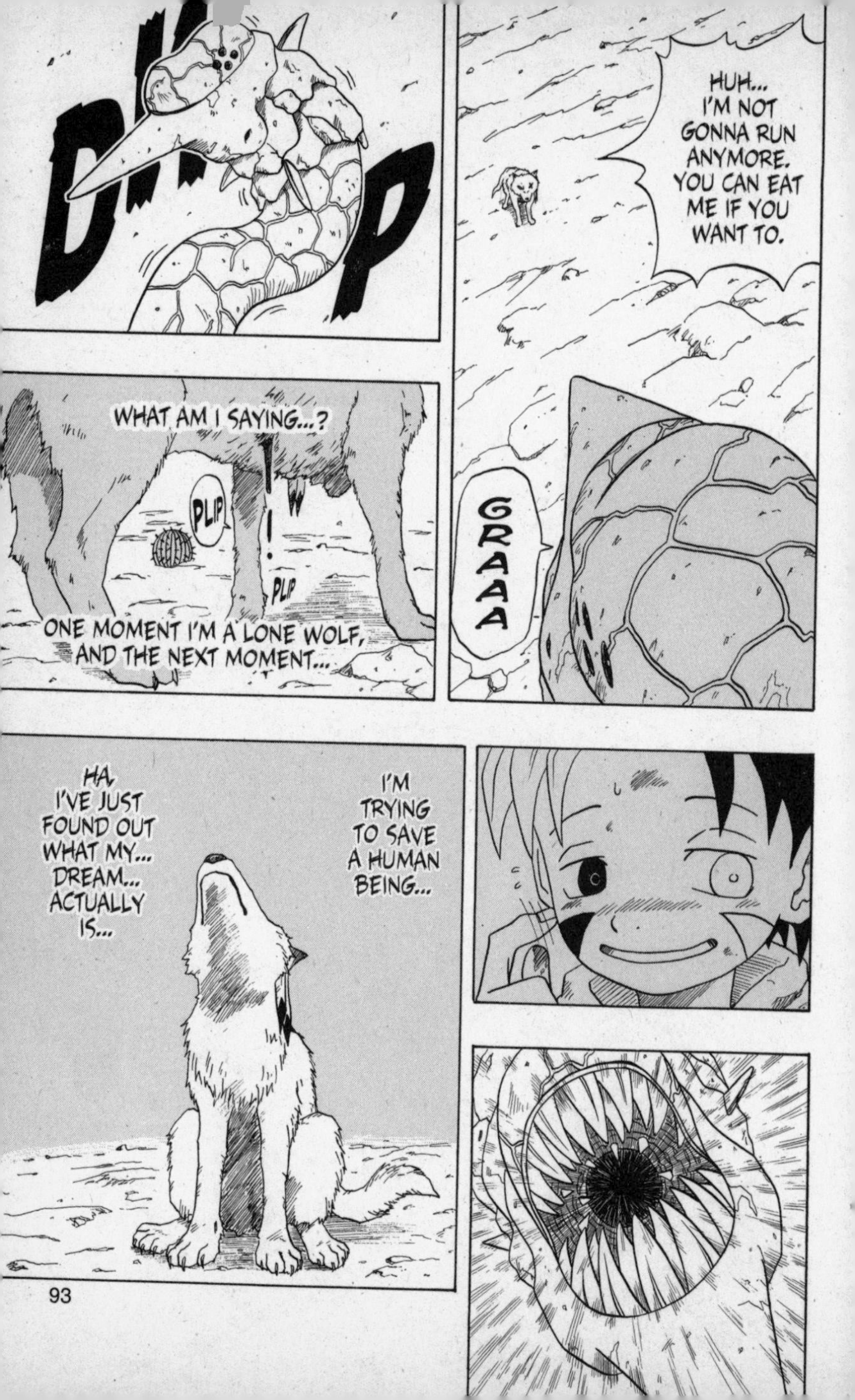
HUH... I'M NOT GONNA RUN ANYMORE. YOU CAN EAT ME IF YOU WANT TO.
GRAAA
WHAT AM I SAYING...?
PLIP
!
PLIP
ONE MOMENT I'M A LONE WOLF, AND THE NEXT MOMENT...
I'M TRYING TO SAVE A HUMAN BEING...
HA, I'VE JUST FOUND OUT WHAT MY... DREAM... ACTUALLY IS...

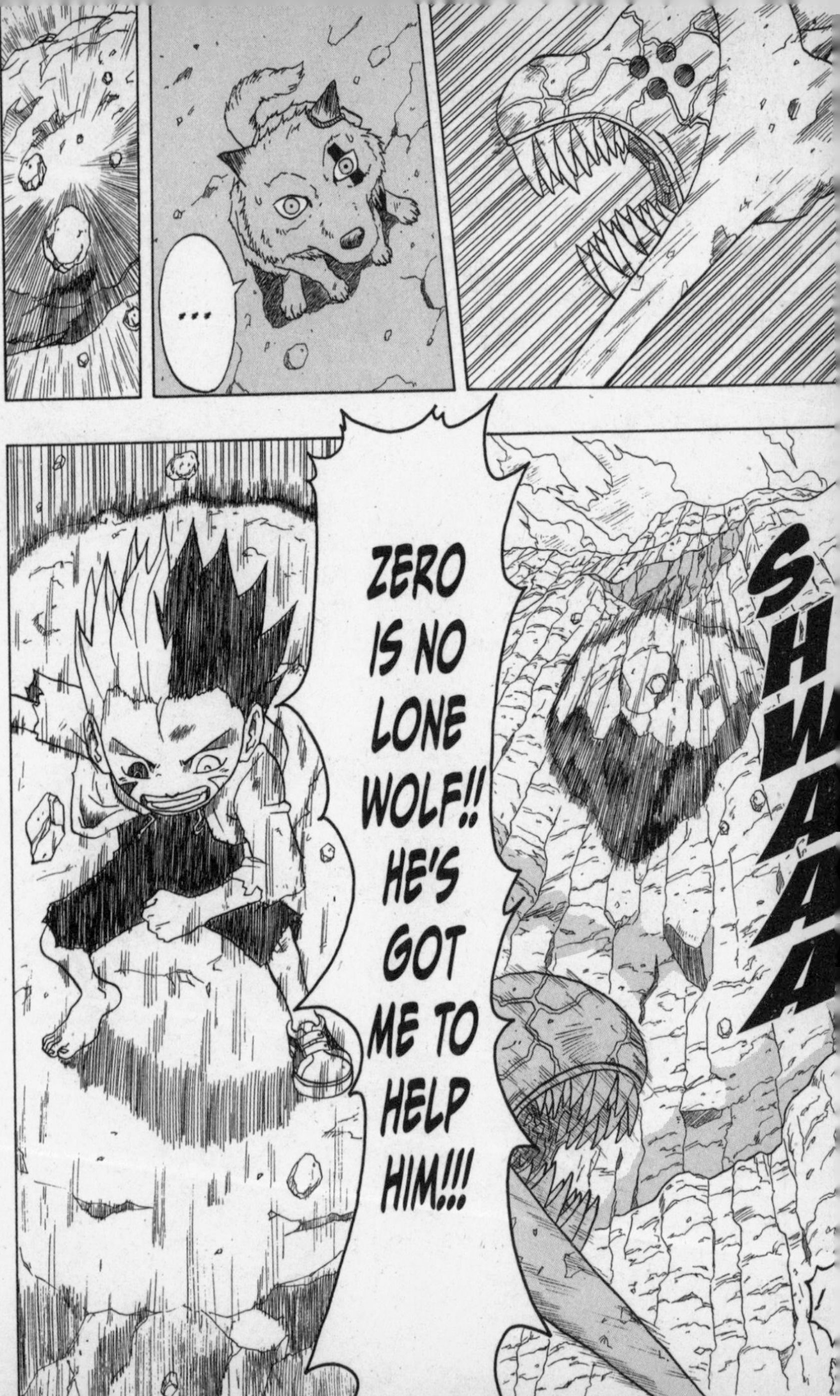
...
ZERO IS NO LONE WOLF!! HE'S GOT ME TO HELP HIM!!!
SHWAAA

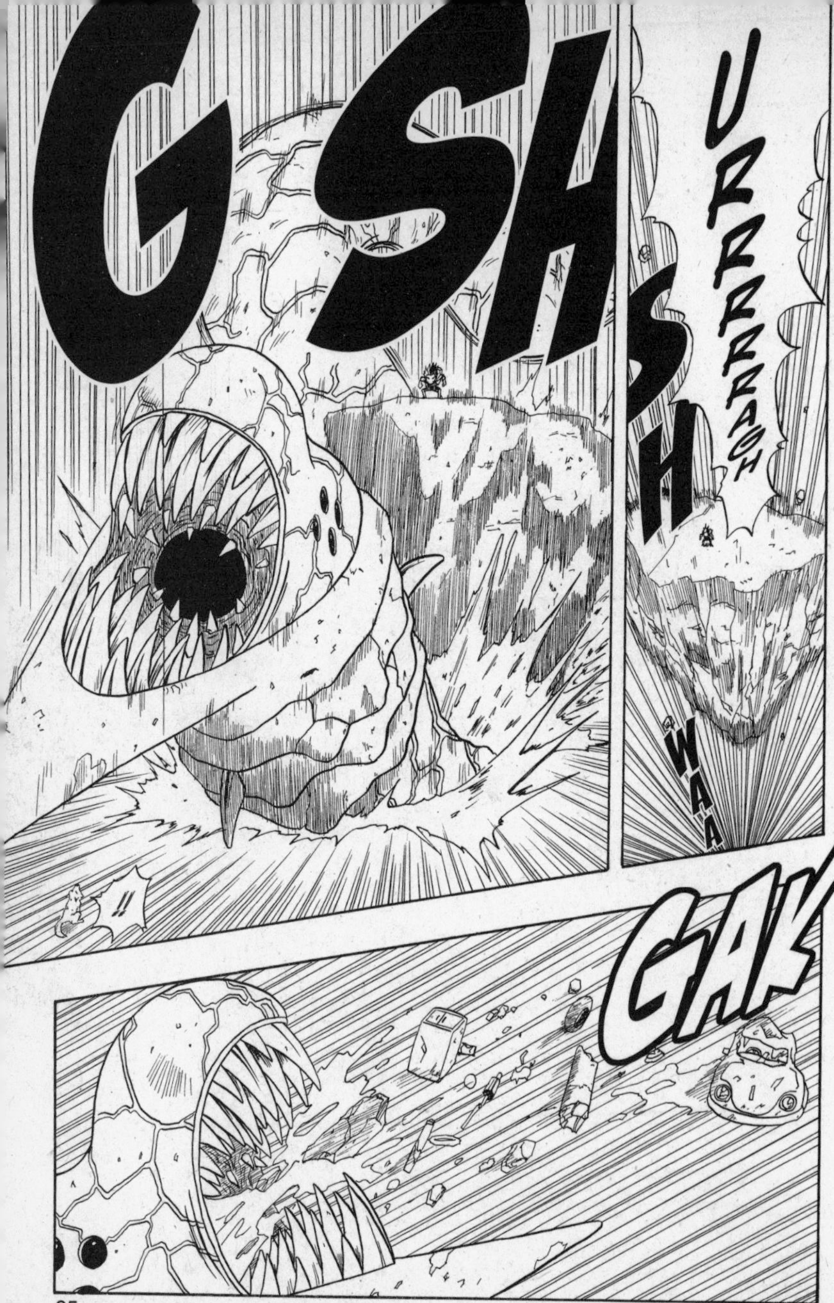
URRRRRAGH
WAAA
GSHSH
!!
GAK

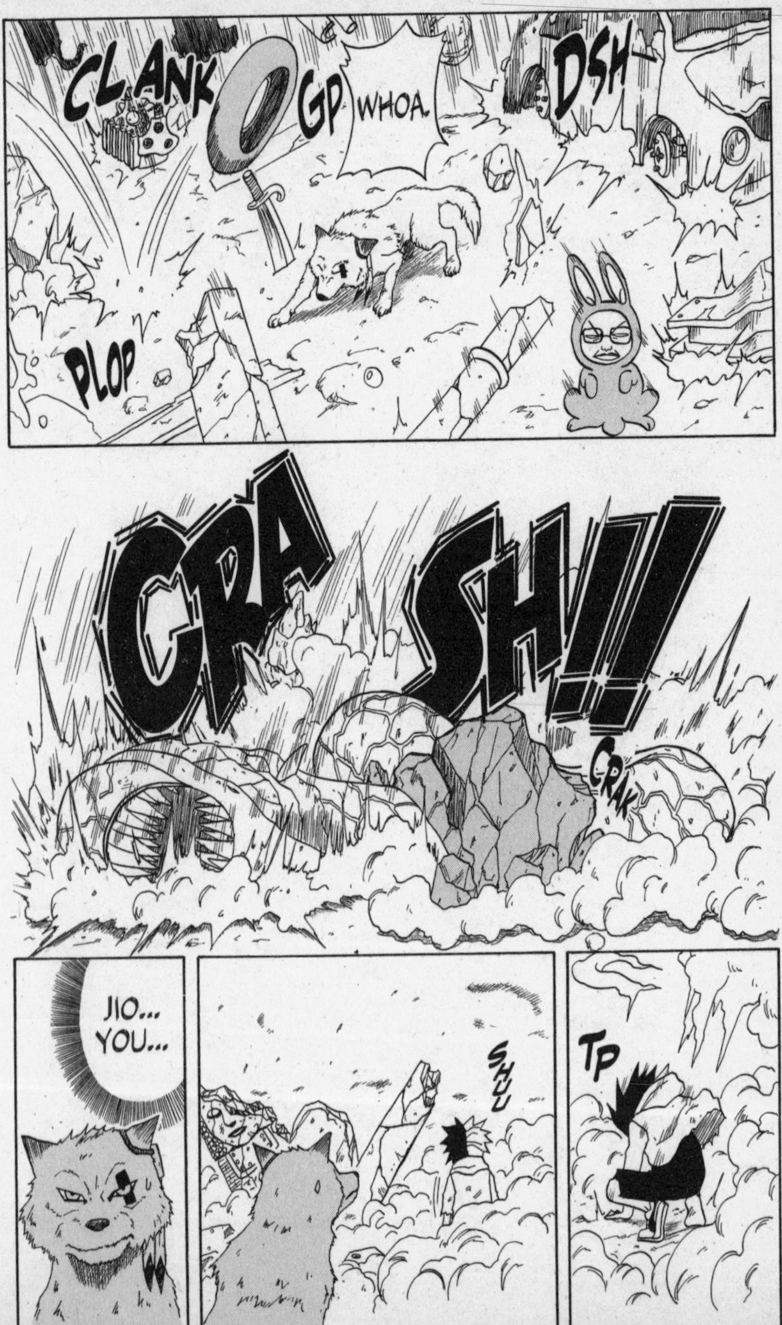
DSH
WHOA
GP
CLANK
PLOP
CRASH!!
CRAK
TP
SHUU
JIO... YOU...

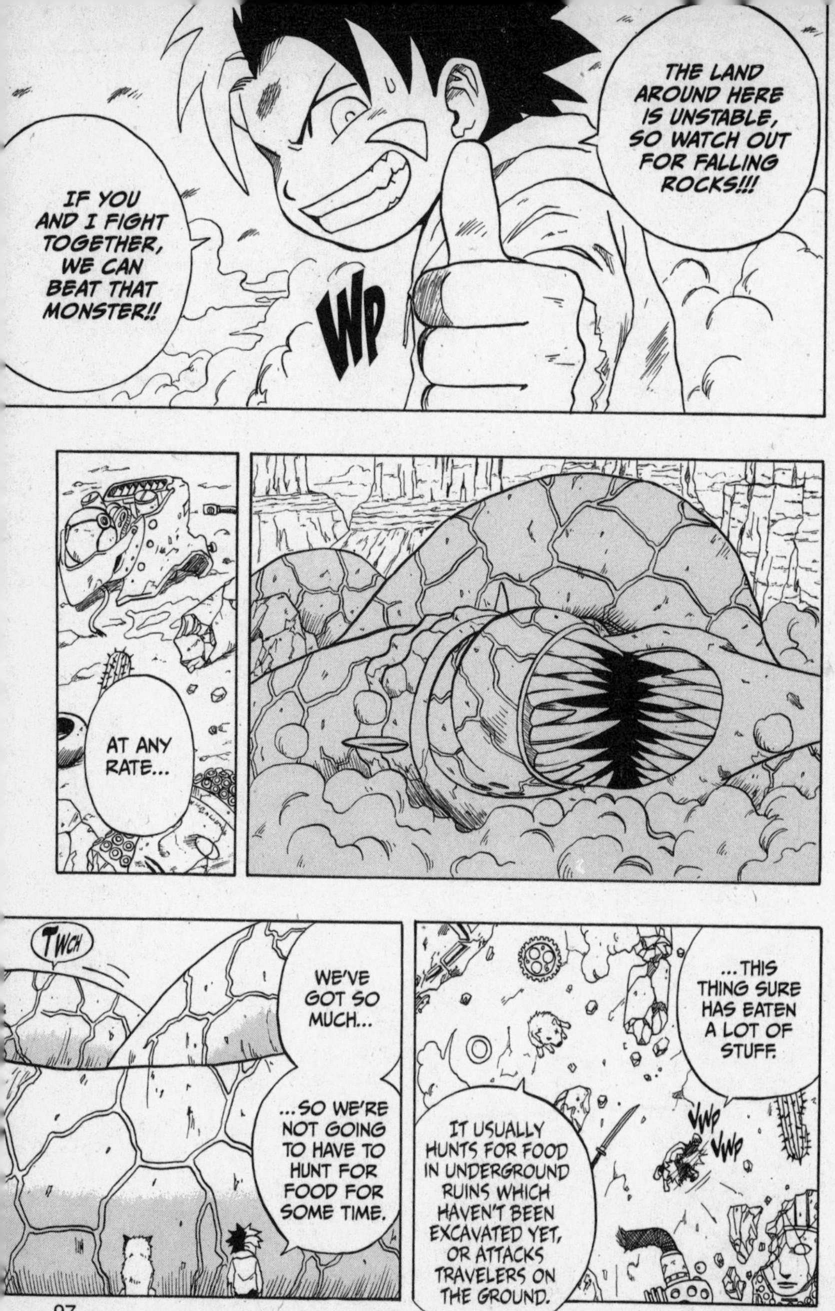
THE LAND AROUND HERE IS UNSTABLE, SO WATCH OUT FOR FALLING ROCKS!!!
IF YOU AND I FIGHT TOGETHER, WE CAN BEAT THAT MONSTER!!
WP
AT ANY RATE...
...THIS THING SURE HAS EATEN A LOT OF STUFF.
VWP
VWP
IT USUALLY HUNTS FOR FOOD IN UNDERGROUND RUINS WHICH HAVEN'T BEEN EXCAVATED YET, OR ATTACKS TRAVELERS ON THE GROUND.
TWCH
WE'VE GOT SO MUCH...
...SO WE'RE NOT GOING TO HAVE TO HUNT FOR FOOD FOR SOME TIME.

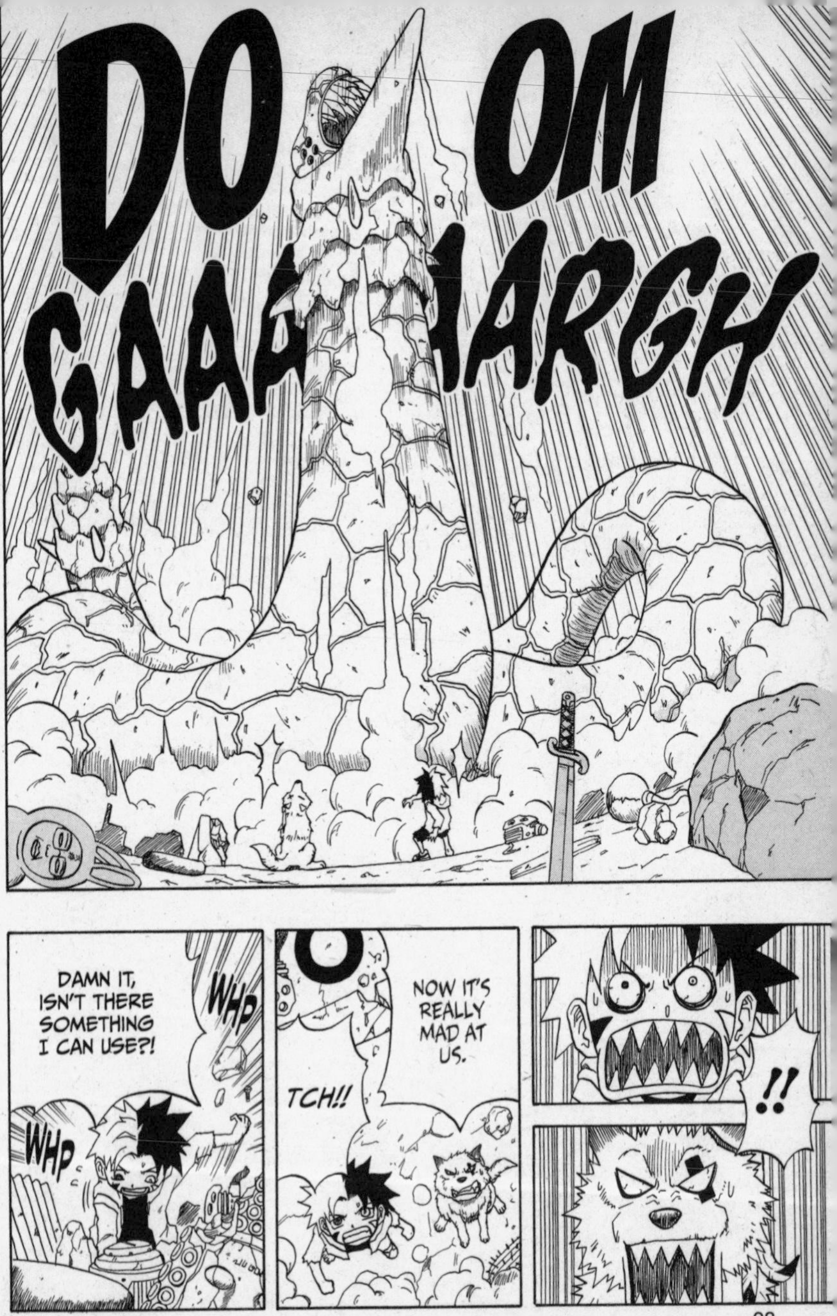

DO OM
GAAA ARGH
!!
NOW IT'S REALLY MAD AT US.
TCH!!
WHP
DAMN IT, ISN'T THERE SOMETHING I CAN USE?!
WHP

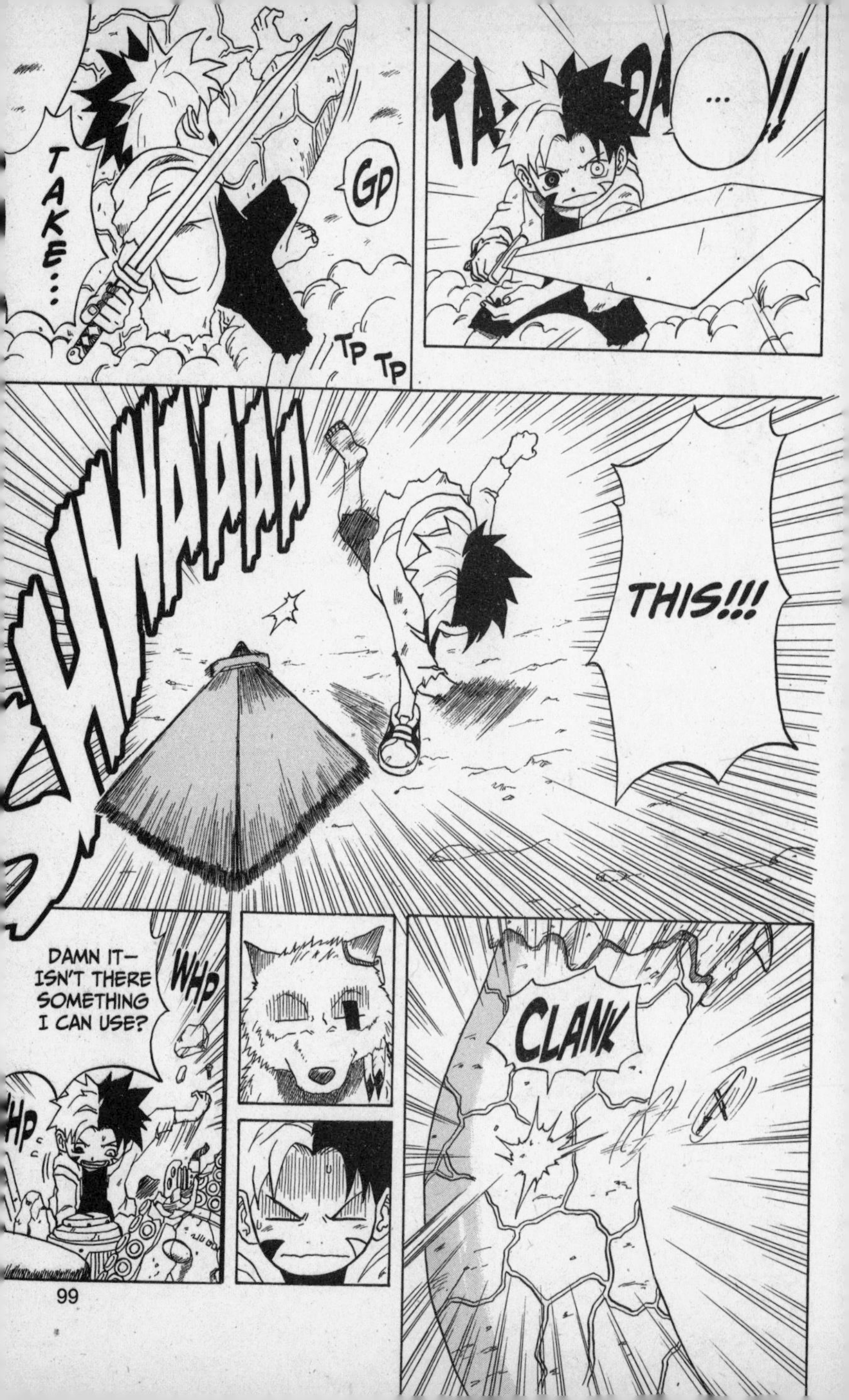

TA DA!!
...
GP
TAKE...
TP TP
THIS!!!
WHAPP
CLANK
DAMN IT— ISN'T THERE SOMETHING I CAN USE?
WHP
WHP

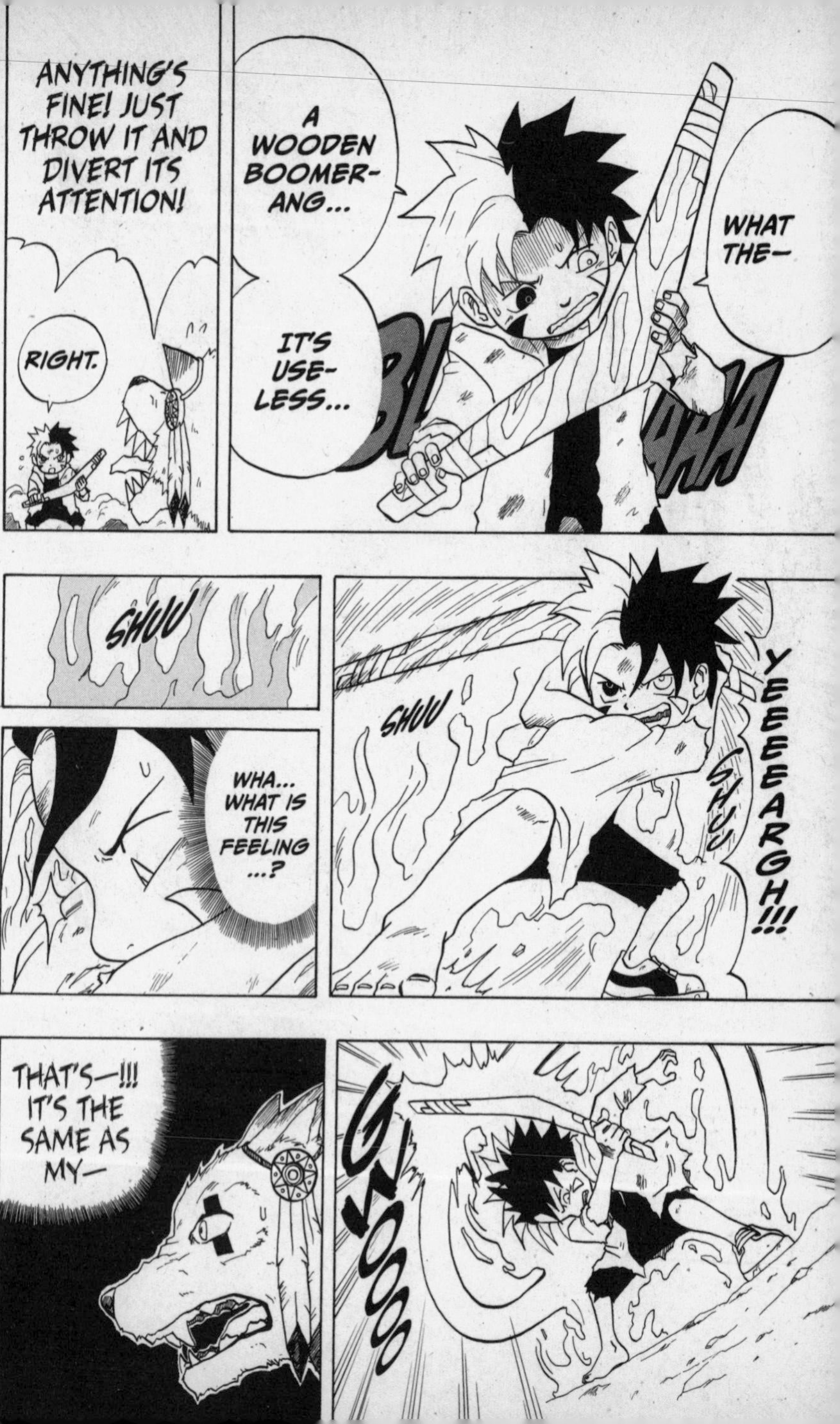
WHAT THE—
A WOODEN BOOMER-ANG...
IT'S USE-LESS...
ANYTHING'S FINE! JUST THROW IT AND DIVERT ITS ATTENTION!
RIGHT.
YEEEEARGH!!!
SHUU
SHUU
SHUU
WHA... WHAT IS THIS FEELING ...?
GOOOO
THAT'S—!!! IT'S THE SAME AS MY—

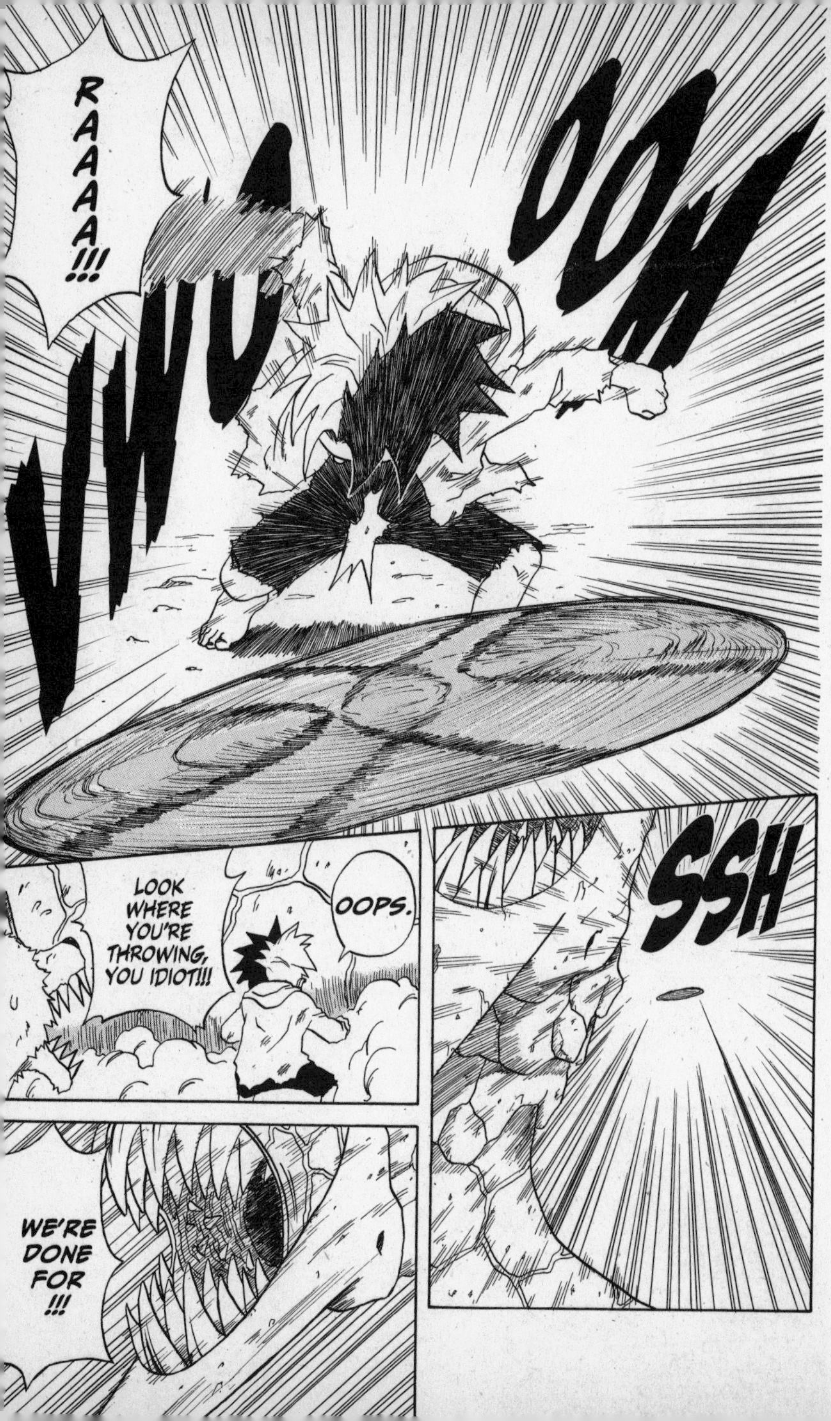
VWOOOOM
RAAAAA!!!
SSH
OOPS.
LOOK WHERE YOU'RE THROWING, YOU IDIOT!!!
WE'RE DONE FOR!!!

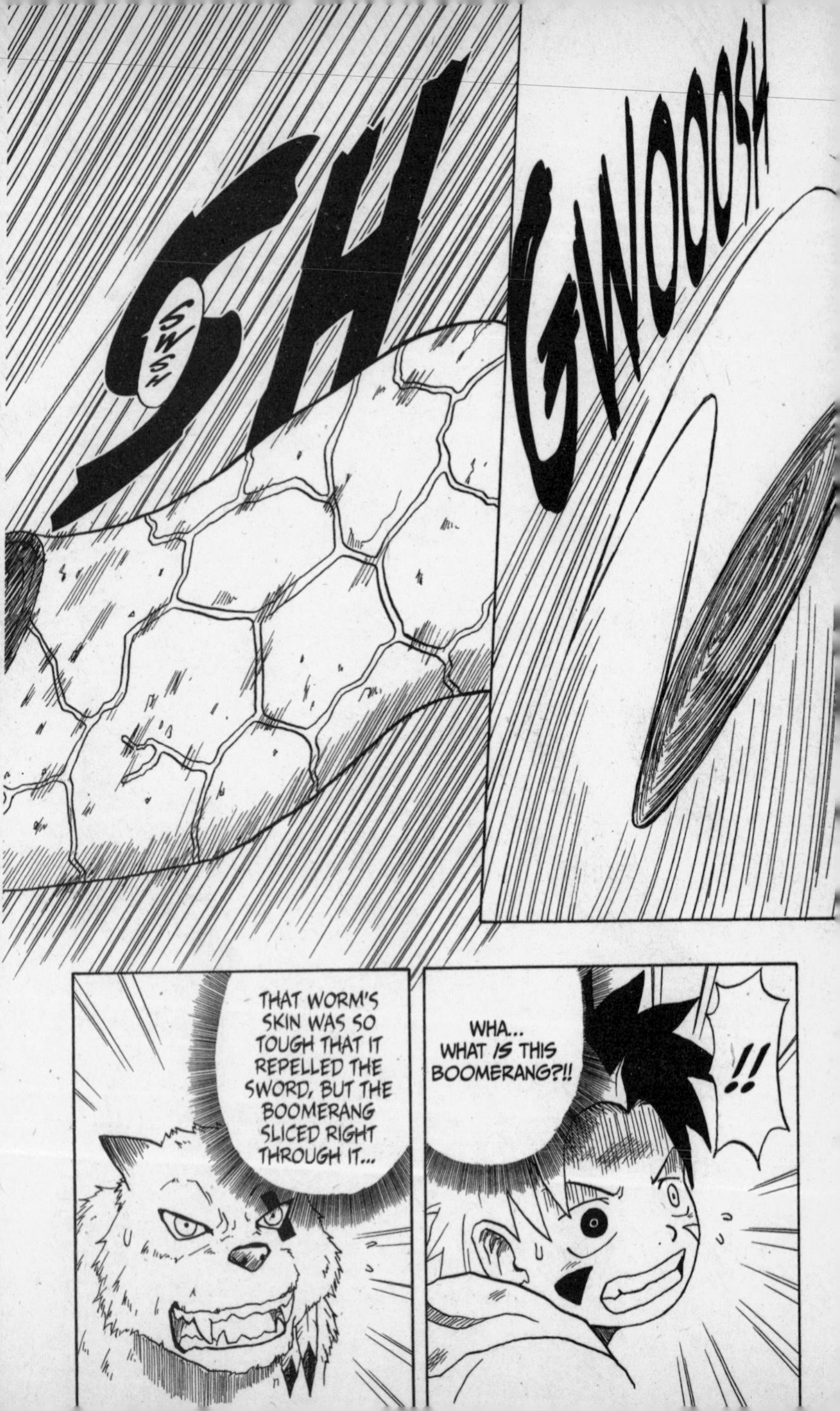
GWOOSH
SH
SWSH
!!
WHA... WHAT *IS* THIS BOOMERANG?!!
THAT WORM'S SKIN WAS SO TOUGH THAT IT REPELLED THE SWORD, BUT THE BOOMERANG SLICED RIGHT THROUGH IT...

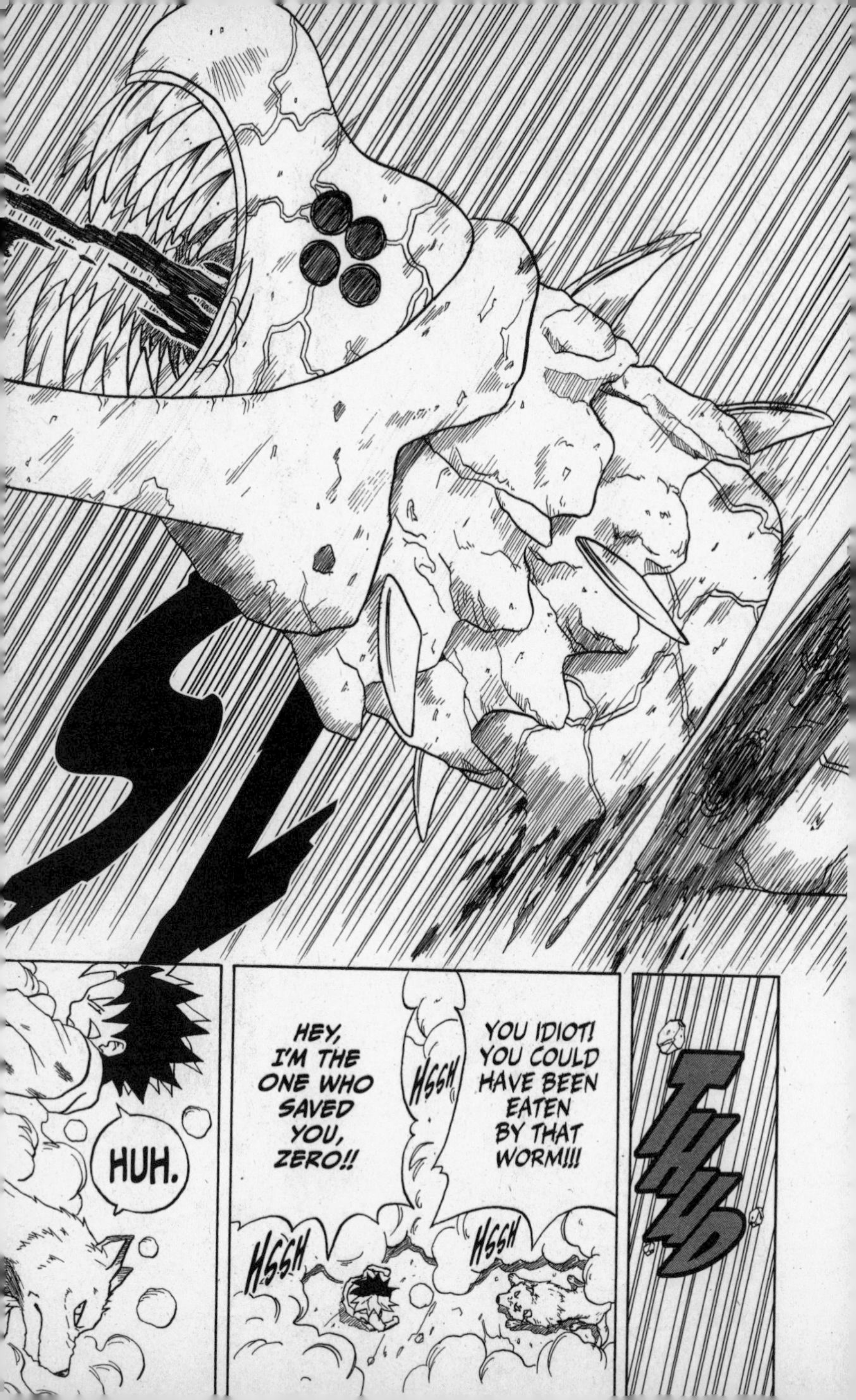
SH
THUD
YOU IDIOT! YOU COULD HAVE BEEN EATEN BY THAT WORM!!!
HSSH
HEY, I'M THE ONE WHO SAVED YOU, ZERO!!
HSSH
HSSH
HUH.

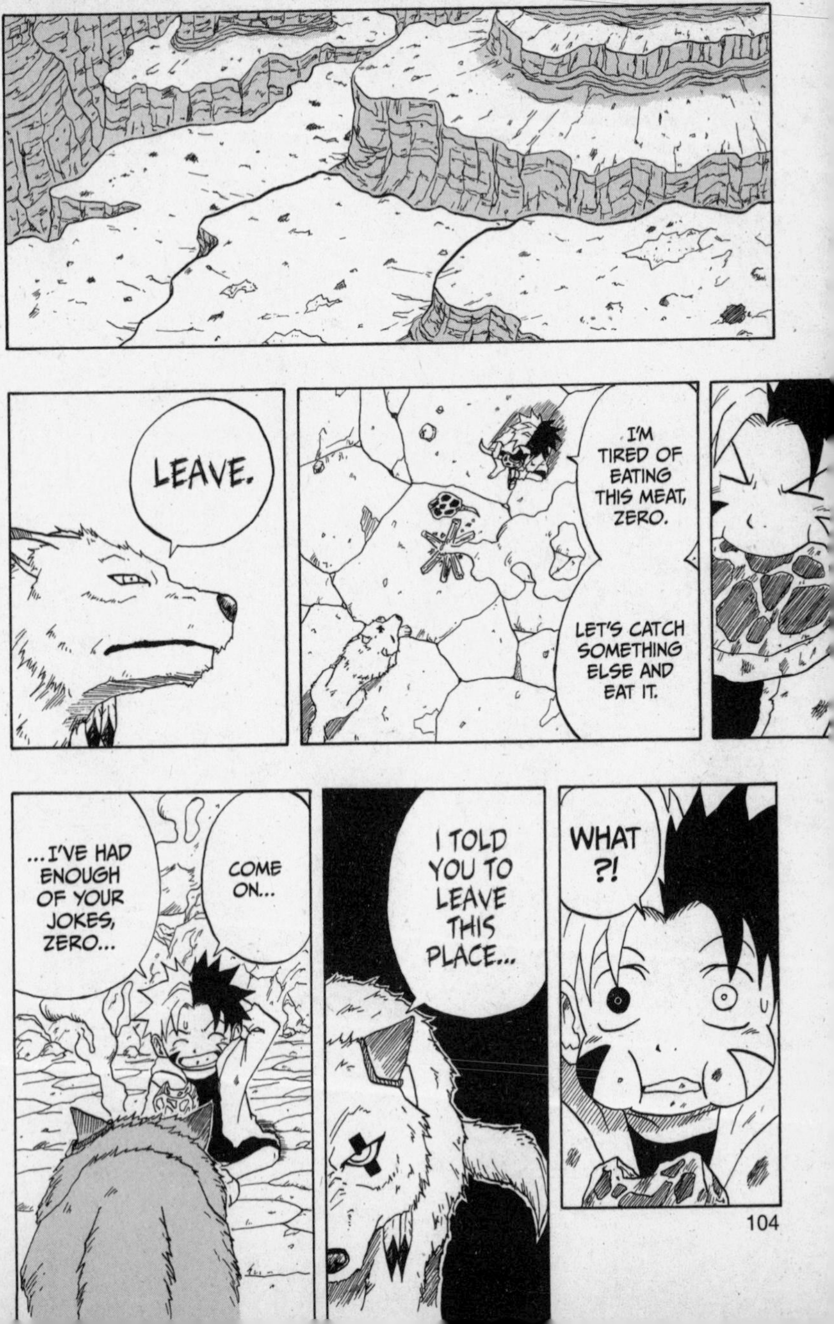
I'M TIRED OF EATING THIS MEAT, ZERO.
LET'S CATCH SOMETHING ELSE AND EAT IT.
LEAVE.
WHAT ?!
I TOLD YOU TO LEAVE THIS PLACE...
COME ON...
...I'VE HAD ENOUGH OF YOUR JOKES, ZERO...

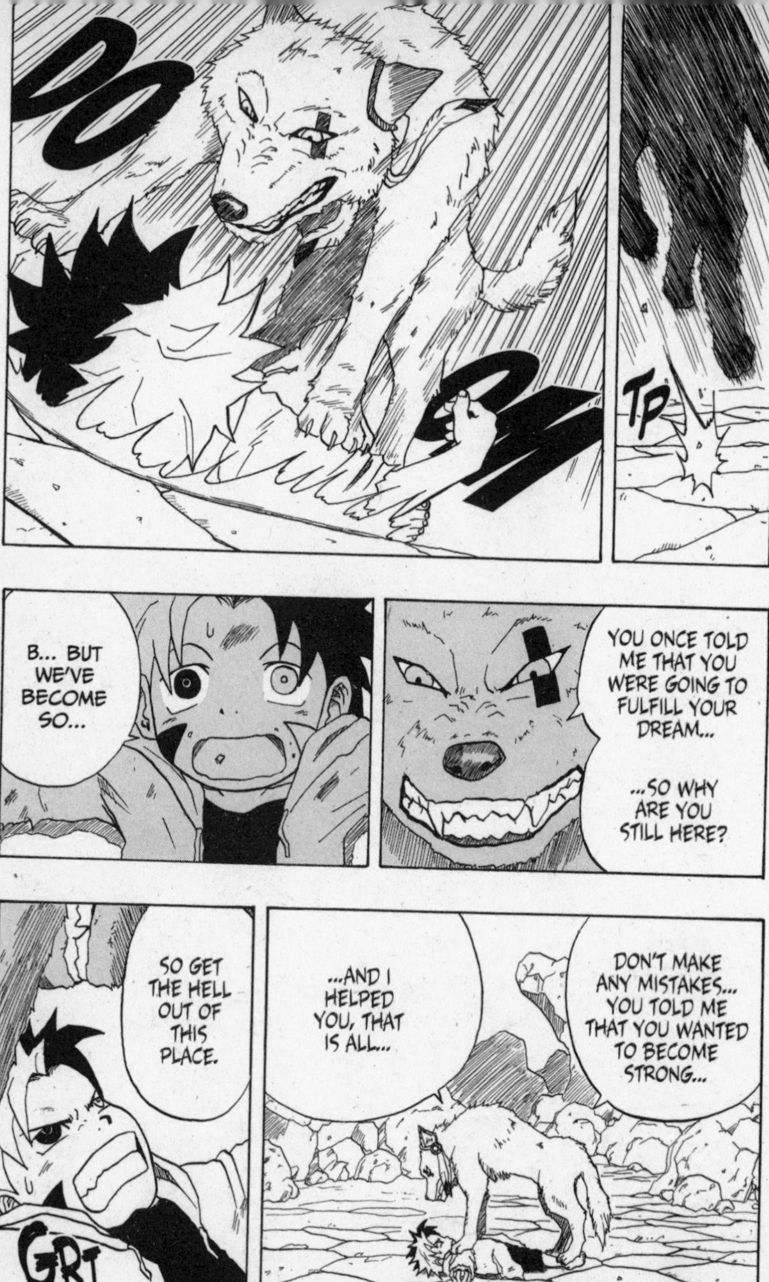
TP
YOU ONCE TOLD ME THAT YOU WERE GOING TO FULFILL YOUR DREAM...
...SO WHY ARE YOU STILL HERE?
B... BUT WE'VE BECOME SO...
DON'T MAKE ANY MISTAKES... YOU TOLD ME THAT YOU WANTED TO BECOME STRONG...
...AND I HELPED YOU, THAT IS ALL...
SO GET THE HELL OUT OF THIS PLACE.
GRT

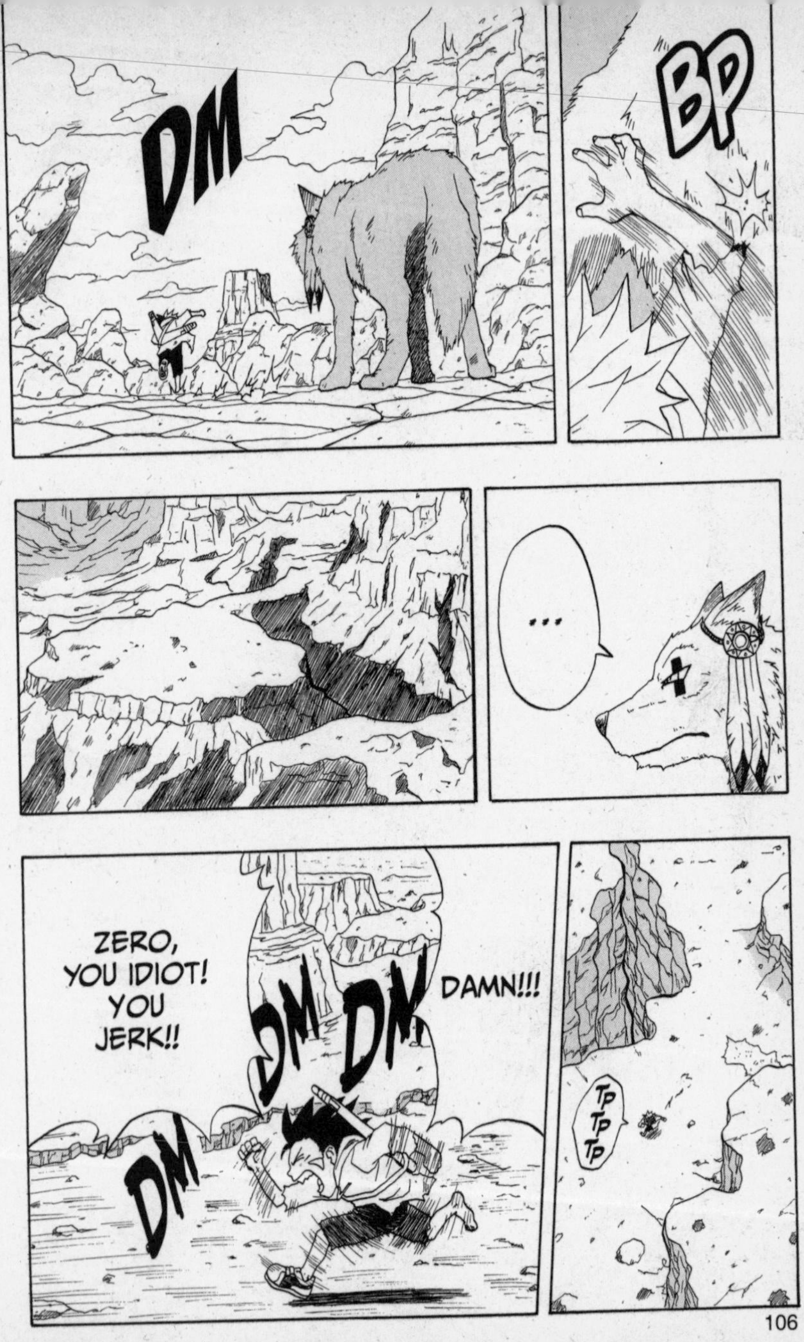

BP
DM
...
TP TP TP
DAMN!!!
DM DM
ZERO, YOU IDIOT! YOU JERK!!
DM

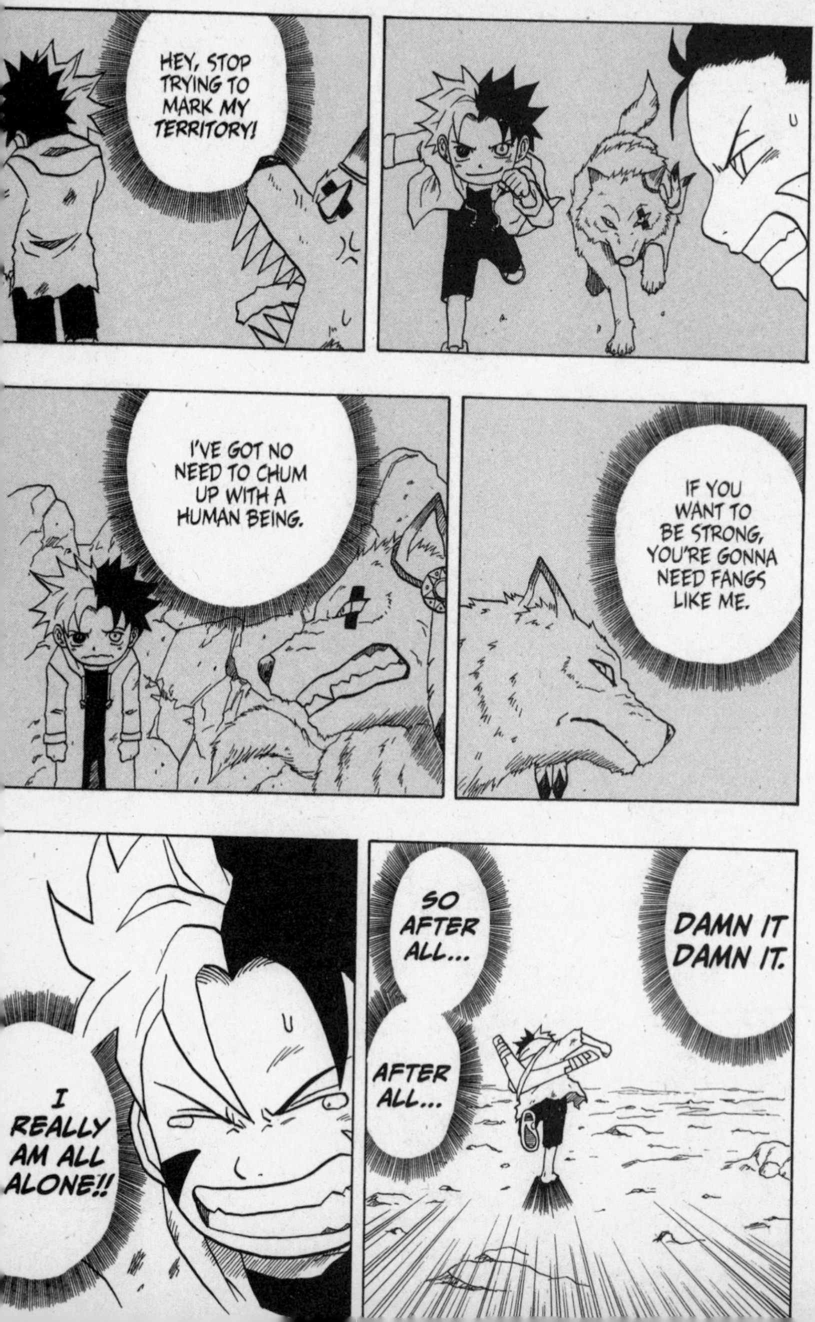
HEY, STOP TRYING TO MARK MY TERRITORY!
IF YOU WANT TO BE STRONG, YOU'RE GONNA NEED FANGS LIKE ME.
I'VE GOT NO NEED TO CHUM UP WITH A HUMAN BEING.
DAMN IT DAMN IT.
SO AFTER ALL...
AFTER ALL...
I REALLY AM ALL ALONE!!

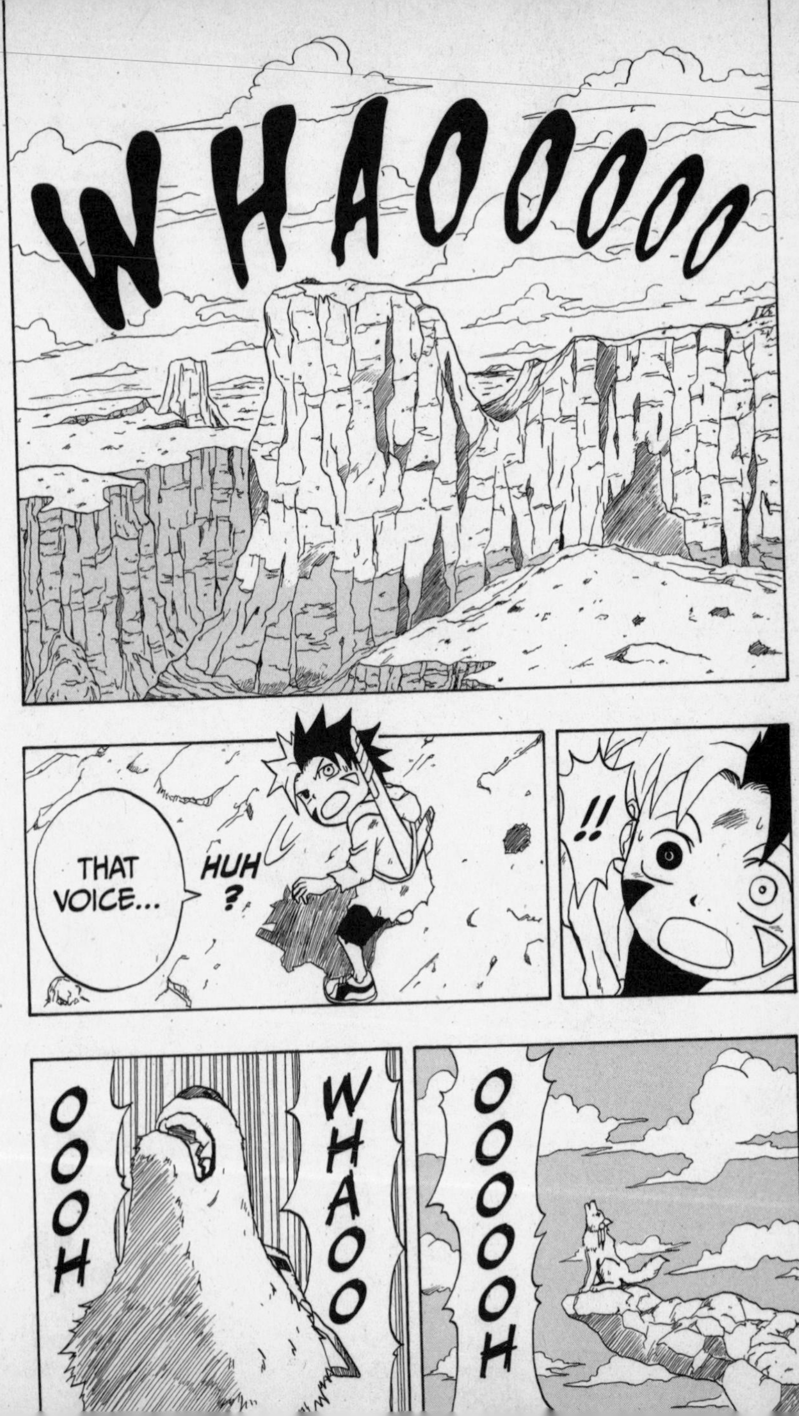
WHAOOOOO
!!
HUH ?
THAT VOICE...
OOOOOOH
WHAOO
OOOH

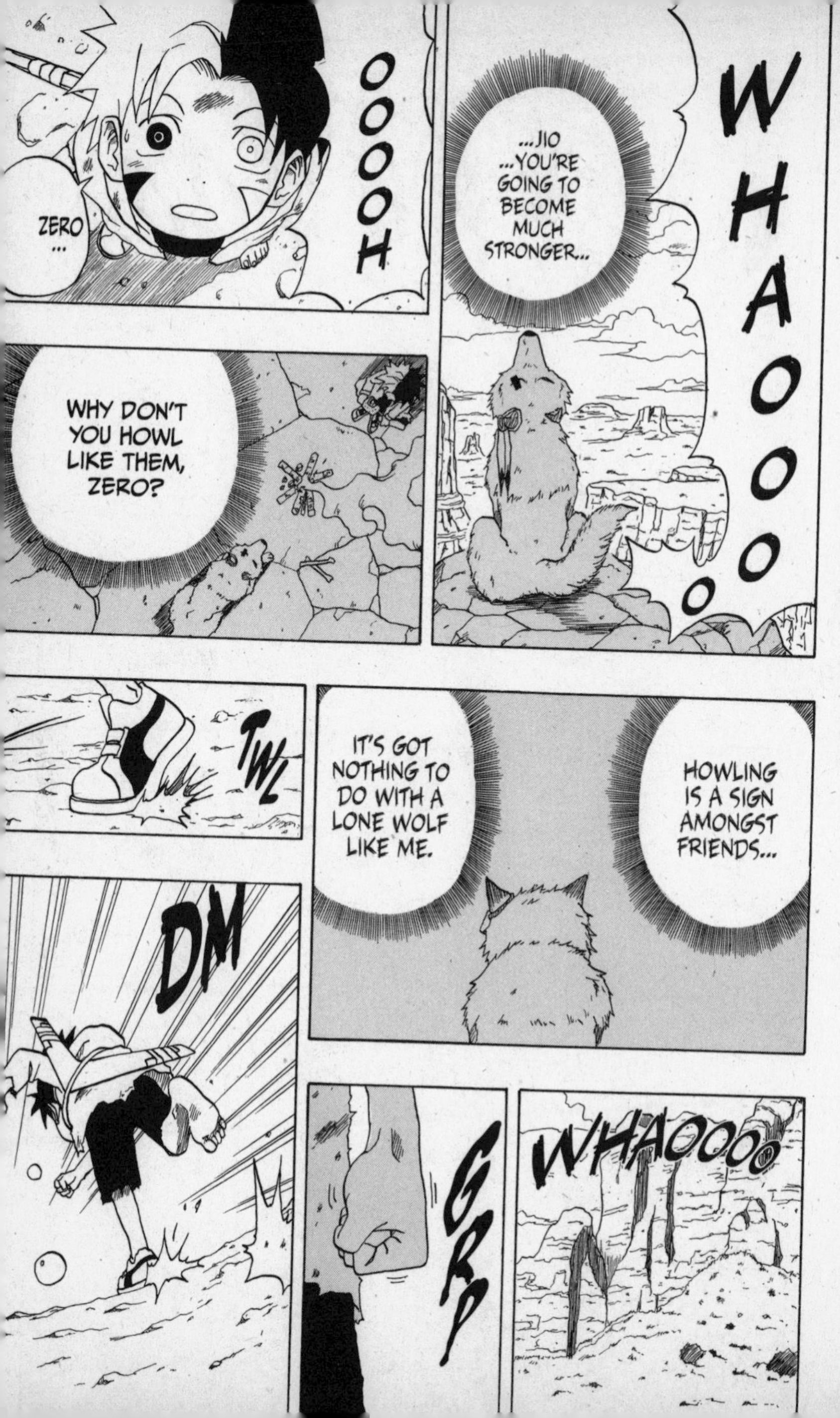
WHAOOOOO
...JIO ...YOU'RE GOING TO BECOME MUCH STRONGER...
OOOOOH
ZERO ...
WHY DON'T YOU HOWL LIKE THEM, ZERO?
HOWLING IS A SIGN AMONGST FRIENDS...
IT'S GOT NOTHING TO DO WITH A LONE WOLF LIKE ME.
TWL
WHAOOOOO
GRRP
DM

YOU'RE A TERRIBLE HOWLER, ZERO!!

HUH... SOME WOLF!!

I UNDERSTAND, ZERO... I WON'T TURN BACK!! I'M GOING TO BE MUCH STRONGER THAN I AM NOW!!!

WHAOOOOOOO

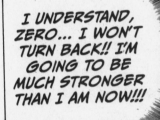

SUU-

OOOOOH

WHAOOO

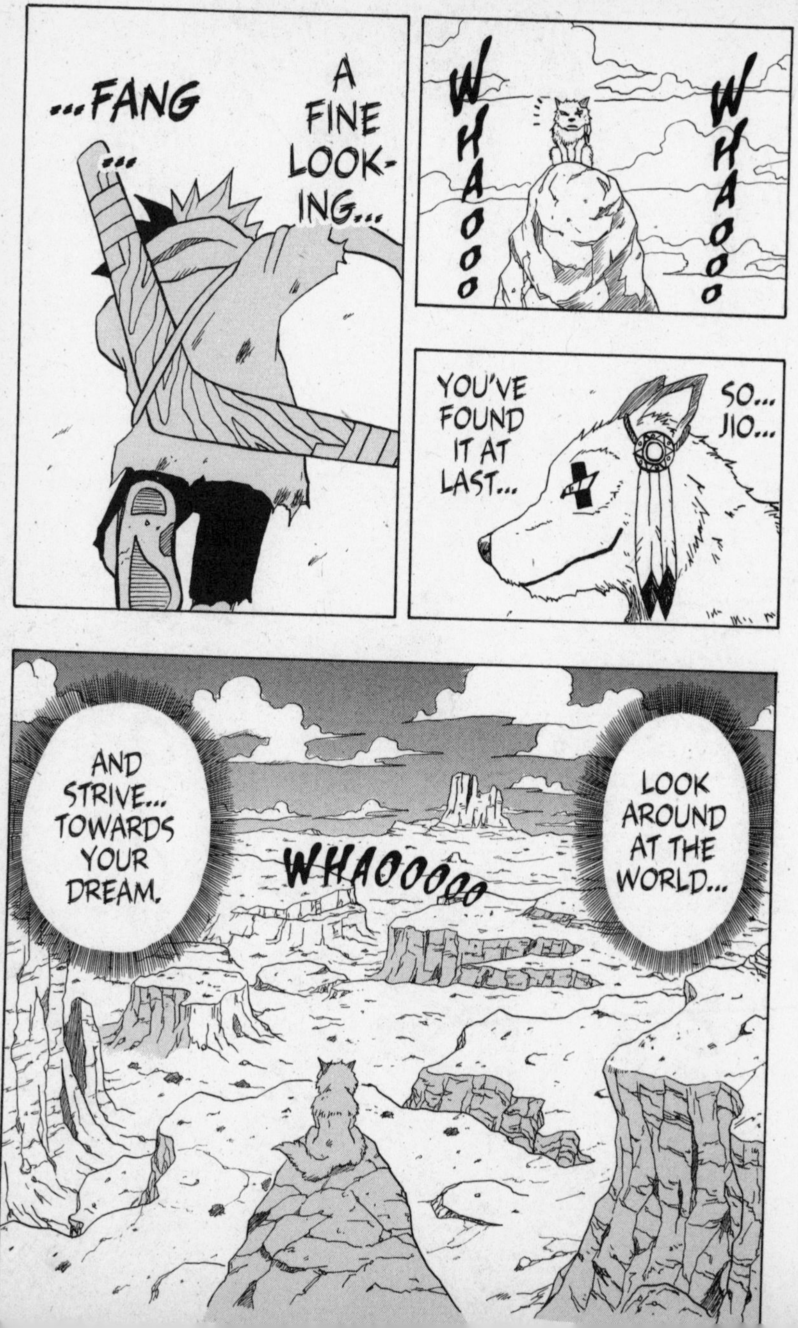
WHAOOO
WHAOOO
SO... JIO...
YOU'VE FOUND IT AT LAST...
A FINE LOOKING...
...FANG...
LOOK AROUND AT THE WORLD...
WHAOOOOO
AND STRIVE... TOWARDS YOUR DREAM.

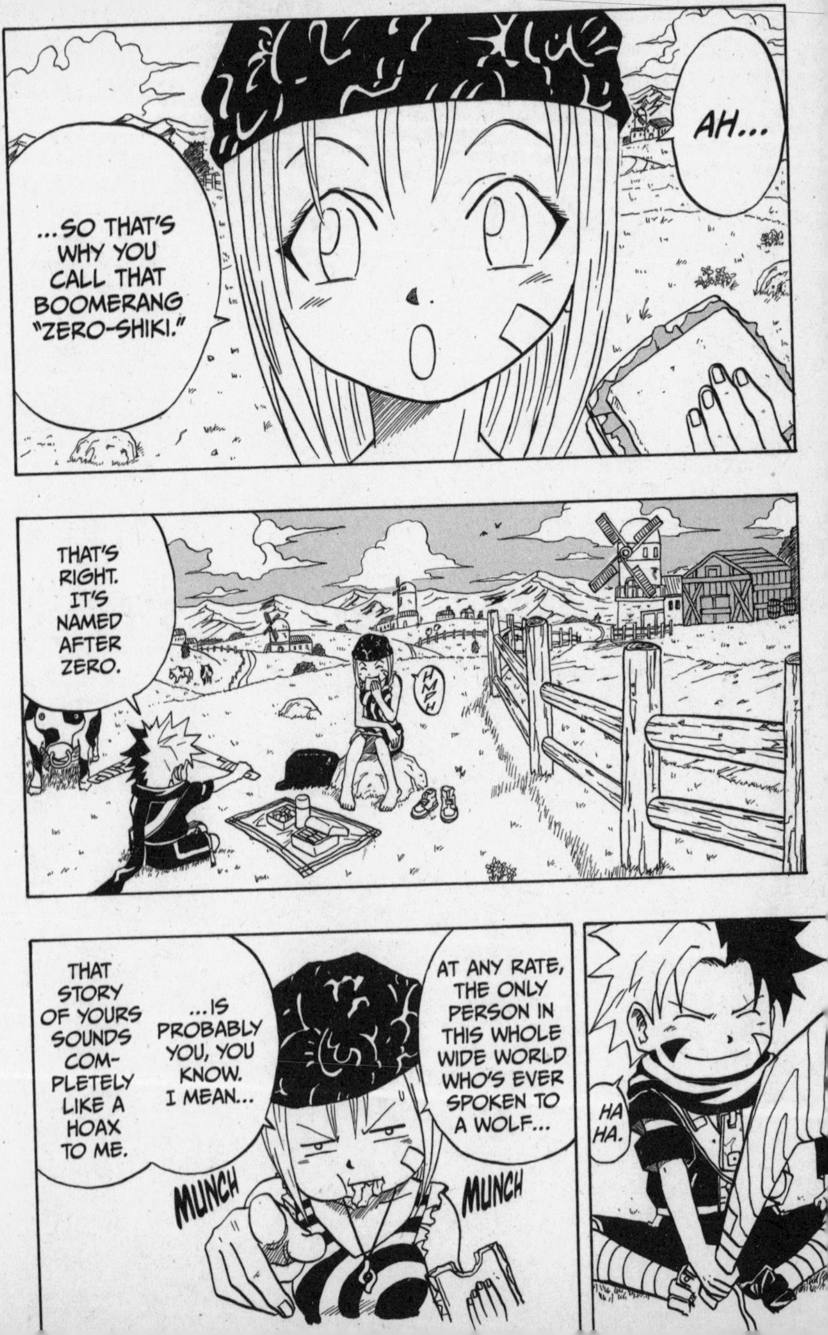
AH...
...SO THAT'S WHY YOU CALL THAT BOOMERANG "ZERO-SHIKI."
THAT'S RIGHT. IT'S NAMED AFTER ZERO.
HMPH
HA HA.
AT ANY RATE, THE ONLY PERSON IN THIS WHOLE WIDE WORLD WHO'S EVER SPOKEN TO A WOLF...
...IS PROBABLY YOU, YOU KNOW. I MEAN...
THAT STORY OF YOURS SOUNDS COMPLETELY LIKE A HOAX TO ME.
MUNCH
MUNCH

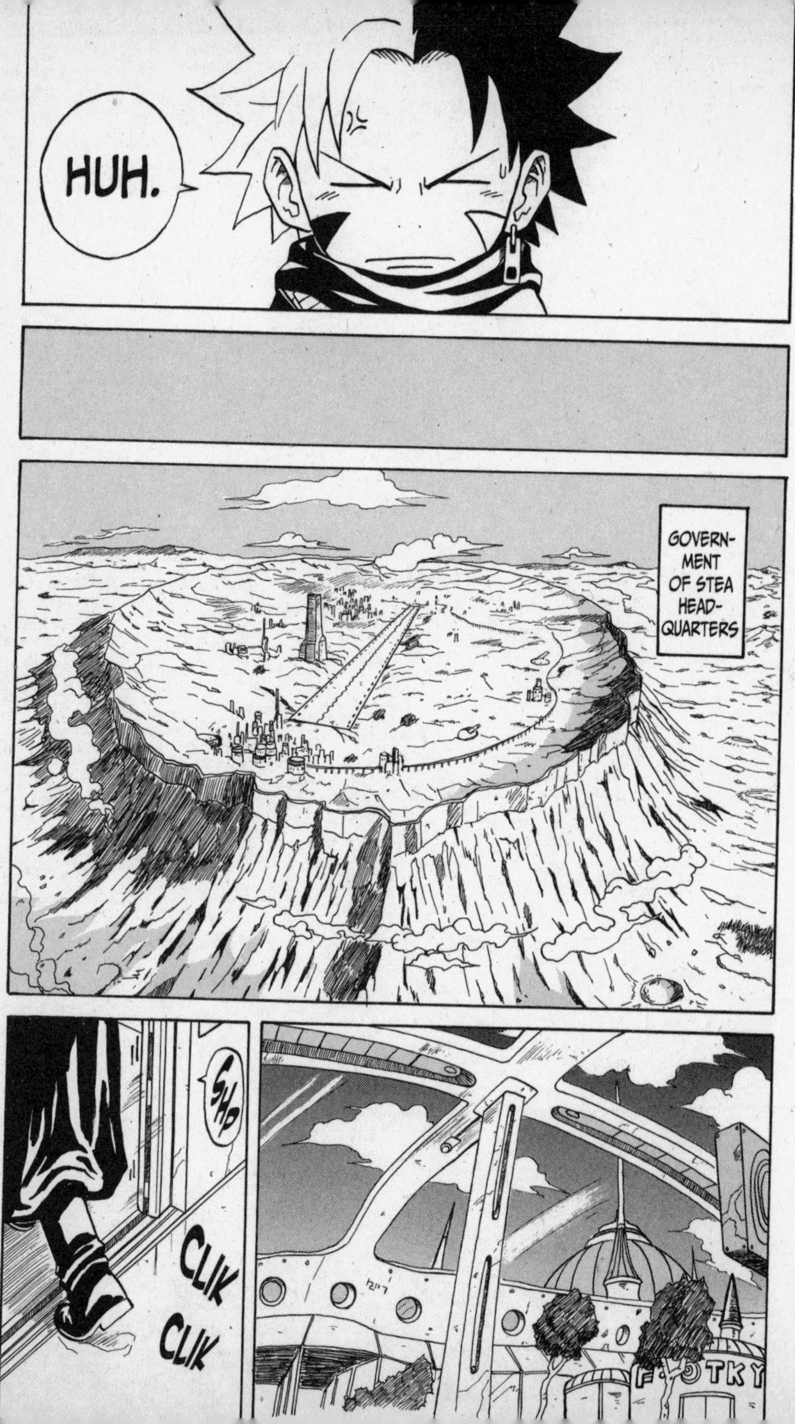
HUH.
GOVERNMENT OF STEA HEADQUARTERS
SHP
CLIK
CLIK

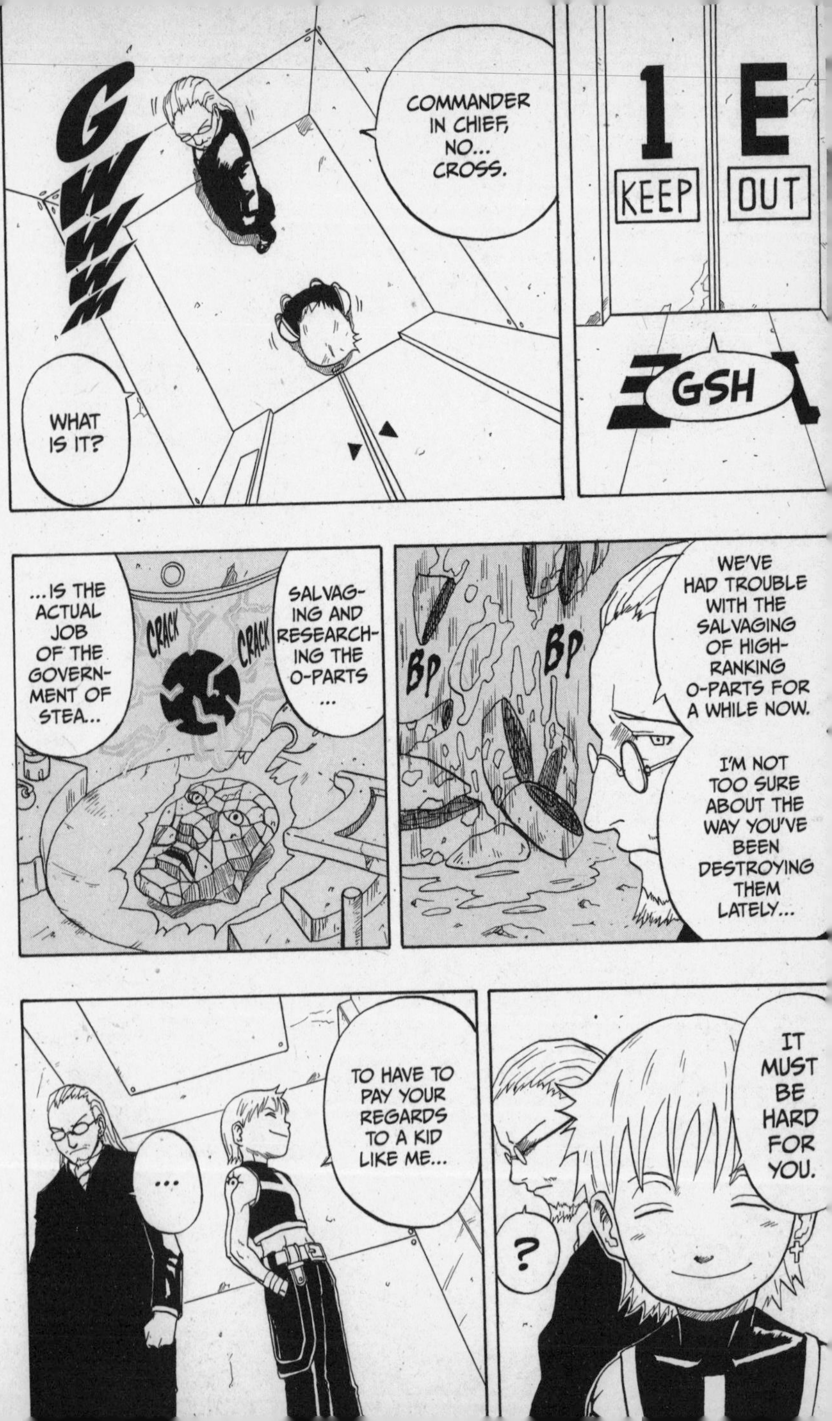
1E
KEEP OUT
GSH
COMMANDER IN CHIEF, NO... CROSS.
WHAT IS IT?
WE'VE HAD TROUBLE WITH THE SALVAGING OF HIGH-RANKING O-PARTS FOR A WHILE NOW.
I'M NOT TOO SURE ABOUT THE WAY YOU'VE BEEN DESTROYING THEM LATELY...
BP
BP
SALVAGING AND RESEARCHING THE O-PARTS...
...IS THE ACTUAL JOB OF THE GOVERNMENT OF STEA...
CRACK
CRACK
IT MUST BE HARD FOR YOU.
?
TO HAVE TO PAY YOUR REGARDS TO A KID LIKE ME...
...

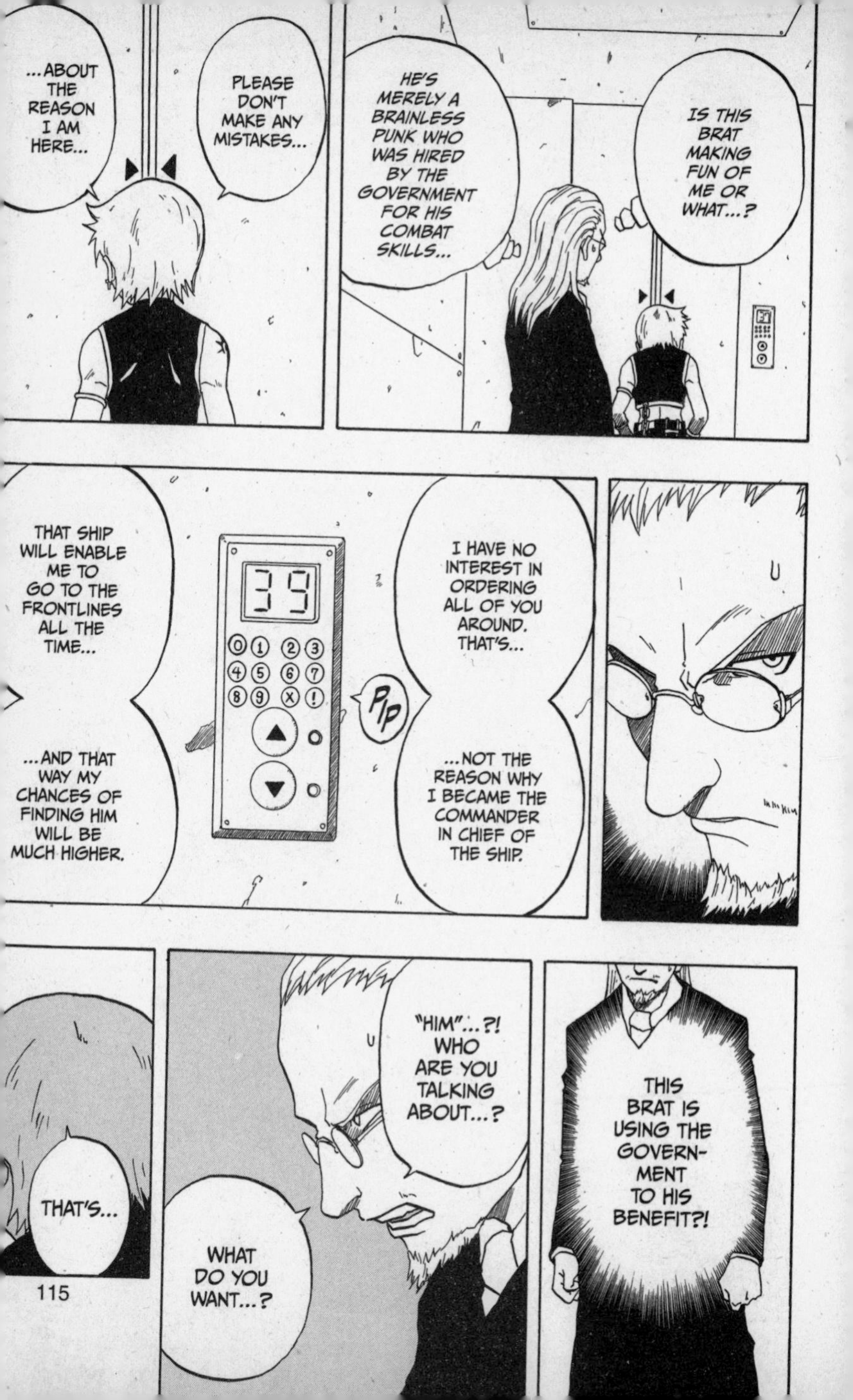
IS THIS BRAT MAKING FUN OF ME OR WHAT...?
HE'S MERELY A BRAINLESS PUNK WHO WAS HIRED BY THE GOVERNMENT FOR HIS COMBAT SKILLS...
PLEASE DON'T MAKE ANY MISTAKES...
...ABOUT THE REASON I AM HERE...
I HAVE NO INTEREST IN ORDERING ALL OF YOU AROUND. THAT'S...
...NOT THE REASON WHY I BECAME THE COMMANDER IN CHIEF OF THE SHIP.
PIP
THAT SHIP WILL ENABLE ME TO GO TO THE FRONTLINES ALL THE TIME...
...AND THAT WAY MY CHANCES OF FINDING HIM WILL BE MUCH HIGHER.
THIS BRAT IS USING THE GOVERN-MENT TO HIS BENEFIT?!
"HIM"...?! WHO ARE YOU TALKING ABOUT...?
WHAT DO YOU WANT...?
THAT'S...

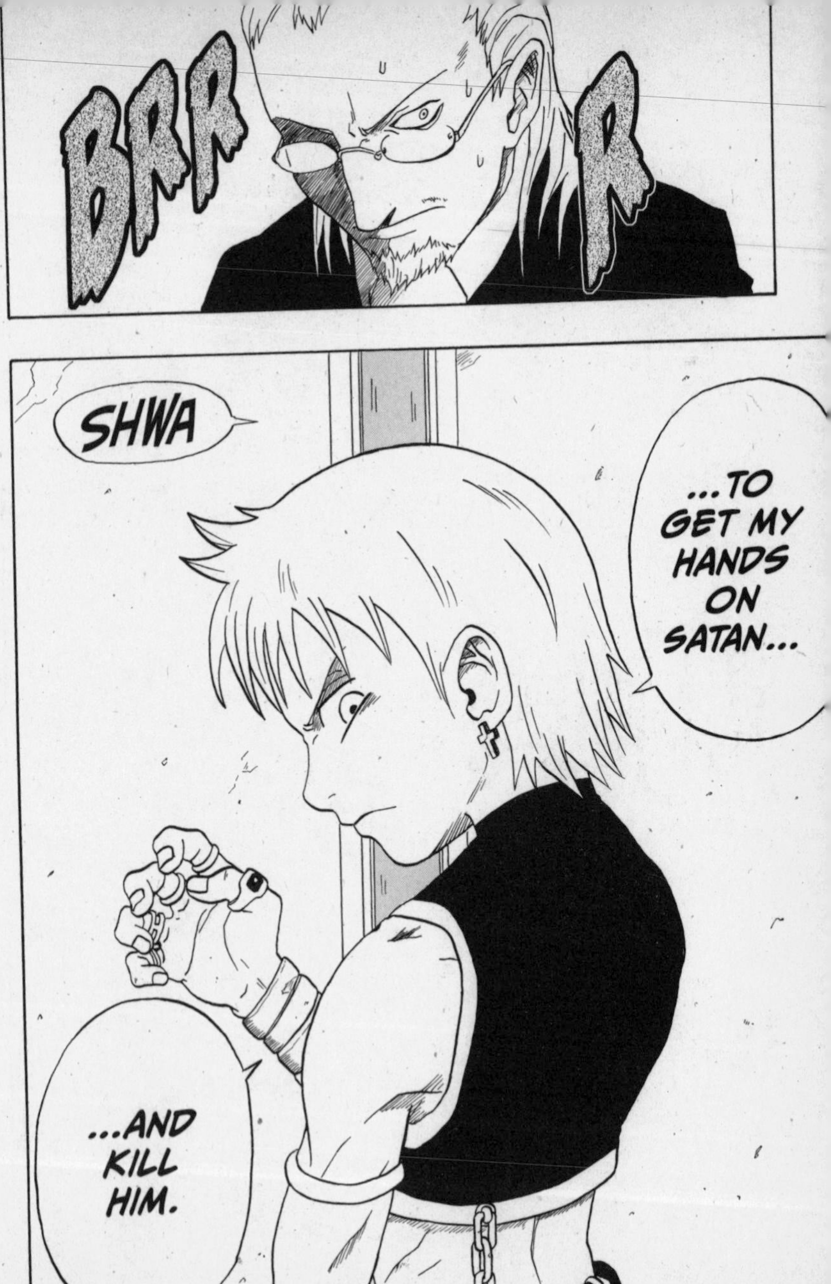
BRR
R
...TO GET MY HANDS ON SATAN...
SHWA
...AND KILL HIM.

CHAPTER 7: THE MISTY CITY

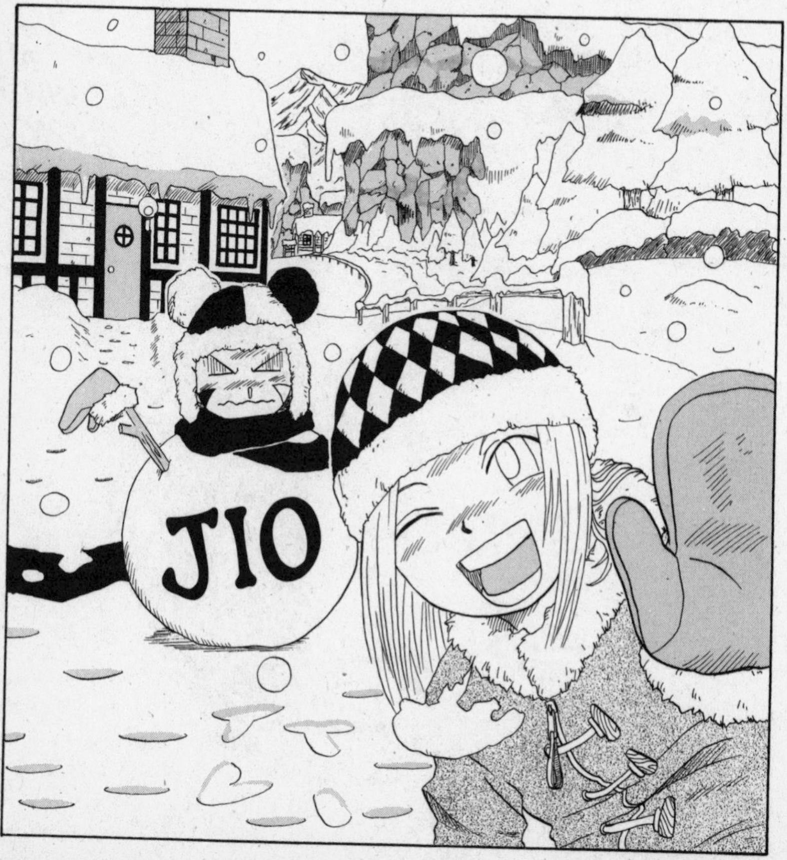
JIO

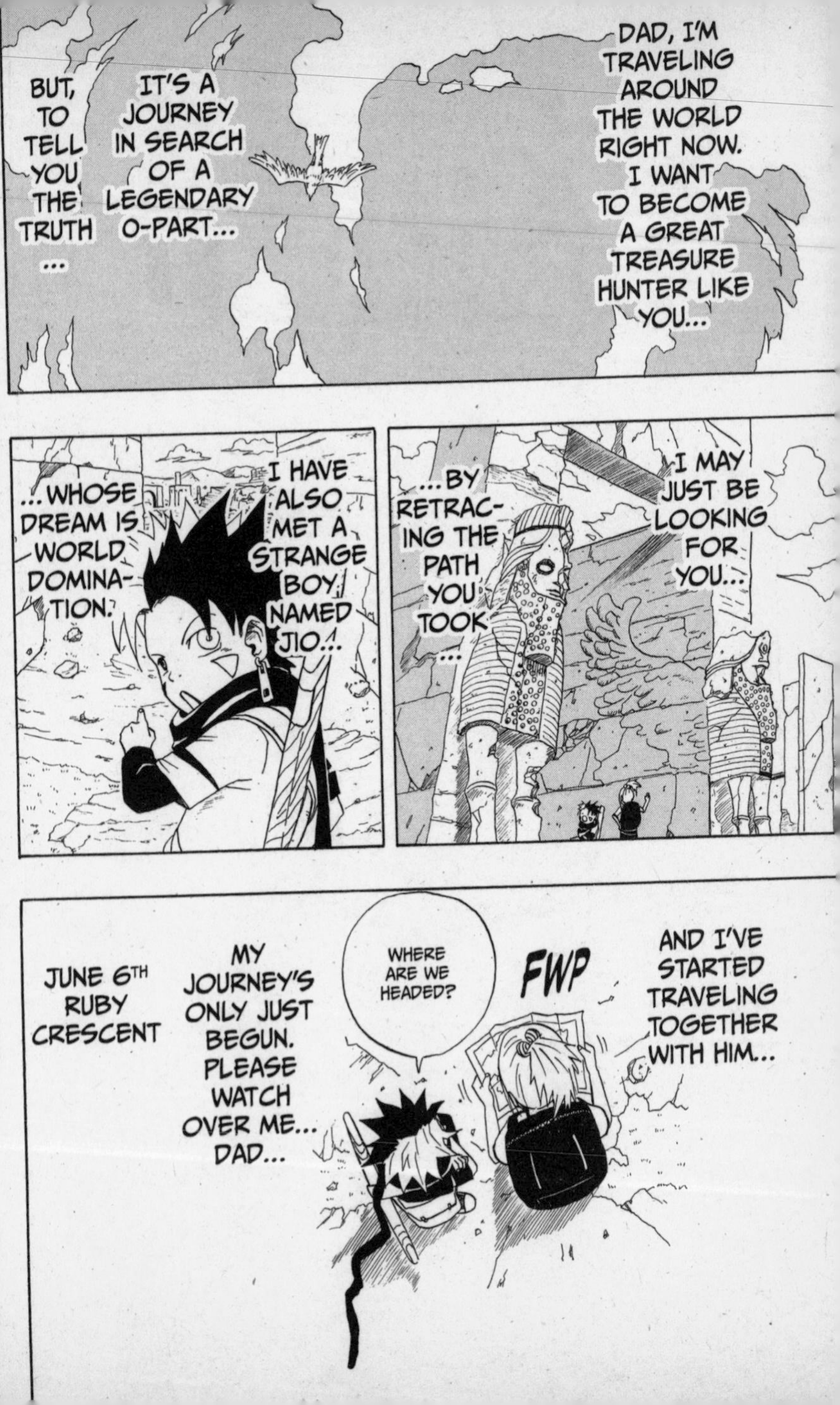
DAD, I'M TRAVELING AROUND THE WORLD RIGHT NOW. I WANT TO BECOME A GREAT TREASURE HUNTER LIKE YOU...
IT'S A JOURNEY IN SEARCH OF A LEGENDARY O-PART...
BUT, TO TELL YOU THE TRUTH...
I MAY JUST BE LOOKING FOR YOU...
...BY RETRACING THE PATH YOU TOOK...
I HAVE ALSO MET A STRANGE BOY NAMED JIO...
...WHOSE DREAM IS WORLD DOMINATION.
AND I'VE STARTED TRAVELING TOGETHER WITH HIM...
FWP
WHERE ARE WE HEADED?
MY JOURNEY'S ONLY JUST BEGUN. PLEASE WATCH OVER ME... DAD...
JUNE 6TH RUBY CRESCENT

SP
HUH?
LOOK.
THIS IS WHERE I MET YOU FIRST, JIO, AND THEN WE WENT DOWN TO THE THORNED RUIN.
TOOM RUINS
THORNED RUIN
(CURRENT LOCATION)
THE TRIANGLE MARKS THE LARGE RUINS.
I'M THINKING ABOUT STARTING WITH THE SOUTH, AND THEN MOVING AROUND IN A CIRCLE TO THE WEST, NORTH, AND THEN EAST.

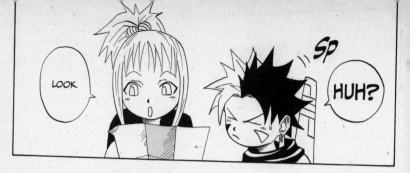

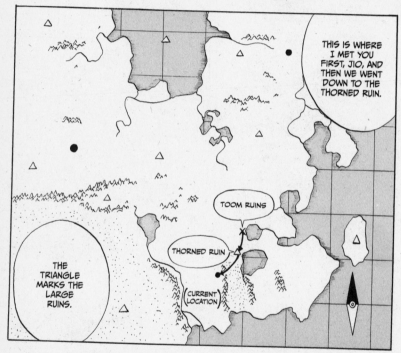

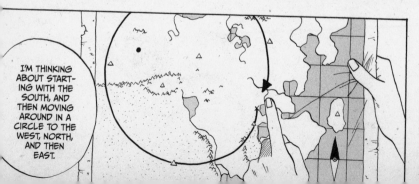

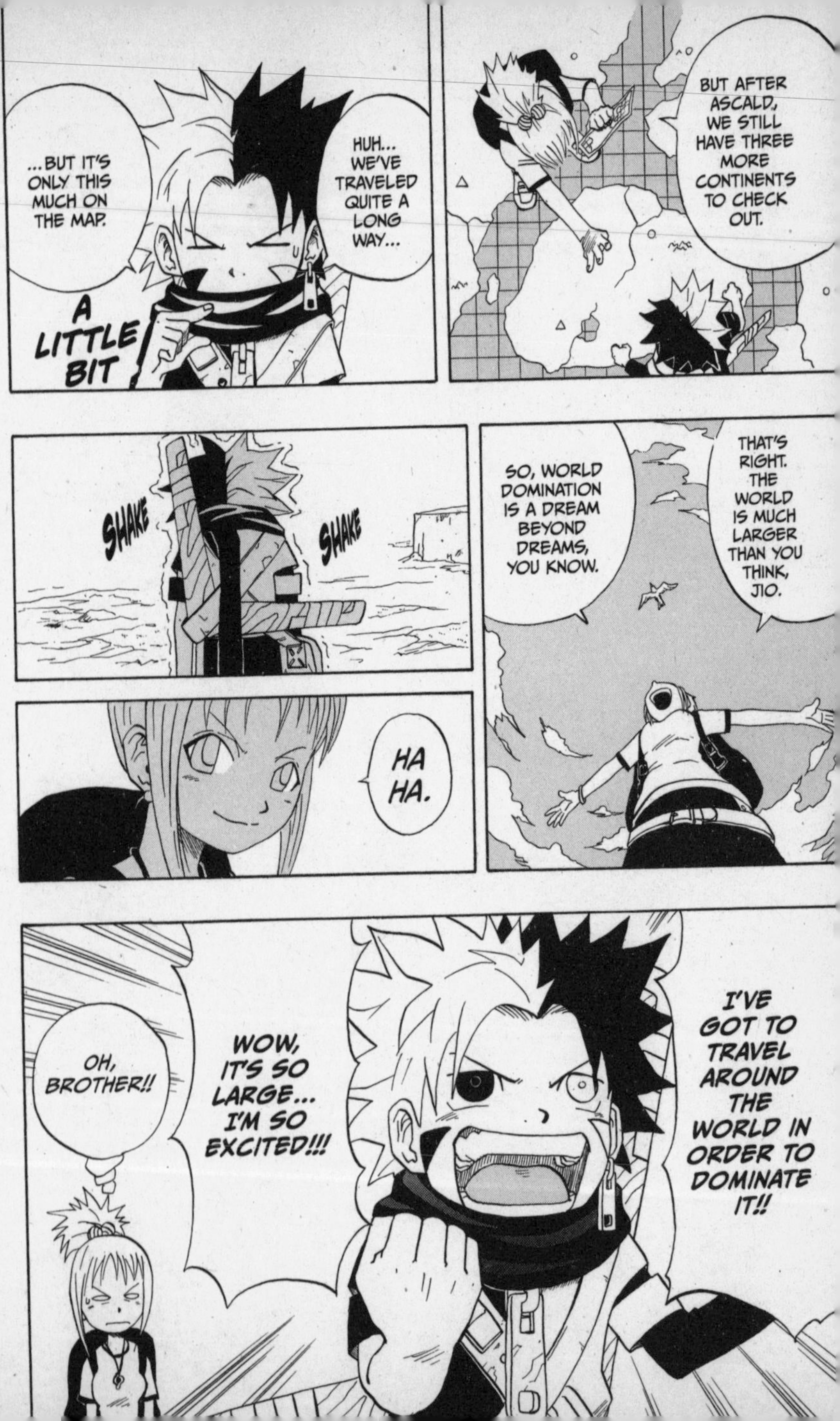
BUT AFTER ASCALD, WE STILL HAVE THREE MORE CONTINENTS TO CHECK OUT.
HUH... WE'VE TRAVELED QUITE A LONG WAY...
...BUT IT'S ONLY THIS MUCH ON THE MAP.
A LITTLE BIT
THAT'S RIGHT. THE WORLD IS MUCH LARGER THAN YOU THINK, JIO.
SO, WORLD DOMINATION IS A DREAM BEYOND DREAMS, YOU KNOW.
SHAKE
SHAKE
HA HA.
I'VE GOT TO TRAVEL AROUND THE WORLD IN ORDER TO DOMINATE IT!!
WOW, IT'S SO LARGE... I'M SO EXCITED!!!
OH, BROTHER!!

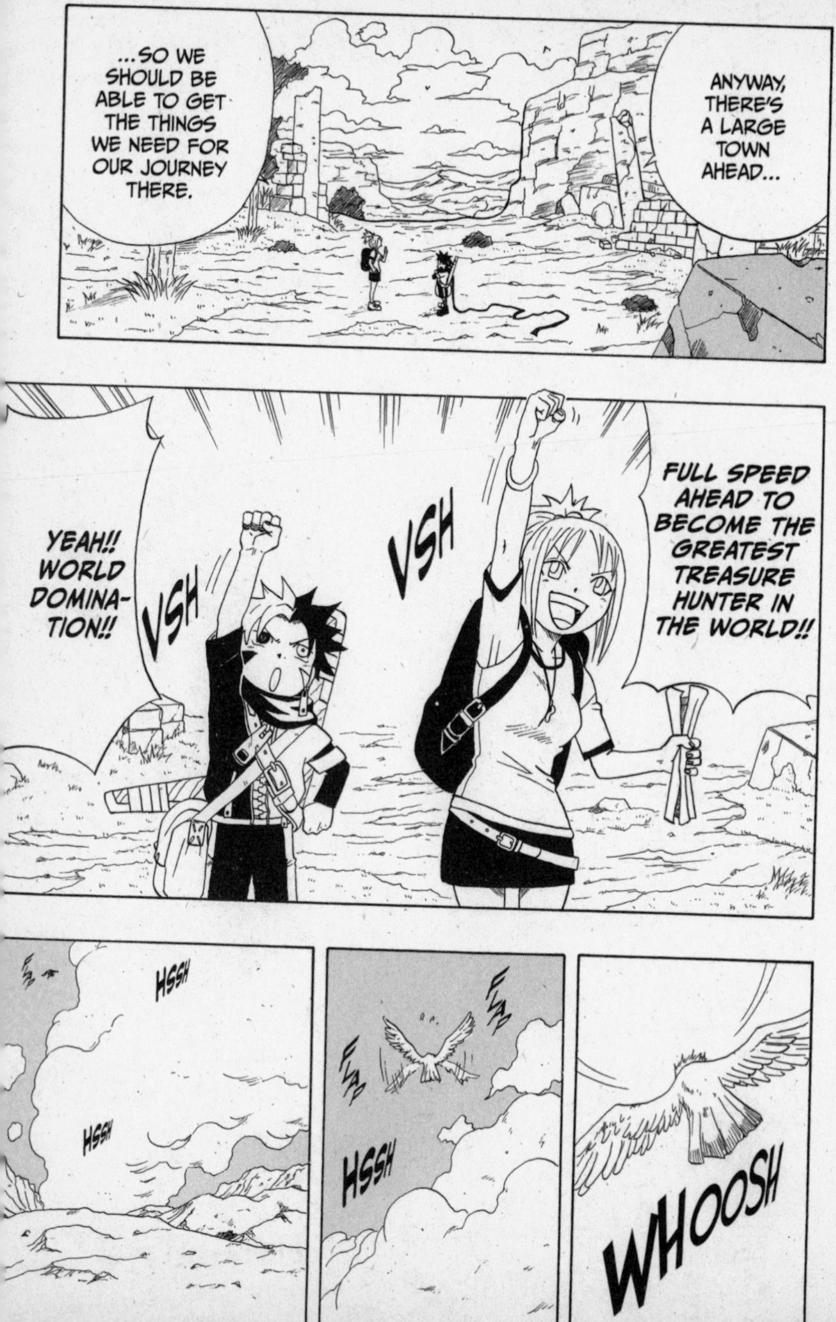
ANYWAY, THERE'S A LARGE TOWN AHEAD...
...SO WE SHOULD BE ABLE TO GET THE THINGS WE NEED FOR OUR JOURNEY THERE.
FULL SPEED AHEAD TO BECOME THE GREATEST TREASURE HUNTER IN THE WORLD!!
VSH
VSH
YEAH!! WORLD DOMINA-TION!!
WHOOSH
FLAP
FLAP
HSSH
HSSH
HSSH

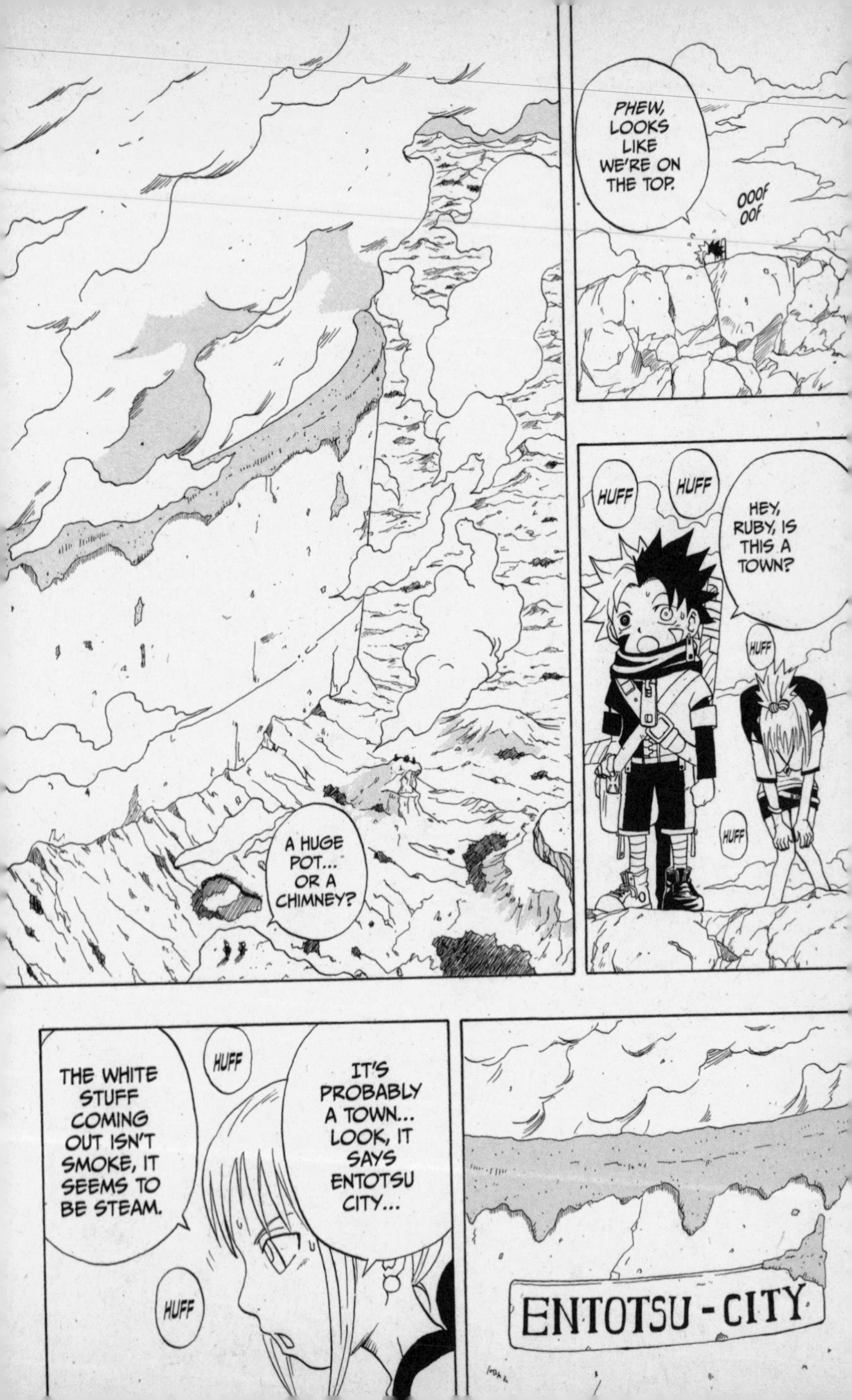
PHEW, LOOKS LIKE WE'RE ON THE TOP.
OOOF OOF
HUFF
HUFF
HEY, RUBY, IS THIS A TOWN?
HUFF
HUFF
A HUGE POT... OR A CHIMNEY?
ENTOTSU - CITY
HUFF
IT'S PROBABLY A TOWN... LOOK, IT SAYS ENTOTSU CITY...
THE WHITE STUFF COMING OUT ISN'T SMOKE, IT SEEMS TO BE STEAM.
HUFF

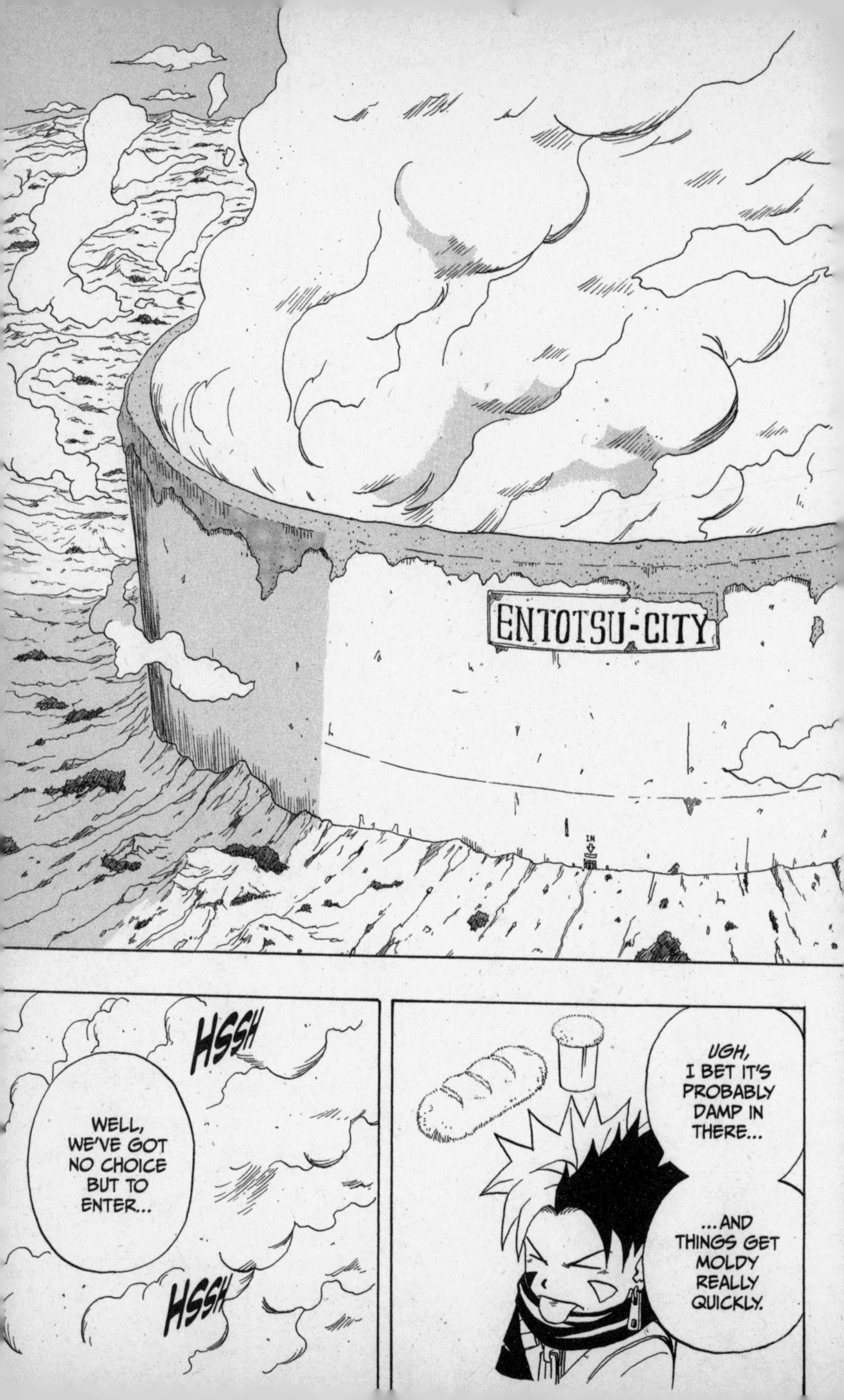
ENTOTSU-CITY
IN
UGH, I BET IT'S PROBABLY DAMP IN THERE...
...AND THINGS GET MOLDY REALLY QUICKLY.
HSSH
WELL, WE'VE GOT NO CHOICE BUT TO ENTER...
HSSH

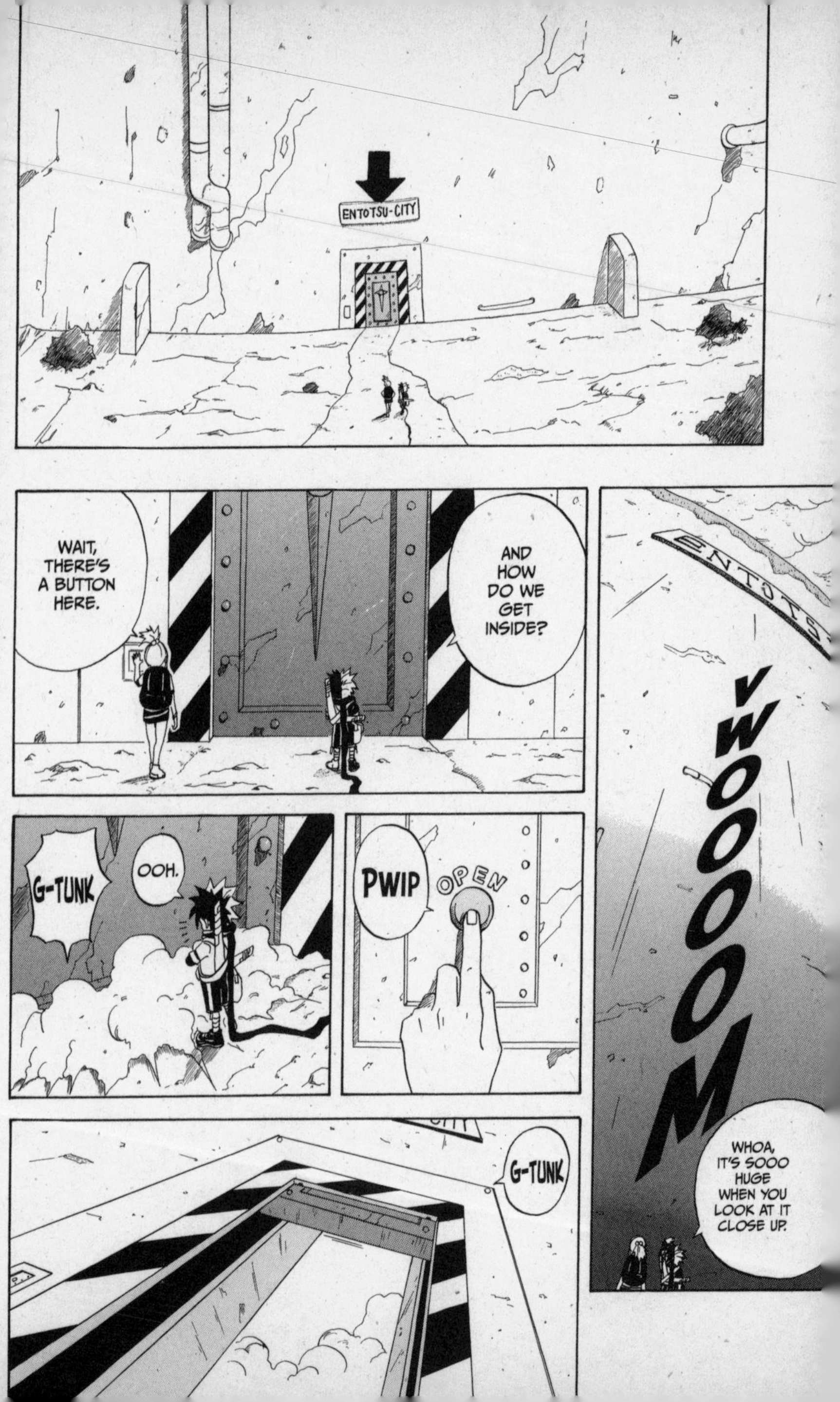
ENTOTSU-CITY
ENTOTS
VWOOOOM
WHOA, IT'S SOOO HUGE WHEN YOU LOOK AT IT CLOSE UP.
AND HOW DO WE GET INSIDE?
WAIT, THERE'S A BUTTON HERE.
PWIP
OPEN
OOH.
G-TUNK
G-TUNK
CITY

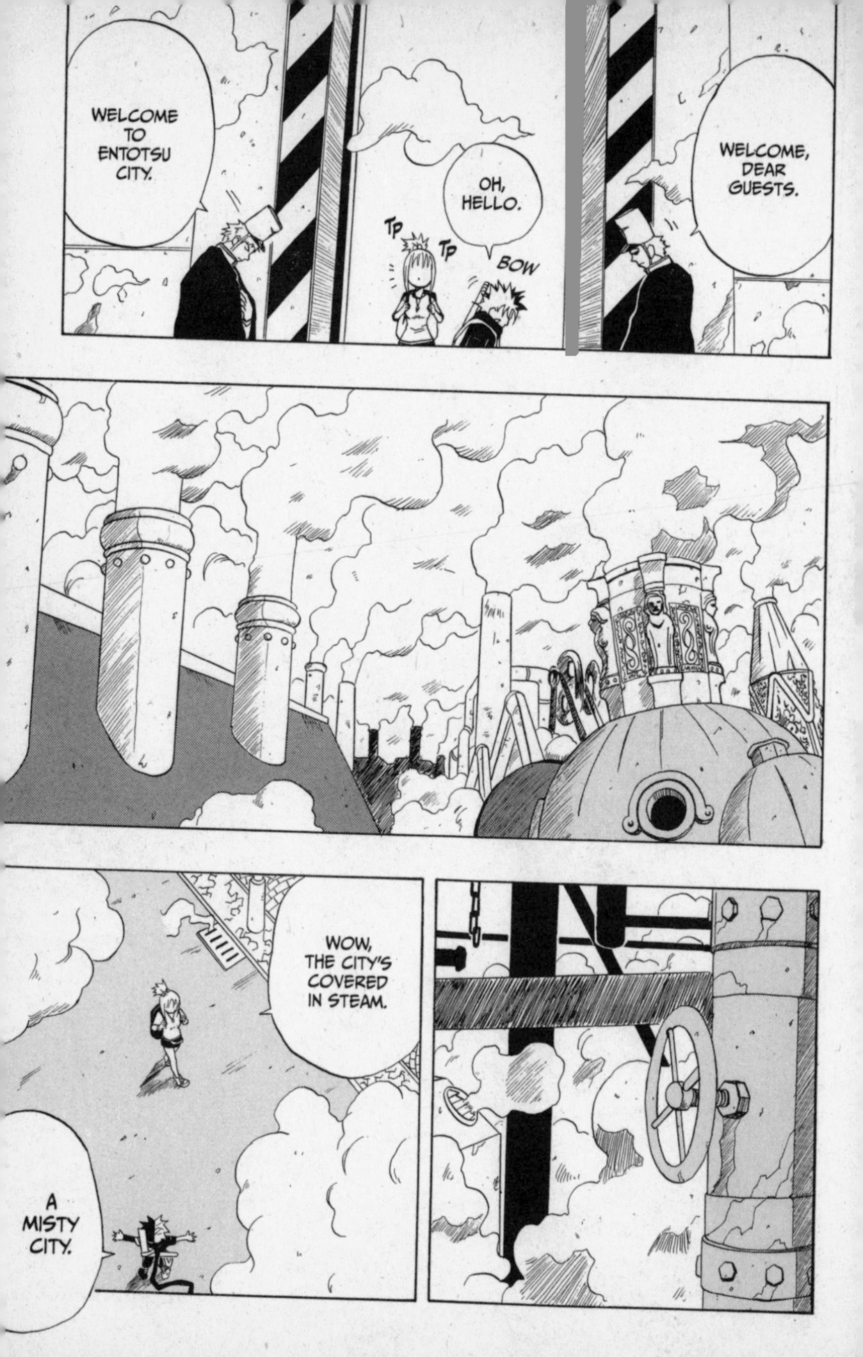
WELCOME, DEAR GUESTS.
TP
TP
OH, HELLO.
BOW
WELCOME TO ENTOTSU CITY.
WOW, THE CITY'S COVERED IN STEAM.
A MISTY CITY.

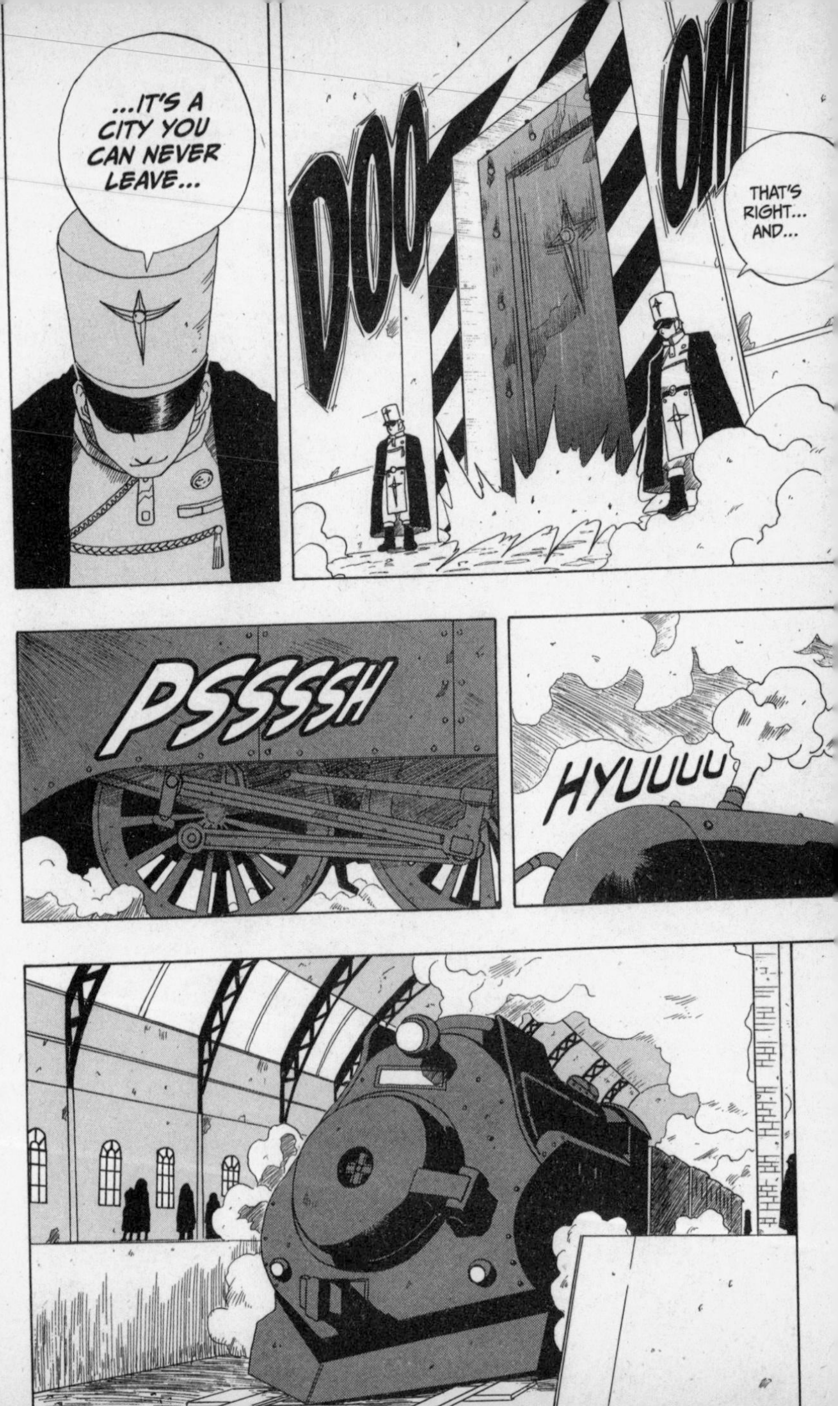
THAT'S RIGHT... AND...
DOOOM
...IT'S A CITY YOU CAN NEVER LEAVE...
HYUUUU
PSSSSH

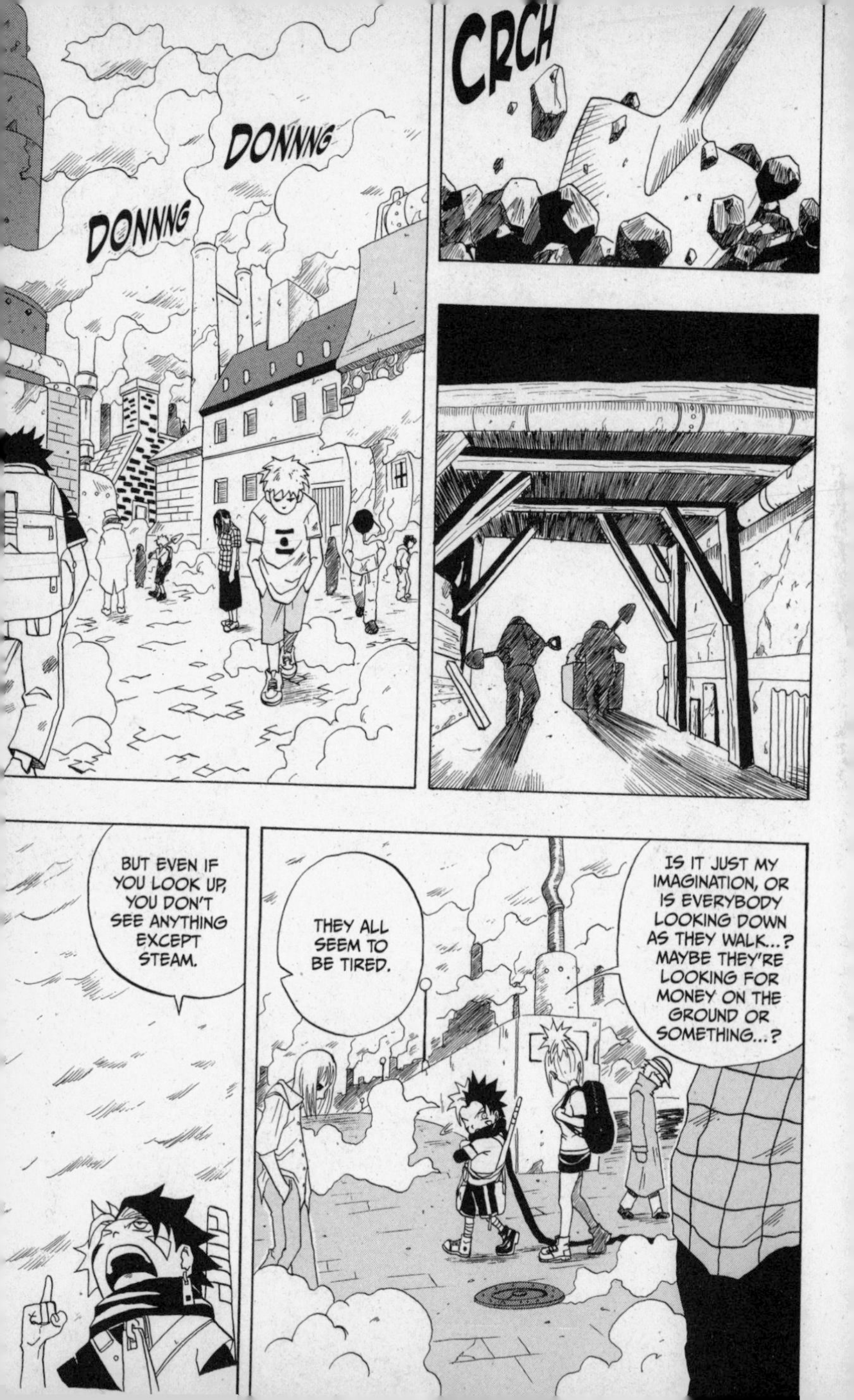
CRCH
DONNNG
DONNNG
IS IT JUST MY IMAGINATION, OR IS EVERYBODY LOOKING DOWN AS THEY WALK...? MAYBE THEY'RE LOOKING FOR MONEY ON THE GROUND OR SOMETHING...?
THEY ALL SEEM TO BE TIRED.
BUT EVEN IF YOU LOOK UP, YOU DON'T SEE ANYTHING EXCEPT STEAM.

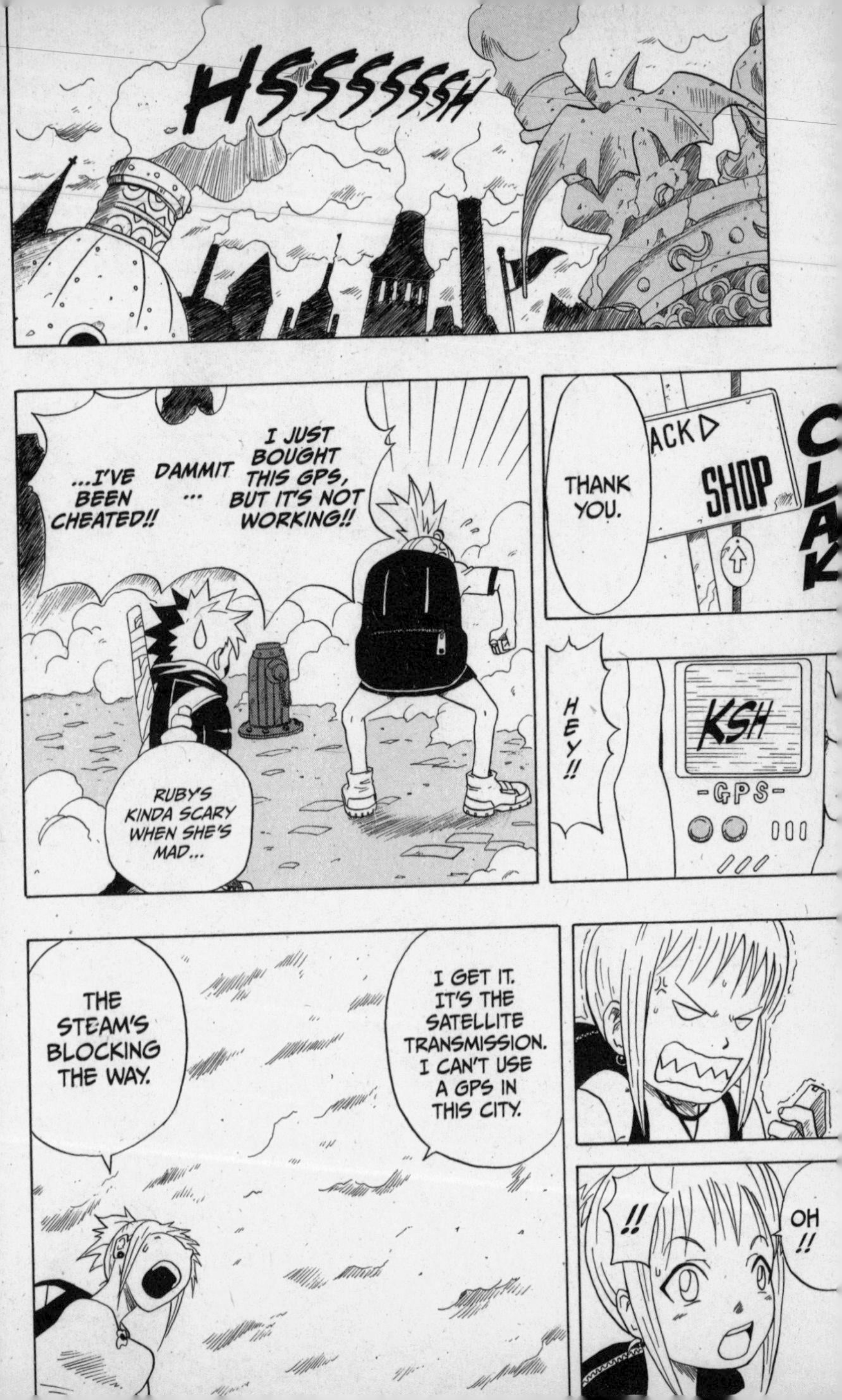
HSSSSSSH
THANK YOU.
CLAK
SHOP
HEY!!
KSH
-GPS-
I JUST BOUGHT THIS GPS, BUT IT'S NOT WORKING!!
DAMMIT ...
...I'VE BEEN CHEATED!!
RUBY'S KINDA SCARY WHEN SHE'S MAD...
OH!!
!!
I GET IT. IT'S THE SATELLITE TRANSMISSION. I CAN'T USE A GPS IN THIS CITY.
THE STEAM'S BLOCKING THE WAY.

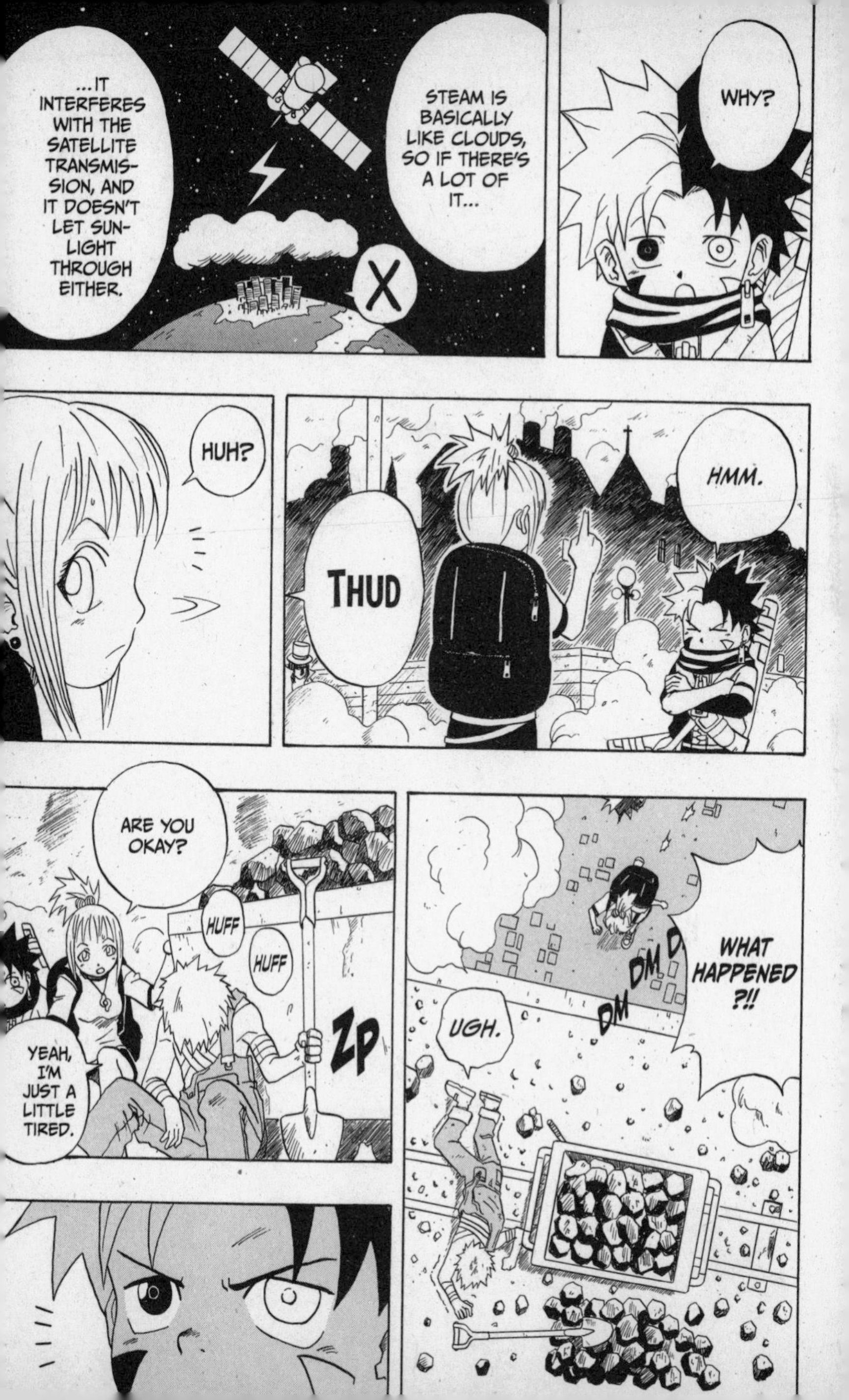
WHY?
STEAM IS BASICALLY LIKE CLOUDS, SO IF THERE'S A LOT OF IT...
...IT INTERFERES WITH THE SATELLITE TRANSMIS-SION, AND IT DOESN'T LET SUN-LIGHT THROUGH EITHER.
X
HMM.
THUD
HUH?
WHAT HAPPENED ?!!
DM DM D
UGH.
ARE YOU OKAY?
HUFF
HUFF
ZP
YEAH, I'M JUST A LITTLE TIRED.

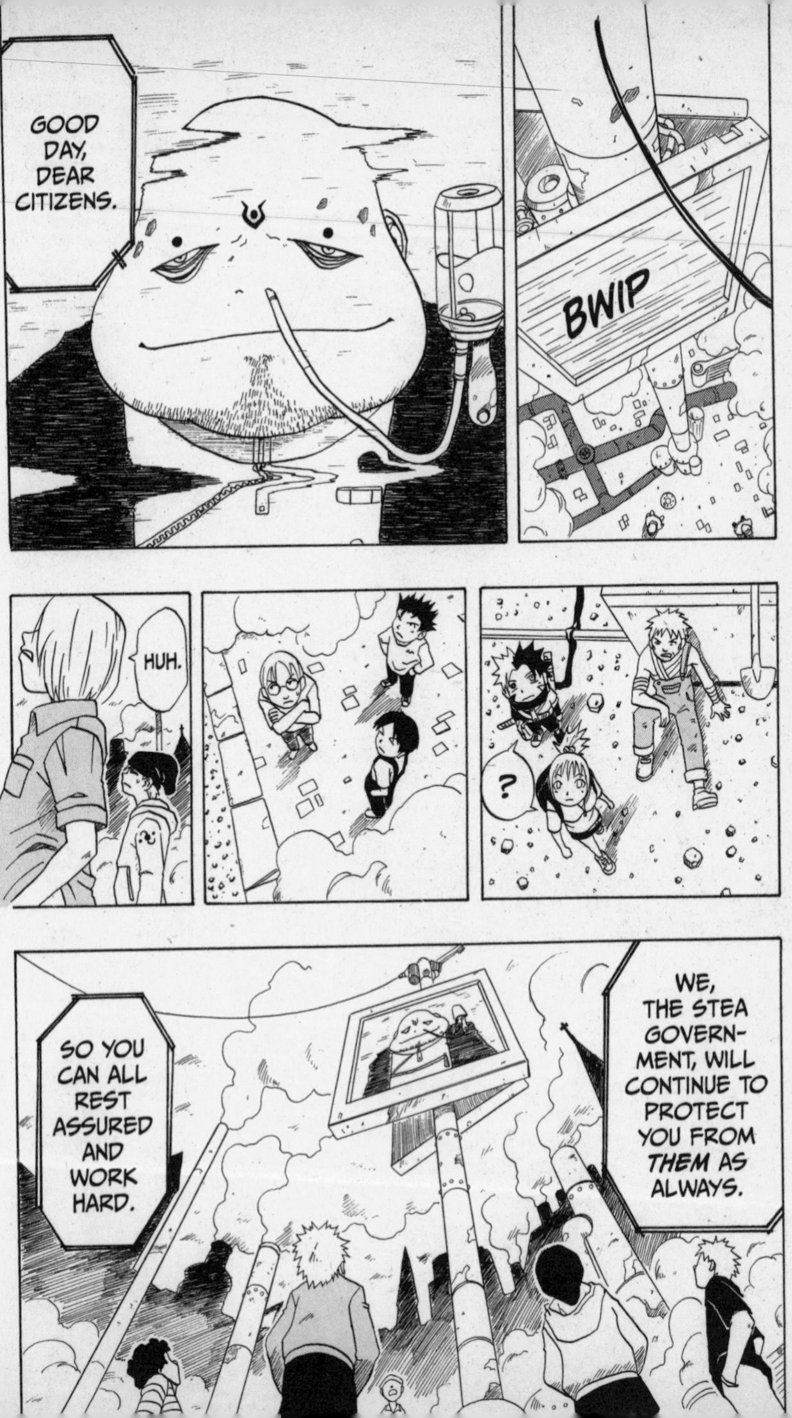
BWIP
GOOD DAY, DEAR CITIZENS.
?
HUH.
WE, THE STEA GOVERNMENT, WILL CONTINUE TO PROTECT YOU FROM *THEM* AS ALWAYS.
SO YOU CAN ALL REST ASSURED AND WORK HARD.

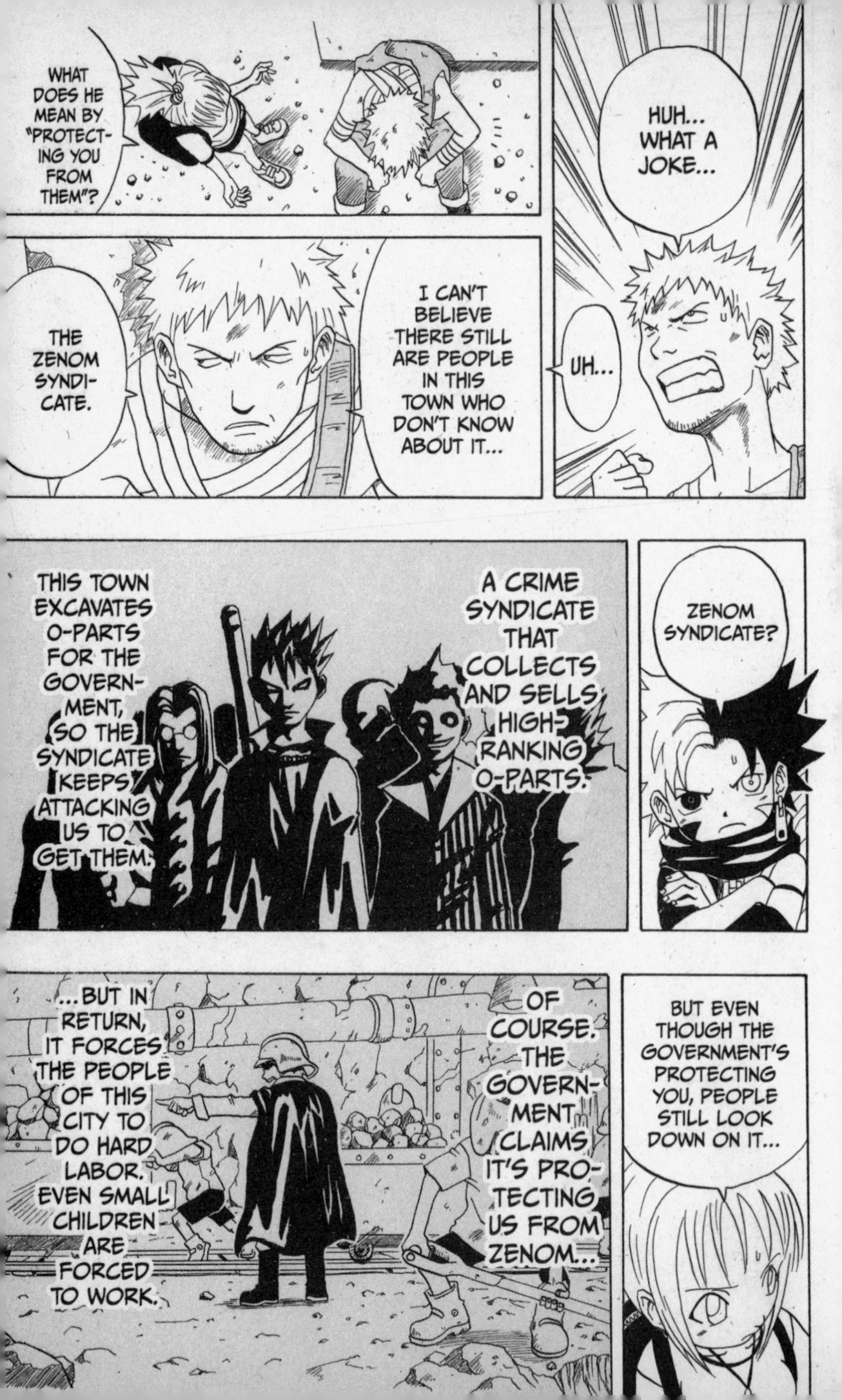

HUH... WHAT A JOKE...
UH...
WHAT DOES HE MEAN BY "PROTECTING YOU FROM THEM"?
I CAN'T BELIEVE THERE STILL ARE PEOPLE IN THIS TOWN WHO DON'T KNOW ABOUT IT...
THE ZENOM SYNDICATE.
ZENOM SYNDICATE?
A CRIME SYNDICATE THAT COLLECTS AND SELLS HIGH-RANKING O-PARTS.
THIS TOWN EXCAVATES O-PARTS FOR THE GOVERNMENT, SO THE SYNDICATE KEEPS ATTACKING US TO GET THEM.
BUT EVEN THOUGH THE GOVERNMENT'S PROTECTING YOU, PEOPLE STILL LOOK DOWN ON IT...
OF COURSE. THE GOVERNMENT CLAIMS IT'S PROTECTING US FROM ZENOM...
...BUT IN RETURN, IT FORCES THE PEOPLE OF THIS CITY TO DO HARD LABOR. EVEN SMALL CHILDREN ARE FORCED TO WORK.

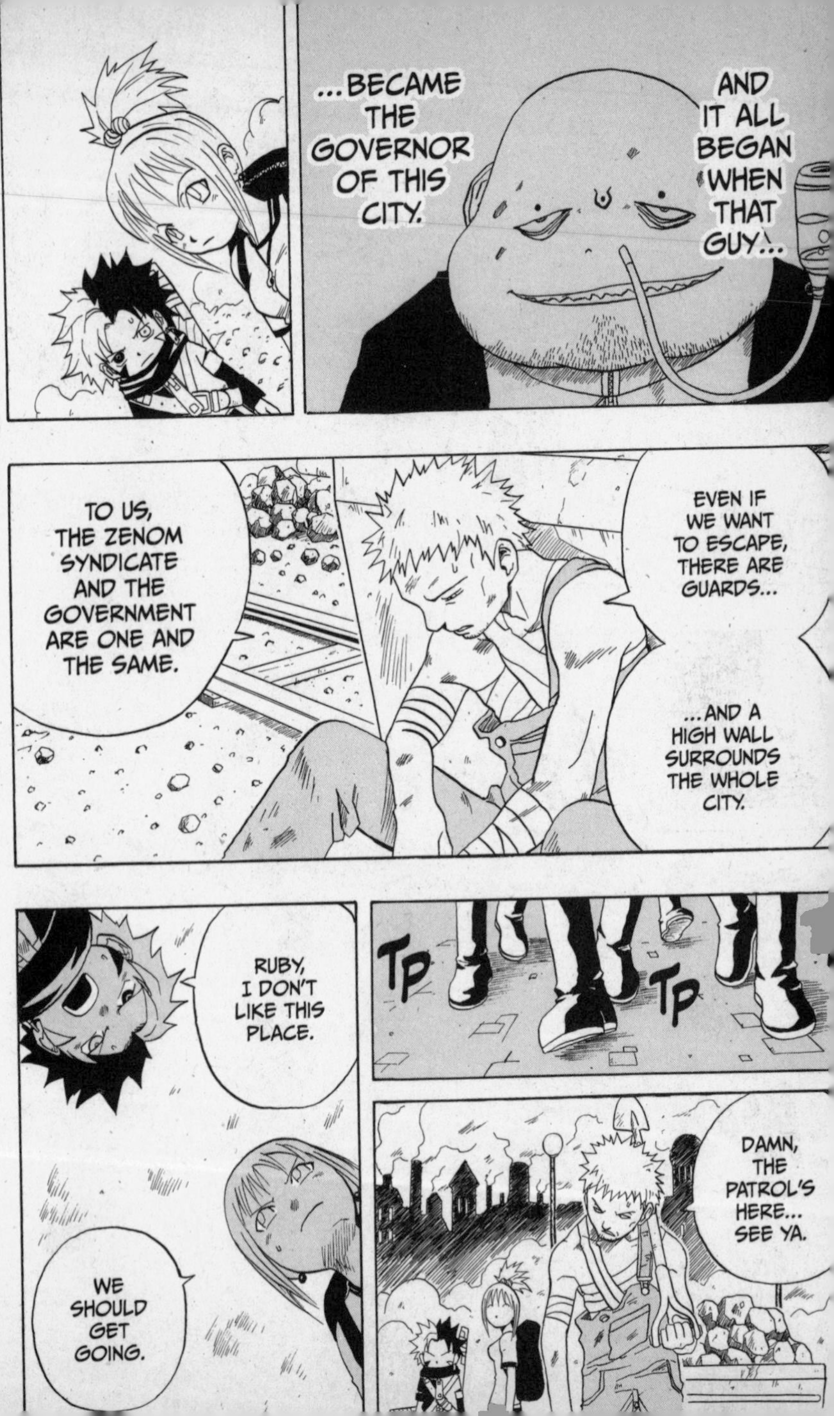
AND IT ALL BEGAN WHEN THAT GUY...
...BECAME THE GOVERNOR OF THIS CITY.
EVEN IF WE WANT TO ESCAPE, THERE ARE GUARDS...
...AND A HIGH WALL SURROUNDS THE WHOLE CITY.
TO US, THE ZENOM SYNDICATE AND THE GOVERNMENT ARE ONE AND THE SAME.
TP
TP
DAMN, THE PATROL'S HERE... SEE YA.
RUBY, I DON'T LIKE THIS PLACE.
WE SHOULD GET GOING.

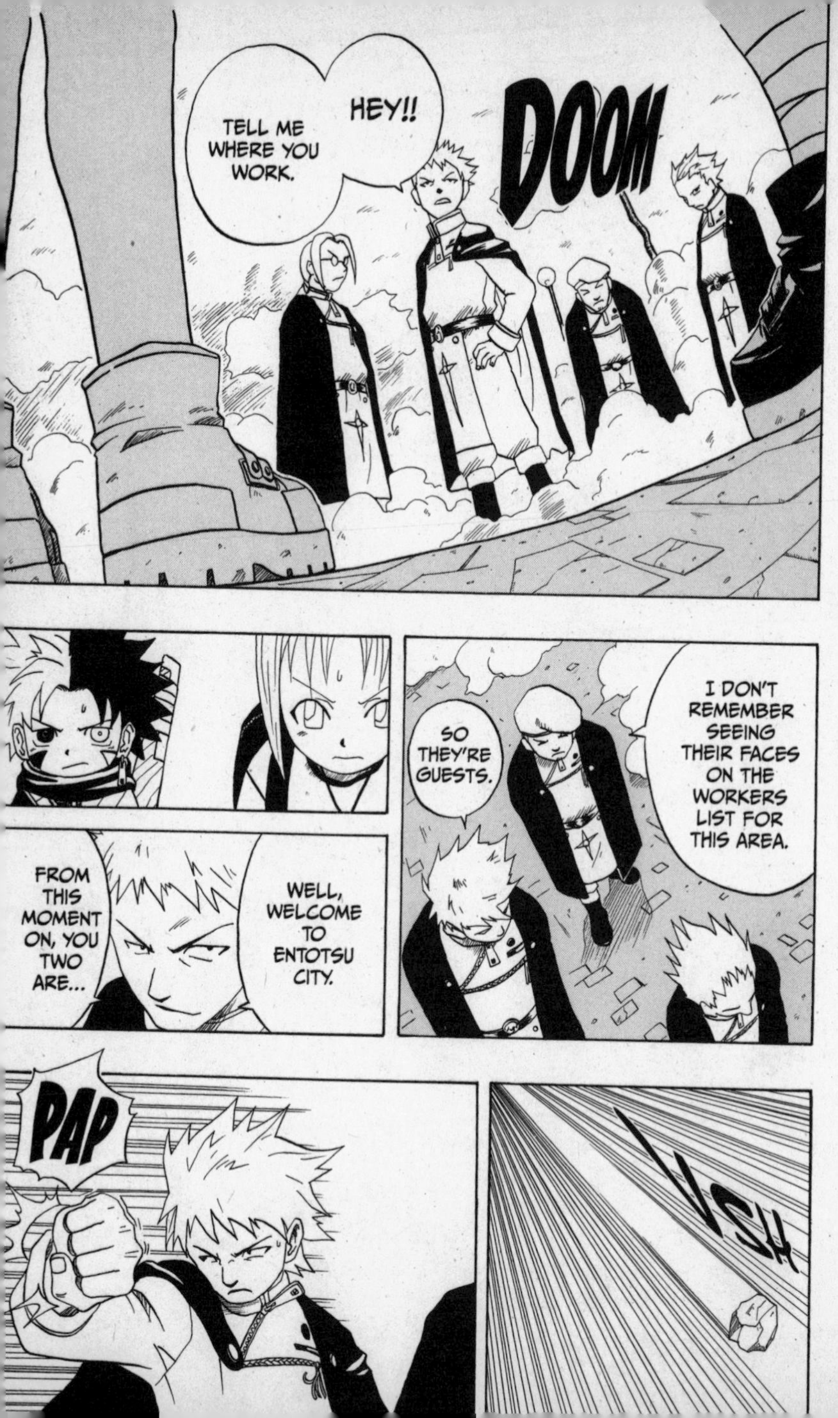
DOOM
HEY!!
TELL ME WHERE YOU WORK.
I DON'T REMEMBER SEEING THEIR FACES ON THE WORKERS LIST FOR THIS AREA.
SO THEY'RE GUESTS.
WELL, WELCOME TO ENTOTSU CITY.
FROM THIS MOMENT ON, YOU TWO ARE...
VSH
PAP

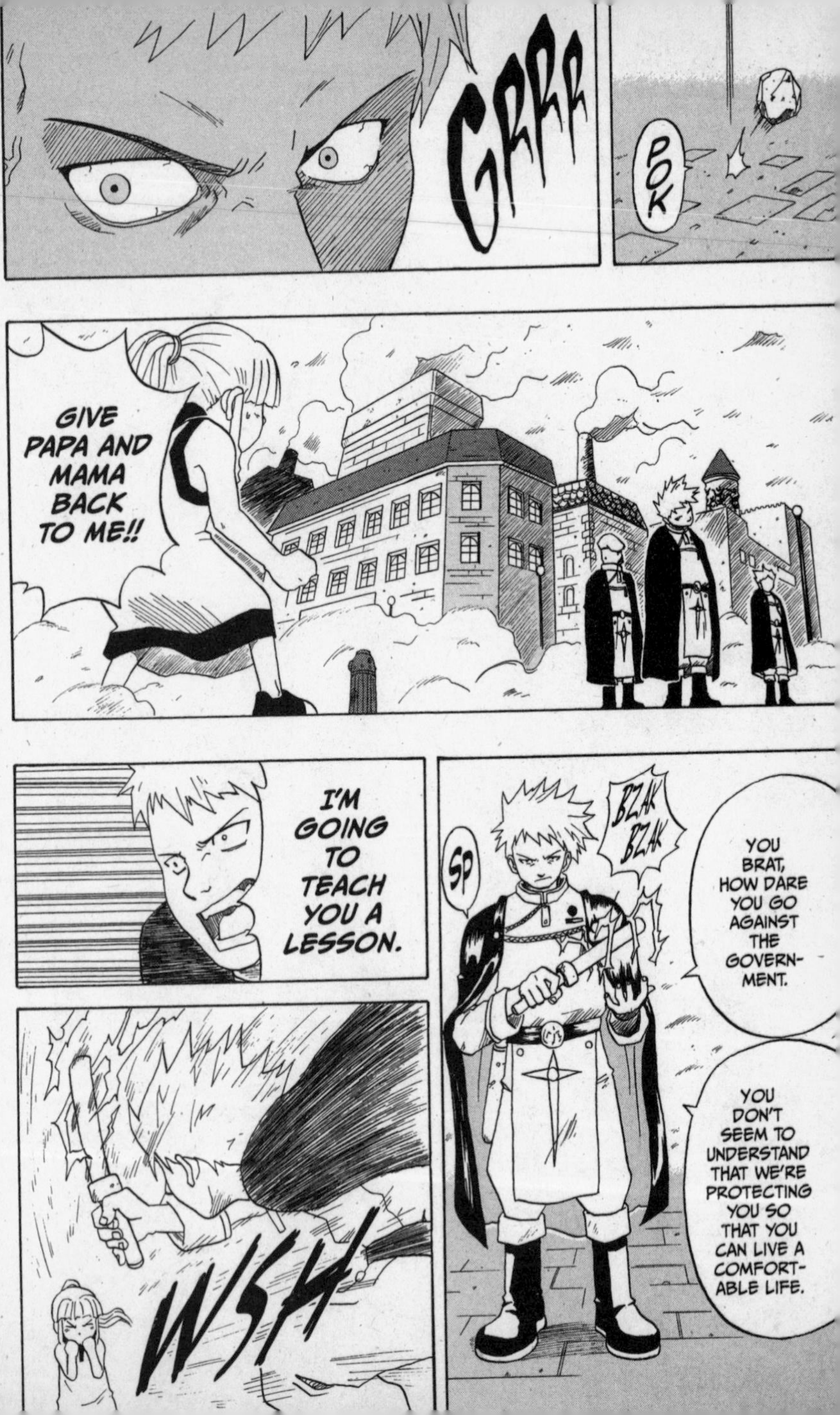
POK
GRRR
GIVE PAPA AND MAMA BACK TO ME!!
YOU BRAT, HOW DARE YOU GO AGAINST THE GOVERN-MENT.
BZAK BZAK
SP
YOU DON'T SEEM TO UNDERSTAND THAT WE'RE PROTECTING YOU SO THAT YOU CAN LIVE A COMFORT-ABLE LIFE.
I'M GOING TO TEACH YOU A LESSON.
WSH

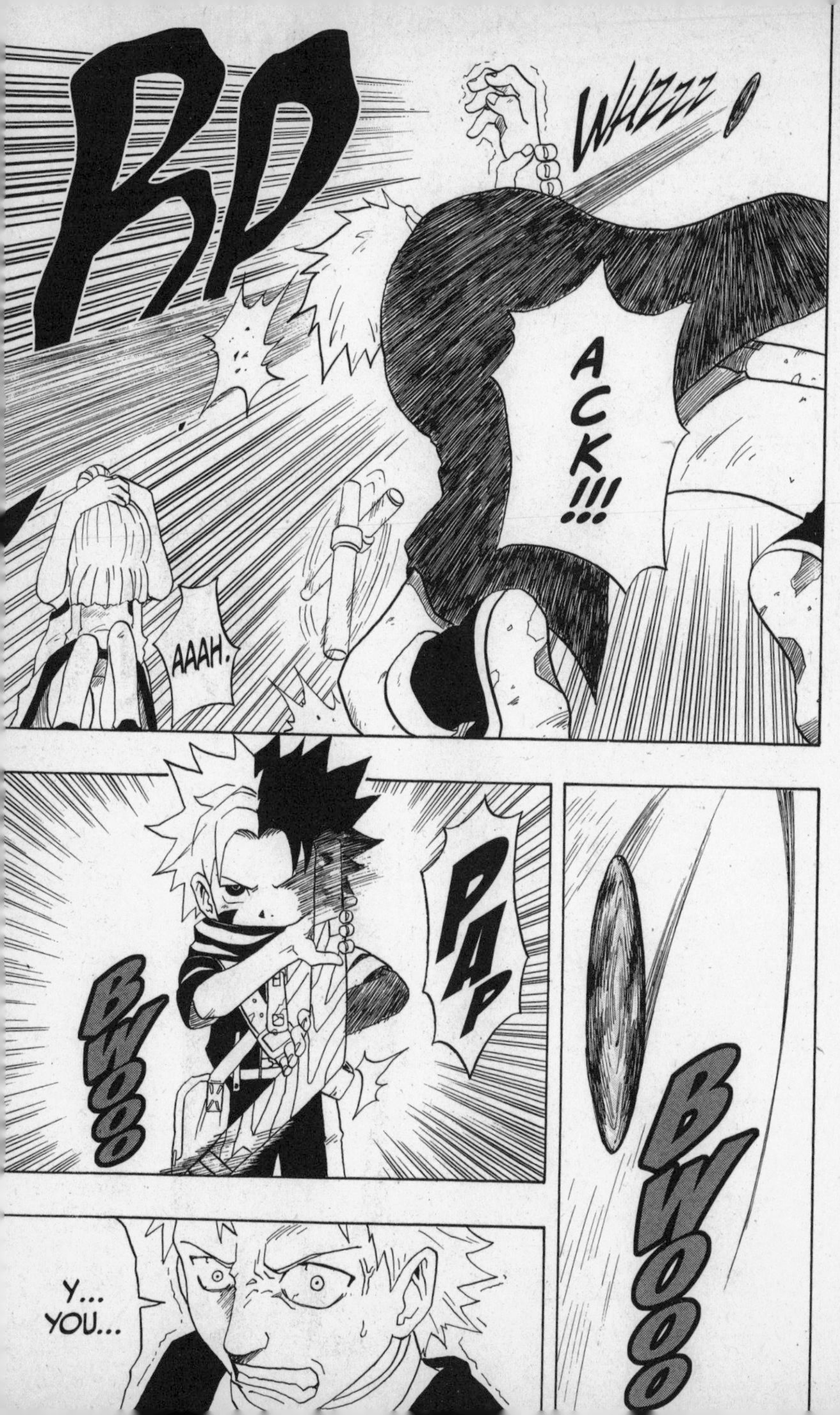
WHZZZ
BRP
ACK!!!
AAAH.
BWOOOO
PAP
BWOOO
Y... YOU...

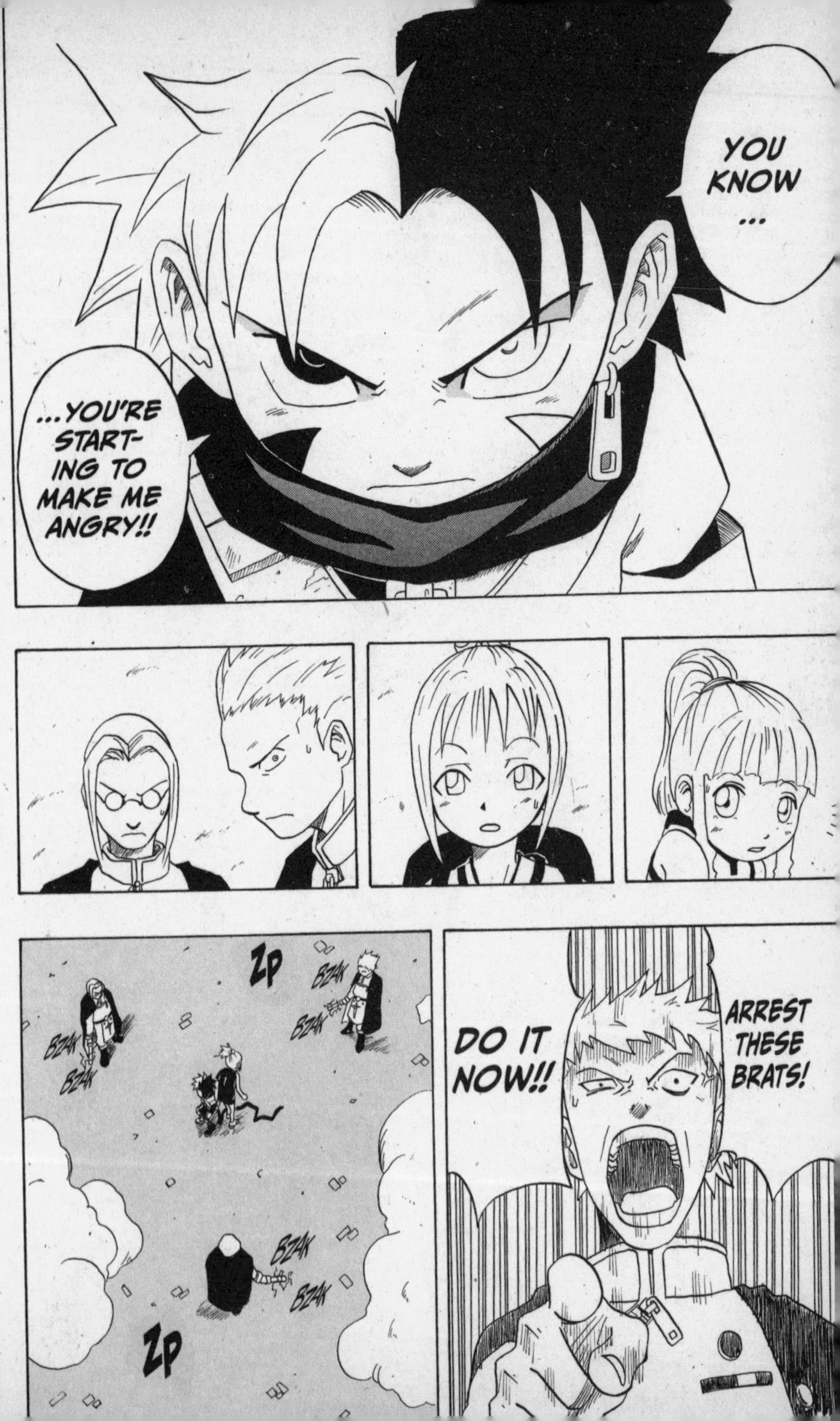
YOU KNOW ...
...YOU'RE START-ING TO MAKE ME ANGRY!!
ARREST THESE BRATS!
DO IT NOW!!
ZP
BZAK
BZAK
BZAK
BZAK
BZAK
BZAK
ZP

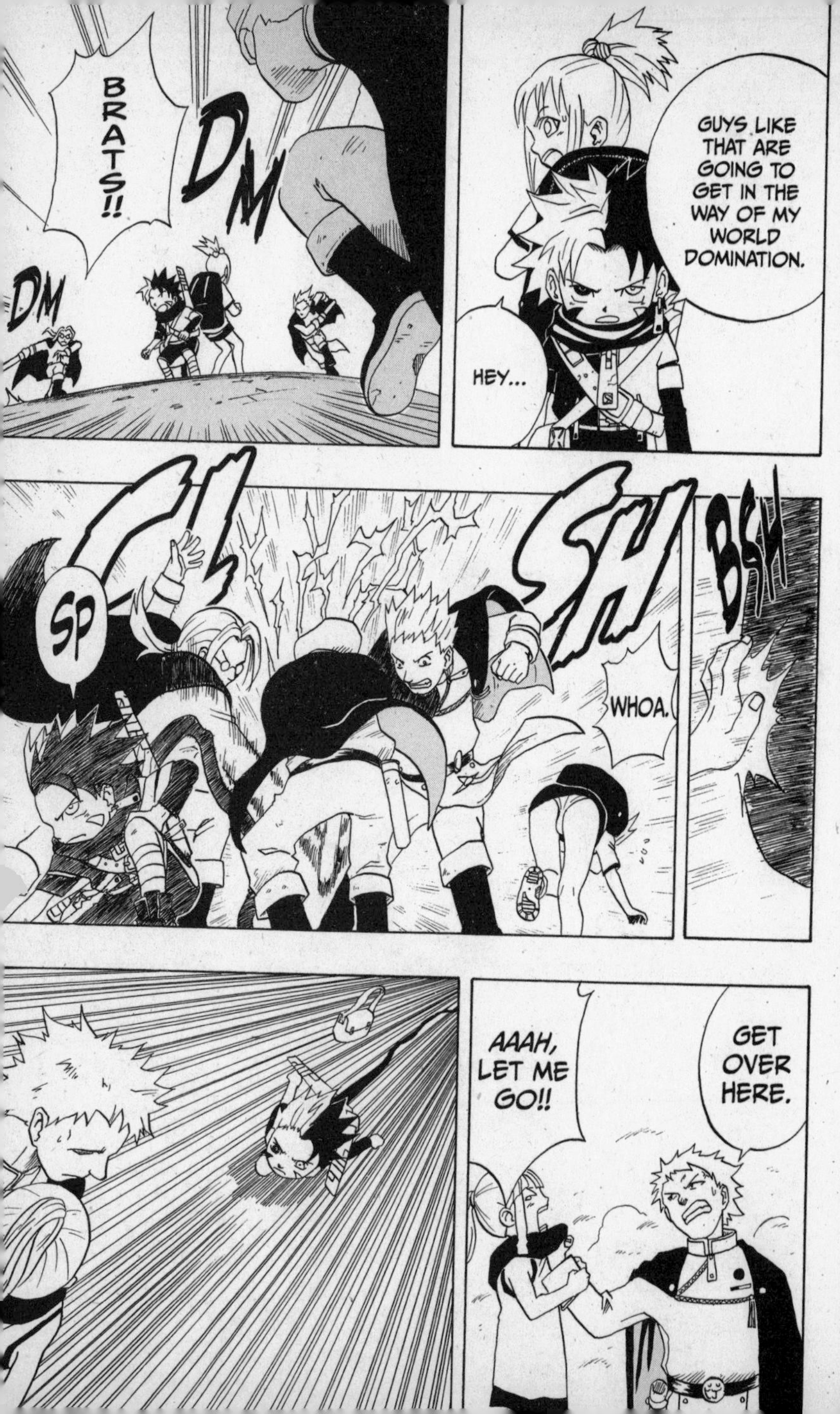
GUYS LIKE THAT ARE GOING TO GET IN THE WAY OF MY WORLD DOMINATION.
HEY...
DM
BRATS!!
DM
BSH
CL
SH
WHOA.
SP
GET OVER HERE.
AAAH, LET ME GO!!

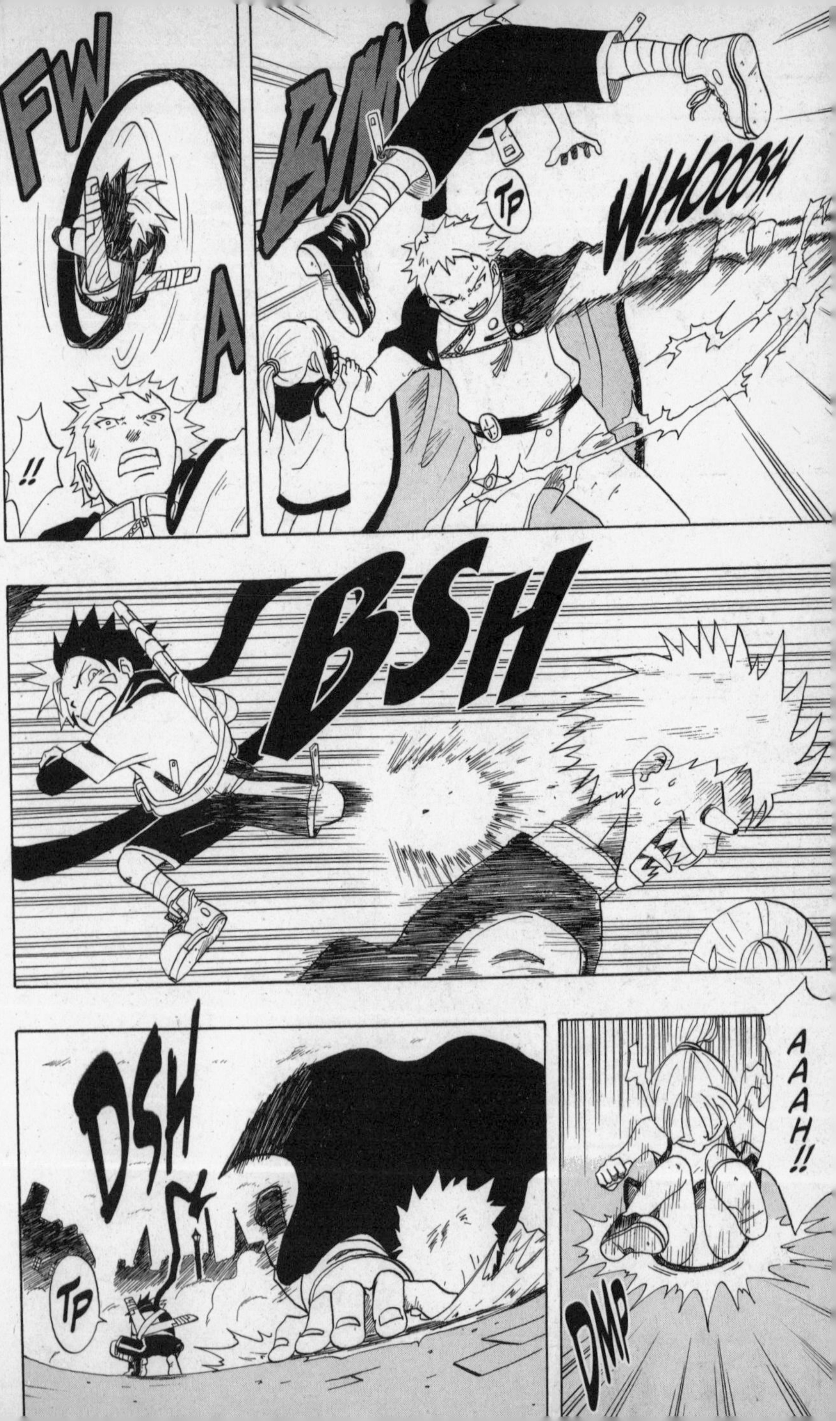
BM
TP
WHOOOSH
FW
A
!!
BSH
AAAAH!!
DMP
DSH
TP

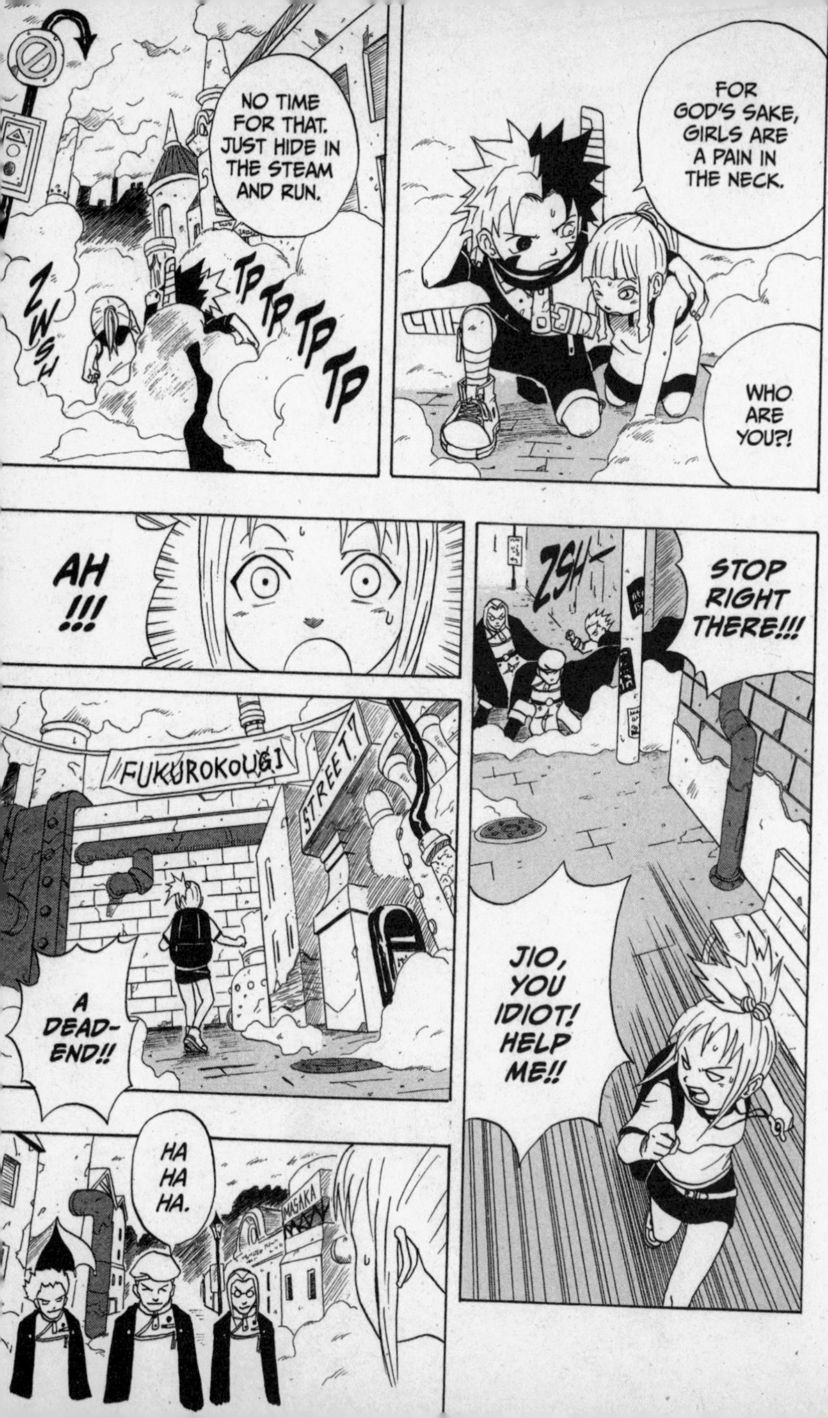
FOR GOD'S SAKE, GIRLS ARE A PAIN IN THE NECK.
WHO ARE YOU?!
NO TIME FOR THAT. JUST HIDE IN THE STEAM AND RUN.
ZWSH
TP TP TP TP
ZSH
STOP RIGHT THERE!!!
JIO, YOU IDIOT! HELP ME!!
AH!!!
FUKUROKOUGI
STREET 7
A DEAD-END!!
HA HA HA.
MASAKA

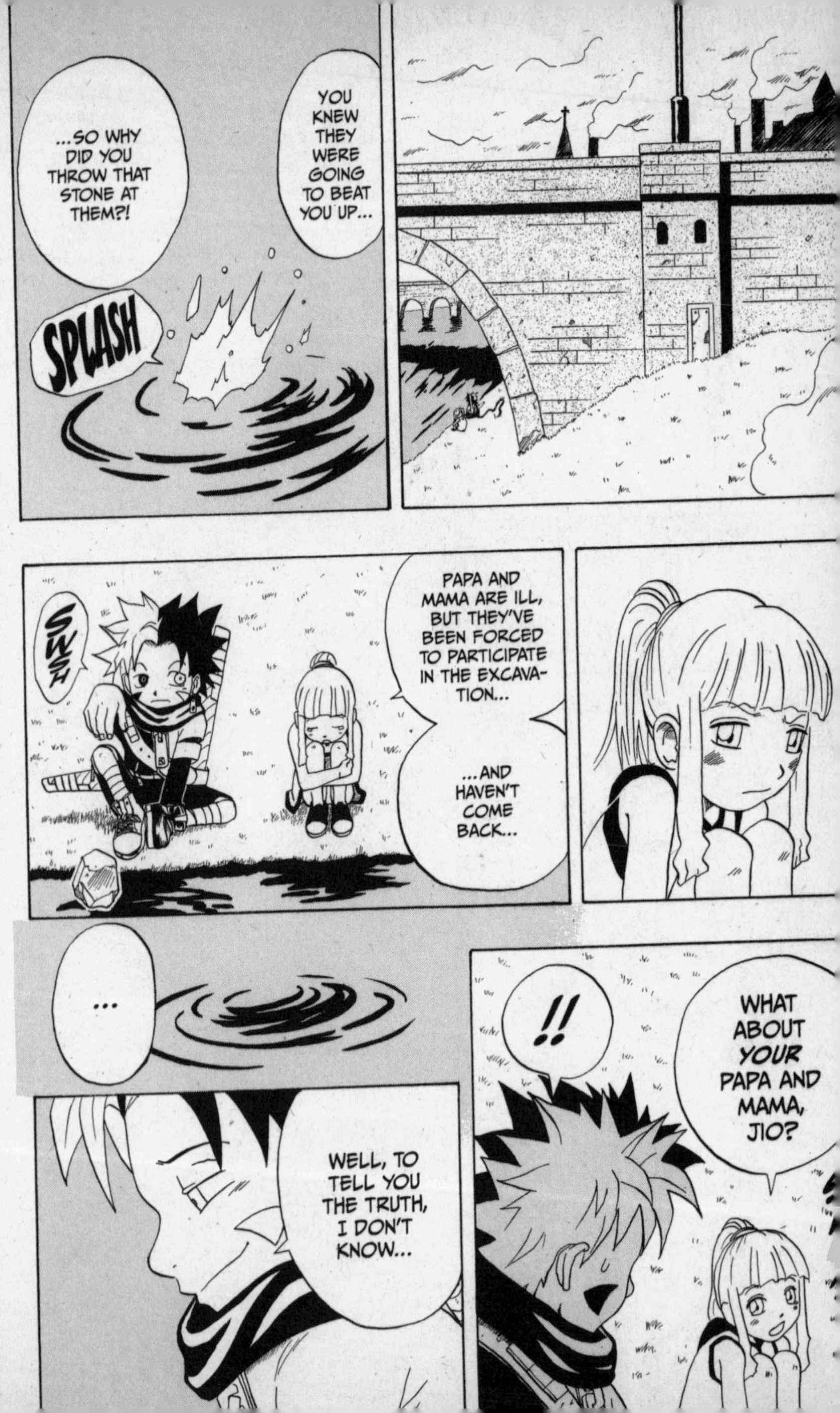
YOU KNEW THEY WERE GOING TO BEAT YOU UP...
...SO WHY DID YOU THROW THAT STONE AT THEM?!
SPLASH
PAPA AND MAMA ARE ILL, BUT THEY'VE BEEN FORCED TO PARTICIPATE IN THE EXCAVATION...
...AND HAVEN'T COME BACK...
SWSH
WHAT ABOUT *YOUR* PAPA AND MAMA, JIO?
!!
...
WELL, TO TELL YOU THE TRUTH, I DON'T KNOW...

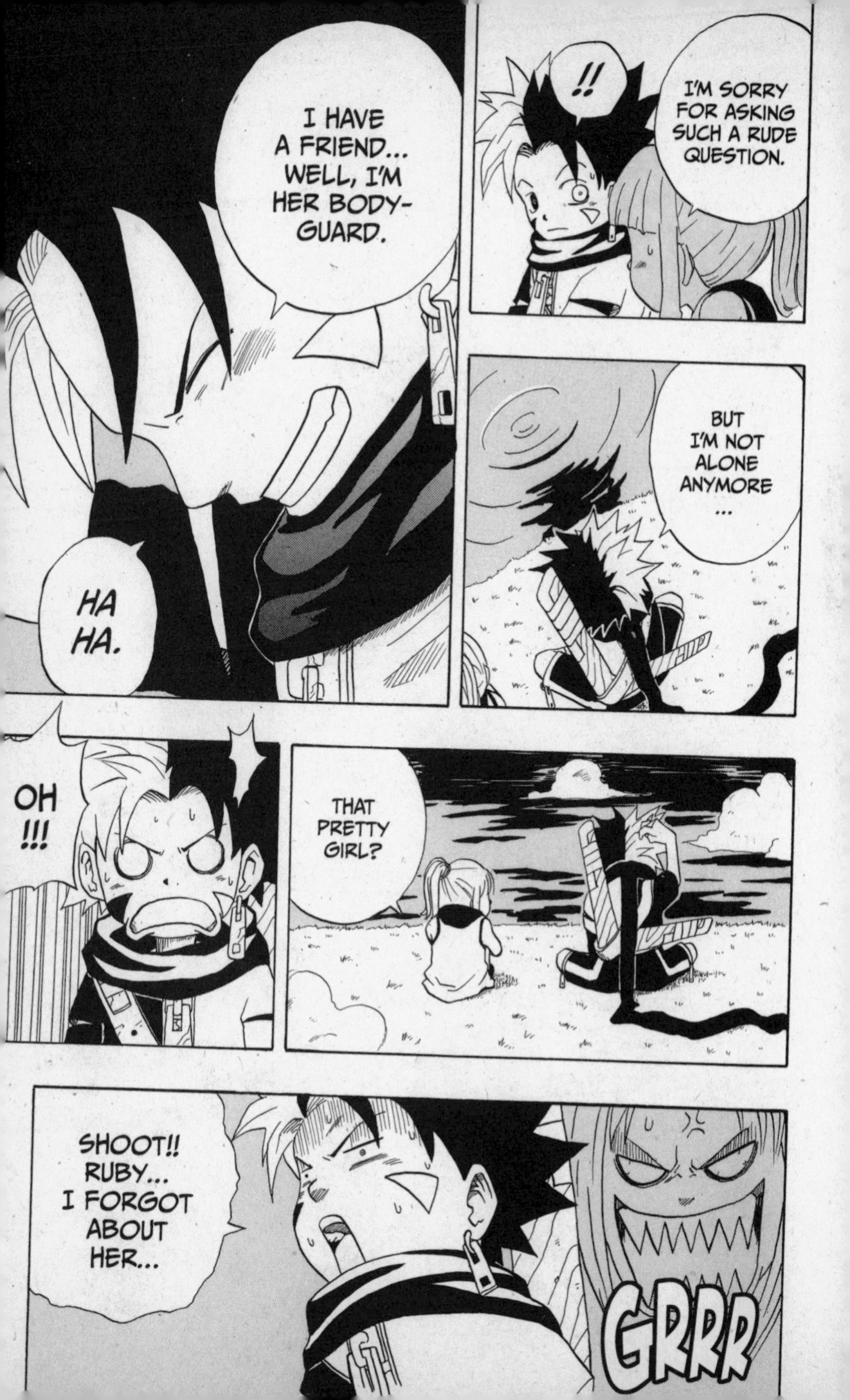
!!
I'M SORRY FOR ASKING SUCH A RUDE QUESTION.
BUT I'M NOT ALONE ANYMORE...
I HAVE A FRIEND... WELL, I'M HER BODY-GUARD.
HA HA.
THAT PRETTY GIRL?
OH !!!
SHOOT!! RUBY... I FORGOT ABOUT HER...
GRRR

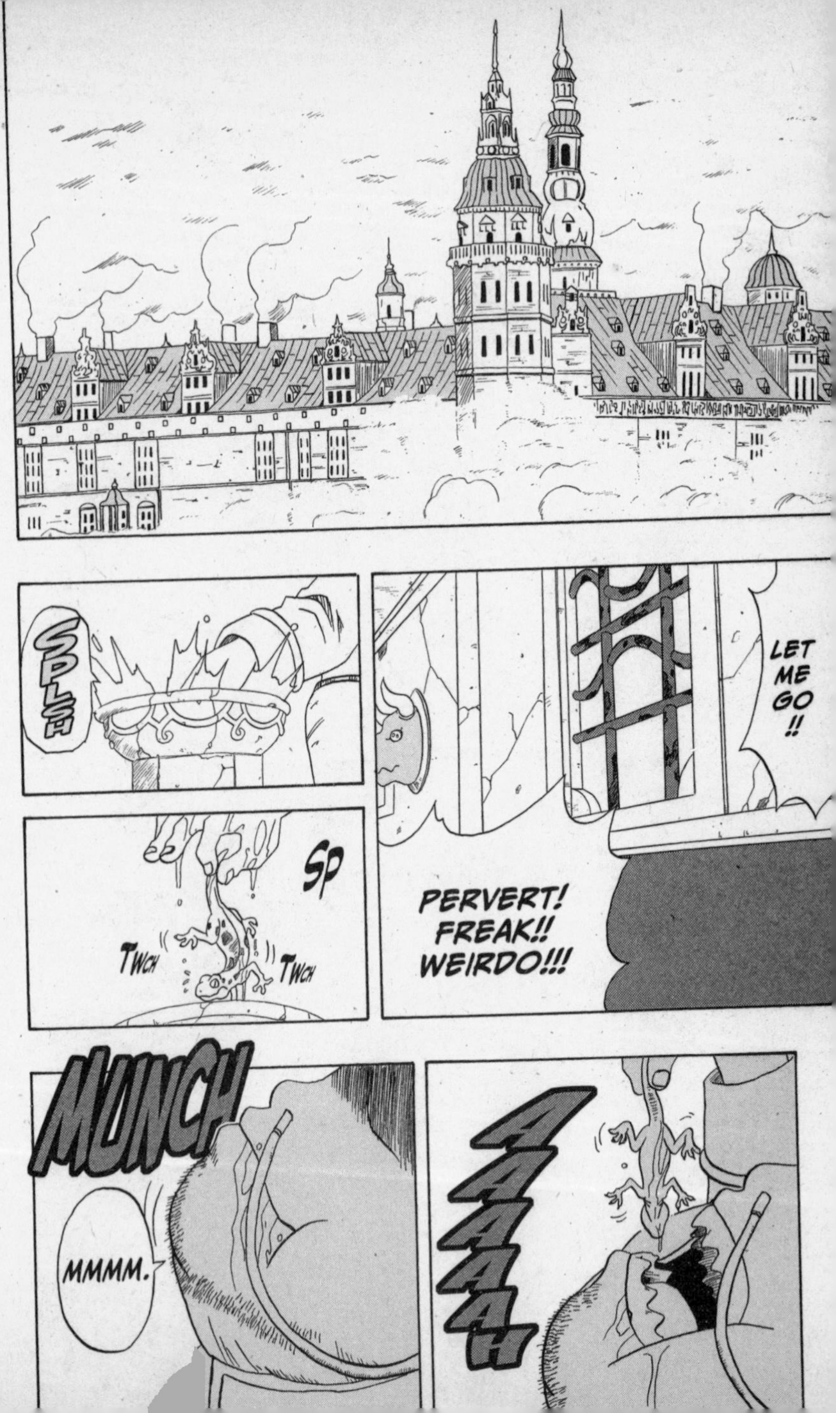
LET ME GO!!
PERVERT! FREAK!! WEIRDO!!!
SPLSH
SP
TWCH
TWCH
AAAAAH
MUNCH
MMMM.

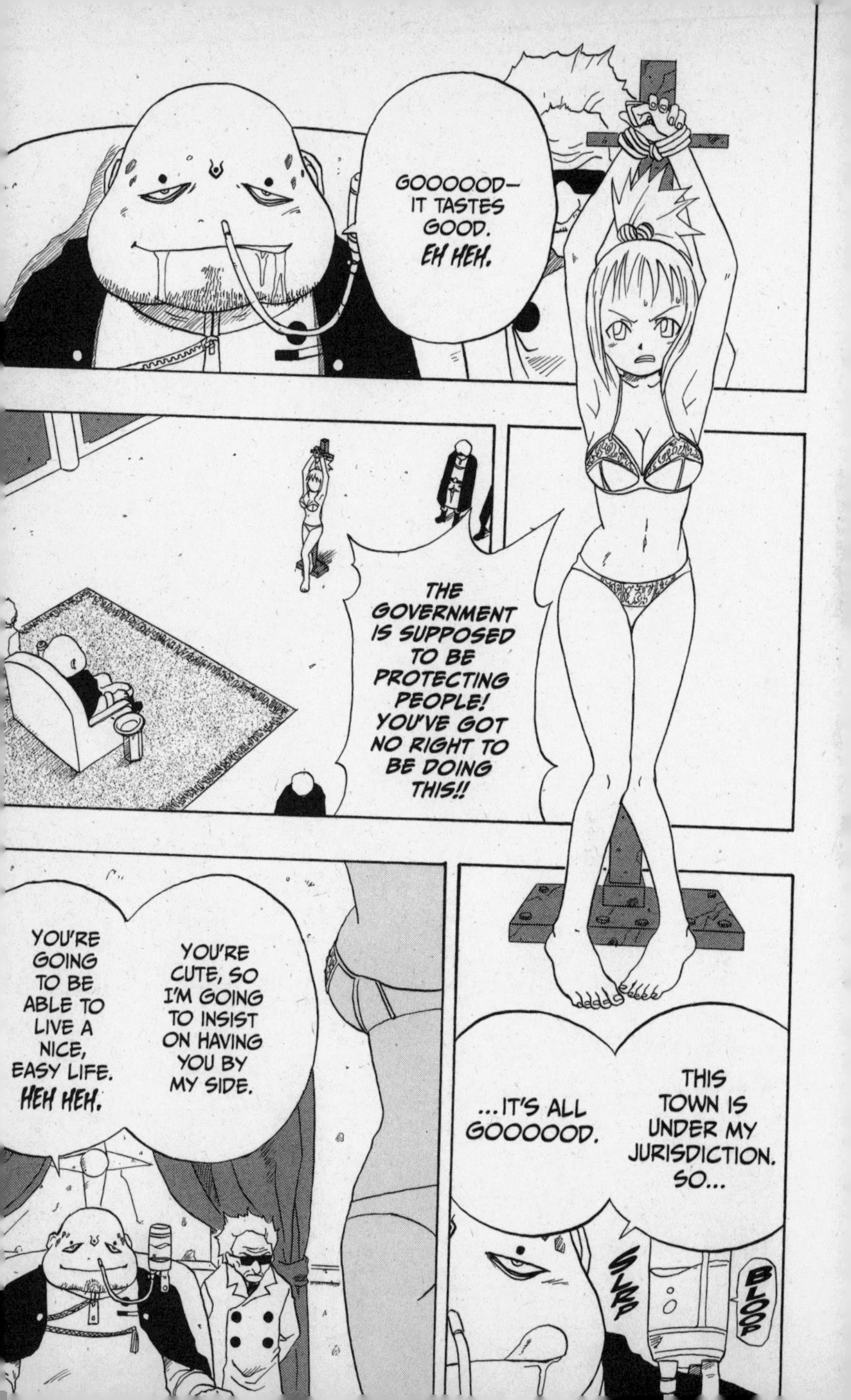

GOOOOOD— IT TASTES GOOD. EH HEH.
THE GOVERNMENT IS SUPPOSED TO BE PROTECTING PEOPLE! YOU'VE GOT NO RIGHT TO BE DOING THIS!!
THIS TOWN IS UNDER MY JURISDICTION. SO...
...IT'S ALL GOOOOOD.
SLRP
BLOOP
YOU'RE CUTE, SO I'M GOING TO INSIST ON HAVING YOU BY MY SIDE.
YOU'RE GOING TO BE ABLE TO LIVE A NICE, EASY LIFE. HEH HEH.

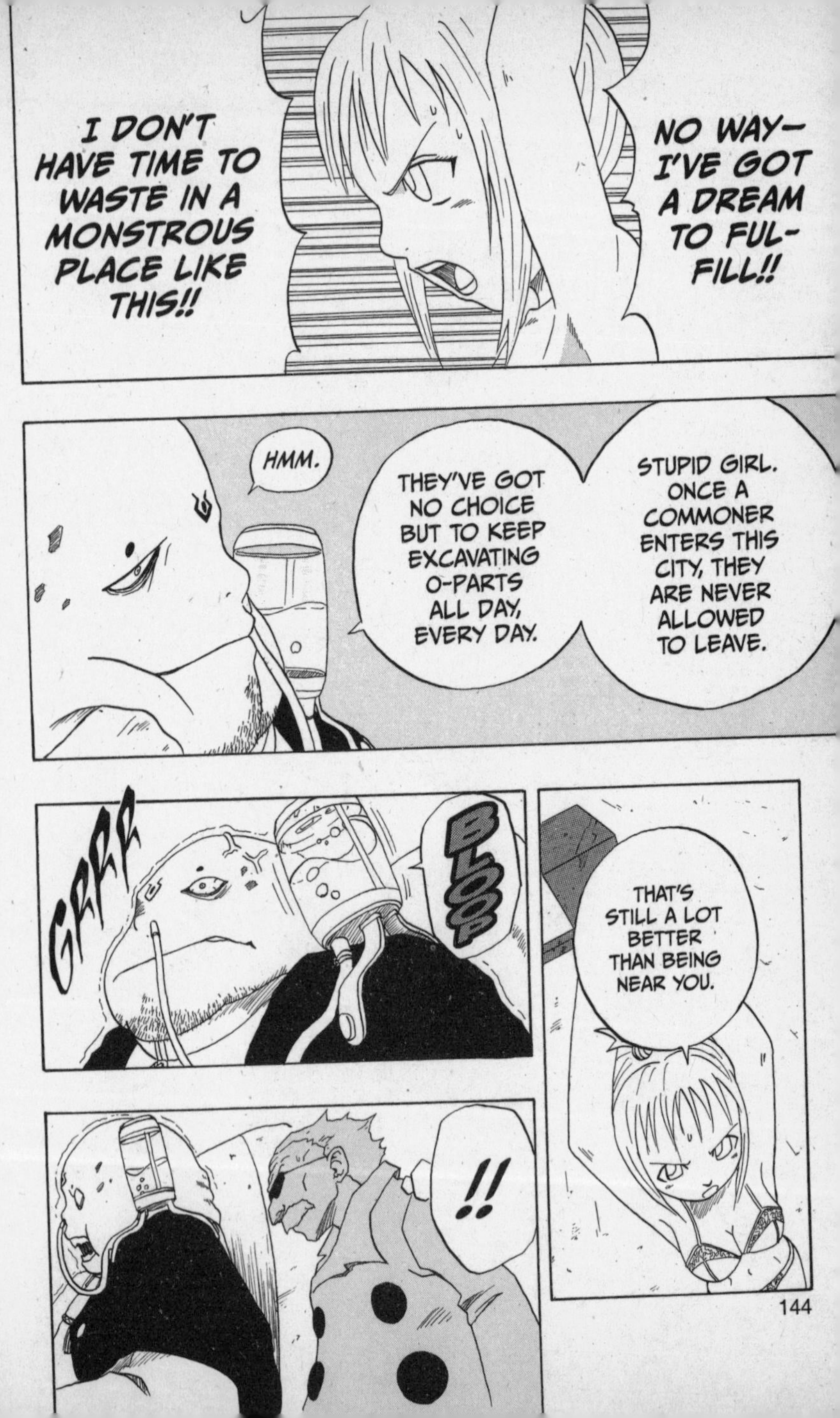
NO WAY— I'VE GOT A DREAM TO FUL-FILL!!
I DON'T HAVE TIME TO WASTE IN A MONSTROUS PLACE LIKE THIS!!
STUPID GIRL. ONCE A COMMONER ENTERS THIS CITY, THEY ARE NEVER ALLOWED TO LEAVE.
THEY'VE GOT NO CHOICE BUT TO KEEP EXCAVATING O-PARTS ALL DAY, EVERY DAY.
HMM.
THAT'S STILL A LOT BETTER THAN BEING NEAR YOU.
BLOOP
GRRR
!!

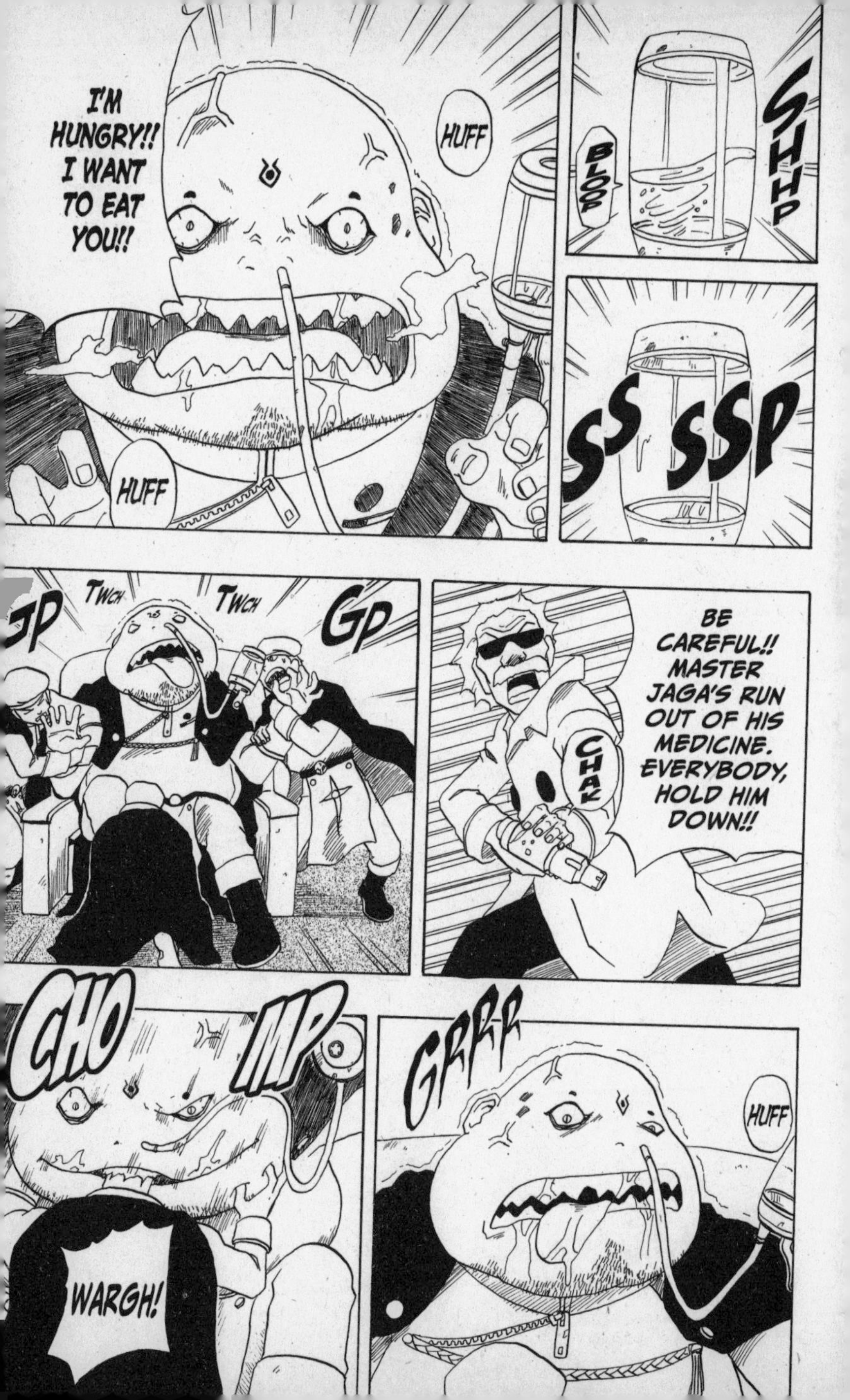
SHHP
BLOOP
SS SSP
HUFF
I'M HUNGRY!! I WANT TO EAT YOU!!
HUFF
BE CAREFUL!! MASTER JAGA'S RUN OUT OF HIS MEDICINE. EVERYBODY, HOLD HIM DOWN!!
CHAK
GP
TWCH
TWCH
HUFF
GRRR
CHO
MP
WARGH!

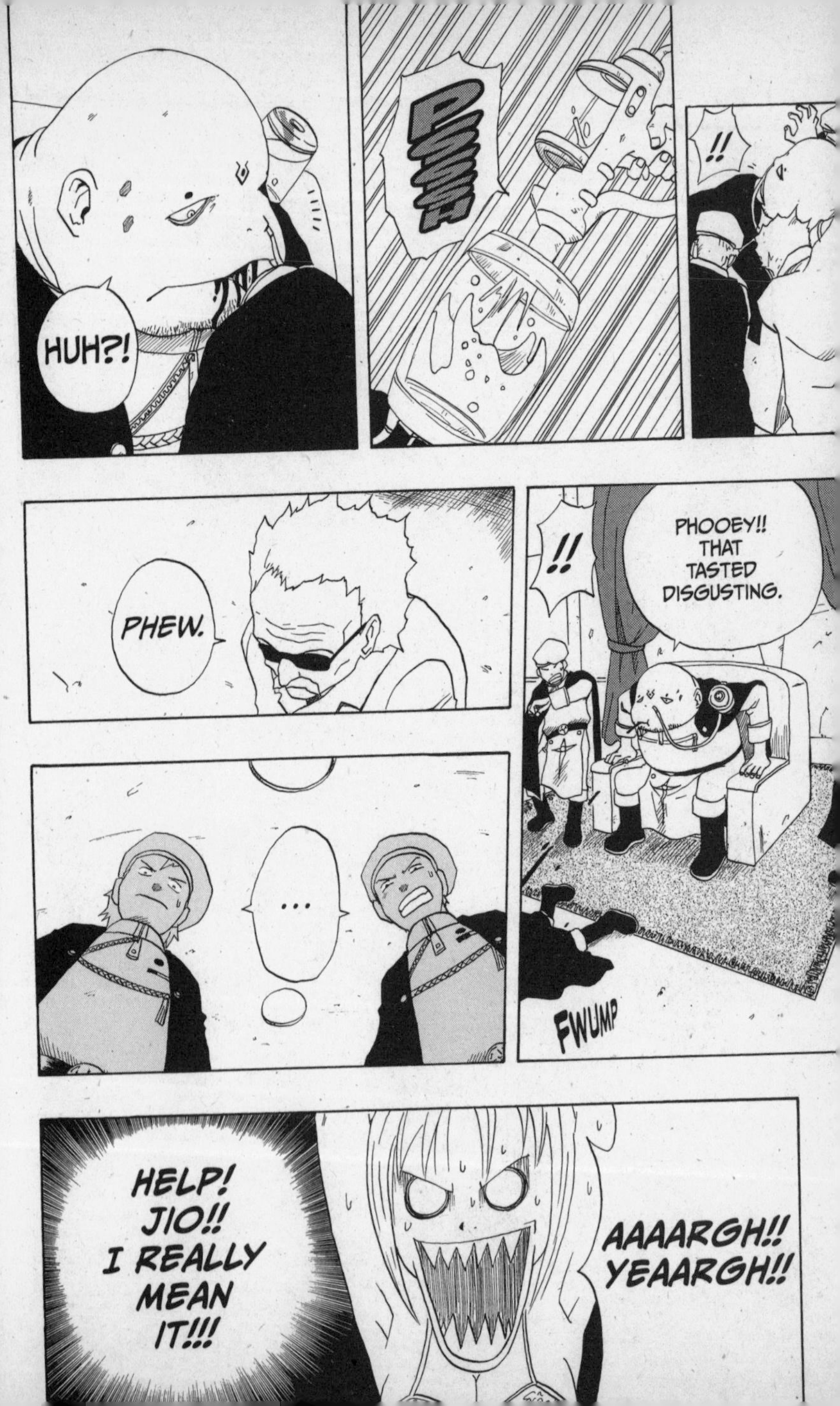
!!
HUH?!
!!
PHOOEY!! THAT TASTED DISGUSTING.
FWUMP
PHEW.
...
AAAARGH!! YEAARGH!!
HELP! JIO!! I REALLY MEAN IT!!!

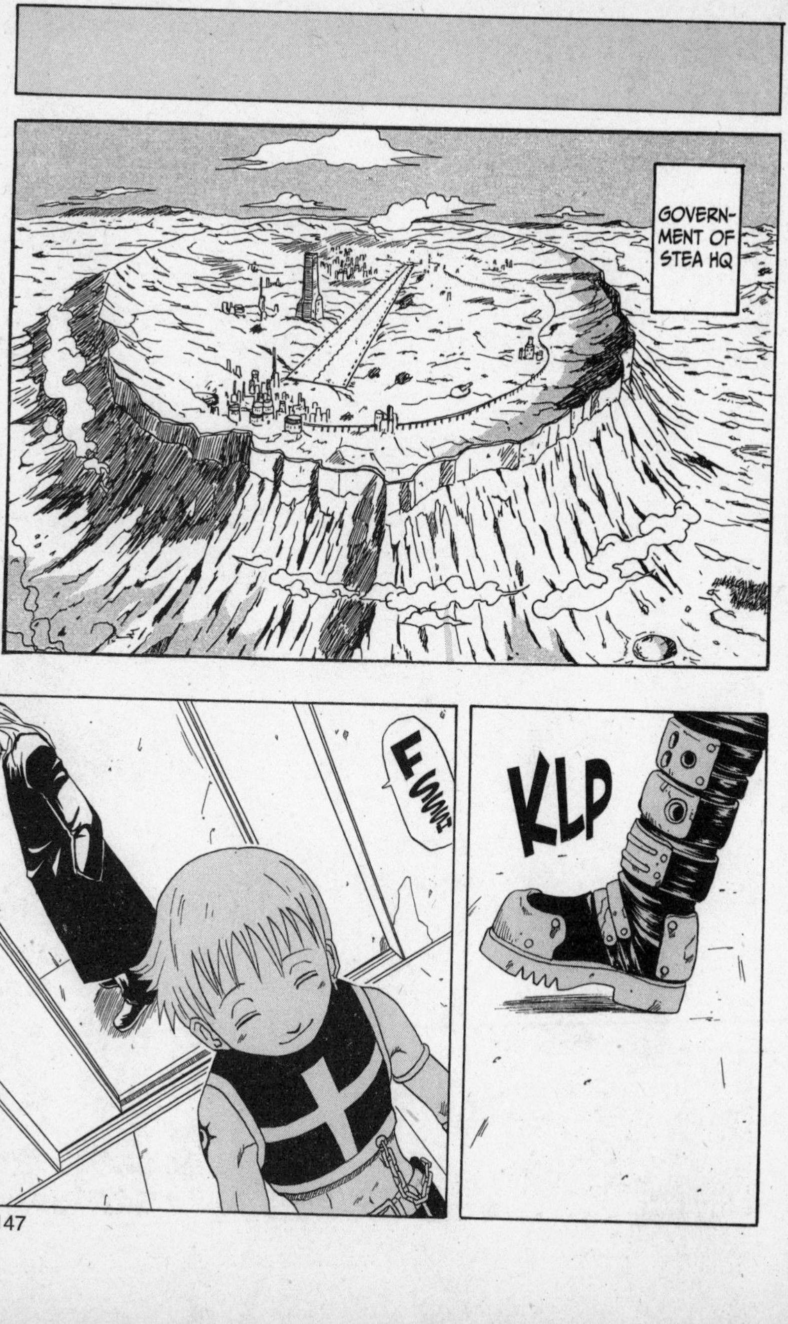
GOVERN-
MENT OF
STEA HQ
KLP

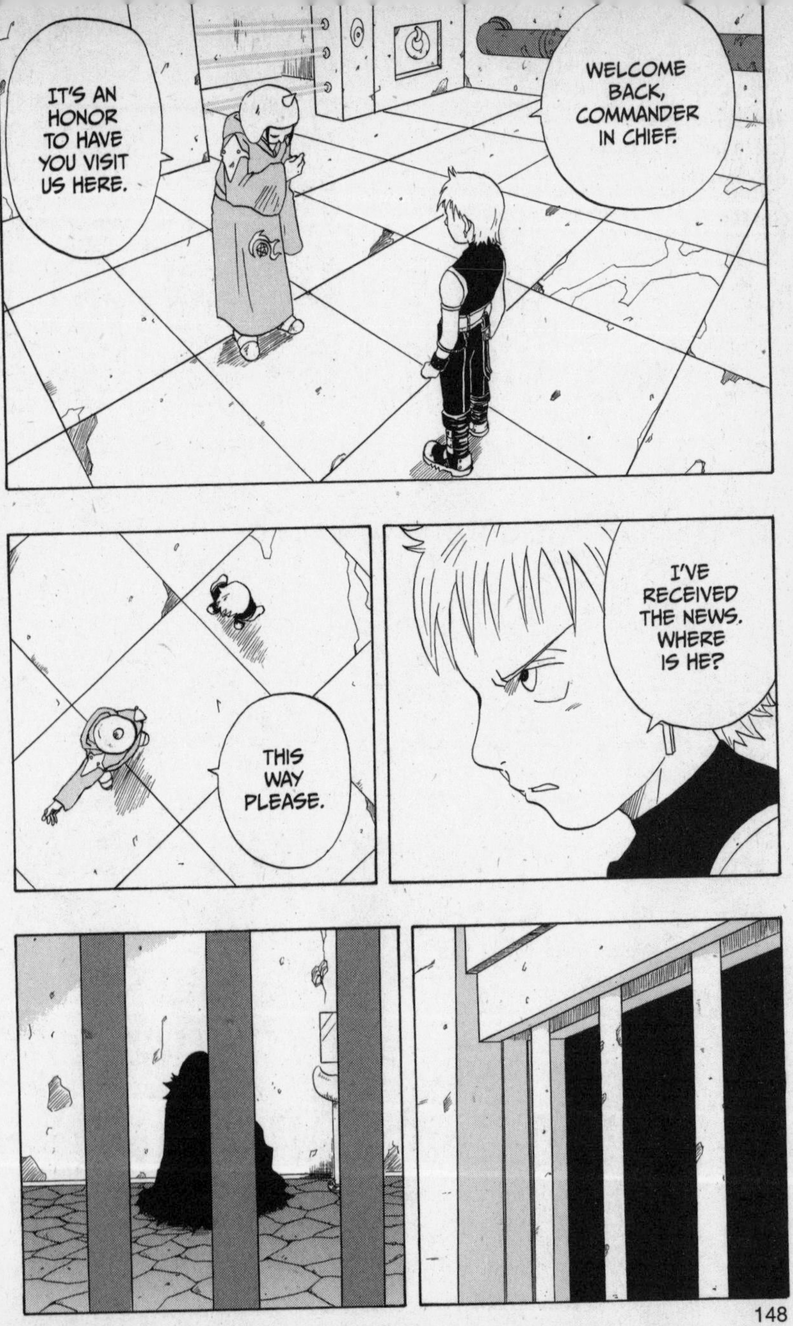
WELCOME BACK, COMMANDER IN CHIEF.
IT'S AN HONOR TO HAVE YOU VISIT US HERE.
I'VE RECEIVED THE NEWS. WHERE IS HE?
THIS WAY PLEASE.

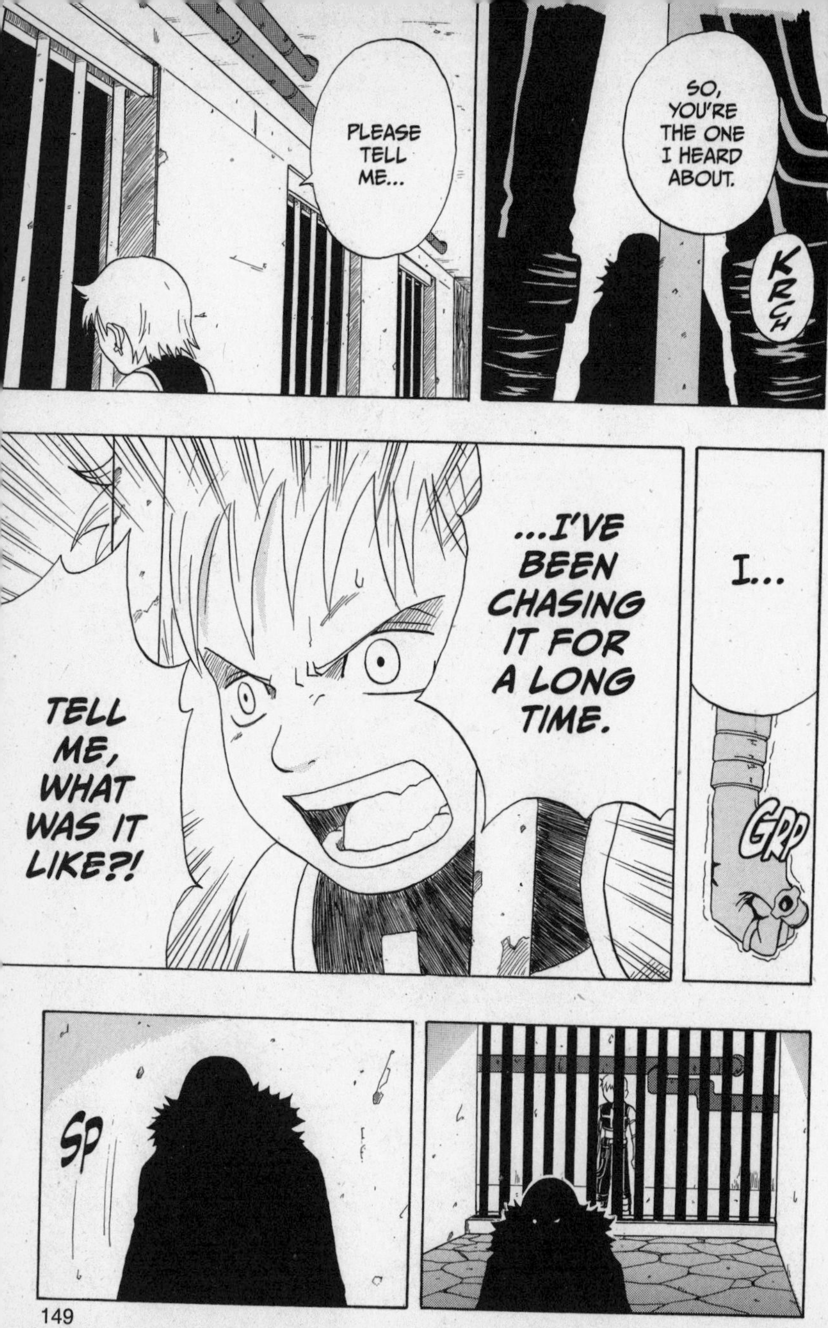
SO, YOU'RE THE ONE I HEARD ABOUT.
KRCH
PLEASE TELL ME...
I...
GRP
...I'VE BEEN CHASING IT FOR A LONG TIME.
TELL ME, WHAT WAS IT LIKE?!
SP

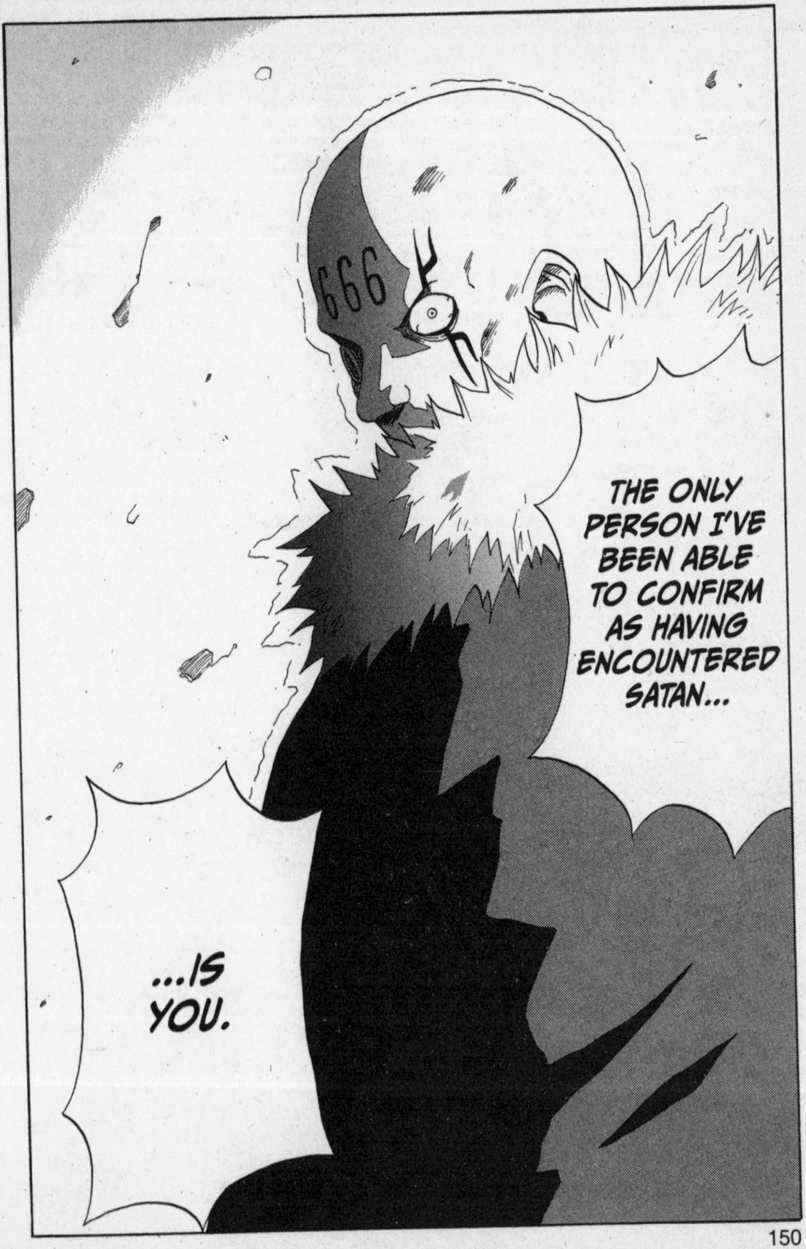
THE ONLY PERSON I'VE BEEN ABLE TO CONFIRM AS HAVING ENCOUNTERED SATAN...
...IS YOU.

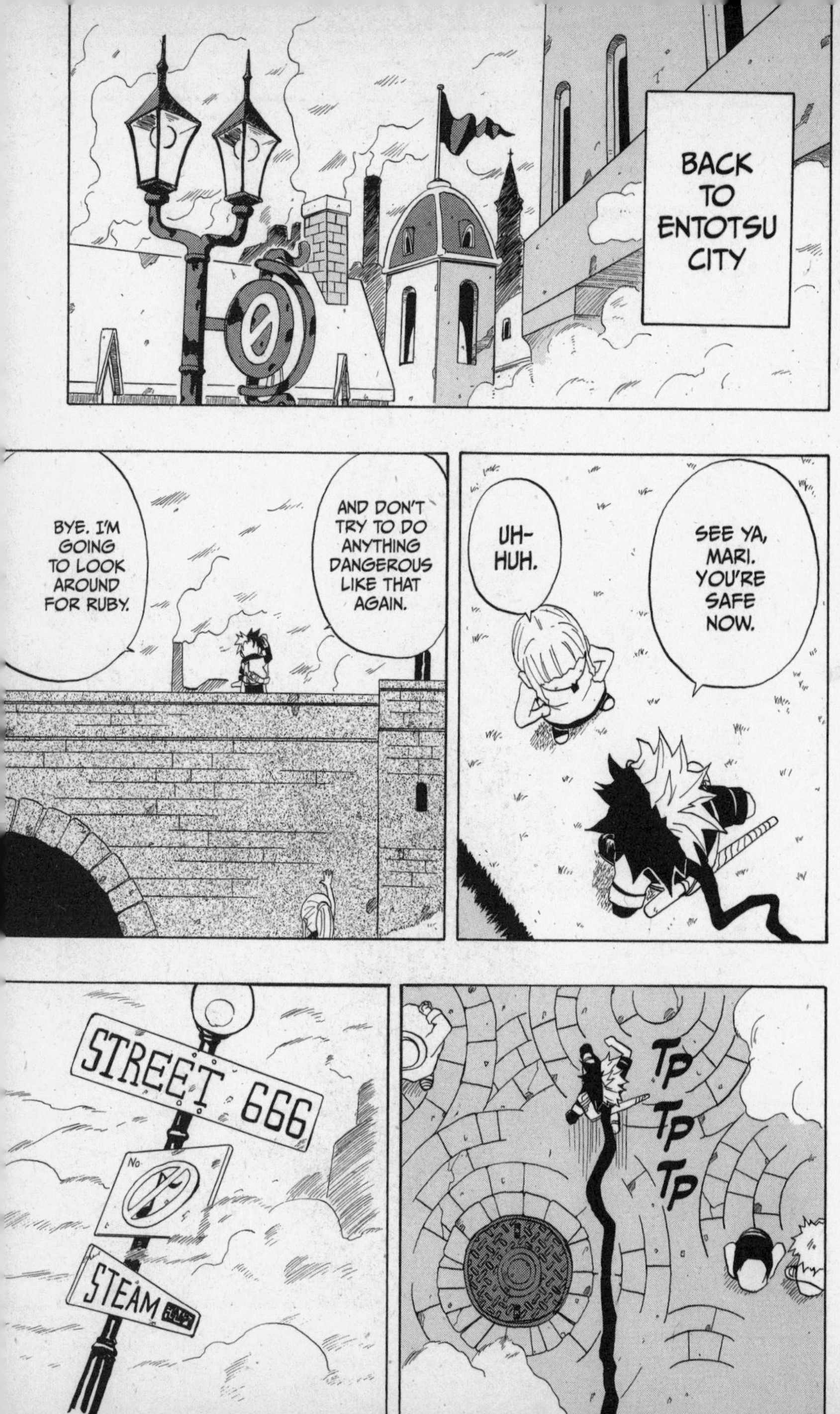
BACK TO ENTOTSU CITY
SEE YA, MARI. YOU'RE SAFE NOW.
UH-HUH.
AND DON'T TRY TO DO ANYTHING DANGEROUS LIKE THAT AGAIN.
BYE. I'M GOING TO LOOK AROUND FOR RUBY.
TP TP TP TP
STREET 666
No
STEAM

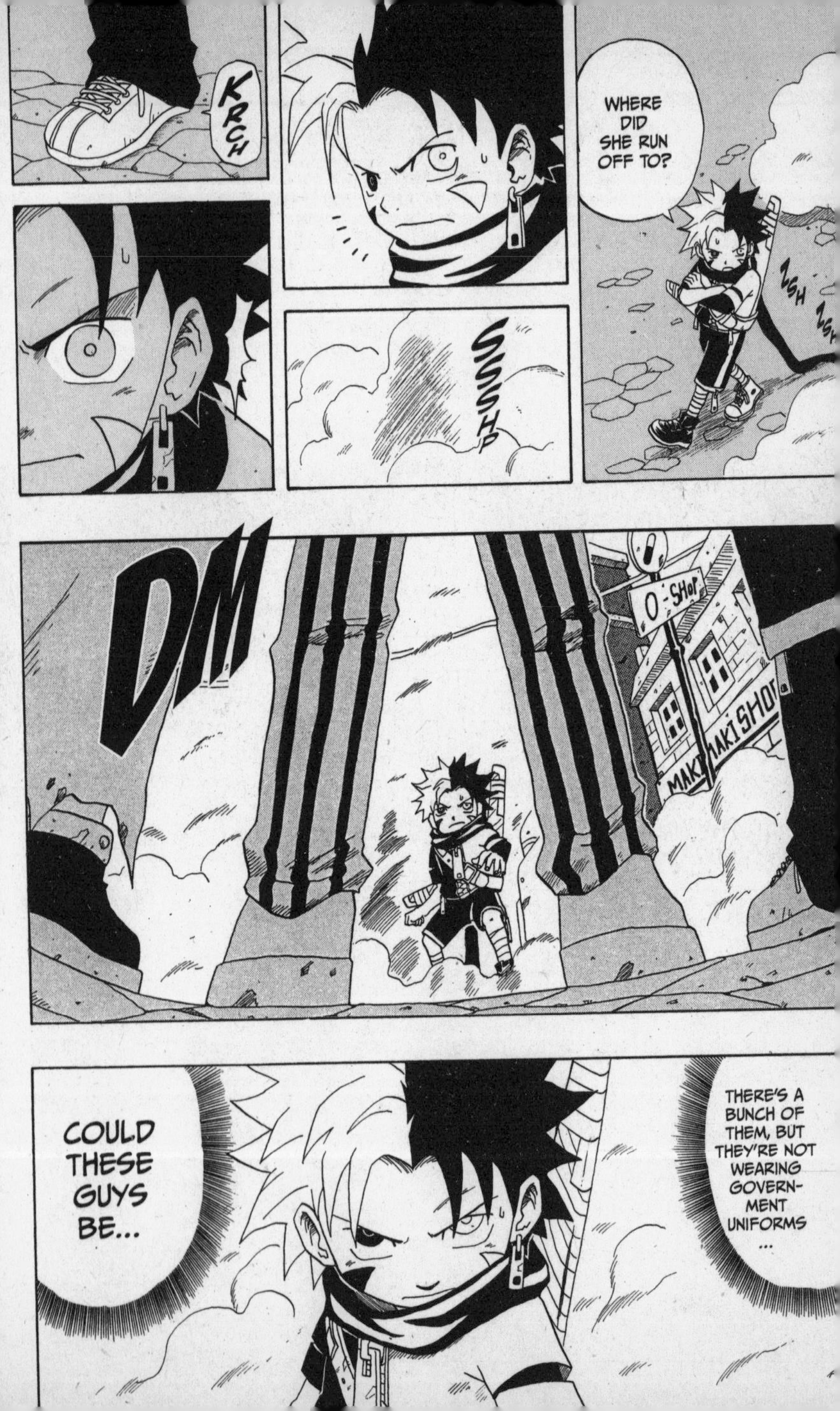
WHERE DID SHE RUN OFF TO?
ZSH
ZSH
SSSHP
KRCH
DM
O-SHOP
MAKIMAKI SHOP
THERE'S A BUNCH OF THEM, BUT THEY'RE NOT WEARING GOVERNMENT UNIFORMS...
COULD THESE GUYS BE...

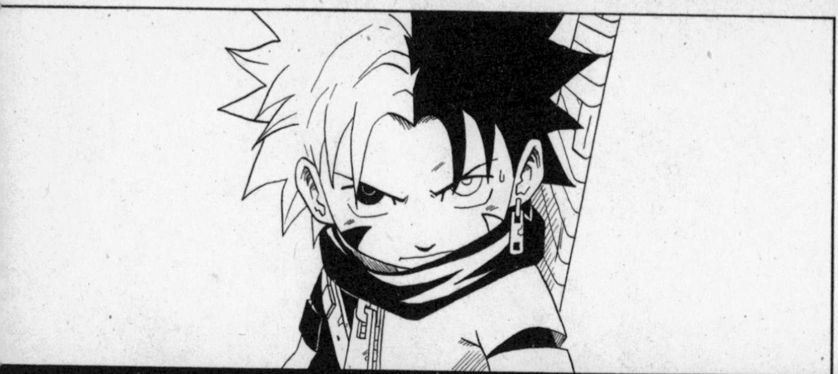

CHAPTER 8: RESISTANCE MOVEMENT

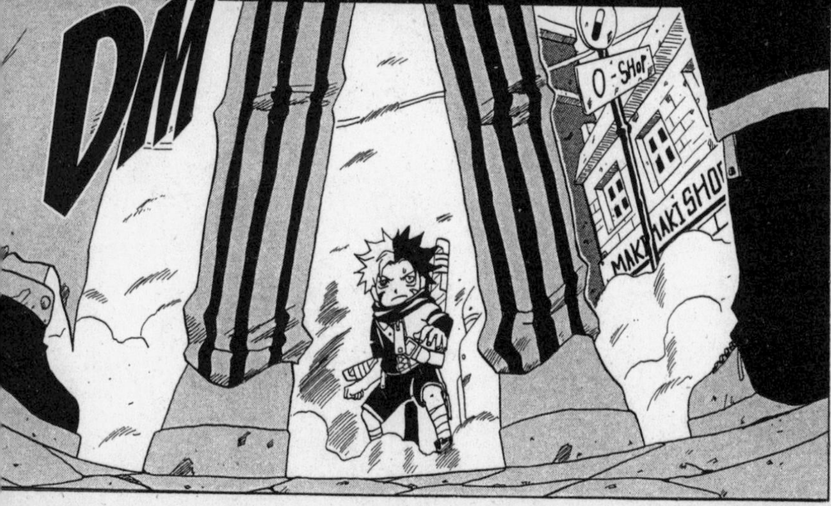
DM
O-SHOP

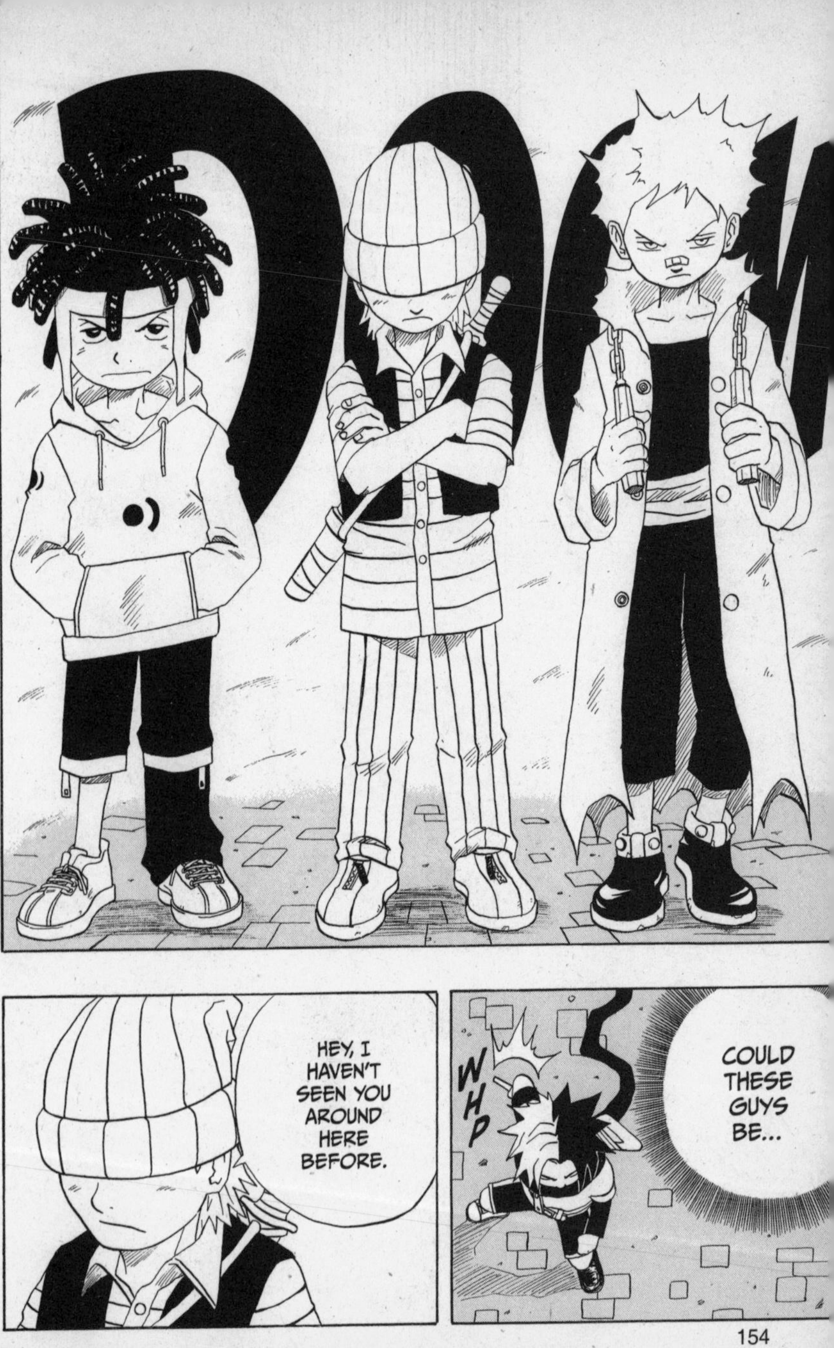
DOOM
WHP
COULD THESE GUYS BE...
HEY, I HAVEN'T SEEN YOU AROUND HERE BEFORE.

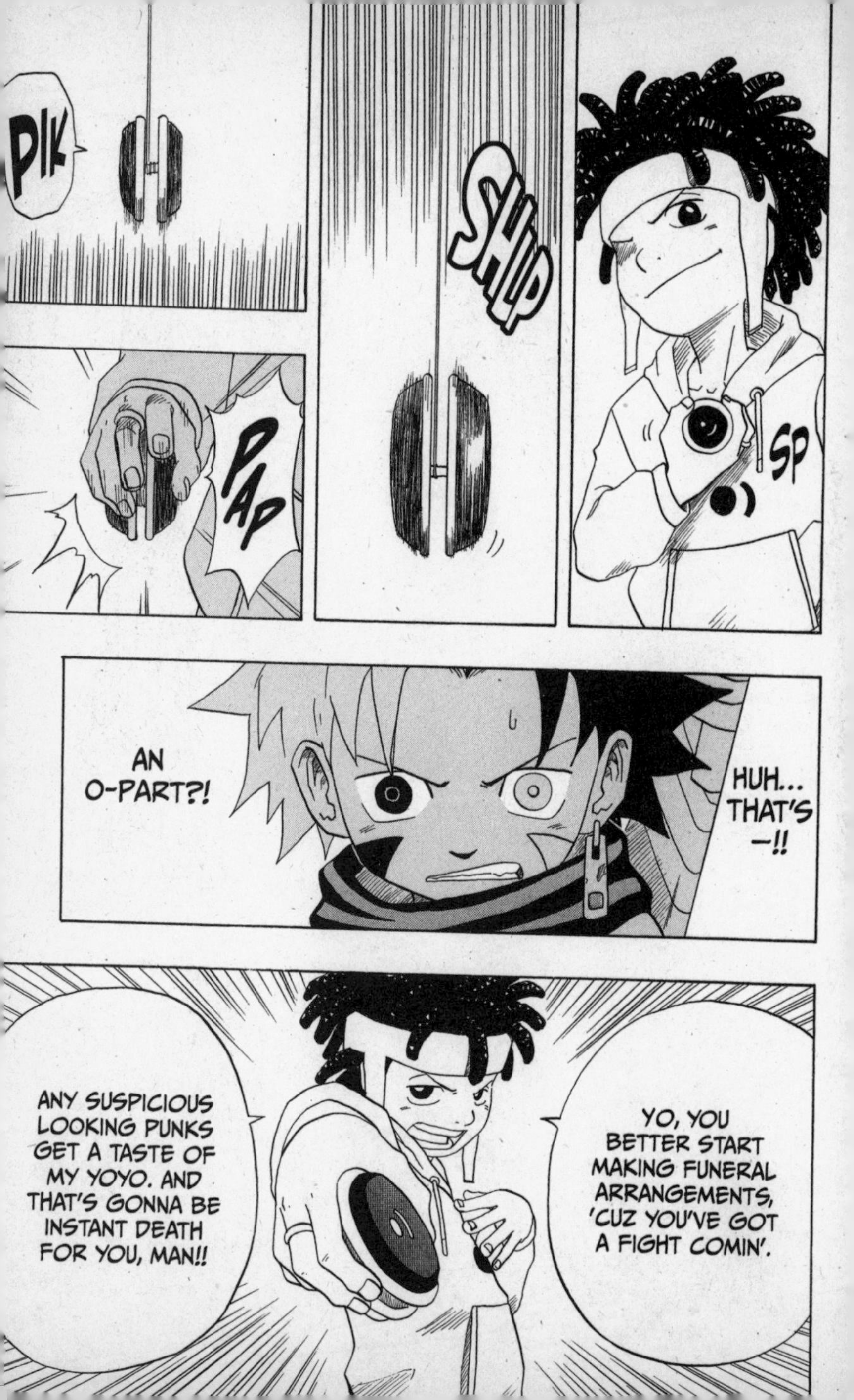
SP
SHUP
PIK
PAP
HUH... THAT'S —!!
AN O-PART?!
YO, YOU BETTER START MAKING FUNERAL ARRANGEMENTS, 'CUZ YOU'VE GOT A FIGHT COMIN'.
ANY SUSPICIOUS LOOKING PUNKS GET A TASTE OF MY YOYO. AND THAT'S GONNA BE INSTANT DEATH FOR YOU, MAN!!

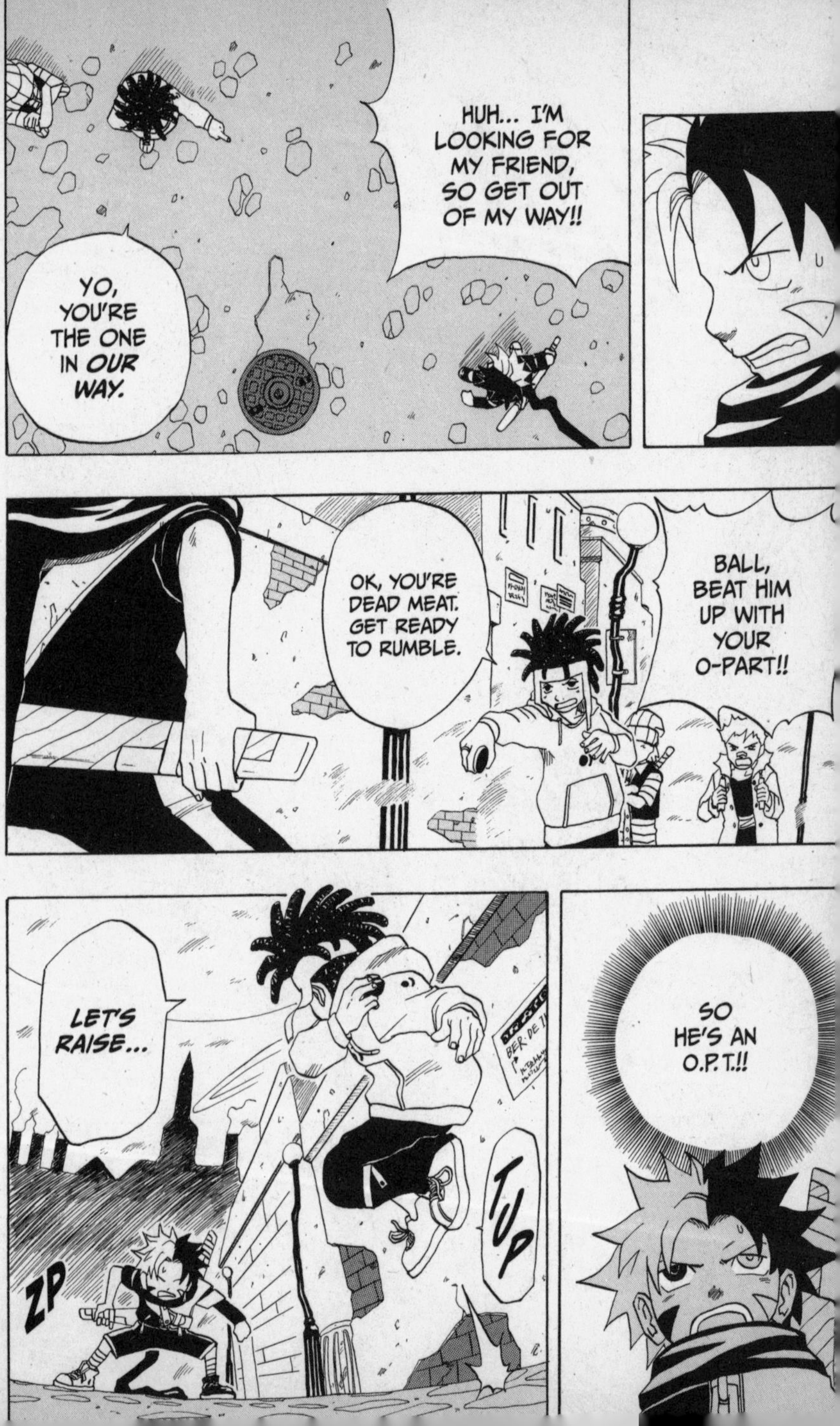
HUH... I'M LOOKING FOR MY FRIEND, SO GET OUT OF MY WAY!!
YO, YOU'RE THE ONE IN *OUR* WAY.
BALL, BEAT HIM UP WITH YOUR O-PART!!
OK, YOU'RE DEAD MEAT. GET READY TO RUMBLE.
SO HE'S AN O.P.T.!!
LET'S RAISE...
TUP
ZP

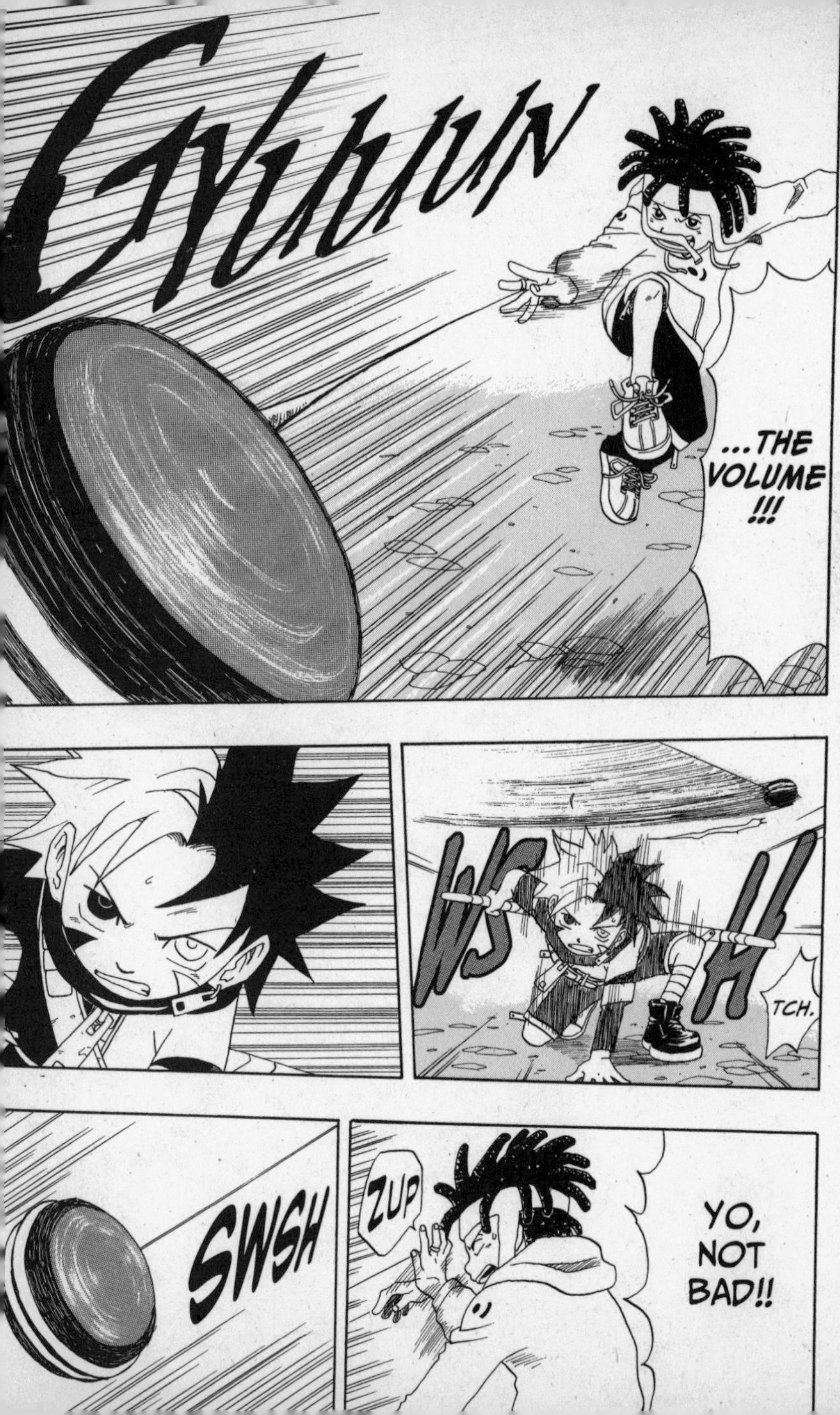
Gyuuun
...THE VOLUME !!!
WSH
TCH.
ZUP
YO, NOT BAD!!
SWSH

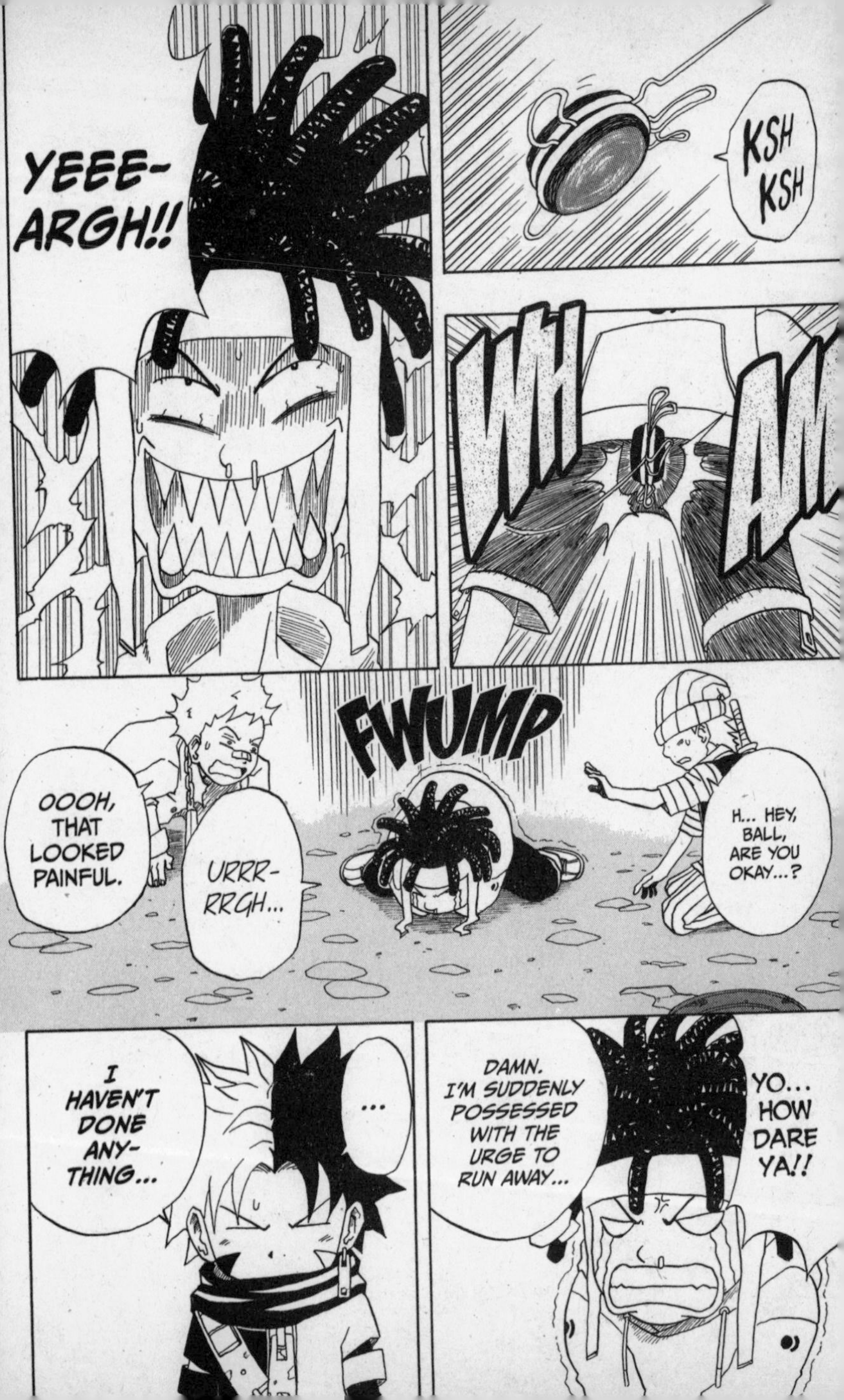
KSH KSH
WH AM
YEEEE-ARGH!!
FWUMP
H... HEY, BALL, ARE YOU OKAY...?
OOOH, THAT LOOKED PAINFUL.
URRR-RRGH...
YO... HOW DARE YA!!
DAMN. I'M SUDDENLY POSSESSED WITH THE URGE TO RUN AWAY...
...
I HAVEN'T DONE ANY-THING...

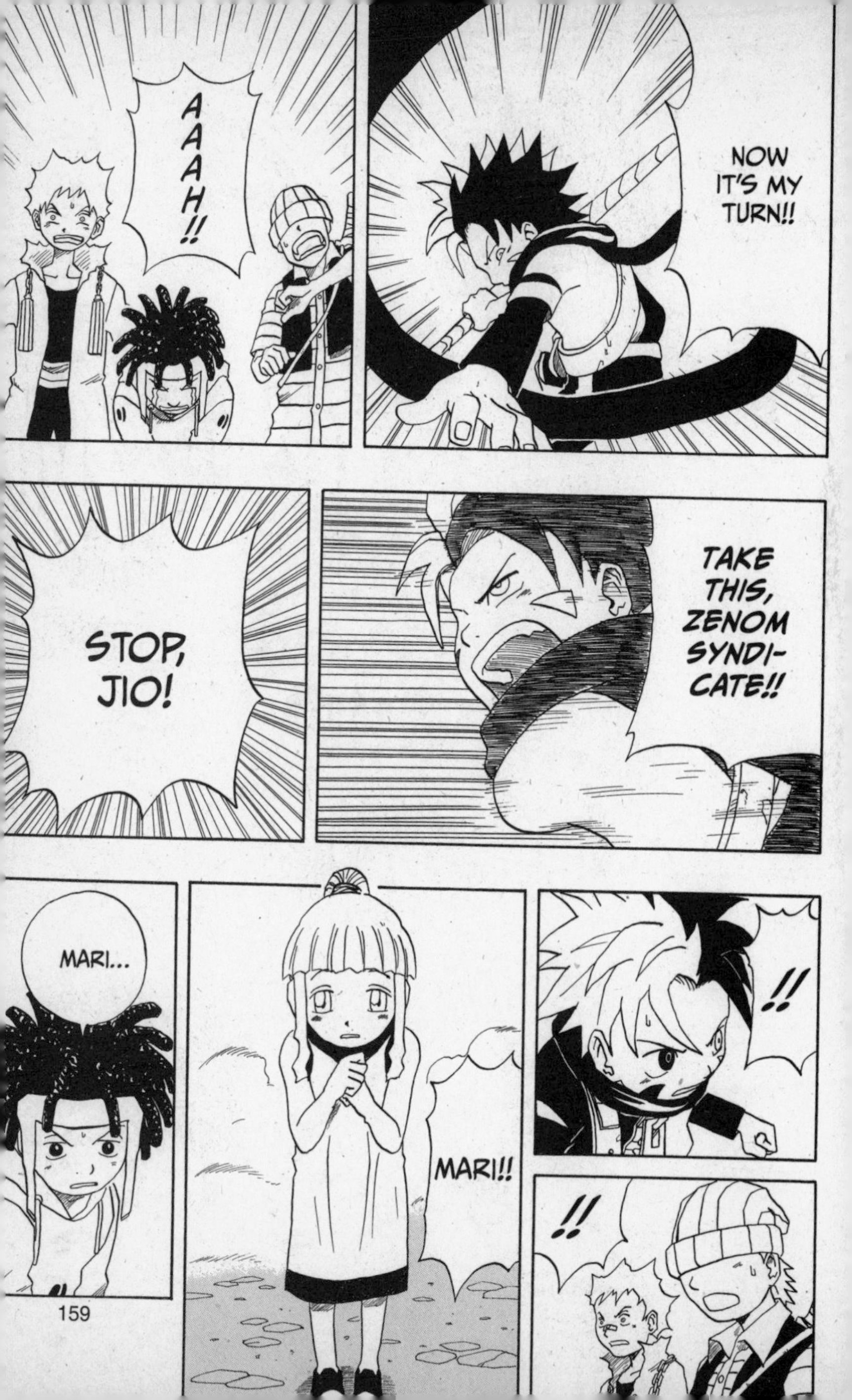
NOW IT'S MY TURN!!
AAAAH!!
TAKE THIS, ZENOM SYNDI-CATE!!
STOP, JIO!
!!
!!
MARI!!
MARI...

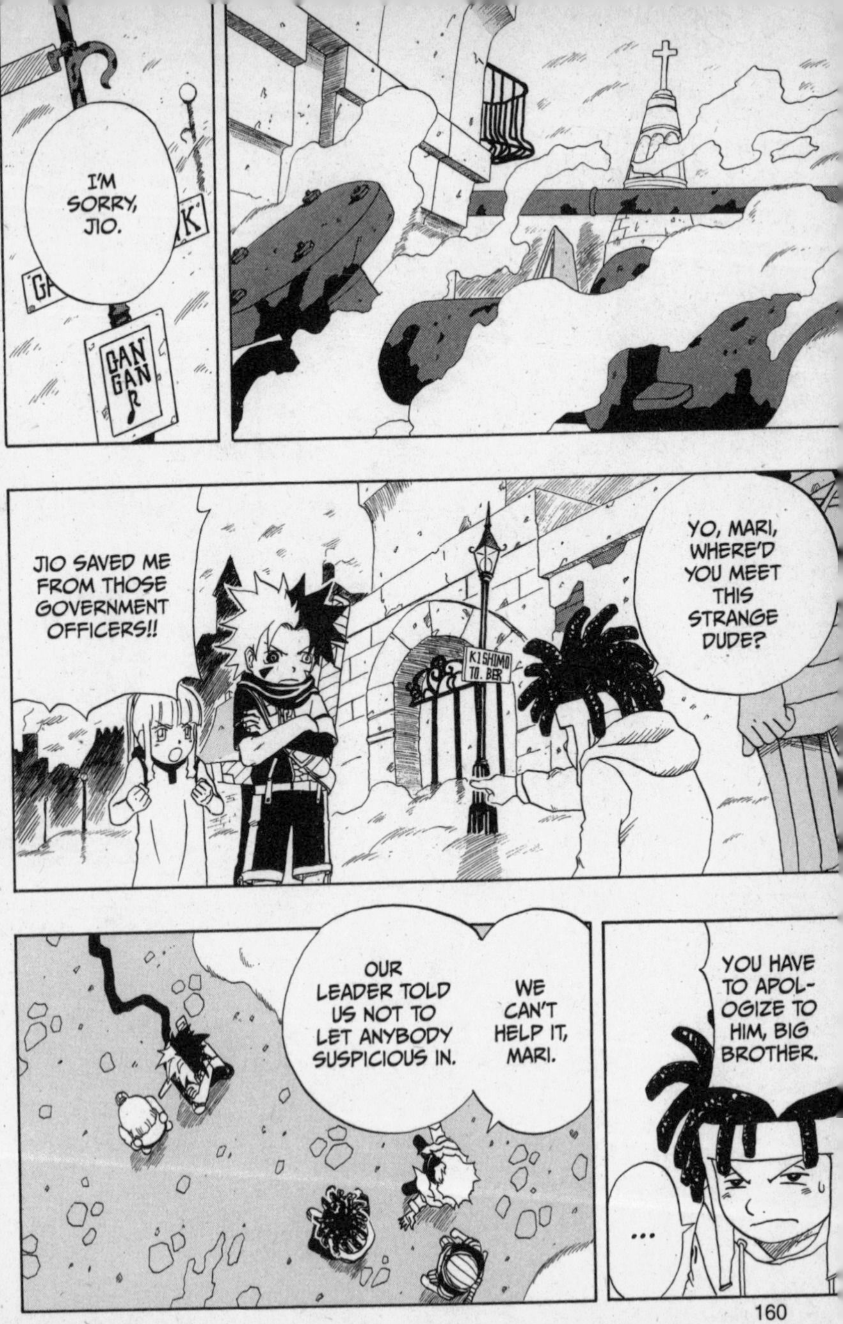
GAN GAN
I'M SORRY, JIO.
YO, MARI, WHERE'D YOU MEET THIS STRANGE DUDE?
KISHIMO TO. BER
JIO SAVED ME FROM THOSE GOVERNMENT OFFICERS!!
YOU HAVE TO APOLOGIZE TO HIM, BIG BROTHER.
...
WE CAN'T HELP IT, MARI.
OUR LEADER TOLD US NOT TO LET ANYBODY SUSPICIOUS IN.

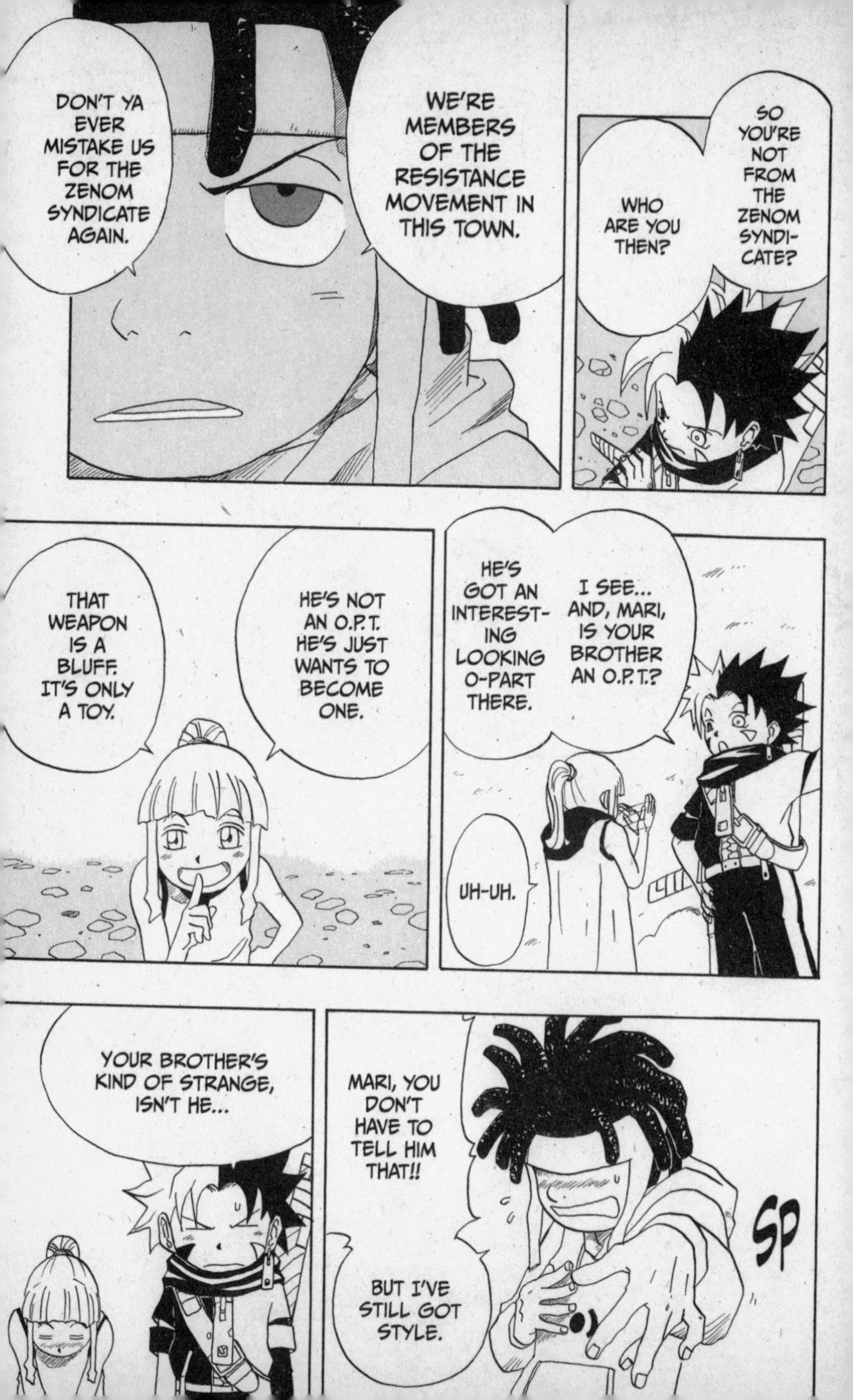
SO YOU'RE NOT FROM THE ZENOM SYNDI-CATE?
WHO ARE YOU THEN?
WE'RE MEMBERS OF THE RESISTANCE MOVEMENT IN THIS TOWN.
DON'T YA EVER MISTAKE US FOR THE ZENOM SYNDICATE AGAIN.
I SEE... AND, MARI, IS YOUR BROTHER AN O.P.T.?
HE'S GOT AN INTEREST-ING LOOKING O-PART THERE.
UH-UH.
HE'S NOT AN O.P.T. HE'S JUST WANTS TO BECOME ONE.
THAT WEAPON IS A BLUFF. IT'S ONLY A TOY.
MARI, YOU DON'T HAVE TO TELL HIM THAT!!
SP
BUT I'VE STILL GOT STYLE.
YOUR BROTHER'S KIND OF STRANGE, ISN'T HE...

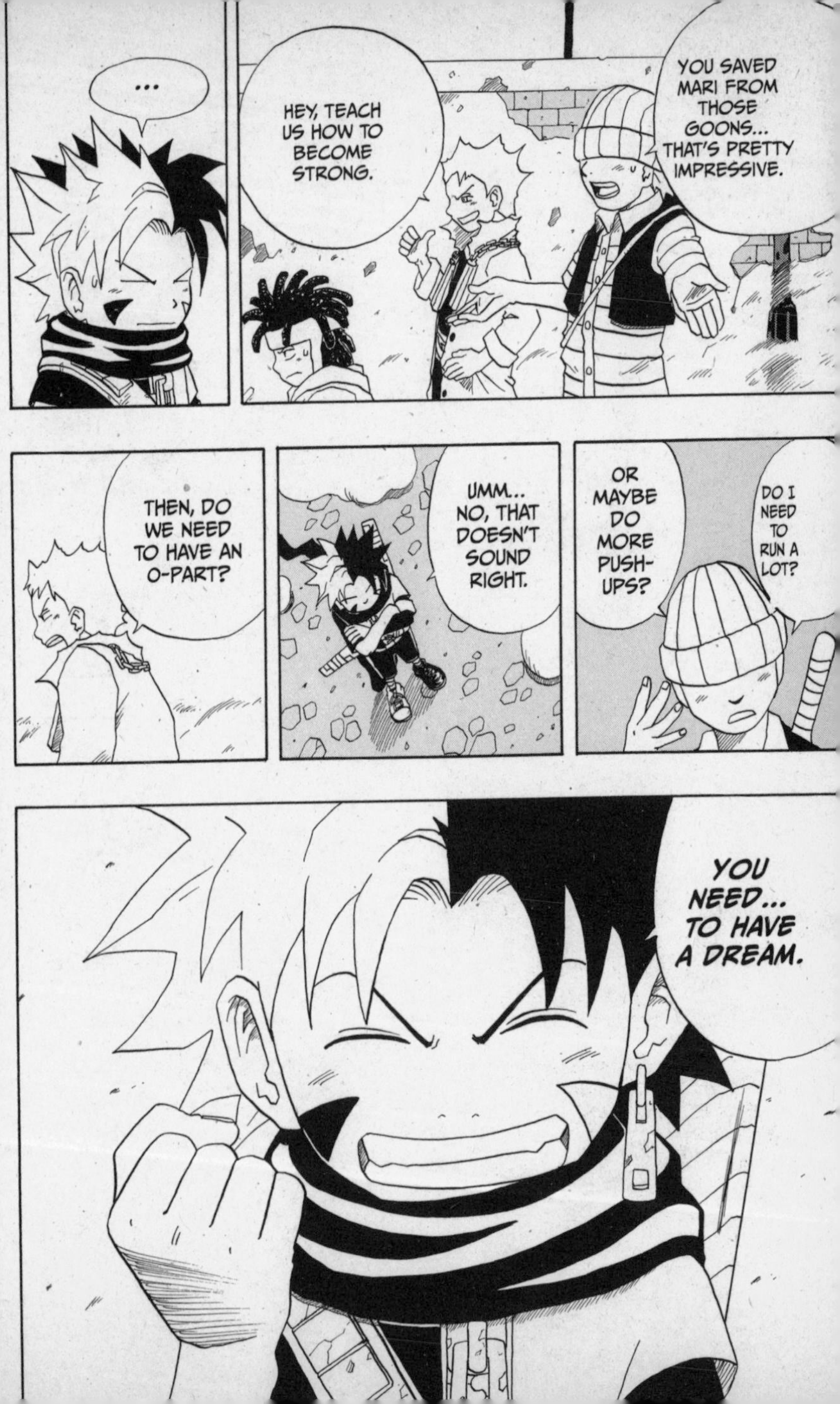
YOU SAVED MARI FROM THOSE GOONS... THAT'S PRETTY IMPRESSIVE.
HEY, TEACH US HOW TO BECOME STRONG.
...
DO I NEED TO RUN A LOT?
OR MAYBE DO MORE PUSH-UPS?
UMM... NO, THAT DOESN'T SOUND RIGHT.
THEN, DO WE NEED TO HAVE AN O-PART?
YOU NEED... TO HAVE A DREAM.

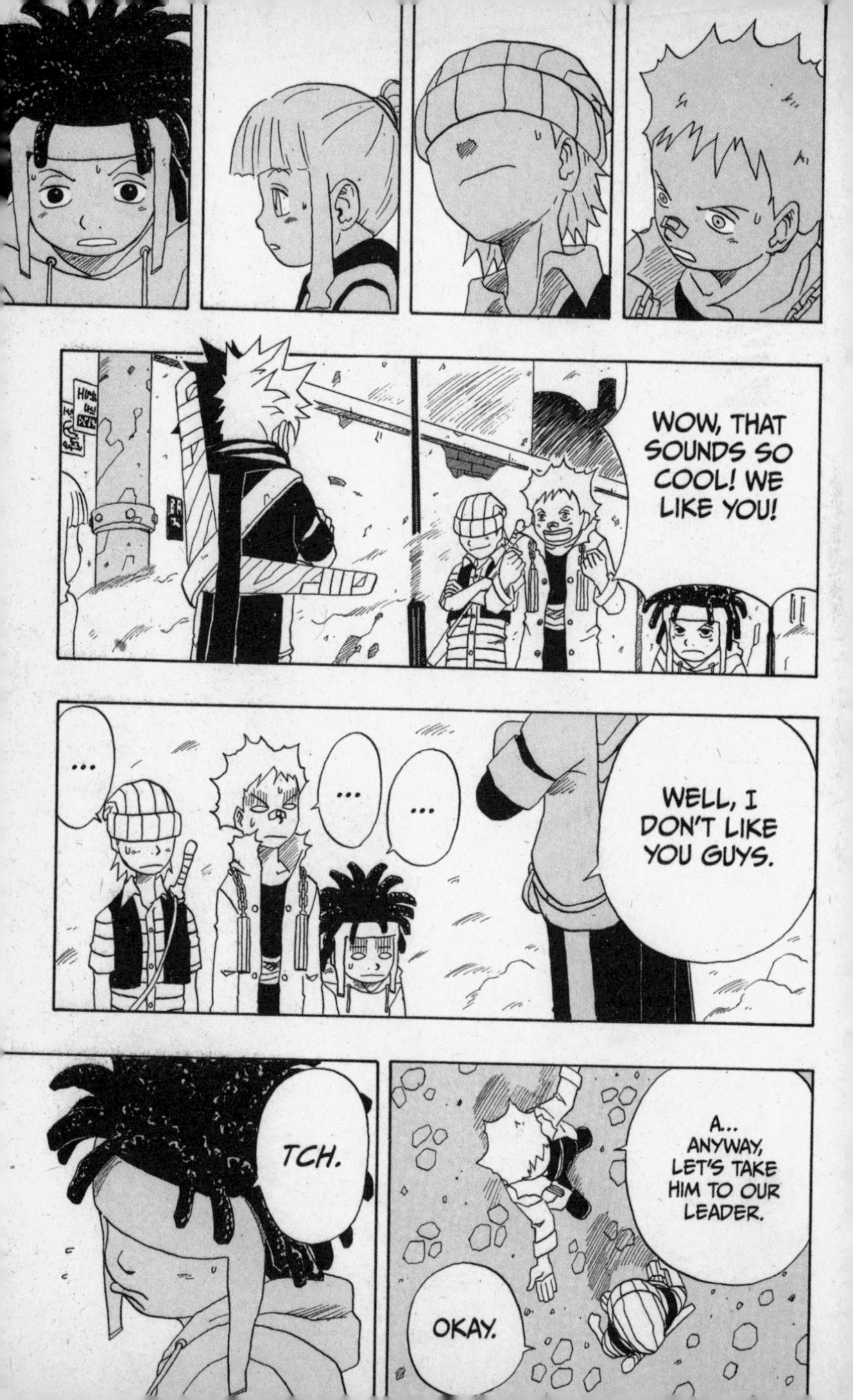
WOW, THAT SOUNDS SO COOL! WE LIKE YOU!
WELL, I DON'T LIKE YOU GUYS.
...
...
...
A... ANYWAY, LET'S TAKE HIM TO OUR LEADER.
OKAY.
TCH.

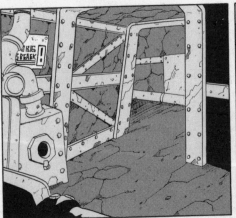

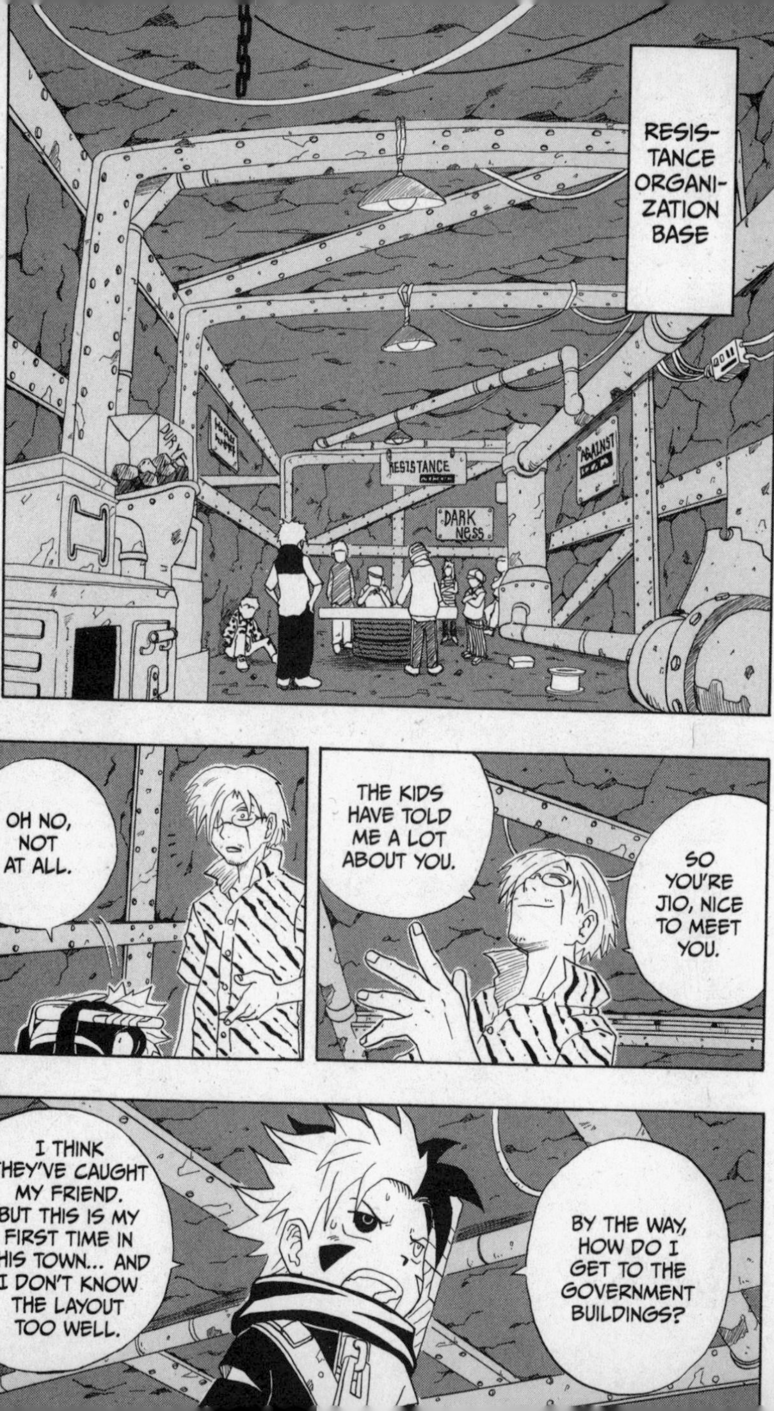
RESIS-
TANCE
ORGANI-
ZATION
BASE
AGAINST
RESISTANCE
DARK NESS
SO YOU'RE JIO, NICE TO MEET YOU.
THE KIDS HAVE TOLD ME A LOT ABOUT YOU.
OH NO, NOT AT ALL.
BY THE WAY, HOW DO I GET TO THE GOVERNMENT BUILDINGS?
I THINK THEY'VE CAUGHT MY FRIEND. BUT THIS IS MY FIRST TIME IN THIS TOWN... AND I DON'T KNOW THE LAYOUT TOO WELL.

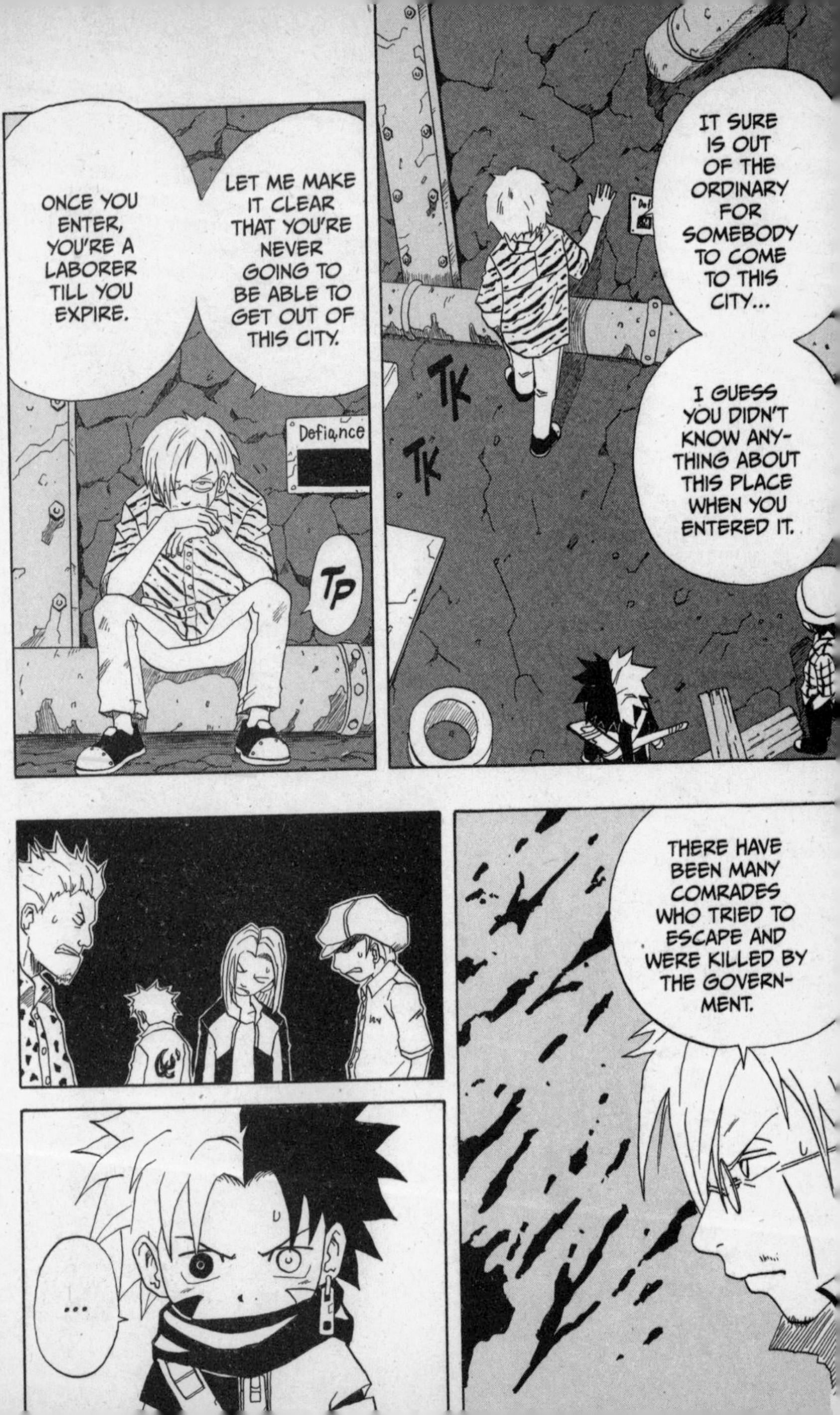
IT SURE IS OUT OF THE ORDINARY FOR SOMEBODY TO COME TO THIS CITY...
I GUESS YOU DIDN'T KNOW ANY-THING ABOUT THIS PLACE WHEN YOU ENTERED IT.
TK
TK
LET ME MAKE IT CLEAR THAT YOU'RE NEVER GOING TO BE ABLE TO GET OUT OF THIS CITY.
ONCE YOU ENTER, YOU'RE A LABORER TILL YOU EXPIRE.
Defiance
TP
THERE HAVE BEEN MANY COMRADES WHO TRIED TO ESCAPE AND WERE KILLED BY THE GOVERN-MENT.
...

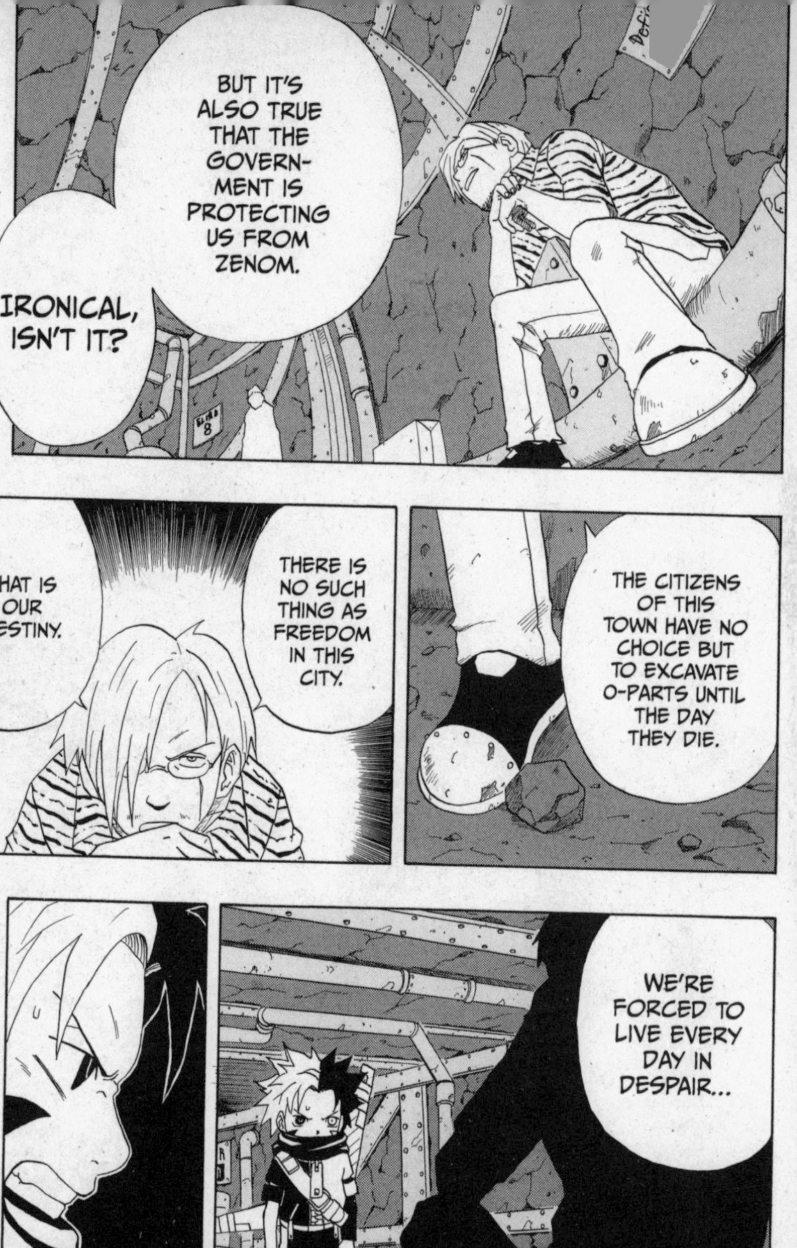
BUT IT'S ALSO TRUE THAT THE GOVERNMENT IS PROTECTING US FROM ZENOM.
IRONICAL, ISN'T IT?
THE CITIZENS OF THIS TOWN HAVE NO CHOICE BUT TO EXCAVATE O-PARTS UNTIL THE DAY THEY DIE.
THERE IS NO SUCH THING AS FREEDOM IN THIS CITY.
THAT IS OUR DESTINY.
WE'RE FORCED TO LIVE EVERY DAY IN DESPAIR...

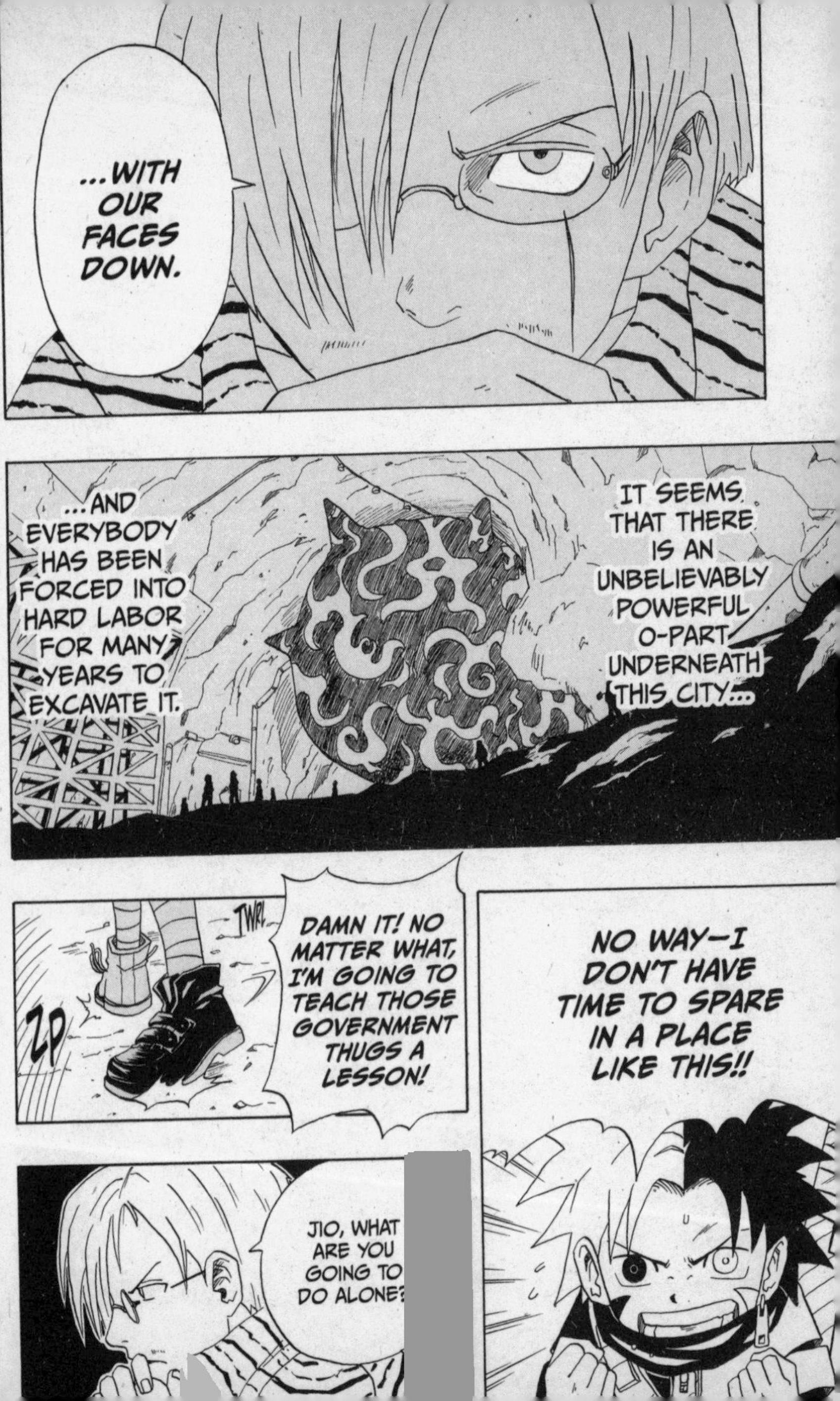
...WITH OUR FACES DOWN.
IT SEEMS THAT THERE IS AN UNBELIEVABLY POWERFUL O-PART UNDERNEATH THIS CITY...
...AND EVERYBODY HAS BEEN FORCED INTO HARD LABOR FOR MANY YEARS TO EXCAVATE IT.
NO WAY—I DON'T HAVE TIME TO SPARE IN A PLACE LIKE THIS!!
TWRL
DAMN IT! NO MATTER WHAT, I'M GOING TO TEACH THOSE GOVERNMENT THUGS A LESSON!
ZP
JIO, WHAT ARE YOU GOING TO DO ALONE?

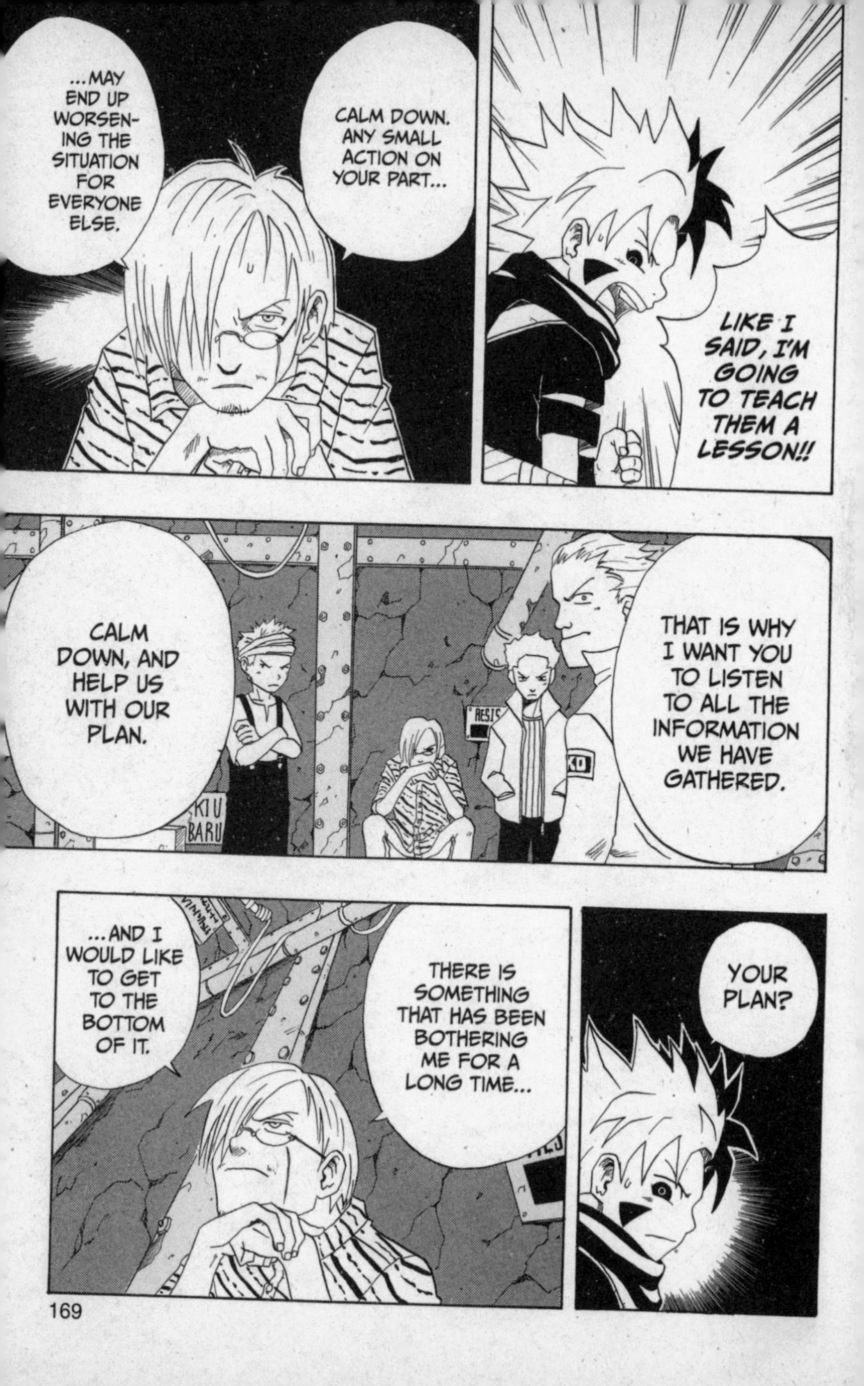
LIKE I SAID, I'M GOING TO TEACH THEM A LESSON!!
CALM DOWN. ANY SMALL ACTION ON YOUR PART...
...MAY END UP WORSENING THE SITUATION FOR EVERYONE ELSE.
THAT IS WHY I WANT YOU TO LISTEN TO ALL THE INFORMATION WE HAVE GATHERED.
CALM DOWN, AND HELP US WITH OUR PLAN.
YOUR PLAN?
THERE IS SOMETHING THAT HAS BEEN BOTHERING ME FOR A LONG TIME...
...AND I WOULD LIKE TO GET TO THE BOTTOM OF IT.

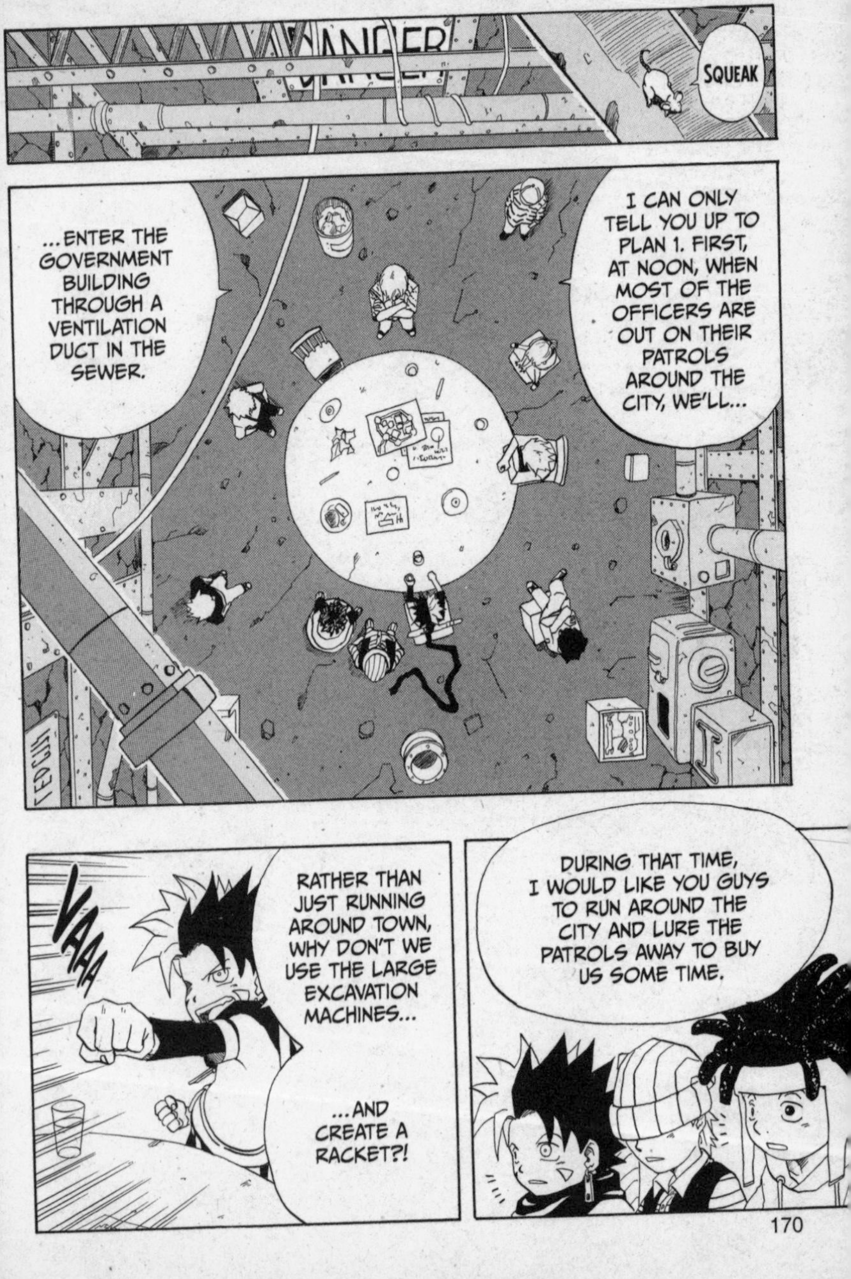
SQUEAK
I CAN ONLY TELL YOU UP TO PLAN 1. FIRST, AT NOON, WHEN MOST OF THE OFFICERS ARE OUT ON THEIR PATROLS AROUND THE CITY, WE'LL...
...ENTER THE GOVERNMENT BUILDING THROUGH A VENTILATION DUCT IN THE SEWER.
DURING THAT TIME, I WOULD LIKE YOU GUYS TO RUN AROUND THE CITY AND LURE THE PATROLS AWAY TO BUY US SOME TIME.
VAAA
RATHER THAN JUST RUNNING AROUND TOWN, WHY DON'T WE USE THE LARGE EXCAVATION MACHINES...
...AND CREATE A RACKET?!

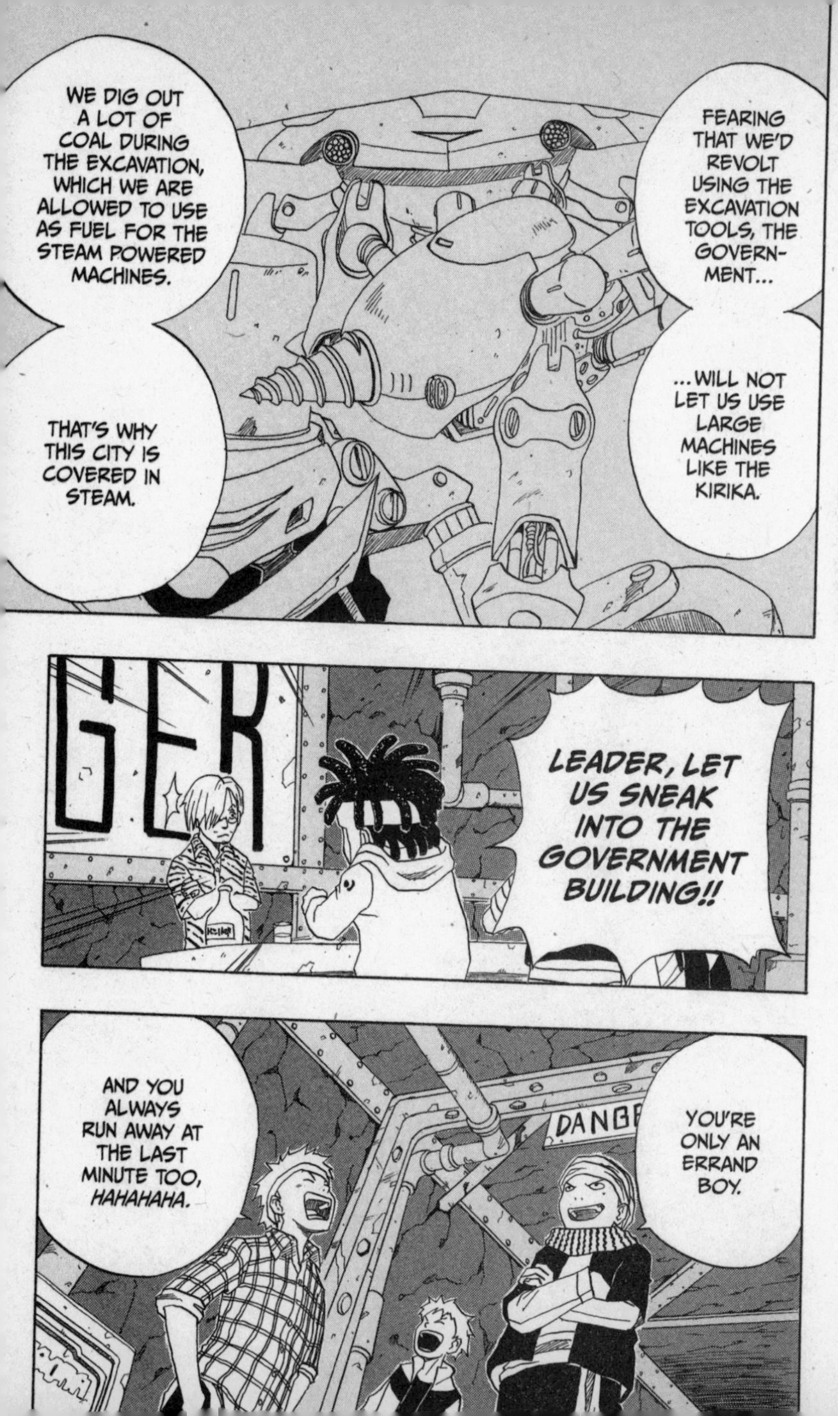
FEARING THAT WE'D REVOLT USING THE EXCAVATION TOOLS, THE GOVERNMENT...
...WILL NOT LET US USE LARGE MACHINES LIKE THE KIRIKA.
WE DIG OUT A LOT OF COAL DURING THE EXCAVATION, WHICH WE ARE ALLOWED TO USE AS FUEL FOR THE STEAM POWERED MACHINES.
THAT'S WHY THIS CITY IS COVERED IN STEAM.
LEADER, LET US SNEAK INTO THE GOVERNMENT BUILDING!!
YOU'RE ONLY AN ERRAND BOY.
AND YOU ALWAYS RUN AWAY AT THE LAST MINUTE TOO, *HAHAHAHA.*

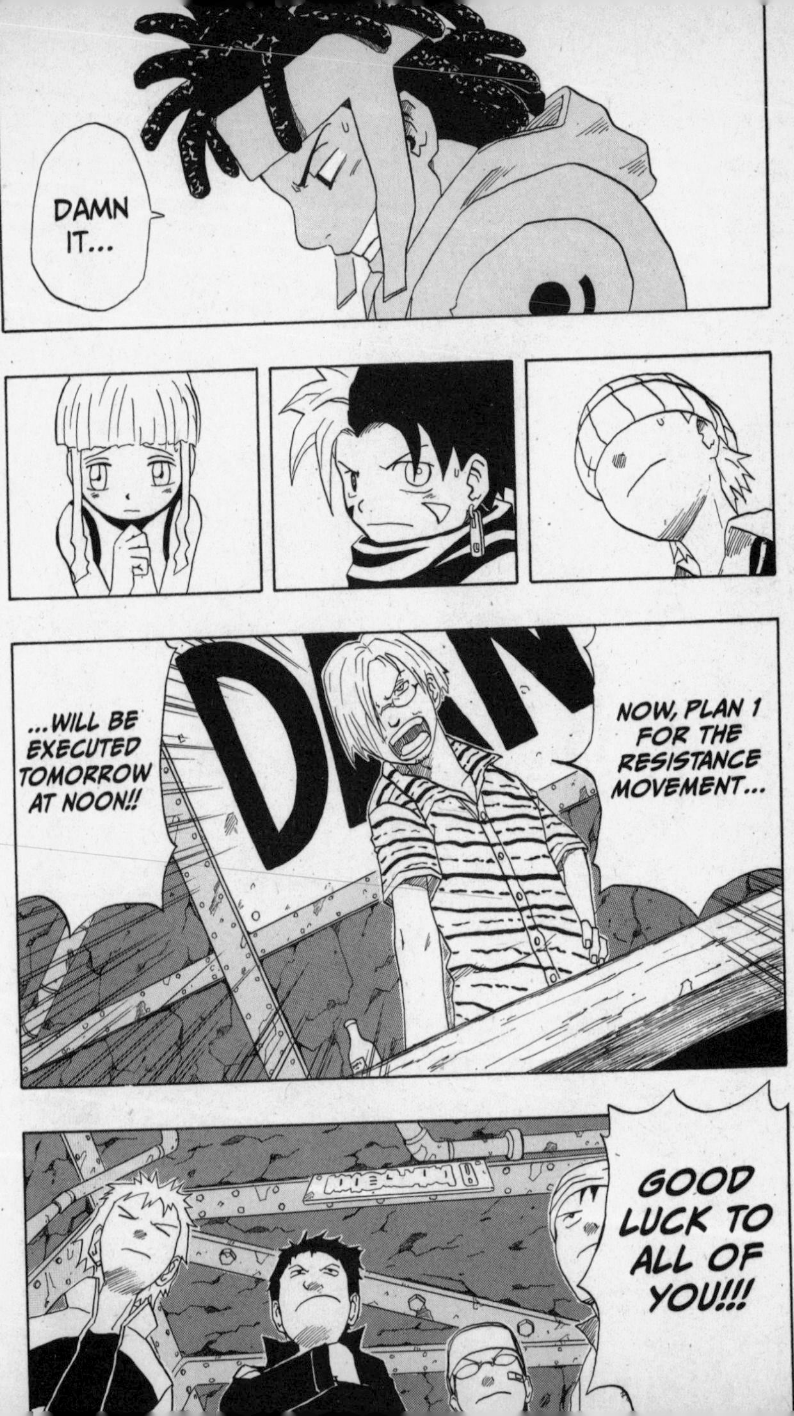
DAMN IT...
NOW, PLAN 1 FOR THE RESISTANCE MOVEMENT...
...WILL BE EXECUTED TOMORROW AT NOON!!
GOOD LUCK TO ALL OF YOU!!!

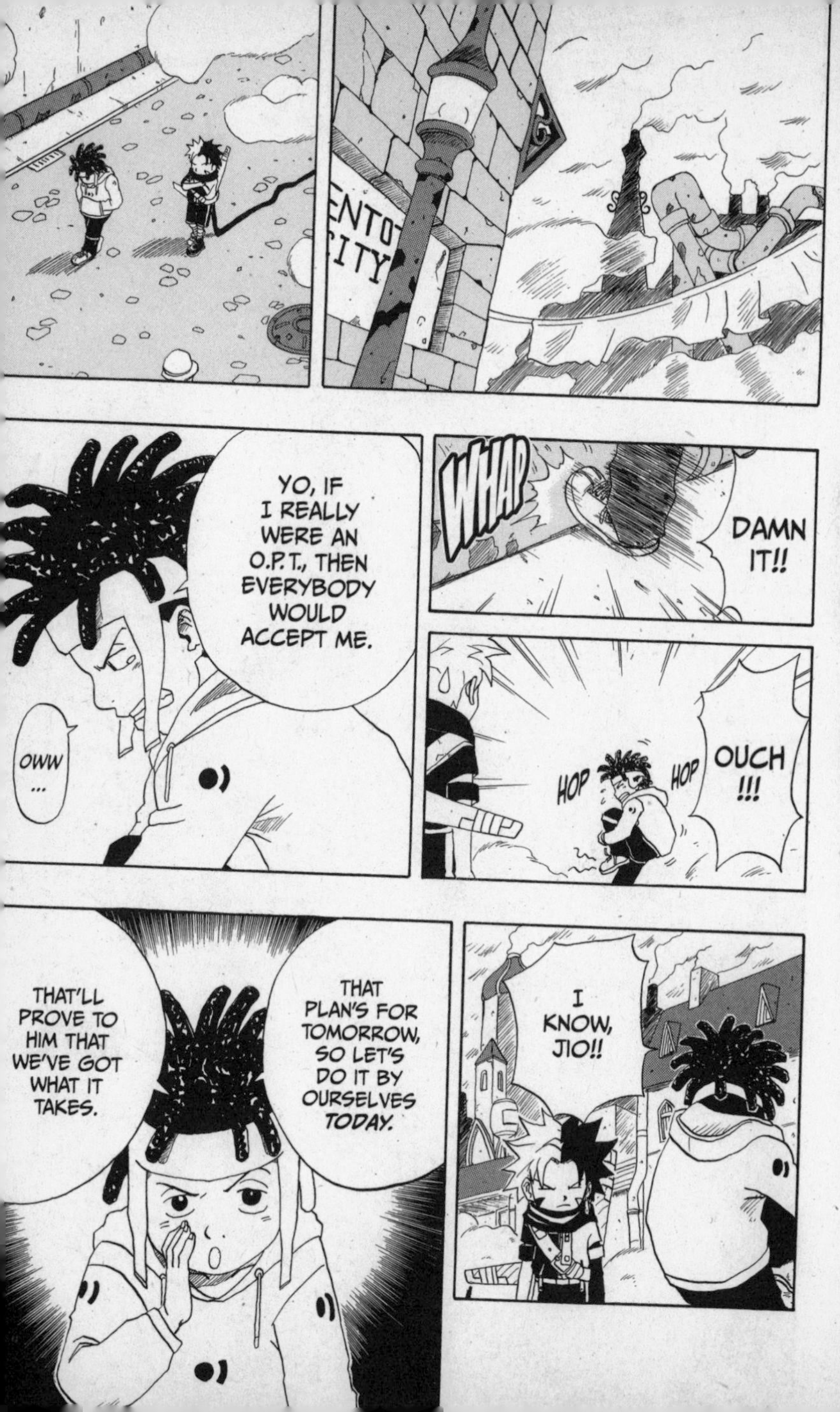
ENTOT
ITY
WHAP
DAMN IT!!
HOP
HOP
OUCH !!!
YO, IF I REALLY WERE AN O.P.T., THEN EVERYBODY WOULD ACCEPT ME.
OWW ...
I KNOW, JIO!!
THAT PLAN'S FOR TOMORROW, SO LET'S DO IT BY OURSELVES *TODAY.*
THAT'LL PROVE TO HIM THAT WE'VE GOT WHAT IT TAKES.

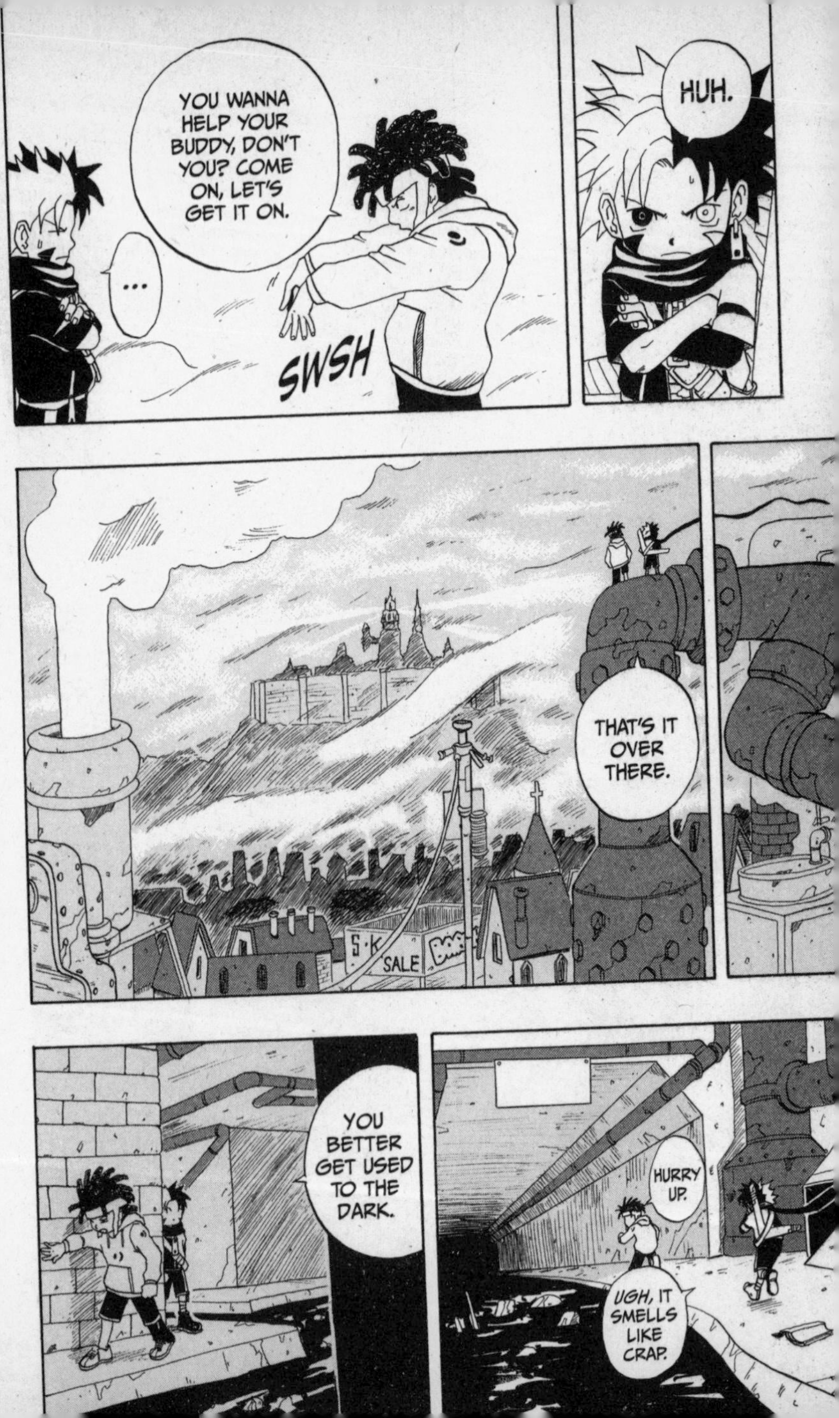
HUH.
YOU WANNA HELP YOUR BUDDY, DON'T YOU? COME ON, LET'S GET IT ON.
...
SWSH
THAT'S IT OVER THERE.
S·K
SALE
HURRY UP.
UGH, IT SMELLS LIKE CRAP.
YOU BETTER GET USED TO THE DARK.

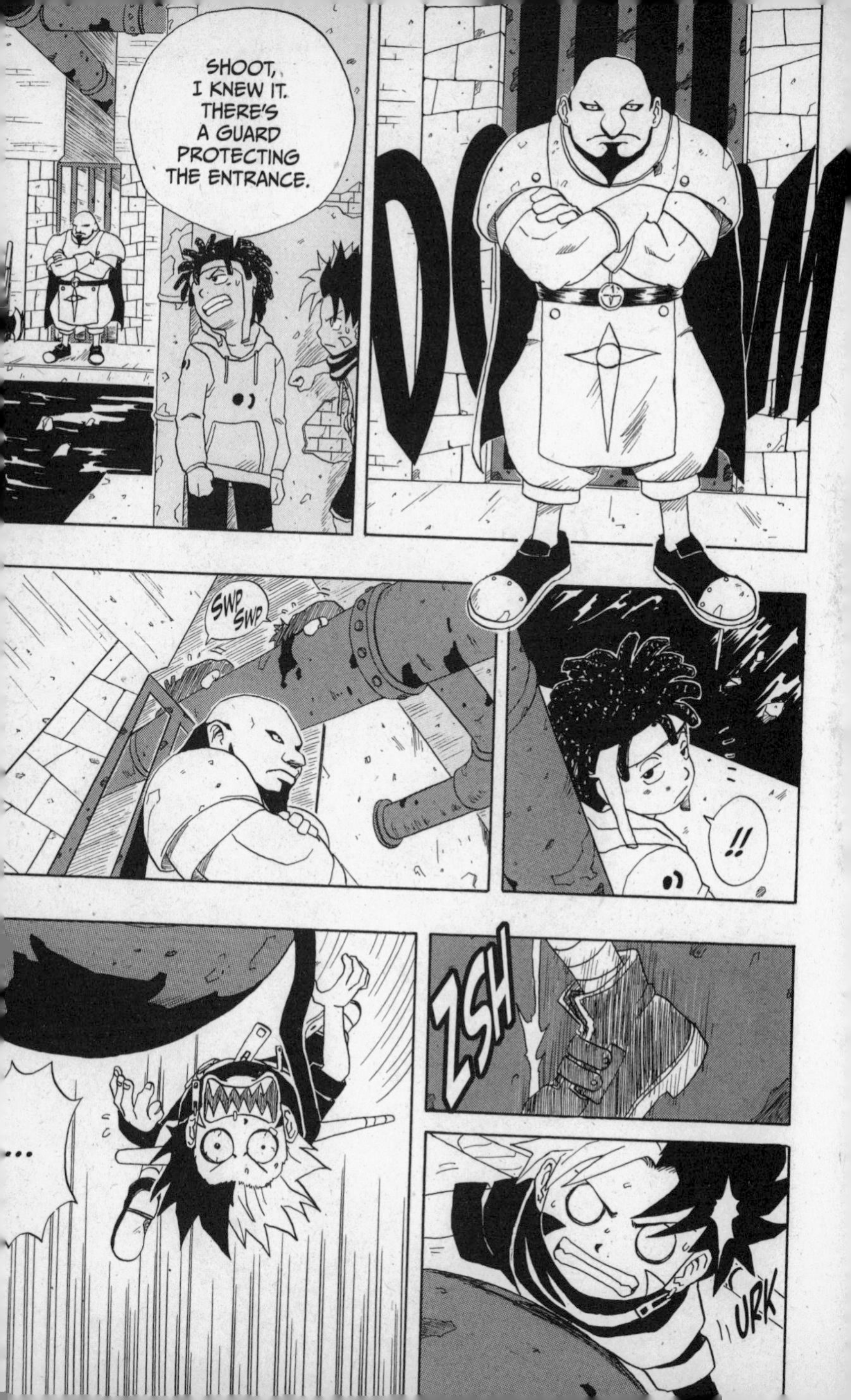
SHOOT, I KNEW IT. THERE'S A GUARD PROTECTING THE ENTRANCE.
!!
SWP SWP
ZSH
URK
...

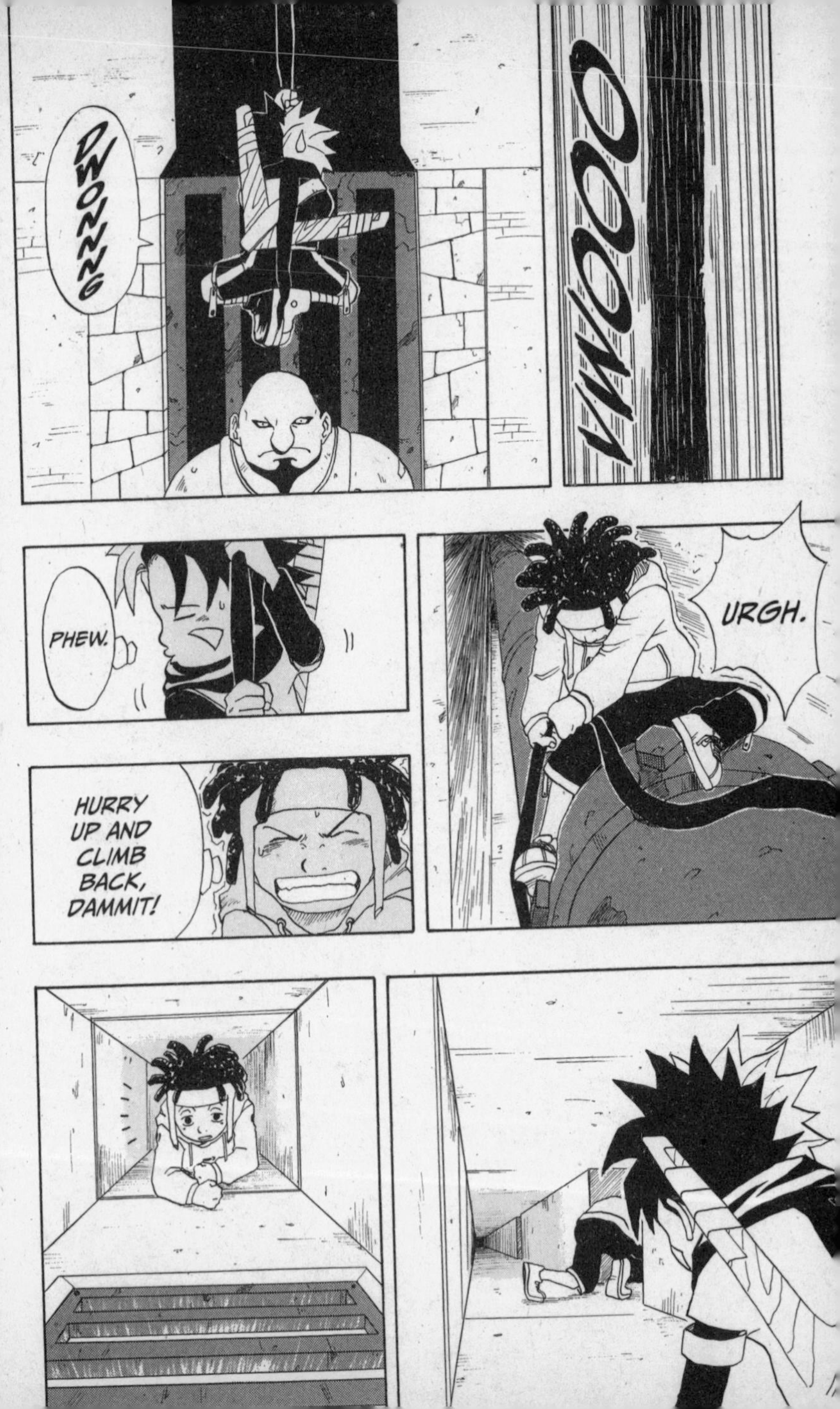
VWOOOO
DWONNNG
URGH.
PHEW.
HURRY UP AND CLIMB BACK, DAMMIT!

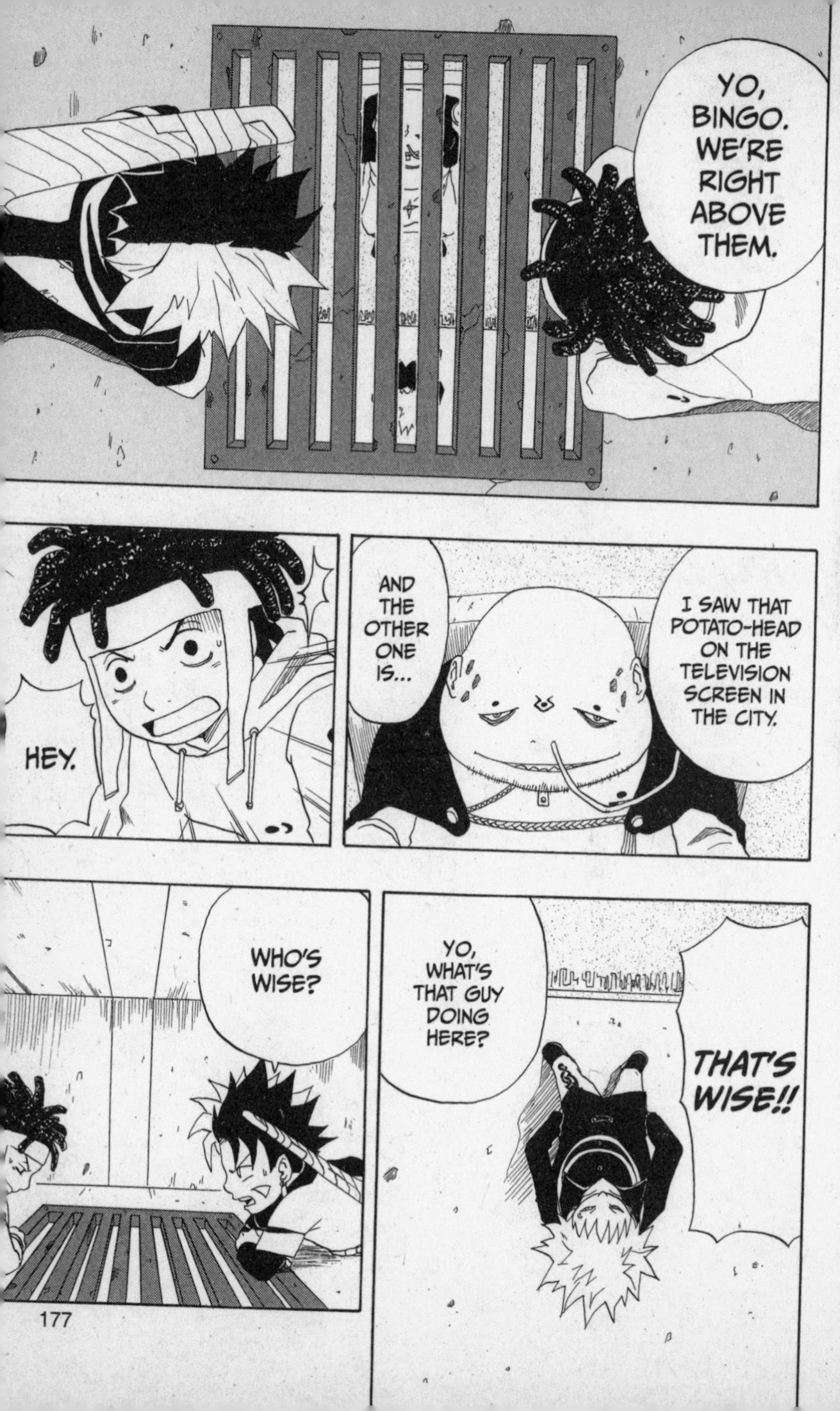
YO, BINGO. WE'RE RIGHT ABOVE THEM.
I SAW THAT POTATO-HEAD ON THE TELEVISION SCREEN IN THE CITY.
AND THE OTHER ONE IS...
HEY.
THAT'S WISE!!
YO, WHAT'S THAT GUY DOING HERE?
WHO'S WISE?

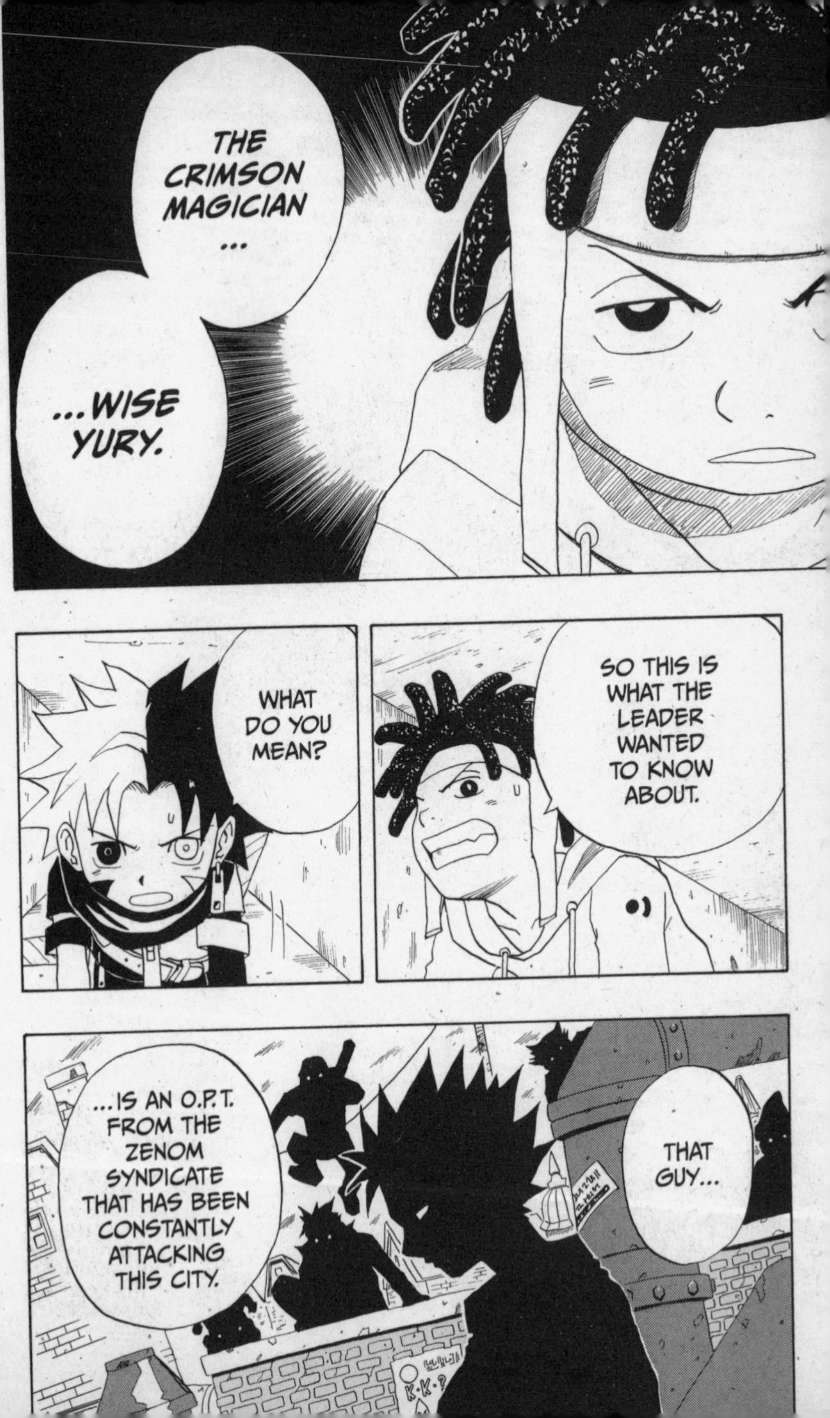
THE CRIMSON MAGICIAN ...
...WISE YURY.
SO THIS IS WHAT THE LEADER WANTED TO KNOW ABOUT.
WHAT DO YOU MEAN?
THAT GUY...
...IS AN O.P.T. FROM THE ZENOM SYNDICATE THAT HAS BEEN CONSTANTLY ATTACKING THIS CITY.

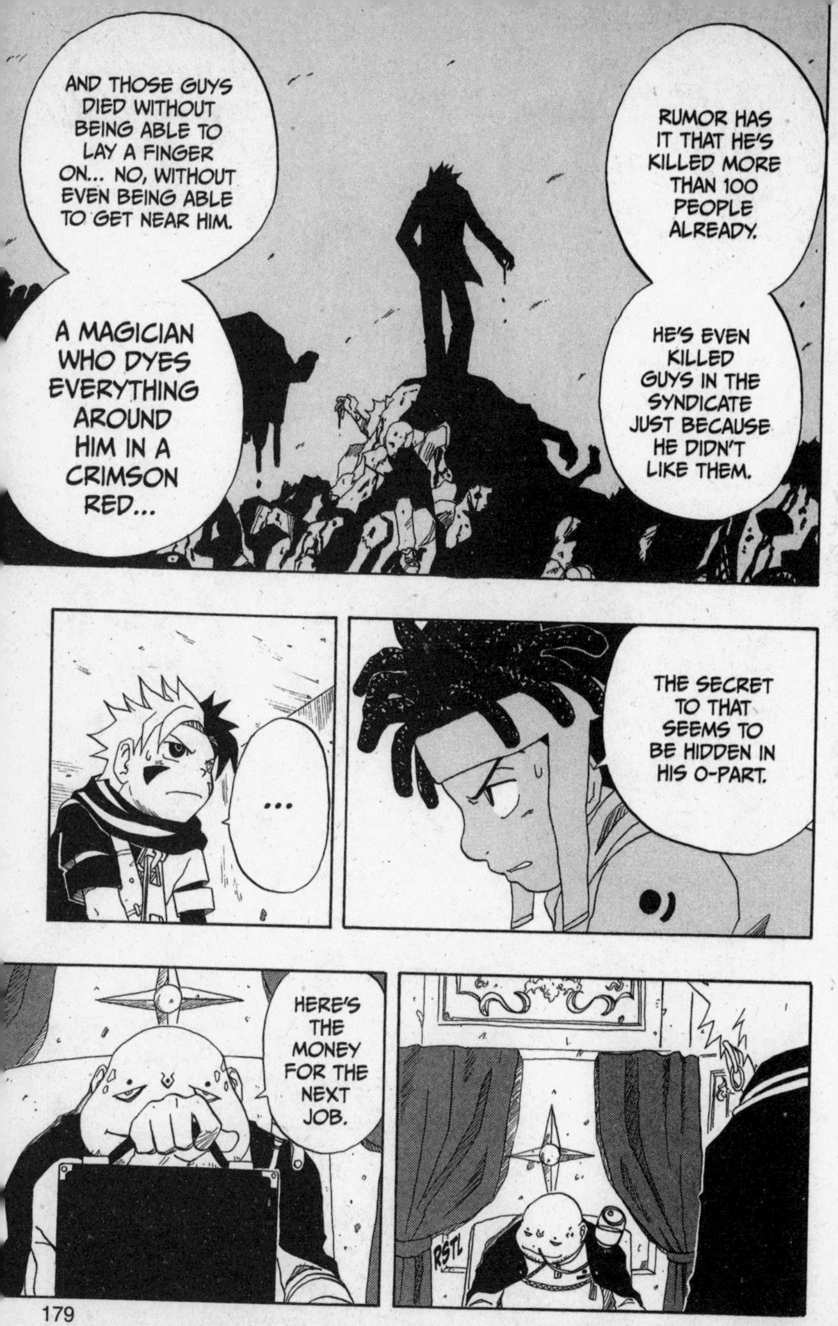
RUMOR HAS IT THAT HE'S KILLED MORE THAN 100 PEOPLE ALREADY.
HE'S EVEN KILLED GUYS IN THE SYNDICATE JUST BECAUSE HE DIDN'T LIKE THEM.
AND THOSE GUYS DIED WITHOUT BEING ABLE TO LAY A FINGER ON... NO, WITHOUT EVEN BEING ABLE TO GET NEAR HIM.
A MAGICIAN WHO DYES EVERYTHING AROUND HIM IN A CRIMSON RED...
THE SECRET TO THAT SEEMS TO BE HIDDEN IN HIS O-PART.
...
RSTL
HERE'S THE MONEY FOR THE NEXT JOB.

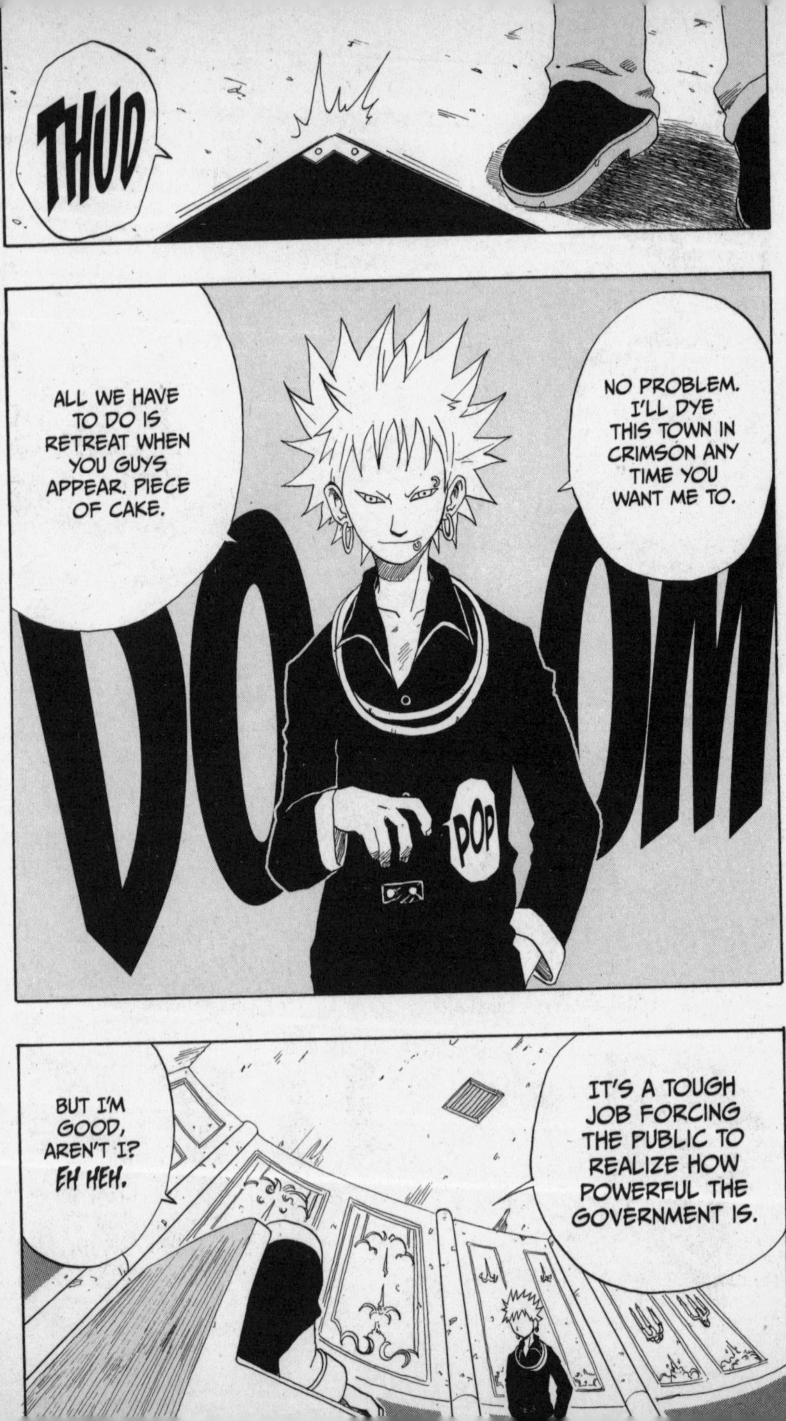
THUD
NO PROBLEM. I'LL DYE THIS TOWN IN CRIMSON ANY TIME YOU WANT ME TO.
ALL WE HAVE TO DO IS RETREAT WHEN YOU GUYS APPEAR. PIECE OF CAKE.
DOOM
POP
IT'S A TOUGH JOB FORCING THE PUBLIC TO REALIZE HOW POWERFUL THE GOVERNMENT IS.
BUT I'M GOOD, AREN'T I? EH HEH.

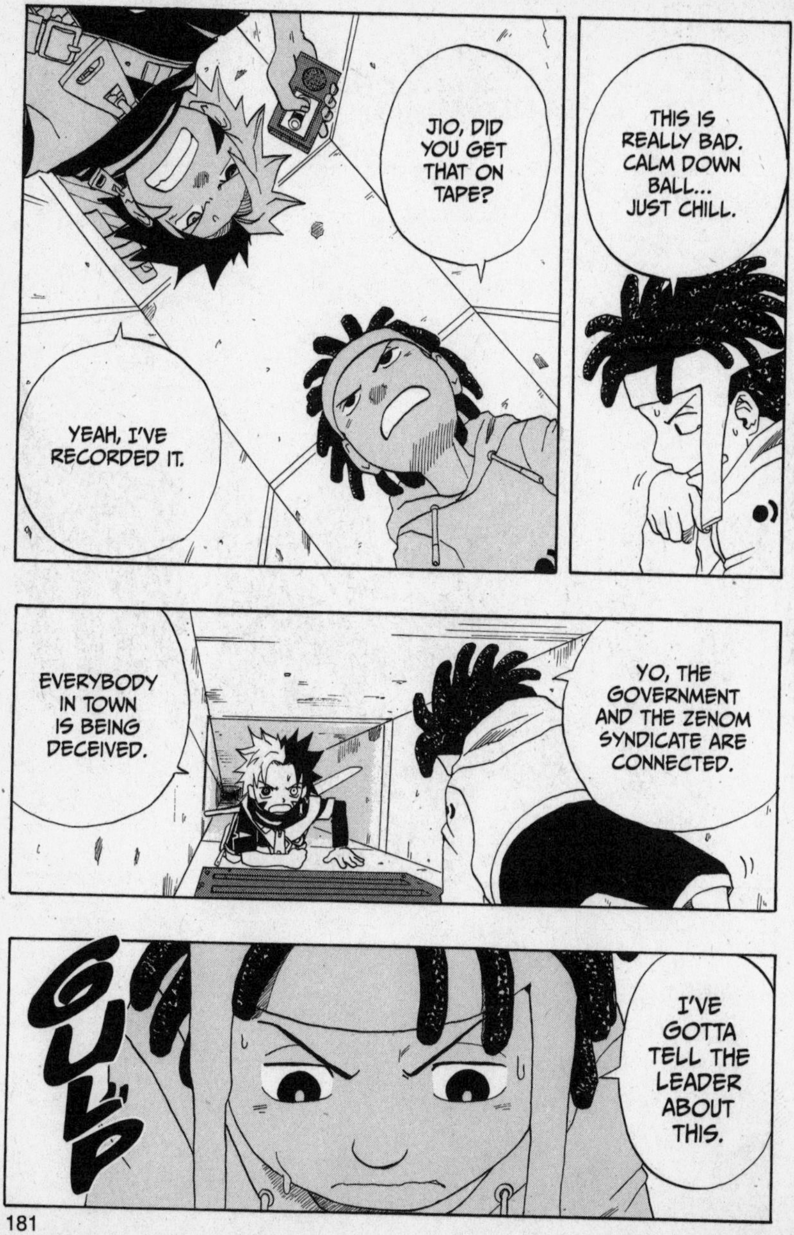
THIS IS REALLY BAD. CALM DOWN BALL... JUST CHILL.
JIO, DID YOU GET THAT ON TAPE?
YEAH, I'VE RECORDED IT.
YO, THE GOVERNMENT AND THE ZENOM SYNDICATE ARE CONNECTED.
EVERYBODY IN TOWN IS BEING DECEIVED.
I'VE GOTTA TELL THE LEADER ABOUT THIS.
GULP

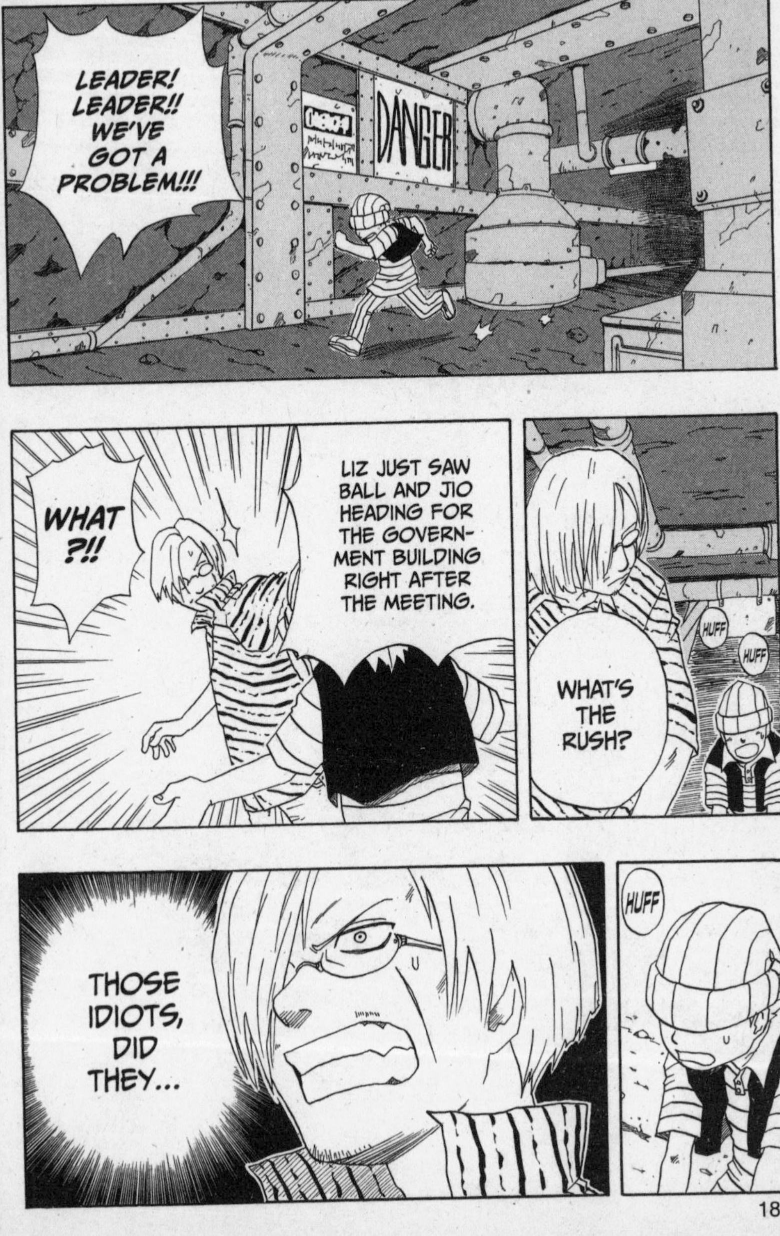
LEADER! LEADER!! WE'VE GOT A PROBLEM!!!
DANGER
HUFF
HUFF
WHAT'S THE RUSH?
LIZ JUST SAW BALL AND JIO HEADING FOR THE GOVERNMENT BUILDING RIGHT AFTER THE MEETING.
WHAT?!!
HUFF
THOSE IDIOTS, DID THEY...

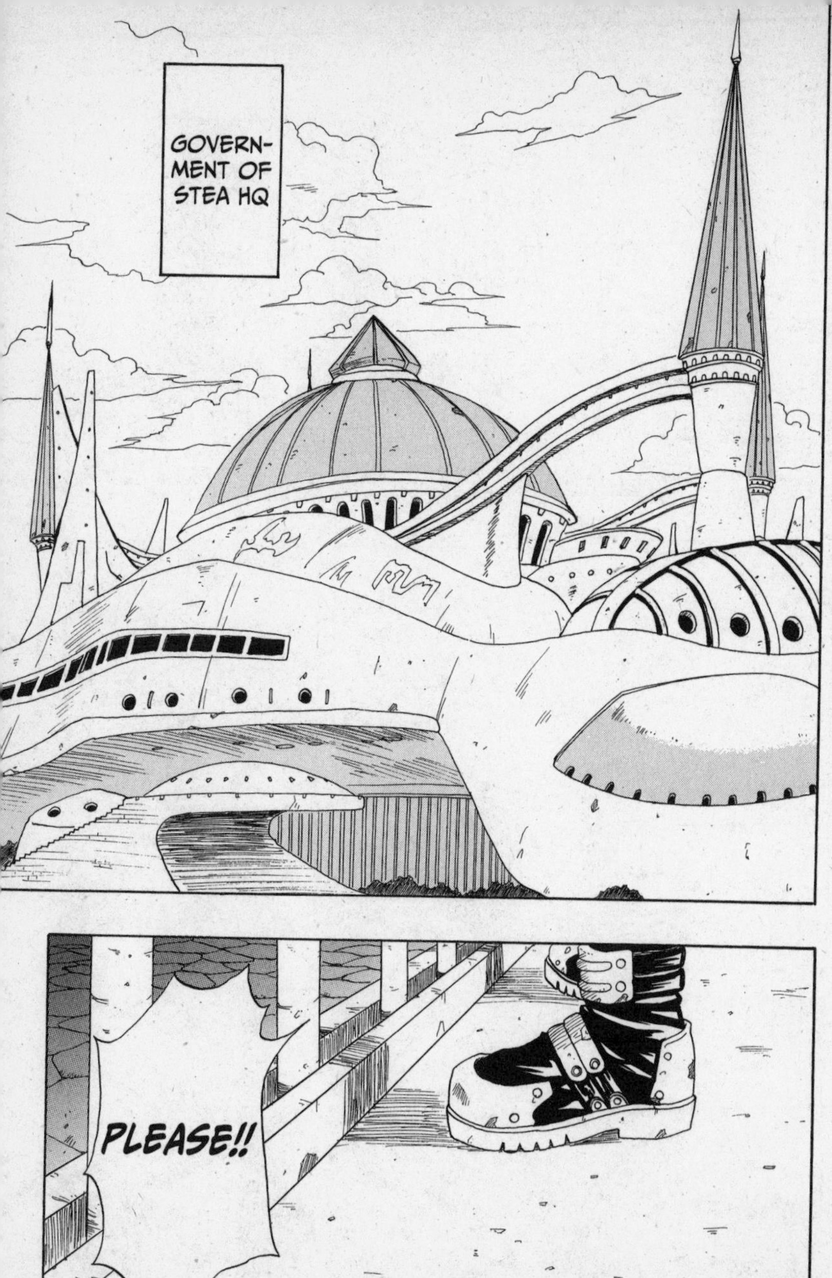
GOVERN-
MENT OF
STEA HQ
PLEASE!!

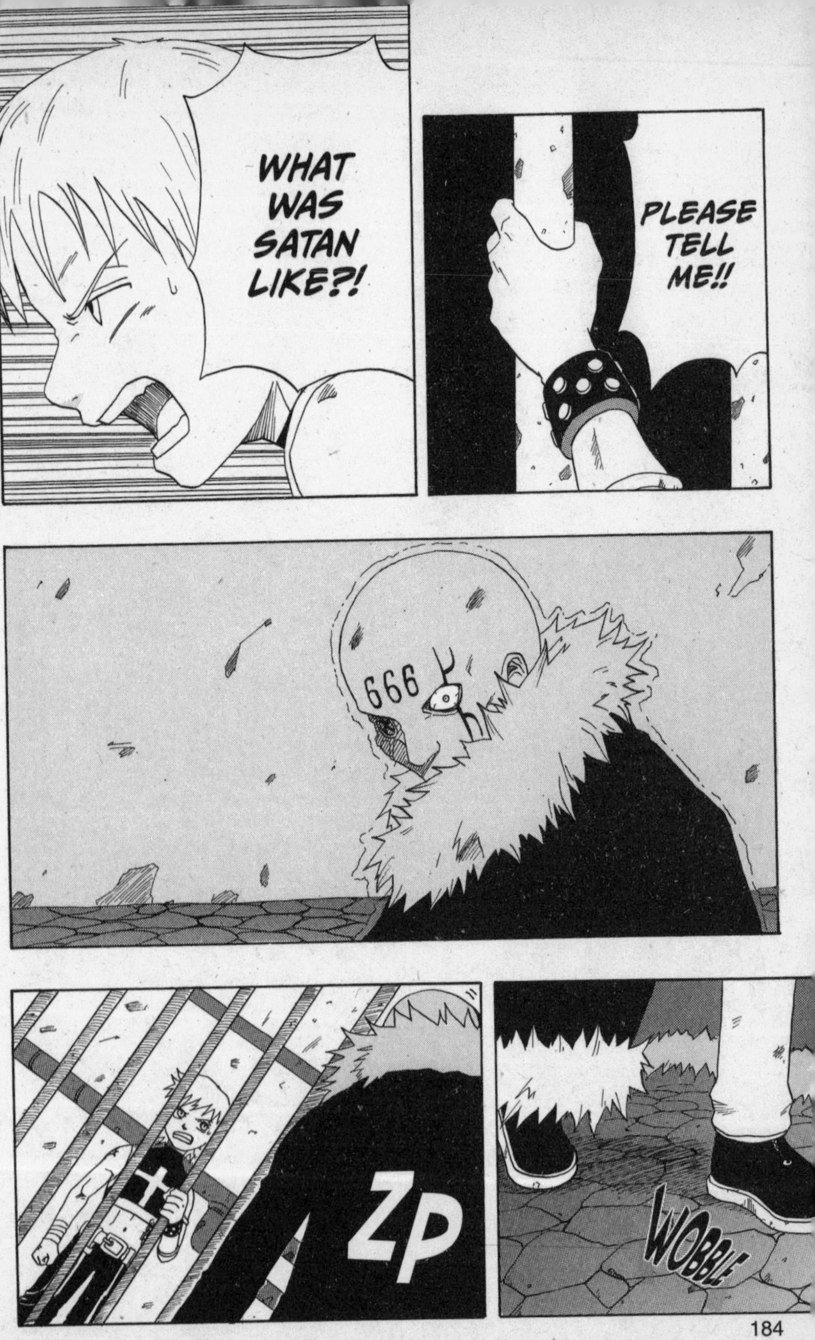
PLEASE TELL ME!!
WHAT WAS SATAN LIKE?!
666
WOBBLE
ZP

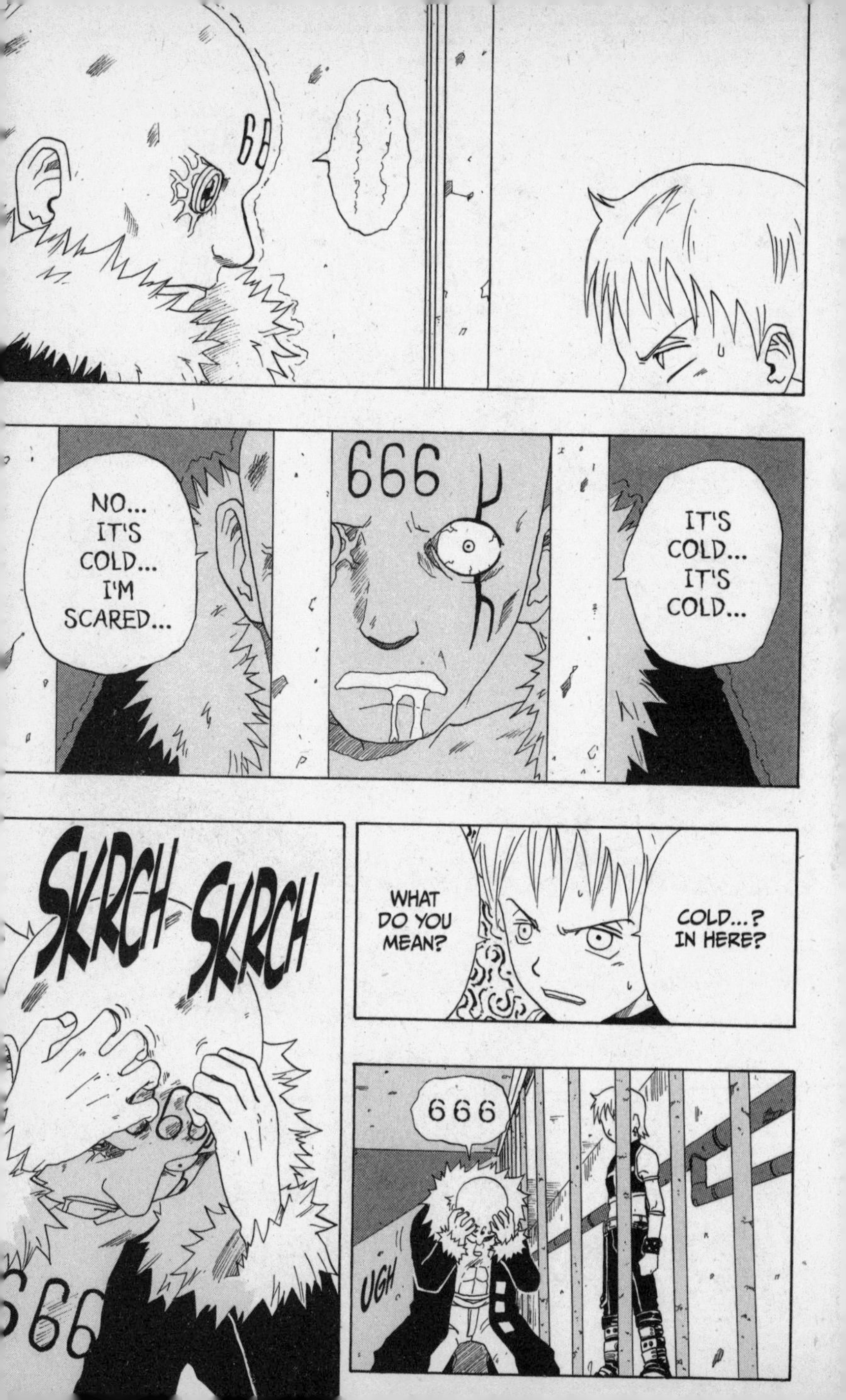
IT'S COLD... IT'S COLD...
NO... IT'S COLD... I'M SCARED...
COLD...? IN HERE?
WHAT DO YOU MEAN?
666
UGH
SKRCH SKRCH

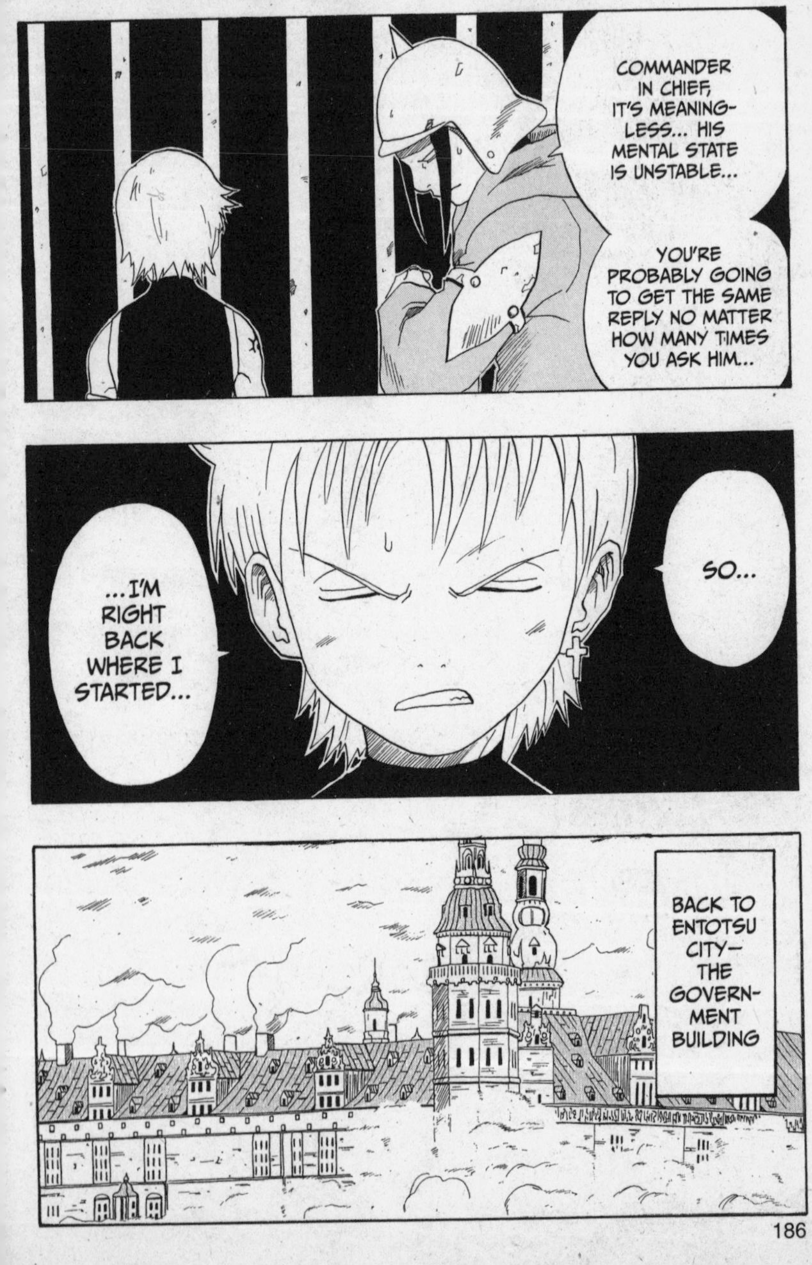
COMMANDER IN CHIEF, IT'S MEANING-LESS... HIS MENTAL STATE IS UNSTABLE...
YOU'RE PROBABLY GOING TO GET THE SAME REPLY NO MATTER HOW MANY TIMES YOU ASK HIM...
SO...
...I'M RIGHT BACK WHERE I STARTED...
BACK TO ENTOTSU CITY—THE GOVERN-MENT BUILDING

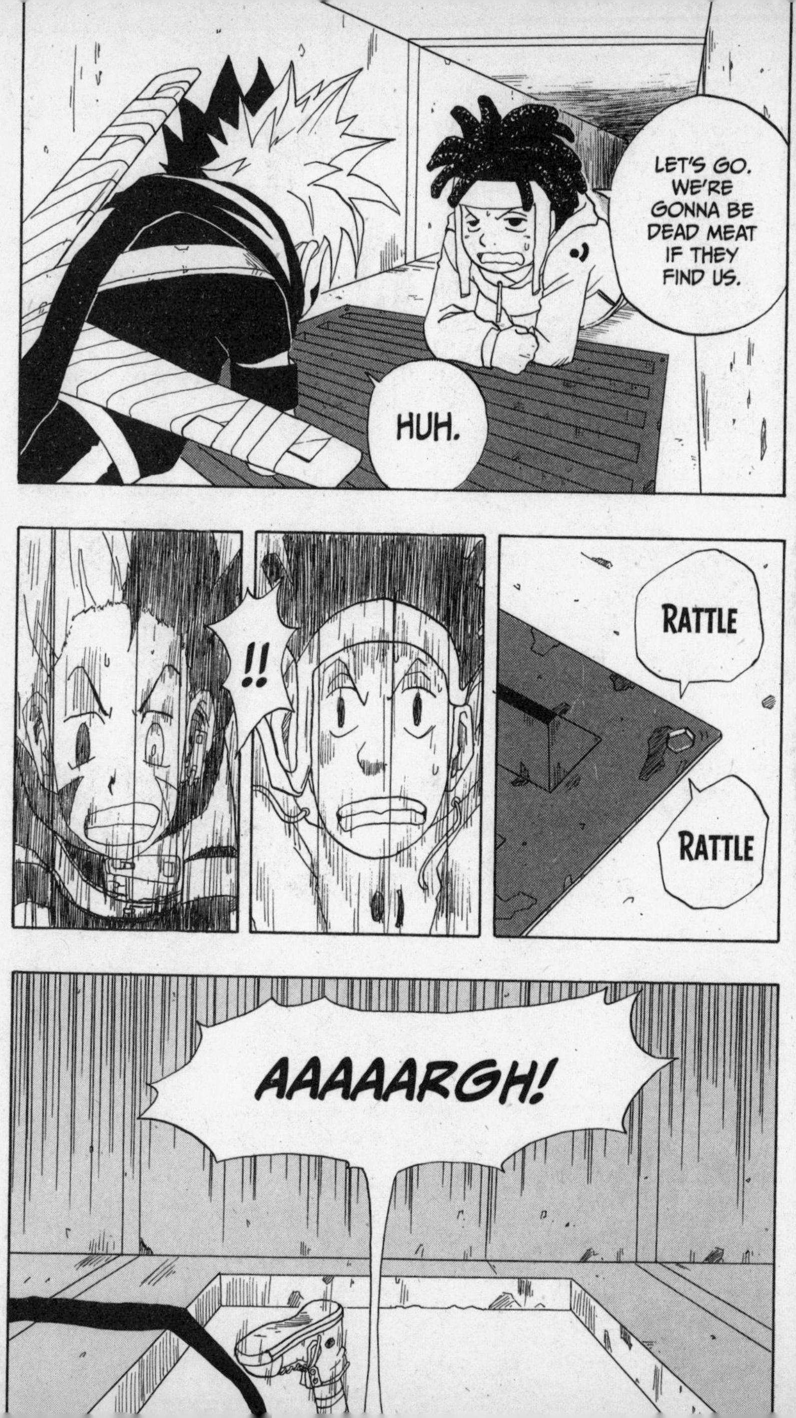
LET'S GO. WE'RE GONNA BE DEAD MEAT IF THEY FIND US.
HUH.
RATTLE
RATTLE
!!
AAAAARGH!

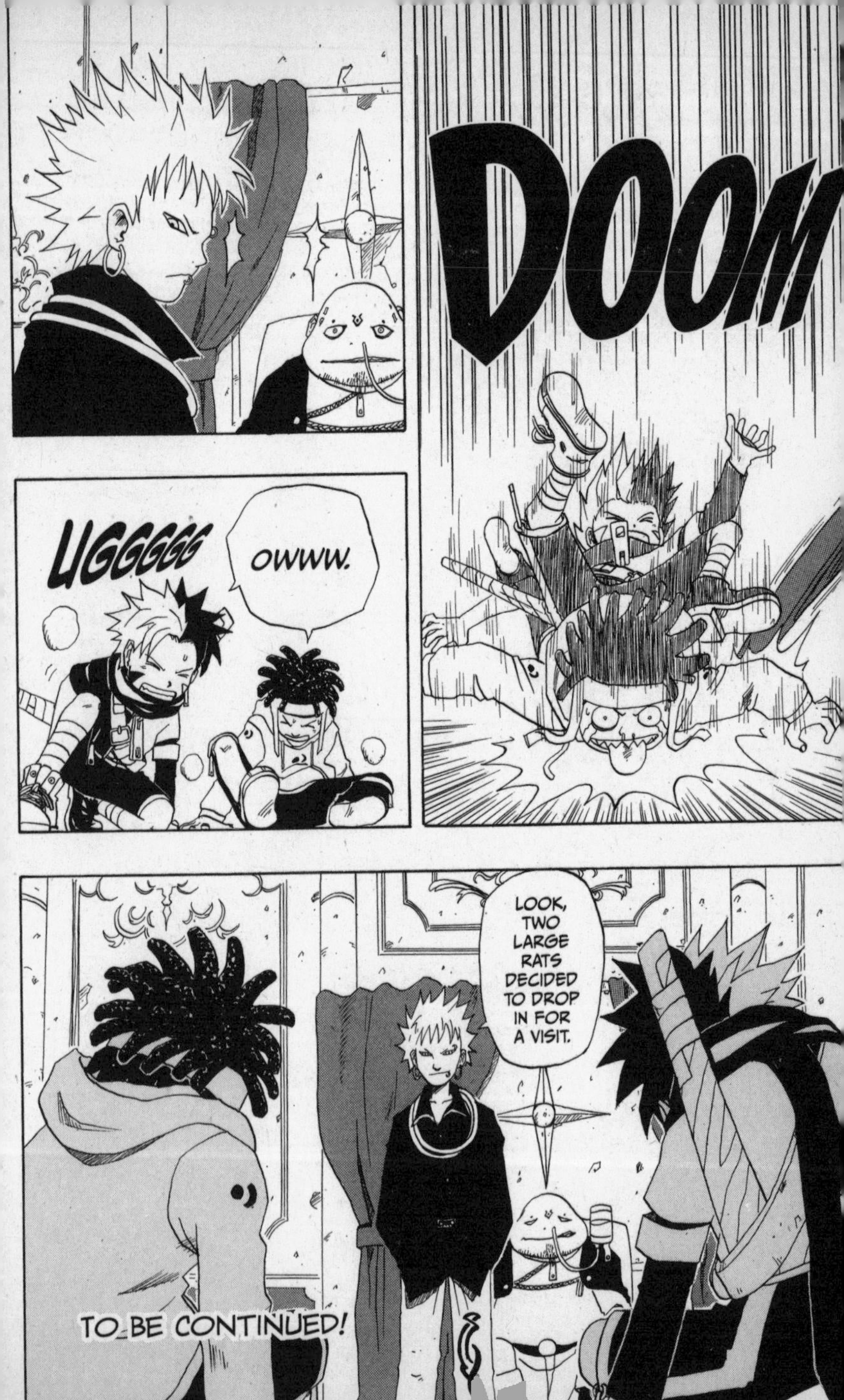
DOOM
UGGGGG
OWWW.
LOOK, TWO LARGE RATS DECIDED TO DROP IN FOR A VISIT.
TO BE CONTINUED!

O-Parts CATALOGUE②

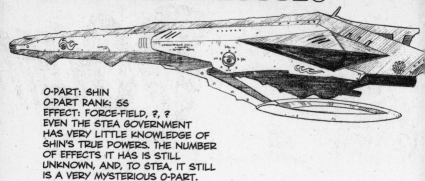

O-PART: SHIN
O-PART RANK: SS
EFFECT: FORCE-FIELD, ?, ?
EVEN THE STEA GOVERNMENT
HAS VERY LITTLE KNOWLEDGE OF
SHIN'S TRUE POWERS. THE NUMBER
OF EFFECTS IT HAS IS STILL
UNKNOWN, AND, TO STEA, IT STILL
IS A VERY MYSTERIOUS O-PART.

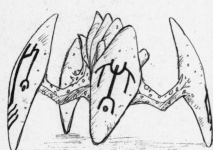

O-PART: MESSIAH
O-PART RANK: A
EFFECT: 1) PARTICLE LASER
2) HIGH-SPEED MOVEMENT
THE O-PART WHICH THE STUPID
AVILANCE BROTHERS USE. THE BIG
BROTHER IS IN CHARGE OF THE
ATTACK EFFECT, AND THE YOUNGER
BROTHER IS IN CHARGE OF THE
MOVEMENT EFFECT. IN OTHER
WORDS, THIS O-PART IS INTENDED
FOR TWO PEOPLE, AND IT CANNOT
BE USED BY ONLY ONE PERSON.
THUS, IT'S THE PERFECT O-PART
FOR THE AVILANCES.

O-PART: ZERO
O-PART RANK: C
EFFECT: HIGH-SPEED
MOVEMENT
ZERO, HIMSELF,
IS NOT AN O-PART.
WHILE THE EXACT
CAUSE IS UNKNOWN,
SOMETHING SEEMS
TO HAVE HAPPENED
TO HIS FATHER A
LONG TIME AGO...
AND, FOR SOME
REASON, THE BONES
IN ZERO'S BODY HAVE
TURNED INTO AN
O-PART.

O-PART: JUSTICE
O-PART RANK: C
EFFECT: ?, ?, WIND, ?, ?
CROSS'S FIVE O-PARTS.
IF IT WEREN'T JUST A
RING, ITS RANK WOULD
BE SLIGHTLY HIGHER,
BUT CROSS'S INEXHAUST-
IBLE SPIRIT AND TECH-
NIQUE MAKE UP FOR ITS
LOW RANK, ENABLING
EVEN ONE RING TO
HOLD DEADLY POWERS.

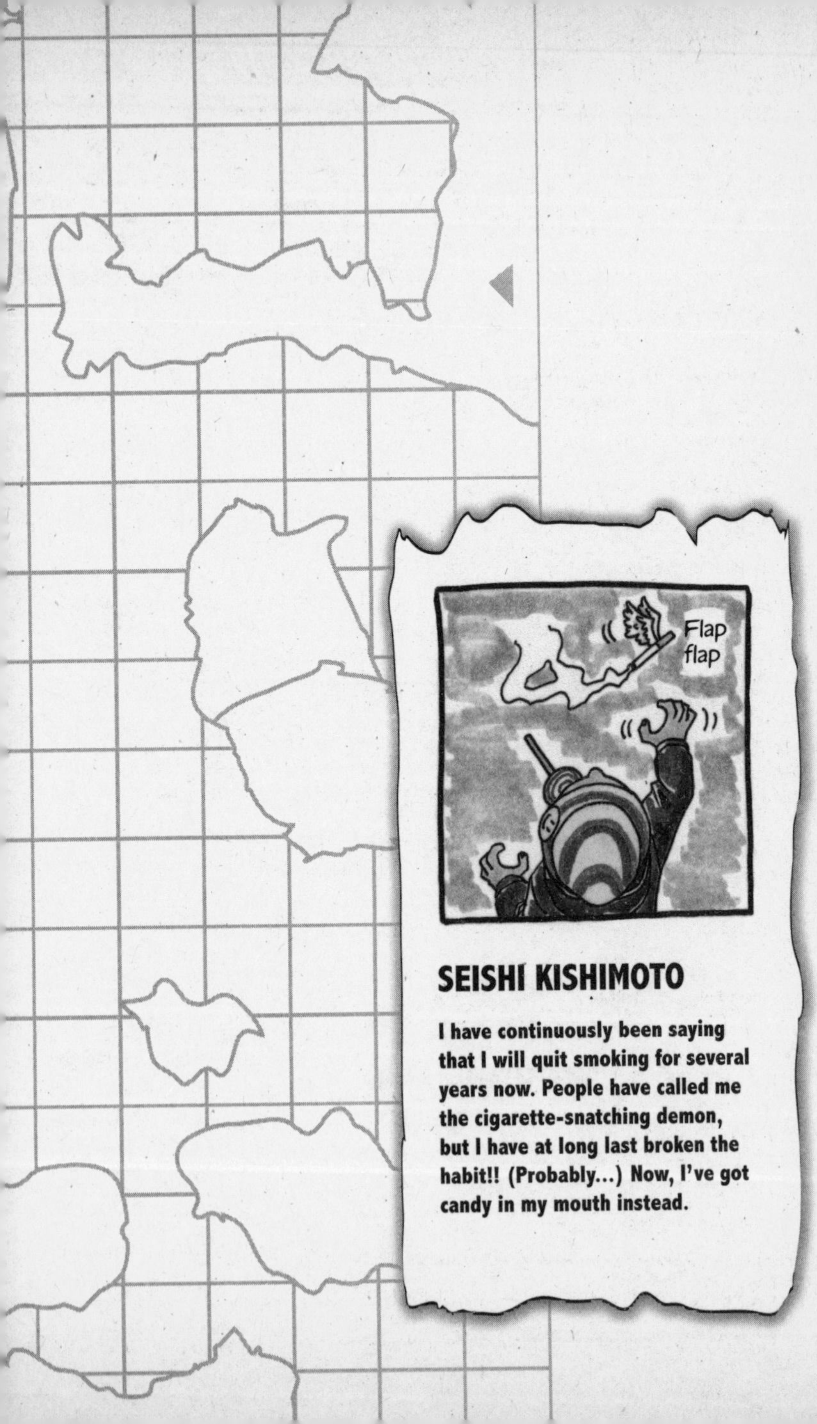
Flap
flap

SEISHI KISHIMOTO

I have continuously been saying that I will quit smoking for several years now. People have called me the cigarette-snatching demon, but I have at long last broken the habit!! (Probably...) Now, I've got candy in my mouth instead.

O-Parts HunteR™ 2

VIZ Media Edition
STORY AND ART BY SEISHI KISHIMOTO

English Adaptation/Tetsuichiro Miyaki
Touch-up Art & Lettering/Gia Cam Luc
Design/Amy Martin
Editor/Kit Fox

Managing Editor/Annette Roman
Editorial Director/Elizabeth Kawasaki
Editor in Chief/Alvin Lu
Sr. Director of Acquisitions/Rika Inouye
Sr. VP of Marketing/Liza Coppola
Exec. VP of Sales & Marketing/John Easum
Publisher/Hyoe Narita

© 2002 Seishi Kishimoto/SQUARE ENIX. All rights reserved. First published in
Japan in 2002 by SQUARE ENIX CO., LTD. English translation rights arranged
with SQUARE ENIX CO., LTD. and VIZ Media, LLC. The O-PARTS HUNTER logo is a
trademark of VIZ Media, LLC. The stories, characters and incidents mentioned in
this publication are entirely fictional.

Printed in the U.S.A.

Published by VIZ Media, LLC
P.O. Box 77010
San Francisco, CA 94107

10 9 8 7 6 5 4 3 2 1
First printing, February 2007

www.viz.com   store.viz.com

LOVE MANGA?
LET US KNOW WHAT YOU THINK!

HELP US MAKE THE MANGA
YOU LOVE BETTER!